Elk and Elk Hunting

ELK AND ELK HUNTING

*Your Practical Guide
to Fundamentals and Fine Points*

Hartt Wixom

Stackpole Books

Published by
STACKPOLE BOOKS
Cameron and Kelker Streets
P.O. Box 1831
Harrisburg, PA 17105

Printed in the U.S.A.

Library of Congress Cataloging-in-Publication Data

Wixom, Hartt.
    Elk and elk hunting.

    Bibliography: p.
    1. Elk hunting.   2. Elk.   I. Title.
SK303.W59   1986   799.2'7357   86-5874
ISBN 0-8117-0600-1

*Dedicated to elk hunters everywhere — and
all who contemplate elk hunting.*

Contents

14   The Elk Camp   181

15   Resident and Nonresident Strategy   188

16   The Extra Edge   199

17   What Is a Trophy?   206

18   Hunting and Game Management   221

19   What of the Future?   245

20   Care of Meat and Mount   265

21   Resources and Contacts   280

       Bibliography   283

       Index   284

Acknowledgments

The author wishes to express appreciation for many persons and institutions who made this book possible. Many are mentioned in the chapters; for those who are not, including my wife, Judene, who typed much of this manuscript, I would like to add a special thanks. Also, to the many fish-game department personnel who assisted, including particular research by the Utah Division of Wildlife Resources, the National Elk Refuge, and the Wyoming Game and Fish Department, and for background material from the province of Alberta. Many local hunters also lent a hand, for which I'm grateful. The mention of anyone in this book is an indication he or she went the extra mile for a resource of particular and charismatic interest: the sight of a wild elk.

Introduction

One reason I've been fascinated with elk is that they want so little to do with me.

They are, perhaps, the most man-shy of all nature's large creatures. Many other game animals running afoul of man, like the timber wolf and grizzly bear, are nearly extinct. But the adaptive wapiti just finds a means, somehow, to remain out of the way. That adaptability now challenges the serious hunter.

But this animal holds more interest for man than merely as a quarry. I admit, however, that my intrigue with *Cervus canadensis* is not as platonic as that of noted ungulate biologist Olaus Murie. He studied elk for years and wrote reams about their behavior. Yet he never wrote of hunting them. I couldn't let the aspen leaves turn ochre without confirming plans for at least one far-country elk quest. But to hunt them only in autumn is too late. A would-be license-filler should ideally "hunt" them year around, yes, even dedicate a portion of his life to the pursuit.

Few hunters score on a big bull wapiti every time out. However, this book is dedicated to those who try! After growing up with elk, and studying them in every state with huntable populations, I'm convinced the fullest enjoyment comes in trying. Success is a bonus.

There's no reason any hunter, veteran or hopeful novice, cannot improve on his "luck" by applying the information (some from experts who have "gotten their elk" nearly every year for half a century) contained herein. Many hunters have said it: "You haven't completed your hunting education until you have hunted a bull elk!"

Let's also envision the hunter taking a greater responsibility in enhancing the future of elk and elk hunting. A giant bull is by all consensus a lordly and majestic animal. My hope is that we can take steps to ensure that our children and theirs have the same opportunity we have.

Besides looking at elk through the eye of a hunter, let's also look at the world through the eyes of an elk.

1

Growing Up with Elk

One of the first, indelible memories I have of elk and elk hunting goes back some 40 years to when I visited an older country cousin. Elk hunting in that part of Idaho was not only a way of life but also contributed heavily to winter meat and basic survival. My cousin and his family had just returned from a successful wapiti hunt, and Jack was credited at the relatively tender age of 14 (legal minimum hunting age) with stopping one of two bulls bagged.

"Jack didn't kill the bull by himself," my uncle was saying, "but on his very first hunt he hit the animal with a fine shot near the front shoulder. That's pretty darn good shooting at a running elk for a kid his age."

I remember the admiration I felt for my cousin. Jack had a proud look on his face I'll never forget. I figured he had a right to feel deep satisfaction in his accomplishment, one I hoped I could duplicate when

old enough to hunt big game. It struck me that this was a physical and, perhaps even more, a mental challenge I wanted to learn more about.

In northern Utah's Cache County (named after the fur-cache habits of mountain-man trappers) where I lived, the minimum hunting age for any big game was 16. It seemed the day would never arrive. There was a winter elk-feeding refuge less than 45 minutes away, plus a university nearby with a major department devoted to big-game management. I had a great deal to learn about this creature before I began hunting it, and I went to work. Judging from the revered and formidable quarry the male wapiti seemed to be, I had the feeling it would be a life-long quest. I was right.

On foothill elk that wintered near my home, I ofttimes attempted to stalk within the length of three football fields. At times, the snow-beleaguered and weary animals would let me do so. But I fooled them not. They heard even my most carefully placed steps in sun-warmed snow or frozen crunch, and they lifted giant heads to mark my progress.

If I avoided a direct line that would mean eventual confrontation nose to nose, the hungry, pawing creatures would sometimes let me approach within the same close range at which I had shot pesky English sparrows. But I knew conditions were not typical here on dependent, nearly starving wapiti. If the elk knew I was around now — with senses less alert than when healthy and hunter-spooked in the fall — how could I hope to sneak up on one during rifle season?

I pondered that mystery as a boy many times while trying to fall asleep. To anchor an elk with a single shot sometimes seemed akin to a native African lad killing a lion with one toss of his spear. In the meantime, I hunted nearly every day during the summer, while school was out, first with a Daisy air rifle on the aforementioned sparrows (six of the grain robbers in a day was deemed good work), and then graduating to my own .22 on rabbits and ground squirrels. I also had an aunt who lectured me on her farm almost daily about shooting at any bird of prey but "chicken" hawks. To me it was a valuable hunting heritage.

That experience was a much-treasured apprenticeship for the day I could sally forth after elk and other big game. I dedicated myself to the goal of improving my stalking and shooting skills. Nor was I aiming merely to reduce my prey to a hump of meat or dead weight. There was something in the very pursuit, the outdoor intrigue, that lifted me into a spirited and exhilarating sphere.

I reasoned that what made the adventure so exciting was the possibility of failure at any time. There could be no guarantee, or it wouldn't be fair chase. It was a duel: the cunning and wild instincts of the quarry against whatever I could legally counter against it.

As for in-season hunting ethics, I didn't consider them altruistic or worthy of any special acclaim. It was just that if I went out golfing, I wouldn't want a funnel to force my every drive into the hole. My hunting joy was in the knowledge that success would depend not on manipulated fate but on my own savvy. If it wasn't up to par, my outdoor opponent would win. Satisfaction like my country cousin's would come only from meeting the foe and outwitting him at his own game. From an early age, I wasted absolutely no sympathy for poaching and no-challenge encounters.

If I intended to succeed on an animal considered the apex of nature's wiliest survival instincts, I decided it would require a year-round learning effort. My outdoor education would need to continue in the so-called off-season, making detailed notes and planning to at least learn more about *Cervus canadensis* than he knew about me. And if this hurdle could be mastered, I would be that much ahead of most other hunting challenges as well.

So it was that I began to bone up on a creature that even 40 years later I still regard as the most wily (I would even call it "intelligent," no matter what the scientists may label it) large creature in the wilds. The bull elk does not live as high or as far removed from civilization as the bighorn ram, nor does he hide as unobtrusively as the whitetail deer. He doesn't pose the threat while you are hunting him that the grizzly or mountain lion does. But many serious nimrods I have interviewed over the years share with me the gut feeling that nothing anywhere is as elusive and matchless as a bull elk *when he knows he is being hunted.*

Split Personalities

As winter approached, I liked to visit Hardware Elk Refuge, where I witnessed the same phenomenon many times. Elk fed there on cured hay each winter like so many docile cattle. Many observers, and even some beginning hunters, talked about how "tame" the animals were and how simple it would be in the fall to find an "easy" bull in the nearby canyons. But when the aspens turned to gold, no sign of a male wapiti could be found — until they showed up the next week or two on the safety side of the refuge.

To be sure, a few license-holders did manage to harvest elk. But success ran only from 5 percent to 8 percent. The percentage wasn't much better when the state allowed unlimited hunting for bull elk for anyone over 15 with $25 in his pocket.

Where did the critters hie to during hunting season? It was as if a flying saucer had absconded with all elk to another planet, only to return them a few days after hunting season. One thing for sure, hundreds of them returned, some with massive antlers, every winter.

If salivating over those racks did nothing else, it convinced me the elk are always there. It's just a matter of finding them where they have always been. Come late November or early December, you can witness elk in almost any mountain state's foothills. Elk are there again for the world to see, as if taunting the hapless hunter who was convinced earlier that the bulls were "all shot out."

Those who hunted with the assurance that elk were about, perhaps nearby, were the ones who scored most often. If they doubted elk were on a given mountain, desert, or somewhere in between, all they had to do was scout a few back roads in winter. Convinced as I was that elk, especially oversized bulls, can and do hide successfully from hunters every fall, my own hunting success later doubled and quadrupled.

While growing up, I also encountered some other truths about elk. One was that it is difficult if not impossible while viewing something akin to the Hartford Insurance stag in your sights, to avoid at least a modicum of buck (bull) fever. I know I had some. While pussyfooting about the hills on my first few hunts as a youngster, I couldn't help but wonder how splendid, even overwhelming, a lordly 7-pointer would look in my open iron rifle sights. I had hit the paper bull in target practice. But could I shoot as well with a trophy perhaps posing broadside in bright sunlight 50 yards away?

I didn't find out. I may never find out. I rarely sneaked up on such an unaware quarry. Oh, in time I did meet a few "gift" elk. Most of my elk, though, were earned with hard work and patience. They weren't so likely to stand like a calendar painting for me as they were to be sneaking off, if at close range. I did learn that a bull might pose for me, but usually at distances no closer than 300 yards.

I didn't fully realize it then, but there never would be any sure permanent cure for bull fever. Nor would I want one. Someone has already said it: "The day you don't get goose bumps on your arms and a lump in your throat at the sight of a magnificent bull elk, it's time to exchange your rifle for the rocking chair." Amen.

Besides, there are ways to put bull fever, or at least the excitement of it, to work in your behalf. It can help you shoot more accurately just as excitement helps an NBA basketball player hit most of his attempts in a crucial playoff game. More about bull fever later.

Another strong impression I received early is the need to stand back and analyze what's happening. On one occasion near a large population center, I remember more than a dozen orange-vesters standing around a dead bull, all claiming to be the owner. Though my approach was considered yet another claim, I quickly dispelled the idea. I let the crowd know I surely hadn't killed that elk, nor was I going to try for any other in the vicinity, thank you. As I departed, I recall they were still quarreling over which bullet hole proved ownership.

Elk, with its intolerance to man, cannot and should not be sought in such a free-for-all circus spectacle. Where it occurs, there is no scouting of game, no lengthy stalk to reach it on opening day, and no reward for the most skillful and proficient approach. The outcome of such a shoot depends more on how long the bull has run, how far, and how tired it becomes when wandering into a hunter. True, the hunter must still actually shoot the elk. But the greatest challenge, that of stalking within range, is totally absent, and any advance attempt to locate an undisturbed bull is wasted effort. Any opportunity for science of the hunt has fled with the spooked animal.

Game managers may be right in saying that such low-quality hunts cannot hurt the resource. They reason that if bulls get tougher to find, license sales decrease until bull numbers return. I don't disagree with

that. But true elk hunting it is not. It's expensive camping.

Some sort of quality control, a limited number of hunters in a given area, is what I mean here when talking about true elk hunting. Otherwise, it deteriorates into an experience like one I had in my younger days when I scouted 13 bull elk in one high park, only to have them all dispersed before opening day. Reason? Improved roads allowed too-easy access. What's more, during the next three days of checking with hunters over that mountain, I learned that only one even saw any bulls at all! One party told me: "We camped right there at the edge of that meadow and staked out our horses *inside* the meadow. It looked like a great place to camp because we saw so many elk tracks around. But during the next couple days, would you believe we didn't see a single bull?"

I believed him.

In the meantime, our own camp two miles lower gave us no advantage over those 13 bulls whatsoever. Our super caution had gone for naught.

It is also a fact that you could glass distant bulls, plan your approach carefully, stalk within rifle range, and nail the trophy with one shot . . . in your mind. But something else unforeseen like a shifting wind current or another far-away nimrod's horse whinnying could quickly create problems. What you need is some rugged terrain, away from the crowd. That combination will give you a chance to put your skills and instincts to best use. Wild terrain is your ally: it keeps the masses away.

I still believe, even after 40 years, that you're better off to turn down a sure "open bull" license for one requiring a drawing, or limiting hunters. The former is all right if the number of applicants allows you an opportunity, particularly in wild back country, to scout your quarry. The elk usually head where man is not. But if there is no such place about, you don't have much of a hunt.

Talk ran rampant, and still does through the 20th Century, that "we should have lived" during the time of Kit Carson or Jim Bridger, when vast herds of elk grazed complacently with bison on prairie grass. Things were undoubtedly better then because of less hunting competition. But unbridled and undisciplined squandering of the "unlimited" resource, without sound game management, actually made hunting poorer by the early 1900s than it is now.

I also hear novice hunters everywhere complain about today's hunting — and "how good" it must have been 40 years ago. Yes, and no. I had a tougher time bringing home elk steaks then than now. Charts and graphs prove unquestionably there were more elk two or three decades ago. But elk hunting is much better for me in the 1980s because I know so much more about the quarry. Acquired hunting skills can, to a considerable degree, offset conditions which are not what they used to be.

No More Dream Hunts?

Is "The Great American Elk Hunt" long gone? Not really. Reports of their total demise are greatly exaggerated. Elk hunting is just tougher in some respects now. There are still many miles of prime elk domain in nearly every western state. The trouble is, some hunters still haven't tapped into it. The elk have done an excellent job of adjusting to what remains. In some hinterlands, I suspect elk are still dying of old age, and certainly little bothered by man. It depends on how far off roads you are willing to venture, how much time you will budget to probe higher and farther, how dedicated you are to hunting a wilderness animal where he yet flourishes.

There are many other "little" things to be learned about elk. Some bands, even herds, do abound in and around the cities or near highways. But there are generally special reasons. As a 13-year-old, I discovered on two occasions that wapiti (including some respectable bulls) had "holed" up almost in my suburban back yard. And during the latter part of the elk hunting season to boot!

Deep snows in Utah's Wasatch Mountains had pushed the animals down one late October to a narrow defile less than 200 yards from Interstate 80. The other band of elk spent the entire fall and winter in one small canyon just out of sight of a Boy Scout camp where I labored unsuccessfully for a glimpse of wildlife to help me pass the requirements for a nature merit badge. What I and apparently my adult leaders failed to discover was that the elk took sanctuary there year after year. After a heavy snowfall, these creatures of habit still migrate to this one canyon. I imagine they'll continue to do so as long as it isn't converted into a summer cabin subdivision or year-around resort.

The two winning ingredients in this elk Valhalla were sufficient south-slope food (rich grasses and browse with ample sunlight and little snow retention) and being out of sight from the roadway. But if you hiked up the slope they were on, the elk could hear you long before you could see them. The best way to study them was to hike up the *opposite* slope, then look cross-canyon.

As for the elk hidden near I-80, they could be glimpsed from the 6-lane freeway if you happened to look precisely at the right time in precisely the right place. The crucial spot was smack in the middle of an exit from a cloverleaf exchange, not the sort of place you ever stopped. You could also observe those elk if approaching from above, but you would have to cross two steep ridgelines to do so.

These elk probably once fled winter onto benchlands above the nearby metropolis. However, continued urban sprawl up the mountainside prevented traditional migration from higher terrain. You had to sit down and ask: "If I were an elk in this situation, where would I go?" Answer: down somewhere out of the highland snow, but still away from easy access by human beings, their traffic, and their dogs. That aforementioned ravine was one of the few places left. It is a monument to the elk's adaptability in taking whatever man leaves him—and to man's insensitivity to elk in taking over the elk winter range in the first place.

Many times I have seen elk "take hold" in a small meadow tilted away from roads or trails—some obscure yet fairly accessible shelf or ledges that for some reason or another man does not care to bother. If man were half so ingenious in taking advantage of every niche open to him, the entire human race would prosper more and complain less.

In many regions where elk were rumored to exist, I rarely saw any sign of them. Yet, analyzing it in my mind, I realized I was sticking to easiest trails. I went where others went, into highland fishing lakes, or scenic overlooks. It was when I determined to go where other boot prints hadn't that I found elk. I climbed over deadfall timber, across rock slides, up steep rims, and into forgotten basins. Some of these places were no more than a quarter-mile off beaten tracks. Up until then, I had envisioned the elk as a mystery animal, a phantom of the woods, even a figment of some downtown game manager's imagination. More often than not, I learned they were also real. Most were a bundle of hot adrenaline, with alert nervous systems and quick hooves. When I went hunting in such territory later, I noticed a decided increase in locating elk. I *knew* they were there. I was not merely walking through the forest with a gun. I felt like a hunter. A bull was expected over the next arroyo or behind the next wall of spruces . . . and very often it was there. With the confidence that they *must* be there now, for they have always been there before, I found shootable elk. Not always, of course, but more than in times past.

Elk Quick to Flee

One of my first forays into remote elk country was by horseback with a federal big-game biologist. He had courageously banned sheep from grazing this steep slope above a certain western community. But continued overgrazing by elk in particular had badly abused the watershed. Spring floods from snowmelt no longer hesitated among plant roots here, for few remained. Floods descended with the first spring thaw.

When we arrived at the target area, it was obvious many elk had just abandoned the hill. Their tracks were etched in the soft mud, and mud was sprayed over crusted snow. The biologist eventually solved the flooding dilemma by planting water-holding grasses on steep areas along the mountain. Then he reseeded with bitterbrush and mountain mahogany to replace chained-out, poor-in-nutrition junipers.

The thing I remember best about that trek, though, was that the wapiti took flight so quickly that we saw none of them. The biologist suggested they heard our horses half a mile before we ever approached sight of the abused slope. On the return trip, we searched widely for elk but never succeeded in seeing any.

From that trip, I learned how intolerant of man wapiti can be. Even the biologist marveled that all could vanish so rapidly. "They'll be back here soon," he said. "They never leave this hill alone for long. But in the meantime, they have probably trotted off to the next county."

Not all such early impressions of wapiti were valid. At times, the big animals seemed extra-terrestrial in eluding mankind. But I was to learn later that even the elk has a few chinks in its armor.

Some "Achilles' heels" are obvious, such as the elk's inclination to crash dead ahead, bowling over spindle aspens or anything that gets in its way. By comparison, a deer (muley or whitetail) is much more surreptitious and difficult to pinpoint by sound. Other wapiti weaknesses are much more subtle, some I learned partly as a youngster. Some weaknesses required years more for me to diagnose and verify. If this sounds like a psychological encounter of the toughest kind, I agree. But I'll explain more about that later in this book.

Some of my early education about *Cervus canadensis* taught me the difference between instinctive reaction and conditioned response. I once accompanied an older hunter who owned an elk permit for a drawing-only topnotch elk unit. When we arrived, however, we were disappointed at the semi-desert landscape. We had to hike hours before daylight to reach a little saddle between two north-slope fir pockets. Hardly classic elk territory.

But scarcely after arriving at the unlikely spot and still puffing from the walk, we saw a dark apparition appear from nowhere. It was a monarch bull with high, back-swept antlers. They seemed to tower into the early morning sunlight. My mentor, who had scored on many mule-deer bucks with a single shot, fumbled at his safety. I noted awe in his eyes. And although he never said so, I also suspected he was just not ready to see such a grand sight so early in the hunt. He fired his old .30-40 Krag, and the monster kicked both front legs and cartwheeled over backward. Then everything was silent.

We hurried over. There was no blood, only brown earth. Nowhere could we locate that bull. Hours later, my companion and I could only deduce that the slug must have connected with the bull's antlers. From watching other game animals react since, including both elk and deer, I still think that was what happened. In any event, we did not see the elk again.

My friend candidly admitted to me that with deer, he had always been ready to shoot. He had spent long hours at the practice range before most of his big hunts. But in this instance, he hadn't used his rifle just lately. And if there was a moment of confusion because of the bull's grandeur, it was compounded by failure to quickly locate the rifle safety. When he was finally ready to shoot, there was precious little time.

I label this situation a "response" because it was something he had to stop and think about accomplishing.

By contrast, I learned later in the military's basic training what it is like to react from instinct. As would-be soldiers, my infantry company took six days just learning the most fundamental rudiments of shooting a rifle.

We spent nearly four days doing absolutely nothing but aiming and squeezing the trigger. The instant the trigger actually tripped, no shot rang out. We hadn't yet been issued any ammo. But a buddy hit you in the shoulder to simulate rifle recoil. It seemed a colossal waste of time, especially for us "mountain boys" who were practically born with a firearm in our laps. But I never forgot what the army had so deeply "drilled" into my consciousness. The steps of taking a full breath of air, letting some of it out while aiming, and then slowly pulling the trigger until it fired was no longer something that I had to think about. It was from then on an instinct, ingrained almost like breathing itself. With such training, a shooter learns to not only aim as accurately as he can but also to shoot without flinching, for you never know exactly when the round will touch off. Such methodical approach to shooting seemed unnecessary and monotonous to me then, as a teen-ager. But it has helped me with my elk hunting ever since. The same good habits will help you, too.

Shooting—Like Golf

In younger years I also tried my hand occasionally at golf. It seemed much like shooting to me. Without some practice, I couldn't retain the delicate "edge" for feeling the chips and putts so necessary to scoring well. I'm not talking here about the mechanics of shooting without flinching, or even trigger squeeze. I'm talking about the process of aiming accurately. My buddy who missed the trophy of a lifetime had hunted all his life. But he became

rusty in the refinement of shooting under stress. When he couldn't quickly locate the safety, he felt more panic than necessary. There are enough uncontrollables and variables in elk hunting as it is without programming more in.

Ever since that experience, I have always practiced shooting on paper targets exactly as I would in hunting season if an elk suddenly showed. That is, I go from safety "off" to safety "on" with each practice shot. And if I intend to shoot from a sitting position on the hunt (prone may be more deadly accurate, but how often can you shoot from this poor visibility position on the hunt?), that's how I'm going to practice on the target range. Simulate the actual hunt as much as possible.

Something I learned as a kid from older fishermen about the law of averages pertains directly to hunting. I was in the habit of reeling in my line, then gathering coat, maps, and other gear and departing straightaway to the next fishing hole.

"You're missing out on half an hour's fishing a day," a wiser angler told me. "They just might be the very minutes some oversized whopper decides to hit. Don't you think you should take advantage of that lost time?"

I asked him what he meant. He demonstrated by mimicking my actions. "Why not gather your line in last, and also make a couple more casts as you depart—while you're deciding exactly what route you want to take?"

Since then, I've caught many good fish with that extra cast or two per hour. The same philosophy paid off with hunting. One more scan of the hunting grounds as you gather belongings to head out could pay off with an elk. You might spot it on the move as it crosses into a "window of vulnerability" between two bushes or stands up from a bed in thick cover where you can now see him. Will the extra effort pay? Maybe you can't count on it. But never shut the door on it, either.

My association with elk over the years has taught me some hard lessons about not only the how and where of elk hunting but also the why. If you have ever listened to the anti-hunting sympathizers, you'll understand why I mention this point. My second winter living in Salt Lake City, Utah, was a long and rough one, the type that comes along about every five years. The mountains immediately eastward had been a game preserve, a no-hunting sanctuary for deer and elk for several years. This seemed the "humane" way to protect wildlife, anti-hunting advocates argued.

By Christmas, the snow had piled six feet deep in the upper canyons. Skiers loved it. But wildlife was driven down into the edges of the city. It was soon clear that deer and elk were in deep trouble. One more snowstorm, and these animals descended like an avalanche out of control into the city itself. Within 200 yards of my home was a country club's golf course. Deer moved right into the yards and ornamental shrubs in downtown Salt Lake City, and the elk made their home on the city-limit edge of the golf course.

To begin with, these desperate elk hid by day along the trout creek that meandered through the links. Then, they literally took over the 9th hole and 10th tee. Of course, many calls went out to the game department to "come and fetch" these wild animals from such fragile damage zones. All the firecrackers and noisemakers in the world did not a bit of good. There was simply no place else for the creatures to go. They soon destroyed both green and tee areas. And eventually, some destroyed themselves.

Elsewhere in the valley, elk leaped fences around haystacks to either catch a leg and die there, or be eaten alive by dogs. Some of those that did not die that way starved to death.

The deer, which subsisted poorly on small, emergency rations of hay placed along the foothills, died in even greater numbers than the hardier elk. The elk had remained in the mountains longer, since they were able to reach higher for conifer needles and bark above snow level. They also ate all hay placed out. But by March, some 60 percent of the deer and up to 25 percent of the elk had perished. Those few that attempted to commute between golf course and foothills morning and night were often entangled with traffic, causing a serious hazard for man and beast. The same nightmare was repeated in many parts of the West that winter, but perhaps none with the tragic results of this ill-conceived "game sanctuary."

Little Justice for Wildlife

Those people who had built homes in the wintering grounds of the elk and deer demanded, and most of them received, payment for damage caused by the animals. Why had zoning boards allowed developers to asphalt and pave this terrain required by the wintering wildlife? The boards should have done so only with the stipulation that those who take over the winter range be required to feed the starving wildlife.

As the winter wore on, I almost learned the first names of those elk. Many seemed to sense that flight was hopeless. I walked up within a few yards of some. They were resigned to whatever fate nature, and more especially man, might deal them. Younger animals perished right where they were.

Their carcasses that spring were tossed onto trucks and hauled away. Not only had they died much more cruelly than by any method I can think of but also no one benefitted from hunting them or from their meat. The sanctuary idea resulted in unspeakable waste. A few years later, before hunting was introduced, another "unseasonable" winter laid more valuable elk to waste.

When hunting was later allowed here, so-called "animal lovers" decried loss of the game-preserve philosophy. But after hunting began, considerably fewer animals died each winter. Hunting clearly brought three-fold benefits: (1) a healthier range that provided enough food to sustain a lesser number of animals; (2) financial revenues through sale of unit elk licenses; and (3) outdoor recreational opportunity.

Of course, the tragedy of winter-wasted game is one repeated over and over in western wildlife history. On Arizona's Kaibab, a no-hunting edict caused deer herds to multiply to upwards of 100,000 animals. In time, a depleted rangeland could sustain no more than 10,000. The entire herd was nearly lost. The wildlife-management tool of hunting again came to the rescue, skimming off the annual surplus to keep numbers at the range's feed-carrying capacity. Only by reduced total numbers could the remaining population thrive and finally flourish once again.

I don't need to take the word of some game manager in an obscure text book. I saw such disaster for myself, and at an impressionable age. The lessons were stamped indelibly in my mind. I apologize to no one for being a hunter, and especially in rendering the services of a book about hunting. If anyone should lament the shooting of a resplendent and mighty bull elk by fair and ethical means, let him be sentenced to watch the wapiti suffer and then be doomed to die by slow starvation, as I did.

Many winters have shown me how much people care about wildlife. I have witnessed people taking lettuce, grass clippings, even Christmas trees to feed elk in trouble. This is commendable, albeit a belated stopgap measure caused by poor or nonexistent winter range. When it occurs, even more hunting permits is about the only way of resolving it. Trapping, difficult and expensive, is another.

Lasting Impressions

These are the lasting impressions of a young boy who frequently saw things more from the eyes of an elk than from those of a man. Perhaps someone will come along to change my opinion, but they will have to offer more logic and reason than led to my deeply imprinted conclusions in the first place.

Most of all, I gained a great respect for *Cervus canadensis*. All experience crystallized a love for that time of year known as Indian Summer when the wapiti (Shawnee for "light-colored deer") season approached. I've also looked at a few so-called "slob" hunters who rush out for half a day hoping to "luck" into an elk, forgetting to close gates or pick up litter. But for this five percent, there are those dedicated souls I've become acquainted with many times over in hunting and guiding for elk. Most of them are, in my opinion, a special breed apart who know they have taken on one of nature's most challenging creatures. Yet these hunters prepared physically and mentally each year for this special epic event in their hunting lives. In so doing, they grew physically and mentally from the challenge.

Then there are the long-time elk experts like Wyoming neighbor and senior citizen Don Cozzens. At this writing, Don seeks bull elk number 50 come his next fall outing. At his age, Don knows he must rely more on knowledge of the subject than simply the physical stamina to ride and ride and search week after week. Don has reduced elk hunting to an exact science, or about as close to it as you can humanly get. You'll learn more later about how he does it so consistently. You will also gain an insight into the strategy of many consistently successful guides and outfitters throughout elkdom, from South Dakota to Washington and Arizona to Alaska.

You may also ponder upon some of your own youthful impressions of elk and elk hunting. Are you comfortable with your hunting heritage, as well as your hunter-success history? Are you willing to change hunting habits and strategy in the light of additional information?

I know that many times in younger or adult life I've had to readjust my opinions about elk. In most cases, I have had to reevaluate my efforts to outwit him. If you have ever told yourself elk hunting is "just too hard," rest assured that most other elkers have also thought the same once or twice themselves.

The attitude you've grown up with is extremely important, especially your negative or positive outlook about succeeding. No doubt you've been out with older and wiser hunters who wouldn't give up until they tied on a tag. On the other hand, you've likely been out with some who give up quickly. They deem it "wisdom" to complain. But are they the same ones who frequently return from a rabbit or waterfowl hunt empty-handed? Is failing to score blamed on something or someone else, rather than themselves? That attitude can get to be a habit. A bad one.

I also remember forming some early hunting habits that later proved less desirable than they might have been. Some are so much a part of our maturing process that we don't even realize how negative thinking can creep in. But I do know this: most elk hunters are unsuccessful because of attitude, mostly negative, far more often than from lack of game.

Whether you have hunted all your life or are just getting started, I aim to change your "luck" for the better. You won't return home with a tag filled every time. Just more often than in the past.

2

History and Lore

Elk have long been classified by biologists into at least six subspecies. Biologist Olaus Murie, who studied them extensively over a lifetime, catalogues them as follows:

EASTERN (*Cervus canadensis canadensis*)—The same species discovered by the first white men in North America. For simplification here, it is defined as all elk east of the Rocky Mountains, although a few "eastern" elk undoubtedly took refuge in the Rockies when driven from the Great Plains and Black Hills.

ROCKY MOUNTAIN (*Cervus canadensis nelsoni*)—The elk of the Rockies and West, other than Pacific Coast. Most of the top trophies listed in record books (such as Boone and Crockett Club's world annals) belong to this longer-tined species. (Note: This species is sometimes classified *Cervus elaphus.*)

ROOSEVELT (*Cervus canadensis roosevelti*)—The dark species inhabiting rainforests of Washington, Oregon, British Columbia, Canada, and, to an extent, northern California. These elk are often larger (but not necessarily heavier) than the Rocky Mountain variety.

MANITOBAN (*Cervus canadensis manitobensis*)—Elk of Manitoba and Saskatchewan. Some historically crossed the border into Great Lakes states.

MERRIAM (*Cervus canadensis merriami*)—Now extinct species which lived in the Southwest, mainly Arizona and New Mexico.

TULE (*Cervus nannodes*)—The nearly extinct "dwarf" wapiti of central California marshes and tule swamps.

If this rundown seems complicated, let's hereafter refer to all elk as merely *Cervus canadensis*. Most encyclopedias and reference texts do the same. After all, the elk don't care what we call them in English or Latin. But we should know as much as possible about the various species, and differentiate between location and hunting techniques. We will also see how elk were hunted in the past. It may help us locate and outwit them today.

It could be debated how the wapiti arrived in North America. But most ungulate scientists attribute it to migration after the last Great Ice Age from Asia (where elk still thrive) over a "land bridge" into western Alaska. From there they pushed down through Canada into the present-day United States. One of the first to record observations of the "great deer" was Giovanni da Verrazzano in 1542. Others who followed described elk as "fairly widespread" along the Eastern Seaboard.

They were frequently sighted from New England almost into the Deep South. Georgia, Florida, and thereabouts was, in fact, about the only region in the U.S. where elk did not seem to dwell in numbers.

Ancient elk bones were also discovered on Alaska's Afognak Island. But the herds that are there now are of the reintroduced Roosevelt species.

It is well documented that the Europeans named this new member of the deer family "alke" after their Old World moose. Of course, this became confusing later when American moose were also discovered. But by then the name stuck, albeit altered slightly. Only the Shawnee and a few neighboring Indian tribes labeled it something else: wapiti, or "light deer." Scientists later would adopt the Shawnee name to avoid the technical misnomer, elk. Of course, the Piute Indians of the Great Basin used neither appellation, for they were among the few early Americans who had never observed the creature.

Elk flourished from Maine (few early journals mention them, but elk bones were later located there) across the Adirondacks, Alleghenies, and Appalachians, through Kentucky-Tennessee all the way to Louisiana. From there they thrived westward to the Pacific Ocean, save only the desert Great Basin. Michigan, Minnesota, and Wisconsin harbored large elk populations. So did Illinois, Indiana, and Pennsylvania, although wapiti disappeared there more quickly due to a rapid civilization influx. Naturalist Ernest Thompson Seton estimated some 10 million elk lived in North America before arrival of the Europeans. But numbers plummeted to about 100,000 by 1907. Populations stabilized for the next two decades, but many of the elk were nonhuntable inhabitants of the Yellowstone Park and Grand Teton ecosystems.

Story of the Demise

Settlers in Iowa in 1856 tell of elk becoming so "pesky" and bothersome in a severe winter that they were destroyed with axes and corn knives. That year's tough winter made them particularly vulnerable, for there were no "remote" or unpopulated hinterlands they could escape to. Most disappeared within a few years. In Kansas, sharpshooters often set wagers on how many bison and elk they could kill in one day, although the wapiti fared far better than the buffalo. Reports say the elk survived by their wits in the less accessible, broken, wooded canyons, especially upper headwater sectors. Like dying embers in a rainstorm they vanished from the plains but continued to hold out in states like Missouri, where the Ozark Mountains offered refuge. A large population of "stags" seem also to have lived furtively with the whitetail deer in western New York's deciduous forests right up until the mid-1800s.

Some of the greatest eastern populations lived in Virginia and the Carolinas. Virginia reflects this episode in her past with place names like Elk Garden, Elkton, and Elkwood, as does Pennsylvania. In North Carolina, natural history records dated 1754 indicate that elk resided "in droves" with buffalo. They were nearly exterminated early in the 19th Century due to unlimited market hunting, loss of habitat, and absence of game laws. (There was no poaching, technically speaking, since there were no hunting regulations.) It may be difficult today to picture New Jersey, Maryland, Massachusetts, and other highly industrialized states as carrying "numerous" elk herds, but so the early records prove.

Four species of elk resided in pioneer times in the backcountry of Canada. The Roosevelt fared well (and still does) on Vancouver Island and mainland British Columbia. The Rocky Mountain species crossed boundary lines frequently from Idaho and Montana. The Manitoban variety occupied much of that province eastward to Quebec. The Eastern elk prevailed from southernmost Canada into New England.

Actually, elk maintained "pocket" populations almost anyplace man wasn't. The areas elk best adapted to were clearly wherever they could find cooler climates in summer and lower elevations in winter — places where they were not in conflict with mankind.

Elk first vanished from areas readily accessible to men by train or stagecoach. As the horse was used more and more, com-bined later with the introduction of the repeating Winchester rifle in 1873, Eastern wapiti were in deep trouble. Although they were not decimated as rapidly as the bison was devastated by professional hunters like "Buffalo Bill" Cody, many were shot to feed hungry railroad and work crews. Like today's elk, those animals stalled wholesale demise by their characteristic mobility and wary nature. Nez Perce chief Joseph told his hunters to approach the elk with utmost caution, "for they will travel 10–12 miles before stopping" in wilderness terrain, and then "place out pickets" to watch for danger on their back trail.

That, too, sounds like the wapiti of modern times.

One midwest surveyor in 1860 put it this way: "The elk is very wary, and difficult to shoot at times, but is often taken on the small prairies near heads of rivers where it feeds evening and morning."

Some of the most proficient hunters during those early times were the native Americans. Indians did in an elk any way they could, driving them on foot or horseback into pits, over cliffs, into water or deadfall timber or deep snows for easier dispatch with spears, bows, or clubs. A favorite tactic of the Assiniboin, Cree, and Arapaho was to snowshoe alongside animals floundering along late fall migration lanes. The Iowas like to ride pell-mell into the middle of a herd, selecting tender cows and calves that were unable to shift into high gear due to the nearness of other elk. Some hunters approached silently in canoes as elk fed at dusk, then shot from close range as the ungulates lumbered from soft mud. Many of these Indians used the most primitive of bow and arrow weapons. According to accounts by the Lewis and Clark Expedition of 1804–06, elk were sometimes found with superficial body wounds and scars that hadn't yet healed.

Indians Wasted Little

The Indians had specific needs for their kills. In addition to meat, elk shoulder blades were used for heavy digging. Hides were fashioned into robes, coats, ground cloths, tarpaulins, and waterproof canoe covers. Every part of the elk had a use for tribes like the Cheyenne and Sioux. There seemed no end to the imaginative ways squaws could utilize teeth: bracelets, necklaces, and dress adornments. Decorative elk tooth dresses could bring up to eight ponies in barter. Many old hunters refused to part with an impressive rack of antlers at any price. Some were highly prized items of inheritance associated with nobility, popularity, and sexual prowess.

The shooting of a monarch bull, naturally enough, was proof in itself of macho skills and masculinity. It is not surprising that the bull's acumen in commanding a large harem impressed many tribesmen. Some seemed to worship the male wapiti, considering it "good medicine" to have him around, dead or alive. Larger bulls were studied for their many mystic powers in subduing rivals, shunting off danger with hooves and antlers, and their general lordly appearance.

Elk meat was never as easy to acquire for the midwest Indian as buffalo was, but elk venison was eaten whenever possible. Some Indians are said to have eaten up to 10 pounds of wapiti per day. Elk meat provided much of the protein, minerals, and vitamins needed, particularly during the winter. Crow Indians went to considerable lengths to obtain elk meat in and around the Yellowstone region, monitoring wapiti movements when the animals were most vulnerable. If they were migrating across water, for example, Crows were apt to descend like locusts.

Yellowstone was early recognized as an unusual haven for elk. Crow Indians named the great stream there the "Elk River," although the first white man maps seem to have favored "Yellowstone."

Trapper Osborne Russell wrote in his extensive journal that he observed many elk in that region. When such news circulated back east, trophy hunters (plus commercial meat dealers) descended on the park. In 1875 two brothers were said to have dispatched some 2,000 elk near Mammoth Hot Springs, saving little from each but the tongue and a few hides. Skins were not always utilized at the time, because prices fetched were seldom more than $3 apiece.

Protection as we know it today was not provided for Yellowstone elk until 1894. A series of jurisdictional law-enforcement authority squabbles finally resulted in wildlife coming under Wyoming Territorial game regulations. However, except for a brief period of military vigilance, the extensive wildlife of Yellowstone was really not afforded much more protection than was given to game in the remainder of Wyoming.

By the early 1930s, epitaphs were being written for the wapiti. Hunters lamented that the "great hunts of the 1800s are now over." Said one hunter sadly: "No longer can a man arm himself and go kill whatever game he seeks."

The Turnaround

However, a minor miracle occurred in the next decade when man began promoting hunting for sport rather than meat. Aldo Leopold said in 1933 that "hunting for recreation is an improvement over meat hunting . . . since in addition to skill, an ethical code is introduced."

Then, too, champions of conservation like Theodore Roosevelt persevered with influential organizations like the Benevolent and Protective Order of Elk (BPOE) to limit killing. Elk were no longer destroyed just for tongue or teeth (the latter used almost solely as symbols of prestige, or household knick-knacks). Game laws were also toughened during Roosevelt's rise to prominence. These efforts initiated a substantial comeback for the elk. Michigan was the first state to require elk licenses, in 1895, with North Dakota next.

Unfortunately, many of these changes in thinking occurred too late to save wild herds in Michigan, Oklahoma, Texas, and California. Their hunting seasons closed.

However, if man's westward destiny extirpated the elk in many states, such was notably not the case in others, such as Montana, Wyoming, and Idaho. This was the region Meriwether Lewis and William Clark explored in 1804–06. In fact, Lewis and Clark referred to elk no less than 570 times in their journals. They observed Rocky Mountain elk from western Montana across the Idaho panhandle, and from eastern Oregon into the Pacific drainage, where the Roosevelt species was witnessed.

Of course, wapiti are not as widely dispersed now as then, and observations today are more likely to be little more than glimpses. But modern elk in this region do more closely approximate historic numbers than is the case in most other areas of the United States.

In the Dakotas, wapiti didn't fare as well. Large numbers, including bulls of trophy size, were pushed from strongholds like the Black Hills into the higher Rockies. Some of the Eastern species undoubtedly mixed with Rocky Mountain elk until today's scientists are not sure which herds originated where. Olaus Murie says that only one Eastern elk skin was preserved in a museum for future generations to study.

Why the demise of the eastern species, compared to the relatively wide survival of the Rocky Mountain elk? It wasn't necessarily that the latter was more robust. More likely, it simply had more options available—more unpeopled seams and crevices to hole up in as the human juggernaut advanced. With few exceptions, the Rocky Mountain elk managed more readily to avoid conflict with man.

Elk in Abundance

One of those exceptions was in Jackson Hole, Wyoming. One estimate said 40,000 elk once wintered there. But winter range was commandeered by an influx of settlers in the late 1800s and early 1900s, signaling a dramatic conflict. It was either eliminate the elk or feed them. Local citizens resisted for several years any extensive feeding efforts, choosing at first to make up for winter losses by banning fall hunting—accomplished via establishment of the Teton Game Preserve in 1907. This halted all elk hunting south and east of the Snake River, downslope from the Teton Mountain range. The elk then grew so numerous they literally ate themselves out of house and home. Some estimates said "not less than 10,000 elk" starved to death in the Jackson area in the winter of 1897.

In the tough winter of 1909, elk raided any valley haystack they could find. A few migrated southward, but even those elk moving on through Jackson Hole seemed to spend some time at the feeding troughs competing with horses and livestock. Thousands of elk trampled frontyard shrubs and backyard fitzers. By spring so many died that a stench settled over the entire valley. Clearly, elk would continue to be at least a nuisance in mild winters, and a major disaster during severe ones. For example, records of the U.S. Fish and Wildlife Service conservatively indicated that 2,500 elk died in the winter of 1911, with 75 percent of the calves lost. About that many elk were also estimated lost in the winter of 1917.

Surviving elk, calculated to be as numerous as 20,000 in 1911, caused almost as much complaint among some citizens as those that died. Other citizens went to work raising $5,000 for hay to supplement winter feeding of elk. According to early game biologist E. A. Prehle, many elk died during that time, and not all by starvation. Many succumbed to dogs. Prehle opined that wolves killed as many as a thousand wapiti (most weakened by hunger) in one winter.

Later, when stockmen and governmental agencies made wholesale war on wolves and similar sheep (and elk) predators, even more elk came into conflict with man. It was figured that herds increased by 20 percent annually until the dilemma of elk versus man became so acute that radical change was obviously needed, and in a hurry. It was accomplished by (1) more hunting, and (2) establishment of a National Elk Refuge just outside the town of Jackson.

The small refuge, signed into law in 1912, helped pinpoint a solution, but it was still inadequate to feed elk in a tough winter. Eventually crusaders like first ref-uge manager D. C. Nowlin fought for expansion beyond the original 2,760 acres. Conservation organizations like the Izaak Walton League stepped in to raise funds, purchase additional acreage, and convince federal decision-makers to provide even more. Today the National Elk Refuge includes some 24,000 acres. Although this refuge is only a minor segment of the winter range supporting northwestern Wyoming elk, it was a proud accomplishment for citizens, sportsmen, and professional wildlife managers.

With establishment of Grand Teton National Park in 1950, a new challenge arose: maintaining a balance between protected and hunted elk. It was met in 1958 with "hunting agreements" for elk reduction on the north or "access" side of the refuge. Though a population goal of 20,000 wapiti had been established in 1927, then changed to 15,000 elk on the refuge in 1944, the numbers agreed on later (1974) were 7,500 maximum, 5,000 minimum.

Tule Elk Vs. Gold Rush

The tule elk of California had a more difficult time of it than most other western species. Subjected to the great Gold Rush of 1849, this species for some reason did not flee into the high Sierra Nevada mountains. They appeared better adapted to the lower marshlands and "tule swamps," where they managed to avoid extinction with the help of awakened California conservation efforts. This is a better fate than that of the Merriam elk in Arizona and New Mexico. The Merriam is gone forever.

Demise of the Merriam seems unfathomable, inasmuch as they inhabited one of the most rugged domains in the western

U.S. Even today, elk hunters seeking the re-introduced Rocky Mountain species testify that Arizona's White Mountains are "wild and extremely challenging." Such terrain surely insulated the species against civilization, and the Apache of that time likely killed but few. Neverthe-

less, the species couldn't cope, and were apparently gone by the time Arizona and New Mexico joined the Union in 1912.

The Rocky Mountain elk there today are managed to accommodate a limited number of hunters on an Apache Indian Reservation.

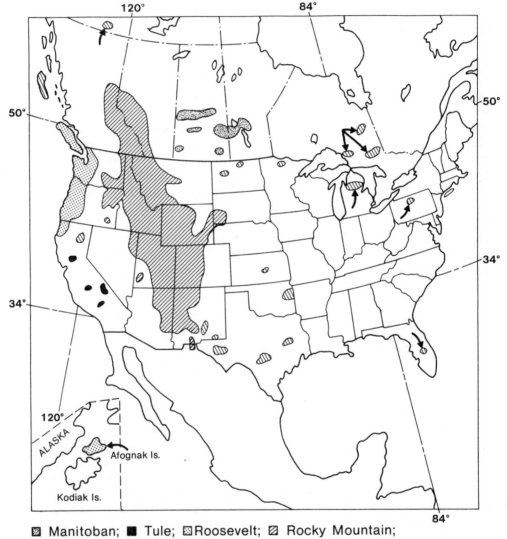

Map showing present distribution of elk in North America. Included are some minor revisions to original map in Wildlife Management Institute's *Elk of North America: Ecology and Management* (1982) edited by J. W. Thomas and D.E. Toweill.

As for the Roosevelt elk, they flourish yet in the jungled slopes of Washington's Olympic Peninsula (some of them non-huntables within Olympic National Park) and into Pacific Slope Oregon. In northern California, meat hunting and civilization all but annihilated them. Only an occasional Roosevelt bull ever graced early Boone and Crockett books (although it is now listed as a separate game species) or Pope and Young archery annals, because the Roosevelt had shorter antlers than the Rocky Mountain variety.

Here is a look at today's remaining wapiti populations and their ranges throughout the continental United States:

Oregon-Washington — Most of the Cascade Range and on the heavily forested Pacific Coast. Rocky Mountain elk hold their own on drainages flowing eastward.

Idaho — All of the vast wilderness north of the Middle Fork Salmon River headwaters to Montana and the Canadian border, and along the eastern border to Wyoming and Yellowstone.

Montana — The entire western mountain sector to the central plains, and northward to Canada and Glacier National Park.

Wyoming — All of western and northern mountains, plus isolated "island" ranges like Snowy and Laramie, and some populations on the undulating sage terrain north of Rock Springs. Greatest concentrations of elk in the world are located here in the Yellowstone and Grand Teton National Park ecosystems.

Colorado — Thriving populations in all mountain bulwarks, with concentrations in upper White River to San Juan Wilderness Area on the southern border. Elk are well distributed in and west of the Front Range.

New Mexico — Classic elk terrain from the Sangre de Cristo Range southward to Albuquerque, and especially westward to Arizona in high and sometimes semi-desert wildlands. Northern habitat is partly controlled by private landowners.

Arizona — Much like New Mexico, with elk found in aspen and conifer forests from Mogollon Rim near Payson to Alpine. Some habitat controlled by Indian tribes.

Utah — Natural populations mainly in Uinta and Wasatch Mountains. Some isolated mountain ranges have huntable populations.

Nevada — Pockets of elk in a few mountain ranges.

South Dakota — Some re-introduced elk. Black Hills herds of the past are gone.

California — The tule species is a "showcase." Little huntable populations.

Much of the above is a tribute to the adaptability of the wapiti. Some modern concentrations owe their existence to transplanting operations via the Yellowstone "pipeline." Some of these successful transplants provide token populations in states like Michigan, Pennsylvania, and Virginia where the habitat holds promise for huntable populations. In states like Utah, much of today's elk hunting is directly due to Yellowstone transplants.

For some reason, remote areas, like parts of the Great Basin in Nevada, always had elk habitat — but no elk. Introductions in such places proved beneficial, and showed that nature doesn't always do a better job than man.

Quite possibly the private ranches of Texas will receive more wapiti, further extending elk hunting opportunities where they have been almost non-existent for a century. Much habitat in the woods of Maine and upper New England also beckons, as do the northern Great Lakes states like Minnesota, where wolves and moose still flourish. Elk hunting may be

Elk antlers in Jackson, Wyoming, city park suggest lore and influence of elk in our lives from historic times. *U.S. Fish & Wildlife Service Photo.*

even more widespread in the latter part of the 20th Century than it was in 1900. According to an "unendangered species" publication put out by Remington firearms, the western U.S. elk population has increased more than 10 times in the last 75 years, to an estimated half million!

Interestingly, as elk have moved into isolated nooks and niches, certain idiosyncrasies have developed, especially in the "island" populations cut off from other herds by human encroachment. In some places calves are born on slopes where trains chug daily. Some transplanted elk tolerate the noises of logging trucks. But if "pure wilderness" elk are transplanted into such an environment, they will likely move elsewhere, refusing to put up with such foreign human intrusions.

Almost all elk transplants these days originate from the Yellowstone area. Relatively docile following years of non-hunting relationship with man, such elk may ask little but immediate living space and may tolerate camera-toting tourists. But as one more credit to their flexibility, most such transplants grow to huntable herds. Another factor is that some of the southern Yellowstone herd are indeed hunted while migrating over 70 air miles to the National Elk Refuge, and thus they learn survival skills that help them later if transplanted. The elk has indeed proven itself indomitable in the challenge of survival.

Consider, too, that it has adapted rather well to life in parks, zoos, and other sanctuaries, often multiplying so much as to cause overcrowding. Yet in the wild, elk seldom tolerate the slightest intrusion by man. Let a hunter put up camp in the same arroyo or ridge, and the elk are gone.

The elk has been the object of many an energetic quest by hunters both ancient and modern. It has held out with a hardy and tenacious stubbornness. In some measure it is this enduring quality that has left its mark on history. Seals and flags in several states and provinces — particularly Idaho, Oregon, and British Columbia — are graced with replicas of this regal and majestic creature. Few animals are so revered.

3

Wapiti Stories — or Myths?

The following article appearing beneath my byline in the November 1983 *Sports Afield* suggests some mythical qualities of the bull elk:

"The distant thump of branches caused guide Mark Wiltse to jump off his mount instantly. 'Sounds like a bull elk to me. And he's headed for the floodplain on Torrent Creek. Let's see if we can get there about the same time he does.'

Mark and I had been riding through a tangle of lodgepole pines high on Wyoming's North Fork of the Shoshone River. I had checked into camp downriver scarcely an hour before. Logic would have dictated that I examine all my equipment carefully to make certain I was completely prepared for a predawn hunt the next day from a high ridge or vantage point.

"But instead I had been admiring magnificent game country for 11 rugged miles. And like many elk hunters before me, I was growing restless thinking about the actual hunt. We had set up camp and unpacked earlier. Then I had persuaded Wiltse to take me out "for a quick look around before dark." Noting my unquenchable enthusiasm, Wiltse led us into shadowed north slopes. 'This is it,' I told myself. 'Terrain where we could see a giant bull anytime.'

"We heard crashing noises ahead. Why not a bull delivered unto my rifle sights the first evening out? I asked myself. And while those who decide such things are at it, I added in my mind's eye, why not broadside against the sunset at the precise distance I zeroed in my 30-06? If such a thing should happen, I could concentrate on two other licenses I held for mule deer and black bear. But I held the slippery illusion only briefly. Deep down I knew all along it was improbable. I had already experienced a 'gift' bull years before — when a thickly antlered 5-pointer (western count) appeared just where I expected him. I suspected that I had used up my allocation of easy elk for one lifetime. Still, I could hope.

"I was not too surprised, though, when Mark and I saw the tracks in Torrent Creek wash. Leading our horses most of the distance in order to better study the ground for sign, we located fresh prints in the glowing sunset. They fairly oozed at us from red clay. But the animal who made them was not only elsewhere; it had moved away via a slate-lined streambed. By the time we could determine an up or down creek exit, valuable seconds were lost. Then I saw tracks heading uphill, and I felt very foolish. Our quarry had escaped up the same sidehill where, just minutes before, we had walked our mounts down! As I slumped into the saddle for the downtrail ride, I once again felt a deep respect for elk."

This phantom quality of the hunter-elusive bull elk only serves to ignite feelings of intrigue and challenge in the breasts of sportsmen. Such feelings are not confined to modern man. Nimrod, the mighty hunter of the Old Testament, may have been the first to stalk the elk or red deer of Eurasia, or perhaps it was Esau ("the cunning hunter" whom Isaac loved "because he did eat of his venison" in Gen. 25:27–28). Yet the greatest legends of the past loom most articulately out of the Orient. Mikhail Prishvin wrote "Jen Sheng; the Root of Life," in which one Lu Weng, an ancient Chinese sage-philosopher (his name meant "searcher for the root of life"), collected game antlers, which he

sold to those who placed a magical or divine value on them. And, it is said, he did a thriving business.

From such sources it is likely the Orientals derived the metaphysical aura with which they shrouded the elk, and more particularly the bull's antlers. So powerful is the Oriental adulation of wapiti head-gear even today that huge sums are spent to buy antlers as an aphrodisiac — some seekers risking long prison terms for stealing or poaching them from national parks. The dictionary defines "aphrodisiac" as "exciting sexual desire; provocative of, or inclined to venery" (from Venus, Goddess of Love), or possessing sexual prowess. No wonder the Chinese call powdered antlers a "love potion."

An element of mysticism also floods through. According to Prishvin, though some ancients merely ground up the antlers to drink as a beneficial potion, others, like Lu Weng, sought possession of antlers attached to the frontal skull bone because they conferred on any Chinese household a promise of "family happiness." In addition, "the sight of them always filled the aged master of the house with the hope that his spent passions would return."

It was never doubted in those days, long before Christ, that the passing of antlers from one generation to another heaped even greater powers upon the new possessor. In fact, antlers were perhaps the most coveted heirloom to be gained in the will of any patriarch.

Presumably, the noble appearance of an adult male elk, along with its sultanic command of a large harem of females, has long inspired man to attain similar macho status. It requires little imagination to see some potentate in the feudal system following the demise of the Roman Empire identifying himself with the lordly bull elk. Certainly the Benevolent and Protective Order of Elk greatly revered the animal's mystique in America. One also wonders what tales of the creature adventurer Marco Polo might have brought back with him to Venice. Robin Hood apparently poached red deer stags similar to the elk (if the game had been deer, the bag would have been identified as a "buck") within Sherwood Forest. Much to the chagrin of the Sheriff of Nottingham, Robin Hood seemed to have little difficulty with the feat.

Taming the Wapiti

In Scandinavia during the Middle Ages, elk were apparently used as beasts of burden. It must have been something of an ordeal, however, to tame the wapiti, for they were replaced with reindeer. Ditto for the legend of Santa Claus, his sled pulled not by elk but by reindeer. It's difficult to imagine St. Nick being borne by eight Imperial-tined elk. But why reindeer? Certainly, a scenario of male wapiti escorting the traditional sleigh would be imposing for "The Night Before Christmas." But it would also imply that elk are willing to do man's bidding. That would be the most difficult part to imagine. Elk in harness? Knowing the animal's disposition, it just won't do. It is too much to ask. Even a legend so warmly embraced cannot support a supposition so incongruous as an obedient elk.

Yet elk do appear domesticated at times. One of them is when deep snows drive herds onto flatland feeding grounds. As hunters ask each year, "How can those elk be so elusive during lengthy hunting seasons and so docile in this situation?"

In order to properly understand this animal, perhaps we need a psychological profile as the animal developed over the centuries. Can we pinpoint some sort of personality pattern?

Elk Kills Horse

We can try. Renowned naturalist Ernest Thompson Seton tells of a western rancher, one John Legg of Wyoming, who confronted an apparently rut-fevered male elk on a narrow mountain trail. Seton's account tells of a skirmish in which the bull ran Legg's pack animal off a cliff to its death. Not wishing to partake of the same fate, Legg pulled a pistol on the assailant and dispatched the elk with several shots. Though Seton was sometimes accused of imparting anthropomorphic qualities to his hero-wolf "Lobo," he did not say much more about the belligerent bull. I wish he had. Possibly he didn't because such tales during his time in the early 1900s weren't unusual. Bull moose charged freight trains. Bull elk attacked pack trains. Apparently, these things happened.

One of the most improbable elk stories involved a farmer who testified he watched a zoo-raised young bull drive several of his domestic beef cows into what appeared to be the beginning of a harem. The account was authenticated by a witness, a zoologist of impeccable credibility. Not explained, though, was whether the farmer managed to retrieve his cows at some point during the rutting season. While farm cattle might go home with just about anyone, I recall a personal incident proving how stubborn a few cows can be. A young moose attempted to run some cattle away from a winter haystack. The cows would have none of it. The day before, the moose had successfully driven off five mule deer, but he couldn't budge those bellicose cattle.

Recently I looked out my kitchen window and saw two young bull elk feeding peacefully with some three dozen black Angus cattle. For days they got along just fine. The elk made no attempt to muscle in directly with the ranch strain, just mingling in unobtrusively to reach the richest hay. I have watched refuge elk compete with local horses for the best hay right out of feeding troughs. It is somehow indicative of an elk's unique ability to fit in wherever he goes, adapting with either intelligence or some super instinct to survive.

The wapiti gives special credence to Charles Darwin's "Origin of Species," in which he advances the idea that the animal best fitted by nature for perpetuation will be the one to adapt and flourish through the centuries. The elk has certainly done that . . . almost as well, it would seem, as the most cunning of them all, the coyote.

Elk Apparition

Let me give another personal example. Not long ago I looked at some 70 elk bedded in the foothills of a hunting area that just a few weeks before had been swarming with hunters, elk permits in hand. Now hunters on the highway gazed in amazement at the scene before them. Was this an apparition? Had the elk been in the nearby mountains all along . . . or did they migrate in from lofty canyons many miles away?

I had hunted these same mountains that season. I had located only a dozen cow elk and one spike bull. They were bedded in thick fir cover at about 10,000 feet elevation. I found plenty of sign, though, including relatively fresh tracks, likely made by night. I knew many elk were some-

where about, but I never saw the 70 that now spread before my view.

It reminded me of a fishing trip I once took into Wyoming's Wind River Mountains. This range is traversed all summer long by anglers and other recreationists. Yet by the muddy shore of one fishing hole, off the usual pathways, I found myself looking down at thousands of fresh elk tracks. I hiked and crept over rims and arroyos, but I never did succeed in sleuthing out any wapiti.

But back to the 70 elk bedded in sage within full view of the highway near a popular hunting unit. It was only the tip of a giant iceberg. A few days later a local rancher tipped me off to some 250 elk in his back hay yard, where he fed hundreds of cattle. For several days he also fed hundreds of elk.

Where did they come from, seemingly overnight? The answer had to be: from the same range that had all the hunting pressure a few weeks ago. The state did not plant elk, least of all here.

As if to rub salt in the wound, the elk included a high-tined 7-point bull that was an easy candidate for the Boone and Crockett Club record book. No one I knew, including local ranchers, had ever seen the critter before. Did he grow from spike to imperial dignity in one year?

Precisely where could all 320 elk have secreted themselves? They hadn't likely traveled here from afar, for the simple reason that it was December. Snow hadn't piled so deeply as to force a desperate march from distant summer habitat. The truth was that these elk had been in the general vicinity, evading this army of hunters all the time. Dozens of rifle-toters must have been near them daily.

But then, anyone can observe the elk's phantom nature by merely visiting a winter feeding refuge where mammoth racks are displayed. Where were they when we had a permit? It would seem, then, as some 80 or more percent of any season's nimrods can attest, that all elk are somehow whisked by shuttle to some other planet. As one licensee put it, "I haven't looked at an elk in over a week. Now I'm wondering what I'm up against. . . ."

Black Hills Mystery

It seems even a dead elk can be extremely elusive. An old hunting book of mine, "America's Number One Trophy" (Jim Bond, 1964), has a picture of a colossal bull elk killed in South Dakota's Black Hills in 1896. The caption says: "Probably the greatest bull elk ever killed anywhere or at any time." The spread: 73 inches, with 13 points on one side, 10 on the other. The base near the burr is, incredibly, just under 12 inches in circumference. The caption also says: "For more than 40 years it rested in a dark attic of a bank building; now it hangs in all its glory in a sporting goods store in Sheridan, Wyo."

Such a monumental specimen ought to be easy to locate. You can hardly hide a rack of those dimensions. Yet it doesn't appear in any record book. The shroud of mystery might be lifted somewhat if the creature had been poached or taken in unfair chase. It would then be ineligible for any record recognition. But why only this one reference in the many reams of literature about trophy elk? Was it grown in someone's back yard?

After many deadends in trying to locate the 73-inch bull (state trophy measurers seemingly hadn't ever seen it), I did discover it in Sam Mavrakis' Ritz Sporting Goods Store at 435 North Main Street, Sheridan. Sam explained that the bull

hadn't been measured, because in the process of splitting the skull for a plaque mount, an antler had been loosened slightly — not enough to make the antler droop in any way, but enough to rule it out for official trophy measurement. Incredibly, Sam said he has another rack in the store with a 77⅛-inch outside spread. "We don't know anything at all about it, except that it was found in a barn in Dayton, Wyoming, and we brought the antlers here to be mounted in another elk's head." It, too, hangs from the Ritz wall.

No effort has proven fruitful in revealing where this rack came from. Sam Mavrakis promised me that he would have the bull checked by Boone and Crockett measurers. It could qualify for the book as a pickup, if the rack is intact. Such stories make one wonder where else might lie an elk that would surpass half the entries in the books.

Every time I ride past a certain rockslide in western Wyoming in the company of certain old-timers, I hear this account, sometimes with a little variation or two.

"See that rockslide?"

"Yes."

"Well, that's where old so and so and I made one of the greatest wapiti drives in the history of elk hunting. Thirteen bulls. That's right. Some big ones, too. We shot 13 bulls, all from one herd, right here in this very place."

I have never been successful in ascertaining whether there were 13 hunters, one license for every one of those bulls, in that hunting expedition or not . . . or even in placing a date on the ambush to determine whether game laws were in effect at the time. But in my mind's eye I can visualize giant bulls wheeling about in confusion — much like the old paintings of Plains Indians stampeding buffalo over a precipice — considering the options, then splintering across the rocks, hooves flailing sparks with each thrust, until the deed was done.

But there is one thing I don't understand. I have helped guide many hunters into this canyon. How come modern elk refuse to get conveniently trapped here these days? Did the direct descendants of that original herd whisper down from stag to son over the years, "Be careful never to go near that rockslide?. . ."

No, probably not. However, maybe some instinct finely honed over the years tells elk to avoid *any* pile of rocks. Come to think of it, I've rarely observed elk associating closely with rockslides anywhere.

Was the original account exaggerated a little? I don't know. Every time I probe too deeply into this wonderful accomplishment of yesteryear, I'm met with stony silence.

Fact vs. Fiction

Sorting out reality from fiction, with or without heroic achievement, is seldom easy when it comes to elk. I've read anthologies in which a fly landing on a hunter carried human scent to a wary old cow elk, which immediately alerted the entire herd. The more I learn about elk, the more I admit this could happen.

I have also been charged by a frenetic young bull I've attempted to photograph. The animal wasn't vicious. Human visitors simply crowded into his living space, and he revolted. Elk, like bears and bison, have been known to charge people in Yellowstone and other national parks. Many elk are docile when human onlookers remain on boardwalks or concrete, but become belligerent when cornered. I shudder to think what might happen to anyone who got in the way of a bull elk bent on fleeing.

Once, when walking to my mailbox in western Wyoming, I noted something strange among the dairy cows in the nearby field. My dog Rascal had noticed too, and was now chasing elk amid the livestock. I vowed to punish my dog, and tie her on a leash. Certainly those wapiti would not return for some time. But they were with the cows again the next day, feeding as nonchalantly as if born in captivity! Where they went in midday, I know not. But they were there morn and eve for several weeks. Yet, I've known other circumstances in which the sight or sound of a dog on the loose expelled elk into the hills for months. "Never try to outguess an elk," might be a motto coined by someone like James Thurber. Thurber, in fact, who wrote so brilliantly about chickens and many other animals never did, to my knowledge, write about elk. I find that difficult to understand. Unless, of course, Thurber just didn't understand them.

Rutting Stories

Of all the wild stories passed on concerning the genus *Cervus,* the tales of rut-maddened bulls have been the scariest. From the pulp paperbacks of the Old West to modern slicks, you can always find a horror story about being in the path of a trumpeting, tree-busting bull elk. Many archers write accounts of taking a huge old codger with antlers out to there . . . that nearly trampled all humans within 100 yards or lowered his antlers to do them in.

I don't believe it all, but there are times when truth is as strange as fiction. For example, I find it fascinating that young bulls, which may not even desire to breed, nevertheless secrete sex hormones that excite nearby herd bulls into issuing a warning . . . stay away from my harem or else! The "or else" part is rarely needed, since a bluffing bull of tender age knows superiority when he sees it. As a matter of additional fact, few of those so-called battles to the death ever occur. One bull usually senses quickly when this dueling business could lead to his getting hurt . . . yet much seems to depend on a bull's sexual intensity.

The sight of a harem boss bull has long inspired mankind. Ernest Hemingway wrote of one this way in "Green Hills of Africa": ". . . a big, old thick-necked, dark-maned, wonder-horned, tawny-hided, beer-horse-built bugler of a bull elk."

Stags of Legend

Irish legend has it that regal bulls with antlers 11 feet wide roamed the highlands. These elk even surpassed the huge elk of the American West folklore, which were lassoed by the old-time cowboys. Elk in Manitoba during Ernest Thompson Seton's time were said to be "Phantoms of the Sandhills" that could subsist where cattle would starve. But the wapiti highly

visible in this bleak setting managed to somehow disappear come hunting season every year. When I look at the arch of elk antlers over western community main streets like that in Afton, Wyoming, I also have to wonder how many stories and legends might be contained in every one of the hundreds of elk racks there.

We're talking here mostly about myths and legends. In the pages ahead we'll try to isolate known facts. Even then, we have to be careful. My standard encyclopedia can generally be trusted, but it says some bull wapiti keep harems of 60 or more cows. That might be stretching it, since few males could keep such an entourage in sight or tow.

Any hunter with the glow of a campfire on his face is also likely to hear about bulls with five-inch tracks, elk incisor bites in aspen bark over a man's head (complicated all the more by the fact that wapiti have no teeth on the outer upper jaw), accounts of the animals wallowing in mudholes and spouting like a whale, plus bugling and torn-up woods that would do credit to an angry bull elephant. We will try to separate pure glory stories from the truth if at all possible. But in the meantime, I also enjoy the legends.

4

Calf-to-Bull Charisma

Few creatures on earth appear as handsome as a fully racked bull elk. But much must happen before any elk attains such noble status.

Sometime in late May a cow about to calve will seek seclusion from the herd she has followed. Usually that spot will be at the edge of timber near the upper limits of winter range. The calf will be born about two weeks later, probably the first week of June. Gestation period is about 8½ months. Twins are far rarer with elk than with deer. Research shows the chances of elk twins are about one-third of one percent. With deer, it may be as high as 40 percent.

A calf enters the world weighing about 30 pounds. One study showed an average of 28.6 pounds. At first the calf is as helpless as any creature can be, but within a few hours it gains use of legs, much like a domestic dairy newborn. In a day or two it can walk and, soon thereafter, run. However, the mother likely will command the youngster with barks and grunts to remain put. A brown coat with light spots offers the ultimate in natural camouflage. But coyotes and bobcats are a constant threat to young elk calves. Idaho studies indicate losses of calves to coyotes, where that predator is numerous, can be as high as 90 percent. Chances are better for elk calves when late spring snow does not bunch animals and make them more vulnerable.

When the young calf can travel (about 2½ weeks old), the cow will rejoin the herd. There the pair will likely follow the lead of an older cow into higher territory as receding snow makes it possible to locate new, tender grass. Observation indicates some cows may trade babysitting duties with each other.

Pregnancy Ratios

Proper nutrition has much to do with pregnancy rates and health of calves. Roosevelt elk seems to become pregnant at only one-half to one-third the rate of the Rocky Mountain species. Why that is so is not known.

A six-year study in New Mexico indicates 69.4 percent of cow elk pregnant in the lowest year, 89.3 percent in the highest. Such fertility rates can depend on weather (and thus length of rut), scattering of elk by hunting, and so on. A study in Wyoming showed that seismographic activity (exploration by helicopter and detonation of dynamite charges) decreased pregnancy rates due to dispersal of cows from the presence of bulls. In addition, such stress could cause cows to abandon habitual calving areas, increasing the likelihood of aborting. Elk, sensitive and nervous animals, can be affected by a number of factors as they try to perpetuate the species.

Motherly instincts can vary. Just as a domestic heifer might well drop a calf in a stream or snowbank, so can a young cow elk. Survival rates may thus vary from herd to herd, depending upon maternal experience.

Pregnancy can happen in the second autumn, but a cow is more likely to bear her first calf in the third year of her life. Cows are fertile for 10 or more years. Pregnant cows commonly drive away any yearling offspring, although after the calf is born in relative solitude, the family group is likely to be sociable again. Not so with sow bears, which seem to realize instinctively the new arrivals are highly dependent on parent-provided food, and relentlessly drive away any previous young ones once and for all. Elk are more likely to keep family members banded together purposely, and contribute to each other's survival. In fact, wapiti are often found in groups of at least seven or more; at any given time six will be resting or ruminating and one will be on its feet to act as a sentinel to warn the others of danger.

A calf may grow almost as tall as a mature cow within one year. But the yearling will have a shorter form, with a blunt face and nose. On the winter refuges, where ungulate biologists have a closer opportunity to study elk growth, it has been found that calves born the preceding June can weigh as much as 250 pounds in January. However, they will likely lose weight during even a moderate winter. The following summer, especially with the males, growth is apt to be particularly rapid with the greater abundance of ready feed.

Bull Growth Rates

Two or three years later, a bull may weigh 600–700 pounds. The record live weight for a refuge-measured bull is 1,100 pounds. (That animal weighed 657 pounds when dressed out for the butcher.) Length of one Rocky Mountain specimen reached eight feet, four inches in one study, with shoulder height at four feet, seven inches. But the *Field Guide to American Wildlife,* Harper and Row, Outdoor Life edition (p. 336), gives this general description: "Bull, length to 9½ feet, height at shoulder to five feet five inches, weight to an average 750 pounds." A cow's weight is more likely to be 450–550 pounds.

Obviously, wapiti in different areas,

The final product, a mature 6-point "royal" bull, probably four or five years old.

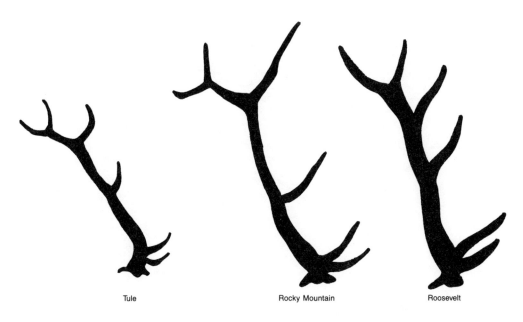

Tule   Rocky Mountain   Roosevelt

TYPICAL PROFILE VIEWS

Antler configuration, three species of elk.

with differing genetics and feed, can vary considerably in weight. Limestone and minerals in any given locality can also affect bone size and antler thickness. Those two factors are a direct reflection of a bull's health, since little antler development occurs until body tissues are properly nourished. One axiom says: good range conditions, good antlers. That's one reason you should hunt the same canyon or ridgeline where you killed a giant bull a year ago — more could very well be nearby.

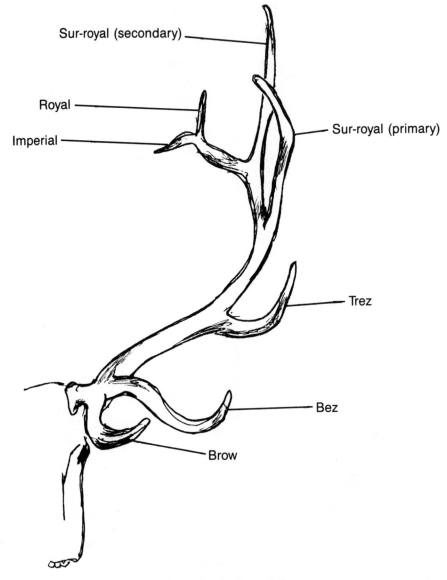

Sur-royal (secondary)

Royal

Imperial

Sur-royal (primary)

Trez

Bez

Brow

Names of antler tines, all elk.

Antlers in a yearling bull will first sprout from knobs or pedicles into thinnish spikes, then grow in circumference and length until they are 15–20 inches long. Branching usually occurs when antlers are around two feet long. Research conducted in Colorado's large White River herd showed that 28.4 percent of 1,839 yearling bulls had more than just spike antlers. While some had forked antlers (called "raghorns"), a few even had four or five small tines per side. Antlers are shed in March-April, and begin growing again by late May. Growth is stimulated by the effect of lengthening daylight on glands.

Tines on a bull elk grow from a main beam much more predictably than with most buck deer. There are few "non-typical" elk, thus no provision for such a rack in the record books. By the third autumn, a bull may have four or five tines per side. Any time after the fourth year, according to most research, a bull might begin to sport the seven-point-per-side Imperial rack. On a private elk hunting ranch in Vermejo, New Mexico, all bulls scoring 300 or more Boone and Crockett points were at least 4½ years old.

Emerging wapiti tines are named as follows: first, brow; second, bez or "dog killers"; third, trez or daggers; fourth, the most prominent tines, sur-royals (primary); fifth, sur-royals (secondary); sixth, royal; seventh, Imperial. A bull may add more tines. Many show in the record books.

Antlers Vs. Horns

Perhaps it would be wise to define here exactly what is meant by "antler" and how it differs from horn. True horns are hollow, while antlers are solid. Horns begin to develop in the immature animal, antlers later in life. Horns consist of a bony core inside an outer sheath. Antlers are always shed once a year, while this is seldom the case with horns. Antelope are one exception. Their horns consist mostly of hardened hair. Wyoming game biologist Harry Harju, who once worked as a taxidermy assistant, explains that an antelope horn is actually removed off the bony core with a chisel for proper mounting. After an antelope loses its horns, new horns push the old ones off the core. This does not happen with antlers.

Horn development may slow during a tough winter and in old age, yet horns continue to grow throughout the animal's life. Antlers diminish considerably in size after the wearer's prime. Harju contests the idea that superior antler (or horn) growth can be attained by killing off the spikes in any herd. "What about the genes which come from the doe or cow—they are a complete unknown," he says. "And what if the second-year spikes are the result of individually inferior habitat and poor food in the first year rather than from genetics?" Harju adds that just as a bighorn sheep may grow only one inch of new horn in a very poor winter, or eight inches in a mild one, antler growth can blossom or stunt. Much depends on body condition, since survival comes before rack. Obviously, most elk trophies result from a relatively mild winter.

How Antlers Grow

The first spike on a yearling bull begins as pulpy tissue. It is fed by blood-bearing capillaries. As the nerve endings are nourished, antlers can grow up to one-half inch per day. Gradually, the "knobs" will project upward to a foot or more. By

August the spike has begun to harden. Capillaries, now no longer needed, dry out. The residual "velvet" becomes an itchy irritant to the young bull. He seeks to rid the outer covering on his antlers by rubbing it against something. A small tree with soft bark seems to provide the gentlest means of doing so without accidentally encountering any yet-sensitive nerve endings.

It is easy to surmise how much rubbing a bull of, say, six years with antlers five feet long and of considerable weight will have to do before he completely eliminates the unneeded and suddenly unwanted velvet. A bull may spend much of August and even part of September (into some bow seasons) in the rubbing process. Young saplings over great distances may be rubbed. A trained eye — and sometimes even a casual glance — can find them. During the late September rut, the bull may also "duel" young trees, but this is done out of belligerence rather than to get rid of a burden.

During the period when antlers are sensitive, a bull is likely to enter solitary confinement. He doesn't want to catch tender antlers on brush or scrape his rack against other animals. Nor is he in a mood to run through trees to elude danger. He may take up residence at or near timberline, or in openings for a time. But as the velvet is rubbed free and the tines "polished" to a clean-looking ivory glow, the bull is ready to enter the next phase of his life, the rut. Now he deserts his self-imposed exile to seek out other elk — as many cows as he can gather at the height of the breeding season.

A bull won't normally begin breeding until his second or, more likely, third autumn. One biologist puts it this way: "The spike bulls stand around during this period like they aren't even sure what is going on." But they enter the process rather enthusiastically, even if not successfully, at age 28 months. However, it may be three or more years yet before they are able to dethrone a herd bull and take his place.

Ideal antler development on wapiti with excellent range (food) conditions and topline genetics was carefully researched over several years at New Mexico's Vermejo Park — 392,000 acres of private ranch land in the Sangre de Cristo Mountains at elevations of 7,000 to 13,000 feet. After examination of 480 bulls taken by hunters, the study concluded that antler size increases up to $10\frac{1}{2}$ years of age, then begins a slow decline.

The number of antler points increased up to $7\frac{1}{2}$ years of age (usually peaking at six on each side). Increase in trophy quality thereafter came mostly in circumference (or thickness) and length of antlers, plus greater weight. Ninety percent of the 6 x 6s were at least $4\frac{1}{2}$ years old. Ninety percent of the bulls scoring at least 300 Boone and Crockett points (considered by most hunters as trophy size) were at least $6\frac{1}{2}$ years of age. The most desirable trophies were from $7\frac{1}{2}$ to $10\frac{1}{2}$ years old. *Note:* to be counted as a point, a tine had to be at least $2\frac{1}{2}$ centimeters (about one inch) long.

In determining weights and measurements of the older bulls, both antlers and skull cap were weighed to the nearest half pound. Antler length was determined by measuring along the outside curve from base of burr to tip of main beam. If antler lengths differed, the longest was recorded. Circumference was measured at the thinnest point between burr and first point, with the smallest of the two antlers recorded.

TYPICAL ANTLER SIZE BY AGE*

Age (Years)	Number of Points	Percentage of Bulls
1½	1 x 1	average
2½	4 x 4	89%
	(some 2 x 4 through 6 x 6, normally thin tines)	
3½	5 x 5	51%
4½	6 x 6	51%
	thin tines	
5½	6 x 6	68%
6½	6 x 6	76%
7½	(no less than) 6 x 6	87%
8½	(no less than) 6 x 6	100%
	trend to decline	
9½	6 x 6	93%
10½	6 x 6	82%
11½	6 x 6	63%

*Vermejo, New Mexico, study on Rocky Mountain elk

Age and Antlers

The study concluded that spikes are the typical antler conformation of yearling bulls. Antler conformation of 2½-year-old bulls showed the widest range of any age, from 2 x 4 to 6 x 6. A total of 89 percent of the 4 x 4 bulls were 2½ years old. The most common (51 percent) number of tines for a 3½-year-old was 5 x 5. When 4½ years old, at least 51 percent of the bulls had 6 x 6 antlers. With the 5½-year-olds, 68 percent were 6 x 6, as were 76 percent of the 6½-year-olds. At 7½ years old, 87 percent had at least 6 x 6 antlers; at 8½ years, 100 percent had 6 x 6. (See table.) Percentages of 6 x 6s at 9½ years were 93 percent, representing the first decline in number of tines. It dropped to 82 percent for 10½-year-olds. Only 63 percent of the bulls 11½ years old or older had the full 6 x 6. In a general summary, a total of 88 percent of bulls at least 4½

years old had the royal 6-point configuration.

Average antler weight began increasing slightly from 2½ years. The heaviest, 10.1 kilograms (22.2 pounds) were attained at 10½ years. Weight declined to 7–9 kilograms for bulls 11½ years old or older. Antler length increased from 2½ years up to 10½, even though number of tines may not have changed. Circumference also increased during that time span. Top circumference (taped at antler base) on any bull was 24.4 centimeters, or 8.1 inches, on a 10½-year-old.

From the previous data, it can be concluded that average maximum antler growth occurs, all things considered, from 6–9 years. It is possible for a 10½-year-old bull to take on longer and heavier antlers while total number of tines diminishes. These results agree generally with the more rapid antler growths studied by

Olaus Murie, and can thus be considered typical for ideal conditions. A severe and prolonged winter in any given year, however, can decrease size of antlers, thus ruling out any faint hope of guessing age by antler points. Other studies on Manitoba and Roosevelt species suggest they may not enjoy the same rate of antler development as the Rocky Mountain species included in the Vermejo and Murie research.

The Vermejo study also offered an opportunity to determine percentage of bulls harvested with 6 x 6 (trophy-size) racks. However, since this private ranch is managed primarily for quality elk hunting (shooting of bulls less than 5 x 5 is not recommended), the ratio of larger bulls is atypical—not within the norm for public hunting opportunities for the average license holder. Percentage of royal (6 x 6) bulls harvested would be considerably less on public land.

Mating Process

In order to better understand Chapter 12 on bugling, and the calf-to-bull-elk growth, let's take a look at the mating process.

A cow is in "heat," or can be fertilized by a responsive bull, only during an estrus period of as little as 12–15 hours. There may be as few as four of these estrus cycles in each autumn rutting period. For perpetuation of the species, nature has given the bull an instinct to maintain close surveillance (usually by scent) to determine when each cow in his harem is ripe for pregnancy. Observation also indicates bulls lick the cow's vulva to determine readiness. A cow's prime reproductive years are from age three to seven years, while bulls seem most likely to effectively impregnate a cow in years 7–12. Smaller

bulls may be sexually mature, but are prevented from servicing cows by older and stronger rivals.

The cow also seems to provide availability signals to the bull in another way. While coquettish prior to approaching heat, she may suddenly turn docile and willing to submit. The actual copulation period is brief, and as naturalist Dean Krakel puts it, "There appears to be no lingering romance."

Bugling is closely tied in with this breeding activity in several ways, as is the vulnerability of a bull during and afterward. Following the rut, a bull is usually in very poor body condition, having lost both weight and energy. One study showed a bull dropped nearly 100 pounds, a fact that can make the animal highly susceptible to the ravages of an early winter. Since the rut can peak in early October, the bulls may be in poor shape by mid-October, when many hunting seasons open. Where I live, elk season begins October 15. Several states have hunts that run immediately post-rut. You will want to examine any elk shot during this time to determine palatability of meat; body weight and appearance may be clues. The coat of any animal is usually a good indication of its health—is it shaggy and poor or shiny and sleek? That's one reason no hunter should be ashamed of taking home a non-breeding spike or raghorn. If your hunt is geared primarily for the freezer, you might have more of a "trophy" that way than you would with the higher antlers.

Over the years, a few cows have been found to carry antlers, as do a few doe deer, but growth seldom advances beyond the spike stage.

A bull is often said to reach maturity at 4½ years, when antler growth reaches six points. But an extremely thick-tined trophy bull is more likely to be 9 or 10 years old. Peak antler growth may not even take place until about the tenth or twelfth year. After that, a decline is likely to happen, much like a deer after its seventh autumn. Elk have been known to live in captivity up to 30 or more years, although a 22-year-old "wild" cow on the National Elk Refuge was considered to be in highly advanced old age, and something of a wonder for longevity.

Since antler growth varies so much from one bull to another, game biologists look to the jaws rather than the rack for accurate aging. Elk never do grow teeth in the forward portion of the upper jaw (seemingly an evolutionary slip), but "whistler" or eye teeth develop on the middle back section. Both sexes have these large, prominent teeth. Elk are the only North American member of the deer family which does.

Aging by Teeth

A sportsman does not have to be a dental expert to make approximate age estimates on an elk no older than four years old. That's because crowns of the central teeth, some of the very first to show wear, deteriorate little in the first three years. Beginning in about the fourth year, however, the last molar shows major wear, and may be flattened.

Biological studies indicate different elk may wear down different teeth at various rates over the years—depending on individualized habits of pulling at or chewing grass and other foods. In most cases, sides of teeth show the most wear.

In elk seven to ten years old, central

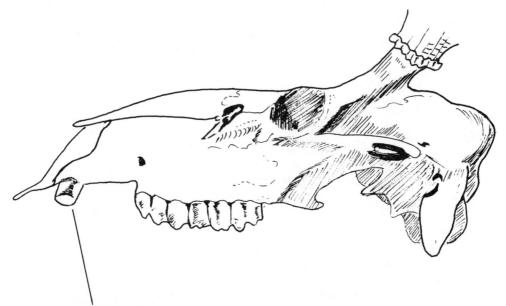

Whistler tooth

Drawing of upper jaw, all elk.

teeth will be well worn. By 12–14 years, severe wear, even a stubby appearance, can result. But some biologists caution flatly: "Beyond the fourth year, aging becomes guesswork." Nevertheless, it is safe to say that if tooth edges have lost their sharpness and are worn and rounded, with some almost smooth, or gone, the animal is well beyond its fifth year. If the animal is a "gummer," it's an old one, perhaps in or beyond the tenth year. After that, the wapiti may have difficulty grasping, pulling, or chewing food, a factor in declining health and eventual death.

The Washington State game department puts out a chart showing elk aging that can be obtained by writing to 700 North Capitol Way, Olympia, WA 98504. Briefly

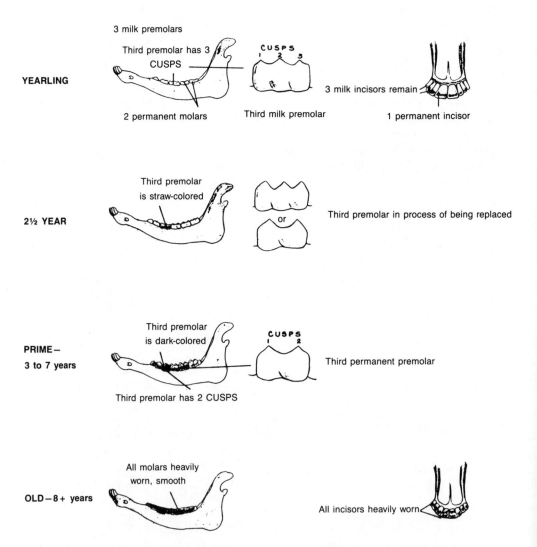

Examination of lower jaw, and aging of teeth, all elk. *Courtesy of Washington State Game Department.*

it states: "Deer and elk have 'milk' or baby teeth and permanent teeth. Elk and deer lose these baby teeth at predictable times, making examination of tooth structure an accurate aging method. Discoloration of teeth and general state of 'wear' are guides in helping you determine the ages of your elk or deer."

The accompanying chart shows a yearling elk with three milk incisors, or front cutting teeth. One is permanent. After 2½ years, the third premolar (counting from the front of the lower jaw) is straw-colored. By three to seven years, the same premolar is dark colored. By about the eighth year, that molar and all its neighbors are dark and heavily worn. The permanent incisors are also heavily worn.

Such age "measurements" are taken when you display your elk to game biologists at a check station. Most will also be happy to tell you of their findings.

For more complex determinations of the age of older animals, it would be wise to send a tooth or teeth to experts for the technical process known as "cementum aging." One such lab is Matson's, Box 308, Milltown, MT 59851.

To help lab personnel obtain such information from an elk tooth, you must make certain to remove both the tooth and the root system. To do this, you can use boiling water to loosen the jaw. Use a gentle rocking motion to pull each tooth free. Keep teeth as clean as possible, and in a cool place. Send them as soon as possible after collection, and mail them in a porous material like paper instead of plastic. Label with everything you know about the animal.

Matson biologists say they don't know why cementum aging works. ("It's a mystery," admits Gary Matson.) And it does not pinpoint age well for some big-game species. But it is highly accurate on deer, bear, mountain goat, and elk, Matson says.

Some other methods of aging elk by body or antler size are employed, but none is as scientific as the dental procedure. In some states, particularly Idaho, bagging a bull may also mean automatically saving the entire jaw for examination by game biologists. Check the game laws closely before you discard the head of a spike or smaller bull, as well as antlerless animals.

Age and Leadership

While a bull may be considered sexually mature by its fifth year (some breed before that), it can be a long haul before the animal reaches the apex of the established pecking order. Any group's leader probably will be an old cow doing sentinel duties for the herd. (Most of the studies on this subject have been conducted on European red deer, close kin of the American elk.) But old-time elkers don't need to be told that they had better not overlook a nearby cow while they're stalking a bull. An alerted bull will almost always prod harem cows away from danger with antler tips at their flanks. The sultan bull will usually bring up the rear of the group. If the younger bull hasn't previously been "weeded" out, the herd bull will likely try to accomplish it now. Of course, some sexually mature bulls can be expected to remain on the fringes, hoping to lure a cow or two away from the herd master. The younger bull seems to exert little influence on the other elk, except possibly as an annoyance. Before taking his place as boss during the rut, he may well spend much time alone. From a hunting standpoint, this fact means you may come across a shootable bull even if you don't locate large numbers of elk. However, one thing even the young bull can do is add one more nose and another pair of ears and eyes in the constant vigilance for danger.

Mental Factors

The mental and psychological development of cow or bull elk seems somewhat different from other game animals such as deer, moose, or pronghorns. Consider the adaptability factor.

None of the other creatures is considered as difficult to find during hunting seasons. Wyoming muzzleloader expert Rocky Moore, who has taken many deer and antelope with his musket, says he has "stopped trying for elk," even though he can obtain a license each year merely by plunking down the money.

However, why is the elk so restlessly intolerant of man during the fall, yet so seemingly docile and cooperative on the winter feeding grounds? Would deer, moose, or pronghorn allow man to come within a few yards, even in early and late winter, when they're not desperately dependent upon artificial feeding?

I put that question to National Elk Refuge biologist Bruce Smith. He allowed that elk are more highly adaptable, although the reasons are not always clear. "Elk utilize whatever nature or man provides for them. They seem born with the instinct to do so more than most other mammals."

Of course, deer do not subsist on hay nearly as well as elk. But in a recent April, I noted bunched deer, searching the foothills for succulent new greenery, scattered by any human intrusion. Elk could also have left the refuge to seek these tender spring shoots, but preferred to remain on

the grounds where man had made things easier by feeding them. As long as man is helping out, why not take advantage of it? The fact is, deer are not fed artificially—for many reasons. They wouldn't allow man to come among them as docilely as the elk do. They don't let camera buffs approach as closely as do the elk in Yellowstone. Elk seem more able to indelibly memorize or "pattern learn" what is safe. My conclusion: elk are more observant and sensitive ("attentive" might be the most appropriate term) to their surroundings than deer or most other mammals. Over the years this factor has contributed to their winter sustenance.

As for moose, they are tall enough to subsist quite nicely on bottomland willows near the Elk Refuge without actually entering it. If it was necessary to artificially feed moose, a man doing so would risk limb if not life. The bellicose, unyielding nature of old bull moose might lead them to charge the wagon that feeds them, just as they have done in Canada when a locomotive got in their way. They are not as flexible (tolerant of man's proximity) or as evolutionarily endowed with escape tactics as is the elk.

Pronghorns are well equipped with eyes and legs superior to the elk's. But attempts to feed antelope have not worked out. In winter the animals even perish along range-blocking fences, which they have the physical capability of leaping. Elk, efficient machines for taking what man gives them, would never hesitate to jump fences much higher than those that block antelope.

Man in general is just beginning to realize a psychological fact about elk that hunters suspected long ago: elk are "goal-oriented." New scientific articles, including some put out by the Smithsonian

Institution, are revealing more and more that elk (and some other animals) can do more than merely react to danger stimuli. It appears elk are capable of setting goals for survival that almost require thinking — that is, working out a plan that requires determining complex escape routes and strategy. Certainly it all fits in with what I know about elk.

I have seen elk run toward a known human presence (brusher or driver) in order to avoid unseen hunters waiting with rifles at a far clearing. Admittedly, it is difficult to conclude whether this is a thought-out program or whether the elk simply have an excellent memory, recalling that they were more frightened in the past running from drivers than against them. However, I believe elk are capable of debating which risk is greater, and deciding to take a chance with the "pushers" rather than with the unknown beyond. I submit that deliberately moving toward a man-made noise, rather than fleeing in the opposite, silent direction, constitutes at least primitive reasoning about the consequences of an action.

Old Bull Savvy

Does a young bull — say a spike or a small 2-3 pointer — have all the danger-eluding faculties of an older bull? I'm convinced his legs, ears, nose, and eyes are equal to the older animal's. What he lacks is the wisdom to interpret what he smells, hears, or sees. He has not gathered as many tools in his bag of experience. I remember one spike bull, fourth in line among a procession of mostly cows, approaching a pass between timbered canyons where I lay in wait. The range was only about 100 yards, and the lead cow sensed something amiss. She stopped, as

did the cow behind her. After two more steps, the third cow halted. The young bull knew something was not quite right, yet he continued mincing forward until I could see his neck. That was all I needed to score.

I seriously doubt, although I was perfectly happy for the supply of tender young meat in a lean winter, that an older bull would have kept pressing onward. Most young elk can be impulsive, thus more vulnerable to danger.

I have witnessed smaller bulls playing the role of "hangers-on" along the fringes of a late September harem. But only until the herd bull drives him out. Then those young bulls hang their heads, looking for all the world like sheepish teenagers who aren't allowed to drive the family car until they grow up. No, I don't know for sure what such an upstart challenger is thinking, but I'll bet it is something like, "I'll show that bully who is who in a couple more years." This is not meant to apply any anthropomorphic qualities to the genus *Cervus*. I'll leave that to the filmmakers. But it is important for any hunter (or nature-lover or wildlife photographer, for that matter) to know that his quarry is developing evasive skills just as the pursuer is developing hunting skills.

Learning and Instinct

How much of what an elk does is related to pattern learning and how much to instincts? I emphasize in Chapter 7, "Tactics in Locating Elk," that the animals tend to remain in high terrain, often along northeast-facing slopes, on warm days in order both to avoid hunters and to stay comfortable in the cooler climate there. I believe that elk in my locality, accustomed to generally cold weather, do just that.

But Prof. Michael L. Wolfe, Department of Fisheries and Wildlife, College of Natural Resources, Utah State University, says research indicates that "elk may be better able to cope with warm temperatures than previously supposed." Professor Wolfe cites studies showing rather frequent occurrence of a thriving elk herd in the shrub-steppe region of eastern Washington, "where summer temperatures are very high and there exists little or no protective 'thermal cover.' This is offset by the fact that the animals in this area are not subject to human disturbances."

There's that adaptability (pattern-learning) factor again—elk taking what man gives them. I have not witnessed this phenomenon (elk tolerating extremely warm temperatures) in Wyoming or in most of the remote Rocky Mountains. Here they can both elude man, and find cooler temperatures, by going higher into northeast conifer slopes. Yet Rocky Mountain elk in eastern Washington likely find man almost everywhere, so they squeeze into those regions where man is least numerous and bothersome. The Evergreen State has vast conifer forests, but they are frequently invaded by man for logging and are less remote than conifer forests in, say, the high Rocky Mountain states. It is a case of elk using their pattern learning to elude humans. They would be adaptable enough to do that from Alberta through New Mexico if man numbers increased in remote areas. Elk have learned where man is not likely to go, and that is their first preference.

Several other game biologists in the Southwest have told me of elk putting up with warmer temperatures than they are apparently inclined to tolerate in the northern climes. But wherever weather is cold and harsh is often an excellent place to begin looking for wise old bulls. They got that way by avoiding conditions comfortable to mankind. I believe elk are creatures that dearly love heavy cover, but if man vacates vast tracts of sage or even semi-desert, elk are capable of filtering in and living there. Yet they will tolerate less man intrusion there than they will in heavy cover because they feel more vulnerable in plains terrain.

The May 1985 issue of "Wyoming Wildlife," official publication of the state game and fish department, speaking of once-thriving elk herds in the open sage north of Rock Springs, says: "Desert elk don't enjoy the cover forest elk do. They can't be as tolerant of human presence. The buffers (trees, hills, rocks, etc.) are not present in the desert. As a result, desert elk are more aware of human presence. That causes stress. If there's enough stress, the elk disperse. . . ."

Much of this human stress is due to just-introduced gas-oil exploration development. More about that later.

The article also points out that wilds-dispersed elk are apt to cause crop damage and therefore attract more hunters to reduce their numbers. Man's presence can thus do more than "thin out" elk populations in the desert (not a true desert here, as in the Southwest); it can stress the remaining animals and cause even more elk to depart areas lacking heavy cover.

In any event, the elk has learned where he can safely go; and if conditions change, he can also adapt in the opposite direction. It is one of the factors a hunter must take into consideration whenever he "just can't find bulls where they were before." Why aren't they there . . . what has happened in the interim? Given what we know of an elk's instincts and pattern learning, what would move him elsewhere? Many of these questions will be answered in the chapter on scouting. But here we need to know what constitutes the psychological makeup of a mature bull, exactly what stresses him, and how his "constitution" copes with it.

Personality Quirks

It appears that the elk's personality causes him to constantly seek out emotional and physical security. A hunter hiring a guide would like to think that a given large bull can be pinpointed by a certain canyon or ridge, yet even game managers attempting daily surveillance are seldom capable of doing that. I can remember one hunt when several big-game biologists tried to help me find the animals on opening morning. "This is where they were day before yesterday," one told me. But they were not there today.

We did eventually locate the elk—two days later. They had left the aspen slopes for higher ground, possibly due to warmer temperatures, or possibly because of elk hunters arriving for the hunt opener.

Another time a conservation officer who had been watching wapiti for weeks suddenly admitted on an oak ridge, "I don't know where they've gone; all I know is they aren't here." Noticing that a bulldozer had been digging at gravel a quarter mile away, the officer discovered why the elk had moved. They just wouldn't tolerate man's presence, even though they had spent most of the summer there. In that regard, *Cervus* is much different than, say, a mule deer, which would simply lie low until the man noises departed. There is little patience in a wapiti's makeup, especially an old bull which has experienced man danger over several years. How unpredictable they can be was also dramatically shown me one day when I searched cover while, I later learned, elk remained in the open.

One personality trait of a larger bull is that he is gifted with superior "radar" sensitivities in ears and nose, and uses them. Many other wild animals are not, at least in so many of the five senses. From my own experience with elk, I see them as an animal that can be outraged even by the presence of a child picking flowers at the far end of a meadow. It is not the truculent anger showing in a disturbed bull moose's eyes; the moose is ready to do you in, now. An elk seems to take the arrogant attitude that since you now have despoiled this place and ruined its tranquility, "I will find another with untrammeled purity where man cannot intrude." And, head held high, he journeys away. It is a personality, it would seem, of smug aristocracy intolerant of others. If an elk wore clothes, I'm sure they would be royal purple, a symbol of snobbish antipathy to man and his mundane doings.

Elk and the Disturbance Factor

Research conducted by the University of Wyoming (titled "Response of Elk to Seismic Exploration in the Bridger-Teton Forest, Wyoming") indicates that man-caused helicopter and dynamite noises can do more than drive expectant cow elk out of a traditional calving area. It can affect the unborn calves. The report says that displacement of range can cause a disturbed cow to use a habitat with "reduced food-intake opportunities," resulting in lesser reproductive rates, small body size, and so on. "Excitation and social pressures from meeting established animals on the new range can result in reduced feeding, and feeding on poorer-quality foods."

The poor feed also requires an elk to feed longer to fill the rumen, with reduced passage rates complicating proper nourishment. "Cows entering autumn in poor condition breed later, and produce late-born calves lighter in weight. Both experience nearly twice the normal mortality rate."

Interestingly to hunters, if in time the disturbance becomes "patterned" or expected, the elk are disturbed less. But if a helicopter deviates from a repeated procedure, elk are more likely to panic.

The University of Wyoming report also indicates that stress causes actual tissue damage in elk and other animals. Abortion may increase, and ovulation may be reduced. Panic may cause first-time mothers in particular to abandon or trample calves. Apprehension may also "elevate glucocorticoid levels, which decrease antibody production" (reduce number of white blood cells), thus inhibiting healing of body tissue. The elk may then suffer reduced resistance to pneumonia and other diseases. When excited, ruminants also select the quickest foods, often inhibiting the food-intake drive itself, reducing body nourishment as winter approaches.

Displacement, especially in winter, can also result in harmful expenditures of energy, according to the report: "Hard running can exceed by 20 times the cost of basal metabolism, and climbing requires about 12 times as much energy as locomotion on level terrain. . . . The cost of such high energy expenditures is usually thought to be highest in winter, when ungulates are in an energy conservation mode."

Failure to conserve energy at this time of year, of course, could cause any animal to use up fat reserves needed to survive a severe winter with little available food. Tremendous energy influx occurs in summer, when elk must get rid of large amounts of heat. Thus they utilize higher elevations, and cool, moist thickets. "During warm summer days there is a tremendous cost of movement, which, if excessive, could cause thermal damage to tissues and organs. This is particularly true for large bulls that may be forced to run uphill." It is suggested that "if a bull already shedding heat maximally under a hot sun was disturbed by a helicopter, it could collapse from heat stroke after running away."

Thus we see that though an elk is a rugged, flexible animal, it is also in some ways delicately fragile. There are limits to what it can do.

This information is more than academic. It can help anyone not only to become more of a hunter and naturalist, but also to better understand elk management and perhaps help to ensure better local elk hunting.

5

Nature of the Beast

"In more intelligent mammals, the size of the brain's cerebrum is relatively greater than in the less intelligent mammals."

So says the World Book Encyclopedia. In *Elk of North America: Ecology and Management,* edited by J. W. Thomas and D. E. Toweill, Stackpole Books, the editors say: "Elk have large brains . . . compared with other ungulates of comparable body size." Of course, North American elk hunters have always labeled the animal "intelligent."

In many ways the elk's physical makeup is closely connected to its intelligence and psychological behavior. As the owner of a highly developed nervous system, the elk has a "red alert" system fed by superior senses of smell and hearing, better eyes than most hunters realize, and something you can only call "feel." That last is akin to the ability of some sport fish to sense

tremors in the ground and water to warn them of a fisherman's less-than-careful approach. An elk does not possess a lateral line to detect such tremors, but heavy steps seem to alert them in much the same way. Their eyes are not as keen as the nose and ears, but just try and walk a skyline two miles away from a bedded bull. He won't be there for long.

Add a monumental intolerance of man and his artificialities, and you have a rather accurate personality profile of almost all wapiti everywhere. A friend of mine once offered to bet his ranch and future rights to any windfall Super Bowl tickets that no one would ever discover a bull elk asleep. It is a bet I would never accept. Some biologists and hunters talk of finding caribou bulls or other ungulates in slumberland, but never a bull elk.

Just how good are the ears and nose

of the wapiti? Worldwide wildlife lecturer and photographer-hunter Jim Bond compared elk with other game animals in his "America's Number One Trophy." Of a possible 100 points for nose, Bond gives the elk 80, behind only the Canada-Yukon moose and the grizzly bear. The elk garners 100 for hearing. Eyesight is 70, surpassed only by that vigilante of the high country, the mountain sheep. Bond rates elk eyes above the mountain goat's. In another category, alertness, the elk also captures all 100 points. This category, in my estimation, includes the trait of "feel" mentioned earlier. I have witnessed a big bull first stand up from a bed, then cup ears and test air currents for whatever had disturbed him.

Bond also refers to "pattern learning," which he pinpoints as any animal's aptness for protecting itself from danger in its own natural habitat. He weights this important classification with 200 points. And he gives the elk all 200.

From the above, it might seem the wapiti is a most formidable creature in both at-birth instinct and acquired habit. This is pretty much the general picture. But it also depends on how much any given individual elk has been hunted, and how many narrow "scrapes" he has lived through. A friend often releases small gamefish with the observation, "There goes a future whopper," meaning that the fish had received a valuable education that it should benefit from in later years. I believe other wildlife is similar. If a 6-point bull eludes hunters once by hiding among old stumps, he has learned something valuable he can use later. If he evades danger by running quickly away as a spike (possibly led by an older cow), he will probably respond that way again.

Thus it may be partly by luck that an oversized bull gets that way. A close encounter makes it wiser. Avoiding man becomes part of his "pattern learning." By digging into a large bag of tactics, he keeps on slipping through the hunting net every autumn.

Few hunters likely fully comprehend just how acute wapiti ears and nose really are. Human scent is wafted about by air currents in ways mysterious to man. We rarely know where the winds take it. Not until we note that the wapiti we seek has fled our meticulous stalk do we suspect an elk's nose has discovered us.

"Spooking" Distances

However, the hearing process is more measurable. I had an opportunity to study an elk's hearing abilities one week while scouting new territory along the Utah-Colorado border. After a horseback ride of some 10 miles from the nearest road, Gary Egbert of Layton, Utah, and I dismounted. As we peered over a steep rim, we made out the forms of elk about 500 yards (one-third of a mile) in the distance. We counted one monster herd bull and 31 cows. Occasionally, an elk raised its head to gaze around, mostly downslope, then resumed feeding. We whispered so low we could scarcely hear one another. The elk were not disturbed. But when we raised our voices to a normal conversational tone only a few feet from one another, an old sentinel cow raised her head. Then the entire band did the same, and all trotted directly away from us into heavy timber. Careful whispering, yes; talking, no.

Another time on a vast Indian reservation, only two other hunters were present besides a buddy and myself. We let the other two choose which half-million acres they wanted to hunt. My companion and

I selected the other half-million. In so doing, we had the perfect opportunity to measure how far away elk could hear our approach, without worrying about their being spooked by other hunters. At this time I had already tagged a thick-antlered bull, and we could take our time conducting some interesting experiments. Precisely how close could we approach elk under three conditions: (1) brittle-dry "cornflake" underfooting; (2) new, frozen "morning" snow; and (3) soft, no-crust snow that same afternoon.

We moved around so as to not alarm the same elk twice. While my partner hiked at a normal two to three-miles-per-hour speed, making no particularly heroic efforts at caution (very much the way most hunters trek forth in search of game), I observed the show from a knoll with 8 x 40 mm. binoculars. My colleague approached no closer than 500 yards in instance No. 1 (dry, brittle ground) before elk streamed away from an aspen patch across open sage. The dust their high-gear exodus raised nearly obscured their flight into another patch of aspens. I jotted in my notes that a 4-point mule deer continued to browse head-down at half the 500-yard distance. In experiment No. 2 (frozen snow), he was within about 600 yards of elk before they fled. In situation No. 3 (soft snow), he had trod within about 350 yards when the animals nervously trotted away. Remember, this was at normal hiking speeds without any attempt to sneak up on the quarry.

Several days later, my friend took advantage of soft snow to *carefully* creep within some 200 yards of wapiti. There wasn't any way we could get any closer than 400 yards on crunchy snow, except by one strategem: sneaking high up a parallel canyon to where we hoped to see elk, then peering downslope over the rim. In so doing, we didn't concern ourselves with game in the canyon we approached. Only in an adjacent canyon did we have any chance to locate elk. But even then we could not stalk closer than about 350 yards. However, we at least had a chance with this ploy to get within maximum rifle range.

The foregoing convinced me never to attempt hunting elk on crusted snow if there is some other way to do it. Research near the Jackson Hole National Elk Refuge indicated cross-country skiers sent elk scurrying off on crusted snow as far as 1000 yards away. They did not later return.

There are some other circumstances wherein dry-ground stalking can bring you within closer range than the 500 yards my friend and I managed during that week. Rain-soft ground with few twigs to snap underfoot helps. I once moved within easy bow range (15 yards) of a giant bull on spongy, soft grass near an old lake bed. But one careless step, and it would have all been over.

Still another way wapiti sense your approach is, strangely enough, when all becomes quiet. When elk move, there is a crackling of leg and knee joints. When one or two suspect something amiss enough to stop and sniff the air, others hear the sudden silence. That can be enough to send a hidden bull scurrying.

Such are the capabilities of elk ears. Treat the nose, too, as though it was just as finely tuned. Hunt into the wind. If a constant wind is at your back when you see elk, forget it. You have only one slight hope: that the bull will become confused with shifting and capricious wind currents. But even then he knows you are about, and will flee in the opposite direction with your first mistake.

You may have a slight chance to score on elk that mill about in indecision until they flatten their backs and raise their heads; they probably don't know the precise location of danger. Cows are usually reluctant to take calves anywhere until they know where the danger lies. Bulls sometimes stay put too. Proceed slowly and quietly. Remain low. If you are in the open or silhouetted on a ridgeline, announcing your exact location, the situation is practically hopeless. One thing that helps is to break up the human outline. Kneel down or hump over. And try to remain perfectly still even though those big brown eyes are taking you apart.

Remember that in most cases, more than one pair of elk eyes are searching for you. Given the gregarious nature of elk—possibly a throwback to the days when many resided on the plains, where danger might appear from any direction—wapiti usually remain grouped. I have witnessed elk in lowland foothills scatter to locate agricultural feed, but almost never does an animal venture forth alone. That would likely occur only with a "social misery" of some kind—perhaps a bull seeking to recuperate from the rut without contact with other elk, or a cow seeking solitude at calving time, or a diseased animal which can't keep pace with the herd.

Studies are not conclusive on whether elk differentiate bright colors like orange or red. However, research does indicate elk note solid orange in a mottled environment of timber, or mottled orange against a background of solid snow. More about that later.

As for the elk's own camouflage, it takes full advantage of the terrain. I have observed large bulls secret themselves in blowdown timber, their reddish summer coats blending in almost perfectly with the surroundings. One such bull was overlooked by eight hunters and three guides who made a "thorough drive" through a patch of firs. Since it was late in the season and the large bull had obviously lived through a number of past elk quests, we could only conclude that the animal had pulled this strategem before. He very nearly got away with it one more time.

To attempt concealment, an elk has to be somewhat convinced it fits in with the natural surroundings. With its "protective coloration," a bull needs only nerves of steel to usher hunters right on by day after day, season after season. Today's elk seem more inclined to hide than in years past, when the main strategy was to put distance between them and danger. For one thing, today there are more likely to be hunters everywhere. In heavily pressured terrain, elk thus appear more likely to use their camouflage as well as their legs.

Skittish Nature

The skittish nature of elk goes far beyond that of a deer. I have watched respectable bucks approach a road in timber and jump across it with no hesitation. If there is no immediate cover, a deer frequently checks out all possible danger, then hurries across. But an elk may balk entirely when encountering a road. An old-timer once told me he observed a cow elk approach a road in timber at brisk walking speed, then stop suddenly. She sniffed all around, then backed off. Encountering the road again farther along, she appeared extremely nervous. In time she jumped over, then fled at a full run. "When she reached a meadow with a road in it," the old-timer told me, "she wouldn't cross at all. She backed off, and vanished into a thicket."

Intolerance is an elk's middle name.

Those that grow up in roaded areas may learn to cope with roads, but only those with little or no traffic. Associating roads directly with human activity can cause suspicious, older wapiti to search out new, less-trammeled territory. New road construction, occurring during summer in foothills while elk are in higher terrain, could block off the animals' normal movement to winter range.

There are few studies to prove how elk respond to the building of roads, but past behavior suggests elk may migrate out of such a region entirely. Research on logging roads in Idaho by that state's fish-and-game department indicated collared and telemonitored elk fled the changes in their habitat. The result was that Idaho closed many back roads. Biologists did not have an easy time convincing nimrods that they directly benefitted — that is, that elk would then remain where they had been. The findings were published in "The Bugle," a publication of the Idaho Fish and Game Department.

Oregon went so far as to ask licensees whether they preferred hunting with or without road closures. Following the closure of 480 miles of back roads, the hunters *favored* by an impressive 87 percent the retention of the closures. Even though banning motorized vehicles obviously made hunting access more difficult, hunters were impressed enough with what they saw to vote by a more overwhelming 93 percent for road closures the year after. Of course, in coastal and jungled Oregon-Washington, the only Roosevelt elk you'll see may be in small clearcuts served by roads.

This isn't meant to condemn any roads in elk country. But it would appear that the psychological construction of most Rocky Mountain wapiti makes them skittish of such things. In most instances, elk and roads just don't mix. The elk's nature seems to require some sort of buffer zone between it and man. Roads are only one way of eliminating the buffer.

Gourmet Tastes

An elk is a restless creature in many other ways. One is likely due to a constant search for foods. The elk stomach (all four compartments) is a rather sensitive organ, one which can take various types of nutriments but will rebel against a full diet of some foods, like coarse fir needles. The animal knows instinctively the needles can compact tightly in its system, causing digestive problems. Therefore it moves about to get variety in its diet.

This quest for more palatable food could lead a big bull to a hunter waiting patiently at the forest edge in the early light of dawn.

Rumination and Restlessness

An hour or so later, the elk may have satisfied caloric needs, and then another need, rumination, takes over. The elk lies down so that the cud-chewing process can begin within the other stomach compartments. The elk will remain bedded for several hours until the entire digestive process is completed.

Some license-holders talk about elk bedding down on a warm day to "shade up" or rest, but the bedding process will take place regardless of weather or other external conditions, simply because that is the way this ungulate operates. Rumination follows feeding. At times, the elk is a most active animal. At other times, it is the extreme opposite.

Elk also have a restlessness born of sheer taste. I have seen elk on a refuge depart their usual meadow hay to walk three-quarters of a mile for a slightly better grade of hay. To do so they must run a certain risk, for the better hay is located along the refuge buildings and corral. Here they must also compete with ranch horses for the favored food, and be willing to mingle within a few feet of domestic stock—so close, in fact, that they frustrated my photographic composition efforts to isolate the wild from the tame.

I have also watched elk literally crash through high-ridge snow cornices during winter to join other wapiti enjoying a change in diet. One particular bull repeatedly lunged into a snowbank as high as his shoulder until he managed to hammer through to grasses and browse in a ravine on the other side. The struggle also said something about an elk's stubborn determination, for as I watched through the glasses, he kept at his task for some time until finally triumphing. Then he settled down quietly to graze with the other animals.

An elk also possesses a certain innate curiosity, although I would say it is not as advanced as the pronghorn's. Hunters often tell of holding their hat up on a sage branch to attract an antelope a few dozen feet closer. An elk, especially a bull which knows it is being hunted, wants to know what is going on in its bailiwick. But it rarely does anything as foolish as walking toward potential danger. It may raise its head to expose more shoulder area to aim at. More likely, it stares in the direction where something unusual is going on. A foreign sound, scent, or sight will generally precipitate immediate alarm. While a deer lays its ears back when about to flee, an elk frequently pumps its head upward a time or two, then digs its powerful legs into the earth. The thrusting motion will launch it into rapid flight. If bedded, the great rear legs gather beneath it, the front hooves anchor into the ground, and it is up. Unlike most deer (muley or whitetail), the elk may not wait to pinpoint the exact location of danger. It is fully capable of thinking on its feet. For the first few seconds while it is wheeling into any cover it can find, it is ready to change directions instantly if any predator presents itself in the flight path. I have watched giant bulls change directions on a dime, even in aspens where a man would have difficulty negotiating in a straight line. Somehow the bull avoids catching its antlers among the fishhook limbs.

In its panic an elk may also knock down a few spindly aspens or brush. An elk's departure is seldom as smooth and silent as that of a deer. If a hunter sits down and analyzes the sounds of elk bowling over small trees, he may get an idea where the wapiti intends to go. Yet it will do little good unless the bull emerges from timber within rifle range. But the rifle toter does have a chance if he scrutinizes any openings along the animal's thundering route and is fully prepared to shoot with little delay. Then, too, how much noise is made can depend on the number of panicked animals. A single bull or cow may slip out more quietly.

How far elk will go after being spooked depends on several things, including how many times they have been pushed. The first time it happens, they might just circle around like a deer so often does. But unlike a deer, elk have no qualms about exploring new hinterlands. And they will do so if convinced man danger is so imminent as to constitute a threat. When that happens, a band of elk can often be seen crossing not just one ridgeline but three or four.

Elk have more than strong legs and

hooves going for them. They also possess strong lungs, although perhaps not as expansive as those of the antelope. Nevertheless, they are capable of tremendous stamina. Such is demonstrated during winter migrations when elk may be on the go for days at a time, possibly moving 90 miles from summer range. During this time the elks' "energy efficiency" usually puts them in a single-file line to take advantage of the trail broken by a leader in deep snow. Many studies of migrations to winter range, or to wilder terrain during hunting seasons, indicate the elk has not only a restless spirit but also the physical tools to match. Such elk may fare well during even a severe winter if the necessary food is eventually found. Of course, elk can be heavily stressed in the winter as precious body fat is used up, and then face starvation. But it is much hardier than the deer.

All of the above are important facts to remember if, for instance, you get it into your head to trail an elk. If it is healthy, you'd better have a pack on your back with several days' provisions. And even then, you may never find the animal standing in those tracks.

Comfort Zones

All elk everywhere follow certain tendencies. One is the search for comfort zones. Part of this is psychological. One winter I watched eight cow elk with their calves hesitate for several days to cross over a road to lowland hayfields. By the end of December, with snow deepening, they did so. For days they bedded furtively in the willows of a river bottom, then moved out into the open stubble, near food. However, they had a most difficult time deciding exactly where to settle for any given night. Once I watched them bed in four different locations, calves protected among their mothers, before the cows tucked in ears and noses themselves. Then a distant dog barking moved them a few hundred yards closer to a cottonwood patch. In the meantime, several bulls remained on the mountain side of the road, stirring only at dawn and dusk to move to the ranchland hay. I never did attempt to determine precisely where they bedded, fearing I might unduly stress them in such a critical cold-weather period. But the point is, they bedded where they felt most secure, not near the daily feed.

There are also physical factors of comfort, vital ones in locating any elk anywhere. Just as fish seek certain temperature zones, so do elk. It is one reason wapiti may seem to be a bundle of nervous energy, restless until they find the right "layer." Elk are homeothermic—that is, they lack extensive sweat glands. Thus, to maintain constant body temperatures they *must* move about. Their thick hide, more often than not, keeps them searching out shade in warm weather, or sunny slopes in cold climes. Murie says, "Extreme cold does not greatly affect elk unless they are sick. Healthy animals do not appear to mind the cold, and do not seek shelter from it. . ."

However, elk frequently do take refuge from heat. While some calories an elk takes in are consumed in the many daily functions, other calories are stored as fat. In the warm weather of early fall this can be aggravated by a heavy inner lining of fur-like hair which becomes the winter pelage. The larger body size of a giant bull, though it better handles cold weather, is less comfortable in what man would term "nice" weather. A heavy, furry bull in early fall is precisely like a man dressed for a cold snap who is required to remain inside a well-heated home. Of course, an elk has options, such as going higher and out of bright sunlight. That is one reason a band of elk which seemed comfortably ensconced in a certain middle canyon may have moved out the day before you got there. It is not so much hunting pressure—the same can occur in any national park; it's just that the 7,500-foot canyon was suddenly too warm on the "cheerful" day you decided to go hunting. The elk, particularly massive bulls, may now be comfortably bedded or feeding at 9,000 feet on a shadowed slope.

This inclination toward comfort zones based on temperature can also depend on health. If an elk is inflicted with scabies (causing loss of hair), the natural insulation against cold is lost. Such elk may then become subject to distress, hypothermia, or even freezing to death. An elk's hair is not hollow, to guard against supreme cold, but it does mat thickly in autumn (the scraggly appearance in late spring is the shedding of this winter coat), and sensitive muscles can project hair outward to protect against lower temperatures (like man's "goose pimpling" of the skin). Exposed parts of an elk—the throat, ears, etc.—are especially woven with thicker hair.

This search for comfortable temperatures probably has as much to do with a bull's being a creature of the highlands, or of remote and "hidden" slopes, as any other factor, including hunting pressure. Fortunately for the elk, it is this type of terrain which man most often shuns for his permanent home. Most often, civilizations are located in lower elevations, where the elk does not come in conflict with man except where his winter range has been usurped.

Cold-Weather Effects

Judging from elk I have observed during winters of 40 and even 50 degrees below zero (possibly 60 below on ridgelines above my vantage point), I conclude elk are certainly right at home in cold weather. A report by the University of Wyoming ("Response of Elk to Seismic Exploration in the Bridger-Teton Forest, Wyoming") concludes: the use by radio-collared elk "of cool north and east-facing slopes was highest in all seasons. In contrast, elk use of warm west-northwest exposures was in lesser amounts in all seasons." It is also true that wet north or east slopes carry more cover for possibly stressed animals.

Elk also visit south and southwest slopes for a major reason: more light there produces more grasses, forbs, and other desired foods. But if hunting pressure mounts, the "kitchen" will be vacated in favor of a more "at-home" living room on northeast slopes. One hunting season, licensees complained to the state fish-game department that the wapiti were "all shot out." As an outdoor writer for a local newspaper, I went along as a witness to what the game biologists saw from a helicopter—some 50–75 elk bedded in northeast snowfields. There was no food there. To reach them, a nimrod would have been forced to don snowshoes. Apparently, none did. There was also little traditional cover on hand, but the elk didn't need it in this case. They found both security and comfort in the same place. Quite likely the elk left that snowbank to feed only at night, thus evading hunters around the clock.

I have come to the conclusion that when hunters gloat about a "beautiful" warm, sunny day to go hunting, it isn't all that beautiful to an elk adapted to finding solitude and comfort zones as far from "nice" south slopes as they can get. They literally flee "sundeck exposure," particularly after acquiring the thick winter coat associated with Rocky Mountain high country by late September.

Research also shows that overhead timber, such as most lodgepole pine, offers "thermal" warmth. Therefore, elk often find winter warmth in timber. Since the trees also act as a windbreak, this is especially true on windy days.

By checking the thermometer on my front porch, I can predict how active elk might be, and at what elevation. When it reads 50 degrees above zero Fahrenheit (more like 40 on the 1,500-foot-high ridge under observation), the elk are sluggish, if feeding in the open at all. More likely they are hidden in the shade of a north slope. When my thermometer reads 20 above (about 10 where the elk are), they are actively feeding near or on top of the ridge. If it is colder, say 10 below, the elk will be more active, and also require more caloric intake. They will be feeding in earnest along the upper third of the ridge. When the climate dips to 20 below, they will move downslope to middle elevations. At 30 below, they will be in the upper foothills, probably on the south-facing slopes, which are warmer and grow more grass and other browse due to the additional sunlight. If it becomes colder still (and temperatures here have been known to drop to 50 below in the lowlands during January), the elk will move into the valley to find the desirable comfort zone and/or feed. To complete the "cycle," they may also seek brushy shelter, if timber is absent.

With more than two feet of snow, even an elk's strong front hooves may not be able to dig out sedges and forbs, no matter what the temperatures. In up to 16 inches of snow, they seem to have little difficulty at all. From 17 to 24 inches, elk tend to grow migratory.

When it is very cold, the ground "glazes" over, and elk find it difficult to paw out grasses beneath the icy mantle. Also, if there are browse shrubs to feed on, the elk may remain in upper climes longer than they would otherwise.

Water is not a major factor, because below 32 degrees any springs and small creeks are already frozen. Elk like to be within one-third of a mile of water, according to studies, but in the winter can subsist on snow to satisfy thirst. In extremely cold temperatures elk may also take refuge and bed for the night against brush, logs, or frequently a tree trunk.

If a falling barometer foretells an advancing storm, elk will often put on the feed bag. Much like humans, they don't want to forage in rain, sleet, or wet snowstorms. It isn't within their comfort zone.

Detailed effects of weather will be discussed later, but elk will often feed through snowstorms, if heavy winds are absent. The winds are helpful, however, in sweeping snow from ridgetops, and are one reason elk are often observed feeding there.

It is also well known that elk will shun warmer temperatures which attract flies and insects. Colder climes do not entirely guarantee relief, but seem to give ungulates like elk some respite from the insect problem.

Grade of Slope

Another factor determining where an elk will likely be is grade of slope. Veteran hunters and guides have long observed that few slopes seem too steep for elk.

They are not mountain goats, and shun cliffs, but anything which has vegetation on it and is less than perpendicular seems frequented at times by elk. I've taken bulls well up on 12,000-foot peaks, primarily on finger ridges with at least a modicum of cover and some footholds for large hooves. Research by a consortium of biologists (*Elk of North America*, edited by J. W. Thomas and D. E. Toweill, Stackpole Books), indicates that a slant of 15–30 percent is ideal. This may not seem like much until you consider that the motorist is given a warning sign on most roads with a seven or eight percent grade.

Other considerations, such as snow depth and available feed, determine where an elk may be. With snow depths of two feet or more, an elk, especially a tough old bull, may remain on favored slopes only if overhead browse such as oak, mountain mahogany, and bitterbrush is present. One conclusion is that elk will remain on relatively steep slopes, the kind a man puffs his way up, unless deep snow (and absence of browse) necessitates their moving to lower elevations with the subsequent dangers but more readily available feed.

In general, I've found elk are often suspicious and unusually wary of canyon bottoms and slopeless ground. One reason might be the increased likelihood of human activity.

Nearly everything about an elk is geared toward eluding danger. At first glance its size (800–1,000 pounds for a mature bull) may seem to work against it. Certainly, a broadside bull presents a large target. But the animal is also built for speed. Tests for speed have been somewhat inconclusive, for an elk rarely races a vehicle over flat terrain for any distance, as a pronghorn does. But horsemen involved in short sprints before an elk sidesteps into timber report bursts of speed to 45 miles per hour. That is faster than any horse can run, and is a reason most elk on the move are blurred targets at best. How they can run through lodgepole pine with antlers twisting free is, as hinted at earlier, a wonder of the natural world. They can also leap fences up to 7½ feet high (an actual accomplishment of a bull escaping a Nebraska enclosure) and swim with ease, despite their bulk.

Elk have a certain personality belligerence which has likely helped them cope in the evolutionary scheme. They rarely are as bellicose as a bull moose, particularly where man is concerned, outside the rut. I've known moose to continue walking up a trail directly into a packstring. Twice I have had to walk around a moose in the wild due to his stubborn disposition. An elk wouldn't do that. I have been charged several times by truculent moose, but never by elk, unless it was wounded. On the other hand, Bond says elk have been transplanted into areas of Canada where there were numerous moose (the larger Canada-Yukon species) and "the elk, being a hardier animal, have driven the moose right out of the country."

This is a different character quirk from that of an elk trapped by man in a tight enclosure. Under such conditions most wapiti can go nearly berserk in an effort to elude man scent, sounds, and sight. If any human is present, the high-strung elk will seem driven by adrenaline alone. But it is not energy channeled against other creatures, as with a moose. It is a desperate fear, one which has helped keep man and elk separated over the years. I have witnessed elk trapped in close quarters beat their heads and legs against log railings in a futile effort to escape confinement. They may be captive, but they have not capitulated. It is as if they were a cross between badger and wild stallion in stubborn determination to rebel. This love of freedom, or will to avoid contact with man, normally keeps elk well away from danger. Research has shown that if man noise or scent is about, as in logging, mining, or recreational activities, elk will in most instances keep at least one-half mile away. One study showed elk disturbed enough at a measured distance of 1,312 feet to seek solitude elsewhere. But loud noises like rifle fire alert them even farther away. I've observed even young bulls seek cover from shooting miles away.

Elk signal danger in several ways. One is a high-pitched squeal, often heard between cow and calf. The animals seem to communicate frequently, albeit in a primitive way, concerning possible danger. (The elk bugle is well known, but it usually indicates a bull in rut warning other bulls to stay away.) One sound elk use to express anger is a sharp bark, sometimes heard when calves do not respond to a cow (such as when they fail to hurry along, or remain camouflage-still) or when a small predator approaches. I've heard such a dog-like bark from fleeing elk, particularly those disturbed from bed or feeding station. The sound is distinctive, readily recognizable after even a little familiarity. With it an alert nimrod can sometimes determine when elk are near. However, most often the communication works *for* an elk, not against it. The gregarious nature of the elk, with a herding instinct likely to include having a cow somewhere watching for danger, is a strong point in their favor. When the barking is first emitted, every elk around is instantly on guard. You will have to be too.

Elk and Livestock

Elk are intolerant of many things. They usually avoid sheep herds. Studies show the presence of either cattle or sheep on a range can discourage elk use. Deer, on the other hand, seem quite tolerant of both, especially cattle. I think one of the reasons elk shun sheep in particular is not so much the grazing competition as that sheep are often accompanied by men and dogs. It is a fear-by-association syndrome. In any event, if you hunt elk near domestic stock, you will have to assess the particular situation. Cattle on the range might also mean the presence of salt, which elk use. Elk can and do get along without salt. Yet they are attracted to it when it's available. I have seen elk utilizing salt placed out by cowboys grow so accustomed to the man movements as to no longer be frightened by them or the livestock. But this is true only when the stockman moves salt about on routine, consistent rounds. If he alters the program, elk grow suspicious and may hightail it elsewhere.

Wapiti are victims of their own ingrained habits. When Flaming Gorge Dam was constructed on the Green River along the Wyoming-Utah boundary, elk just kept using the old migration trails to reach winter range. Only now they had to swim the resulting reservoir for several miles to reach the traditional destination. The new barrier did little to stop them, although the increased activity of fishermen, tourists, and others have had an effect on old habits. The elk are less often seen nowadays. They have tempered their old ways with new nocturnal habits, once again with beneficial survival results. But it was man's presence that did it, not the lake he created. Why should a man-made reservoir be tolerated and not a road? The only explanation I can think of is that the road is linked to man and danger more than the lake is.

Bull Different

Bulls have more individualized habits than cows. One, previously mentioned, is the rubbing off of velvet in late summer, leaving antler tines so sensitive that the bull shuns other animals which might touch them. Observing bulls on any winter feeding refuge indicates the antlered animals like to stay with their own kind. It may be a social order, or it may be that the males feel their feeding and security needs are different than those of the females. For one thing, the bulls will lock antlers at any time, in or out of the rut and without anything seemingly at stake. They apparently just want to test their own physical

strength and prowess on occasion. Peculiarly, even the antlerless males may rise to spar on occasion with animals having well-endowed racks. At such times the bald bull is more likely to utilize front hooves. In fact, however, hooves are seldom used by bulls, possibly because the sparring seems to be more of a male ritual than any attempt to actually inflict injury.

On the other hand, cows learn early and well how to keep coyotes and other predators away, mainly from calves, by using their front hooves. An angry mother is more than a match for a single coyote, but the predator often finds ways to sneak in at the most opportune time. When any elk is angry, it will often show first in a grinding action of the teeth, possibly in tandem with a flailing front leg. The antler tine or hoof has been known, especially with males, to inflict injury or death, sometimes by puncturing a vital organ. It is rare, but it has happened.

An aspect of survival in bulls seems to be antler configuration—the high and

A young bull scratches on lodgepole pines to get rid of velvet on antlers.

Lonesome bull, possibly in late stages of velvet, remains away from other elk, or from cover that might bother sensitive antlers. *U.S. Fish & Wildlife Service Photo.*

This bull, not at all afraid of coyote, runs the predator off in mild irritation. *U.S. Fish & Wildlife Service Photo.*

Two bulls spar, even in winter, well after fall rut. *U.S. Fish & Wildlife Service Photo.*

Typical migration pattern of elk: single file to take advantage of breaking trail by animals ahead. *U.S. Fish & Wildlife Service Photo.*

rearward-tined design reduces chances of antlers locking together during combat. Mule deer and whitetails, with their typical or non-typical racks, seem to more often lock permanently. Frequently, duels between bulls seem to be more of a neck-strength, leg-pushing, shoving match than a direct test of antler size.

Elk lifespans vary, depending on location. A tagged bull in Arizona was found to be over 25 years old. I've heard of cows on the Wyoming feeding refuges being 28 years old, but some of these stories are not fully documented. Research indicates a domesticated 14-year-old bull elk mated with a cow elk, which became pregnant. However, studies cited elsewhere clearly show a bull begins antler decline after the ninth year. Elk in zoos seem to live longer lives, as a rule, than wild wapiti. Winter is the key. During any strenuous December-to-April period, the older animals and the calves are the most likely to succumb first.

Contributing heavily to death is the wearing of teeth after the 10th year, with many incisors nearly gone and the crowns of central teeth worn away. It is not known what effects the lack of upper front-jaw chewing teeth might have on an elk, but since nature did not bestow any, it is a fact that much of the grinding must be done in a smaller area. "Gumming" at grass and browse might be easy in the summer months, but would seem to be much more difficult for the older animals come winter. These oldsters are probably the first elk to head for migration lanes each winter.

Many other traits of the bulls will be examined in the chapter on bugling: wallows, sapling-sparring, etc. One habit of a rutting bull, tossing branches or dead vegetation or even dirt over his head, is observed at other times of year, just as "fighting" is seen all winter. I've read many explanations for this, including one claiming that the bull "seeks to show the world

Nothing is more wary than a bull elk. In each of these five bulls, note alert ears and nose, readiness to flee.

who is boss." That's possible. We may have to accept it until someone learns how to talk to the animals.

Although it is said elsewhere in this book that bulls are not territorial, they do seem to be so at times. I believe they are not defending any given physical area (like a large fish does) but guarding cows or harems within that bailiwick. Studies in Montana have indicated that bulls seem to defend up to a square mile of preferred real estate, yet if the cows move from it, so will the herd bull. A bull, if he is territorial at all, is much less so than a predator like a coyote or mountain lion, which warns all intruders to remain out of his feeding grounds.

Elk appear playful by nature in many ways, including romping around in ponds and streams long after they have drunk their fill of water. The calves may also be observed jumping and running about for no apparent purpose. But in nature's efficient way, they may feel the urge to strengthen and test leg muscles that may well be needed later to avoid predators or to help them rejoin the herd. Even young elk seem to enjoy swimming, another muscle-toner.

Cows are often thought to be simply watchful heralds while the herd feeds, but they often play a much greater role in deciding where the feeding will be done, and in selecting a bedding ground from which

Elk migrating from winter to summer range, Jackson Hole, Wyoming. *U.S. Fish & Wildlife Service Photo.*

approaching movement can be detected. An old cow may be the herd's "interpreter," as when a vehicle stops in the vicinity. Is it a routine stop to which the elk have become accustomed, such as a slowdown needed to negotiate a certain rut in the road, or does it signal danger? The first elk to leave a site is almost always such an "interpreter" cow. She will often be first to bark or flee at any noise, in or out of hunting seasons. Such a herd "nanny" seems to be both a physical and social leader year-round in what the herd does and where it goes.

A Typical Day

The average day in an elk's life goes something like this:

• After three or four hours of sleep, drowsiness has fled. The animal is fully awake well before dawn.

• Feeding and watering time during the autumn may occupy a daily average of some 134 total minutes, more than half in the morning. Rutting bulls may feed but a few minutes, however, and at the height of the rut, probably not at all. Cows with calves may feed more in the spring. Cows have been clocked feeding up to 550 minutes during a 24-hour period. Young elk during the growing, formative years, like boys, may eat much more than mature animals.

• Following an active feeding period comes the rumination time, which is more difficult to scientifically measure. However, elk have been observed to remain bedded for two to three hours after feeding, even in weather which was neither oppressively warm, cold, or windy. The rumination through four stomach chambers requires that food only quickly chewed be regurgitated and re-chewed in quiet security, moving through the "storage" system into the digestive channels. Daily consumption appears to be less if the diet is woody or fibrous, but digestion of such food could mean a longer rumination before the animal is again active.

• In midafternoon, if temperatures are comfortable enough, an elk could do just about anything. He might stroll in search of better food, or just curiously meander to see what is in his domain. Of course, he may remain bedded in extremely warm, cold, or windy weather.

• At dusk, the feeding and rumination periods are duplicated. Obviously, the foregoing indicates that early morning and twilight are the best times to be looking for elk out feeding. If hunting at midday, you'll likely have to seek out the bedding areas, in or near cover, rather than any openings.

These are the physical attributes which make the elk the elusive quarry it is. You will have a better chance of outwitting him if you know where he is coming from—if you understand the challenging nature of the beast.

6

What Is Elk Country?

Elk country?

An elk hunter's first inclination is to visualize scenic meadows or parks interspersed with conifer forests. That is, of course, the classical description, the one you would expect to see as a calendar painting with "American wapiti" written underneath. I can see it now: emerald grass caressed by the cold, clean winds of the highlands; carpeted greenery among high, verdant forests resembling Yellowstone or Yosemite National Park.

But elk haunt many other places as well. In one elk bailiwick I know of, the wapiti are not even up on top of the mountain, or near it, because the ridgelines there embrace a lacework of roads. Elk also remain away from the mountain bottom because warm temperatures and elk hides don't harmonize. That leaves the middle. But the terrain there is not pine or parkland. It is almost entirely oak brush and mountain mahogany mixed with sage.

But it is also elk country. The reasons are threefold: 1) it is cool enough (some 7,500 to 9,000 feet above sea level); 2) food and cover are present; 3) man rarely is.

Elk habitat varies from the coastal rainforests of Washington to the chaparral of northern Mexico. On the coast, the Roosevelt elk don't need high altitudes for comfort, because of the cooling effects of the ocean, and heavy rainfall assures adequate lowland cover. To find this situation inland, you would need at least 6,000 feet of elevation in most places.

Then, too, elk "country" is not the same in different seasons of the year. Here we will limit ourselves to elk residency from early to late fall, during the hunting seasons.

Classic elk country in Utah's Uinta Mountains north slope.

One clue you are in elk country. This young bull failed to make it through the winter. Carcass was found near author's home, with no indication of bullet wound or foul play.

Story in the snow: hungry elk are on the move into lowland riverbottoms. *U.S. Fish & Wildlife Service Photo.*

We must also be aware of elk moving into (or out of) areas where they have seldom ventured before. When I moved into western Wyoming, old-timers told me there had never been elk in the rolling foothills across the river toward the Idaho border. That seemed likely enough, since nothing much grew there except rabbitbrush and an occasional outburst of oak. (This western oak is not like the high, dignified oak of the eastern states; it is a thick, wide bush growing up to the height of a man's head.) In time, though, enough elk resided over across the river to constitute a winter nuisance as they raided valley haystacks and even rummaged around a small subdivision. A hunting season was initiated. However, it soon became evident why the elk took up residence there: man had little reason to go there, except after stray livestock. And the few four-wheel-drive roads bogged down in steep arroyos. Though there was very little vegetation,

wandering gulleys and points undulated up to 8,000 feet in a manner that let a man see but relatively short distances in any direction. Grasses and sedges peeped out of shadowed gulleys.

Why hadn't elk moved there earlier? Apparently they were content in higher and more "classical" mountain terrain eastward, until increasing herd size, along with two consecutive severe winters, sent them looking for lower winter range. When they found it, they also found a permanent home. The elk will quite likely remain there. Winter in this lower margin of their comfort zone is never likely to be so harsh as to push them out. Probably the only thing which could do that would be road improvement to make hunting easy, or a combination of subdivision construction, land cultivation, or something else to bring humans in for more than an occasional visit.

Elk can also flourish in expansive sage

flats. They have in south-central Wyoming near the Red Desert. Hunters drawing permits for the region are seldom certain whether they were seeking wapiti or antelope. Yet hunting there is far from easy. Success figures have been about average for the state, but some nimrods even doubted elk were there.

At first those sagebrush wapiti were not overly vulnerable, despite lack of cover. They adopted some of the pronghorn's habits, relying more on their eyes and legs than they would, say, in coastal jungles. Transplanted elk multiplied in the new habitat. However, increased human activity, apparently from oil and gas exploration, has driven some of these elk long distances into higher terrain, according to Wyoming Game and Fish Department studies.

In some other sectors of the West, elk have adapted fairly well to daily life near civilization. Basically, these are elk which have been there all along while communities built up nearby. Such wapiti continue to hold out in huntable numbers not far from Wind Cave National Park in South Dakota, Denver, Albuquerque, Salt Lake City, Missoula, Boise, Cheyenne, Portland, and Seattle. So long as the elk do not encounter a harsh winter, human inhabitants of these metropolises may rarely see the animals. The elk subsist there because of some obstacle to man such as steep terrain or heavy cover. Food and water are likely found in abundance nearby.

Barren-Land Elk

On the other hand, I have looked at elk in some hinterlands which had little food and water. Elk ranged over great distances to fill those needs. However, those places provided a lonely and desolate expanse. In one region along the Utah-Colorado border, 100 miles of greasewood and sparse pinyon-juniper support a wide-ranging elk population. I was startled there one day at the edge of sand dunes to witness 11 elk, two of them young bulls. Two cows wore blue collars, apparently to allow biologists to monitor just how far they moved about. The animals were just as surprised to see me as I them at midday, 40 miles from the nearest town. They stopped to stare at me for a half a minute before thrusting muzzles to the horizontal and trotting indignantly away.

With little intrusion from man, this is a growing herd, on which a two-week limited-draw hunting season is allowed. But the territory is not easy to hunt. Elk are scattered, since sedges and water are scattered. There are few steep slopes to focus on. All the geography is wild and uninhabited. It would not be particularly profitable to use horses there, because elk can see movement for long distances. Other than roaming a few back roads hoping to find elk by sheer luck, as I did, hunting strategy would be limited.

The best recourse in that situation would be to sit down with the biologist who tagged those elk and discuss their movements at various times of year. Where do they go come deep snow? Where were they tagged, and where have collared elk been sighted? Where have they been harvested in the past?

Cervus canadensis will probably always thrive in such hinterland habitat. But in my opinion, higher and steeper elk country is more readily hunted. It is the kind I look for.

In almost any neglected high mountain meadow, anywhere at all in North America, you are likely to find elk. You can generally count on it if man has not been there for any length of time. The chances are good that the elk may feed each morning and evening in the meadow. Otherwise, they may frequent the edges only.

I remember one week's hunt near an alpine parkland which had only one thing wrong with it — people crossed it on weekends. It remained that way from the Friday before the elk season opened, through Saturday and Sunday to Monday afternoon. Deer appeared in the meadow edges on Monday evening. The elk, possibly letting the deer take the first risk, waited out one more feeding period, appearing Tuesday morning. Tuesday evening the bull showed.

But let's examine a "typical" elk haunt, one resembling Yellowstone or Rocky Mountain National Park. On one such quest, up Elks Fork to Wapiti Ridge in northwestern Wyoming's Washakie Wilderness Area, our party of guides and hunters rode nine miles along a canyon bottom without seeing a single elk or any immediate sign. But we could glance cross-grain up side canyons almost anywhere and look directly into picturesque wapiti habitat. It was recognizable in more ways than just its removal from man: sharp features such as jutting hogbacks, grassy finger ridges, and rugged chasms leading to forbidding ridges rising over 12,000 feet in elevation. A hunter could possibly ride for weeks up and down that north-south main drainage without seeing elk. All the necessary ingredients for wapiti were there, however, just a mile or two either east or west. With all that vast territory for bulls to hide in, it wasn't an easy hunt by any means. But in time we found them.

Game Scarce?

In another wilderness area it seemed we would never locate elk in the week I could hunt there. A carpet of spruce seemingly allowed no open areas where grass or other desirable food could find sunlight. Even elk, with a diet which can include conifer needles, seemed incapable of surviving there. Several new hunters complained it just "wasn't elk country." And if it was, "they had all moved out." Five of them left disgruntled — partly because of inclement weather which had prevented their traveling far from camp. Most of the others had remained in camp to wait out the wet storms. Looking at the magnitude of the terrain, I was convinced elk resided in it somewhere. But I was also concerned that when we did find game, it could melt into the forest before we saw it.

I asked one of the more experienced guides, totally familiar with this region, where we might locate elk.

"Simple," he said. "A few miles from here we've got a number of steep south-slope pockets with browse. Or we can go up near timberline to find the same thing. Then there's the bottom of the snowslide gulches swept clean of trees, where small meadows have taken over. Or we can try old burns . . . places like that."

The next day he led me to those places. If the other license-holders had remained around long enough, they would have seen bulls, as we did. I nailed the second bull we saw. True, we had to scramble over rockslides high on a mountain for half a day. But that is a small price to pay for a respectable bull elk these days.

The thing which paid off for me was that the guide *knew* he was in elk country. Given some patience on my part, he took me to it. I might have found a bull on my own, but it would have required perhaps a few more days.

Interestingly, there are several strips of land near this same wilderness which are non-wilderness public forest, open to any hunter who wants to do it himself. (In designated wilderness in Wyoming, a licensed guide is required for nonresidents.) The trouble is that several of the forested strips are so close to a major highway that many nimrods take the easy route and hunt there. The terrain looks the same, with about as many spruces, as the accompanying wilderness where I scored. But the latter is far better elk country (guided or otherwise) because it is more buffered from human sight, sound, and scent.

The best way to find such remote non-wilderness domain with elk, where you can hunt on your own, is to obtain a good map from the local Forest Service office. Study the areas less accessible to hunters or other human activity. A new permit-holder can spend a hunting week in one of two ways: either taking a few hours to reach the hunting grounds and then searching in vain for 6¾ days, or taking, say, 1½ days to get into terrain which may appear no different — but having less spooked and more unsophisticated bulls — and then scoring in three days or so. Which is the more valuable use of hunting time? The point is to make certain you take time to get in the best elk territory you can find wherever you hold a permit.

Elk are often found with mule deer or Columbia (West Coast) blacktail deer. But it would be a mistake to suppose that since you've found deer, even large ones, you have found elk. For example, I once spent two weeks in the Washakie and North Absaroka Wilderness areas east of Yellowstone and saw elk daily. I never saw a single deer in the Washakie and saw only two in the Absaroka. The conifer-studded Washakie has little of the browse deer must have. To understand why, we need only look beneath the boughs of thickly growing conifers. Because so little sun-

light gets through, it is a barren desert under there. If there are wet bogs or springs, grass and sedges may grow, but relatively few shrubs or browse. Elk get along just fine in such terrain.

If the timber is particularly unrelenting, look for elk in any man-made openings. Power or pipeline cuts which invite sunlight are also good. They act much like south slopes in that they grow preferred grasses and brushy browse. The same is true of small clearcuts in the West Coast's almost tropical forests. Man actually helps elk by creating these openings. You can usually locate them with the help of a detailed map. It should also be pointed out that such cuts in the habitat jungle help but little if man remains around to prevent elk from using them. Human occupancy for more than a few weeks might keep elk out for months.

A Barrier Away

Many times oversized elk may be just a few miles from a road's end, beyond an obstacle of some kind. In 1984 the outfitter I was guiding for decided to establish a new, higher camp. Warm weather during the previous year had kept elk so high that it was about a 14-mile round trip daily to reach them and return to our cabin camp. But where exactly should be locate the new camp?

Most traffic into this higher domain funneled up several canyons from road's end. After some study, we put the camp in at the upper end of a wilderness lake. The lake attracted plenty of fishermen and human activity from a trail on the lower end. However, the upper sector was considered impassable to horses due to steep bluffs directly over the water. But when we worked at it, we discovered a way to "punch" a route through the barrier of nearly vertical boulders, a route safe enough to get pack horses and supplies through.

After setting up our camp where there were no other hunters, it did not take long to find elk tracks and the animals which made them. Five elk permittees took bulls of 4 points or better in a few days. One was a monster royal 6-pointer. The early kills were a major plus for the hunters since it gave them time for fishing and other hunting they wanted to do. The terrain looked exactly like that around it: steeply tilted Engelmann spruce and Douglas fir sprinkled with small meadows, all within an hour's ride of home base. The element here that made the difference between hot and only lukewarm elk country was one "impassable" bluff which wasn't really impassable at all.

Elk Sign

If you aren't certain whether you're near elk, look for the following sign: tracks, beds, droppings, wallows, and bark-rubbed saplings.

Let's first take a close look at elk hoofprints. There is no way you can confuse them with those of moose. Elk tracks are approximately four inches long. Moose run some six to seven inches and are blockier. Mule or whitetail deer (there is some habitat overlap in Montana, northern Idaho, and northern Wyoming in particular) seldom attain hoof size over 3½ inches. A large muley may run four. The elk print has a "heavier," rounder, less narrow outline than the muley's.

Try to determine freshness of the track by noting its edge or "definition." If it is still fine and sharp, the track could be only hours old. If "weathered" for a few days by sun, rain, and wind, the sharpness quickly deteriorates to smoother lines.

An elk bed could possibly be confused with that of domestic cattle if both range on the same mountain, although most range cows "crush" down a much larger area than elk. Elk beds tend to be in steep terrain, while lazier livestock beds on flatter turf.

You can also look for droppings. The end-of-thumb-sized wapiti pellets little resemble cattle or horse manure. Sheep droppings are only slightly larger than those of rabbits. I used to kid younger hunters about "tasting" spoor to determine how old it is, but fortunately you can tell by looking. Droppings a day or two old will retain a wet, black appearance, while pellets older than that will likely fade to a dry-looking gray. A brownish "crumbling" period follows. Such spoor is at least a week old. In addition, large, roundish pellets are an indication of an elk on green feed, while elongated, tightly compacted ones point to browse. Knowing the terrain and the locations of the various vegetation can help you determine where the elk has been feeding.

Wallows are a sure sign of the presence of bulls, although this sign is fairly rare outside the rutting period. Wallows will be covered more fully as they relate to rutting bulls in Chapter 12 on bugling. Even "obvious" wallows are often overlooked. Suffice it to say that any earnest elker should constantly be alert for elk tracks around mud holes and springs, especially if accompanied by "rolls" where several bulls might have bathed, apparently to cool off rutting ardor. Such places also attract elk as watering grounds and should be scrutinized carefully. Elk will sometimes also "play" in remote ponds. A buddy of mine once bagged a giant bull by guessing correctly that it was headed for a small alpine lake.

Elk Rubs

In late summer when elk are bothered by itchy remnants of velvet and dry blood on antlers, they seek to rub all off against trees or brush. Soft-barked young saplings are often selected as "rubbing trees". If you see a young tree swaying for no apparent reason, it could have an elk rack "doing battle" with it.

While the bull is usually finished with this ritual by mid-September, tree rubs do indicate that male wapiti have been around. If there has been no major change in weather, they may still be.

In the absence of deep snow (say, two feet or more), elk sign can be expected from elevations of about 7,000 feet on up. Veteran Colorado guide Bob Burch, of Vallecito, says he often places hunters on mountain passes in the San Juan Wilderness Area up to 13,000 feet, well above timberline. "Those who stay there patiently score more often than those who walk all day in the pines," Burch says.

In some areas of the Southwest or Great Basin edges, it may be necessary to start hunting at altitudes higher than 8,000 feet just to find heavy elk cover and feed.

Now that we have emphasized the value of hunting high and far from man, it may seem something of a contradiction to say that elk can also exist very close to civilization. I know of one ridge just above a community of 20,000 people which has always had elk. The state issued elk permits for the area, but many hunters returned disgruntled, saying that the quarry had been "all shot out." A biologist decided to take a look for himself from a helicopter. I was able to go along for the ride. We saw both hunters and elk aplenty. From our chopper, I noted several vehicles parked at road's end overlooking a precipice. The orange-vesters there, apparently having found nothing, were engaged in a playful snowball fight. But they wouldn't have been so bored with the hunting if they had peered meticulously 400 yards below the rim, where a monarch bull elk lay with his antlers etched against the scrub oak. Intrigued, we noted that the animal moved slightly to keep brush between him and the human activity. We left the bull to his cat-and-mouse game, then flew over another steep and rocky cliff and saw other elk holed up to avoid exposure to hunters.

This plateau was riddled with roads, yet all hunters were along the flatter "table" sections. Elk avoided danger by climbing into the steeper pockets where man would not be as likely to look for him. On another mountain we saw basically the same thing: elk hunched down against a series of ledges. For all I know, they remained there all day for the rest of the season, coming out only occasionally to feed at night.

To locate shootable elk on those ridges, hunters might do well to creep down from the top, checking carefully below. After descending 1,000 feet or so, a comrade could pick him up on one of the flatland roads for a repeat of the entire process.

This is not to imply that elk dwell where bighorn sheep do. Far from it. Most of this terrain only looked like sheep habitat. A close look showed terraces and natural shelves that provided comfort zones with utmost security. But it might be well, at least initially, for elk seekers to pretend they are sheep hunters in determining where to start hunting.

At other times I have observed large

wapiti haunting the edges of river rims— not just any lowland notch, but high escarpments with sharp breaks on the stream side. One such place is in Utah's Book Cliffs. Most of it is on private land, including the Ute Indian Reservation, not now open to public hunting. Some monster bulls and muley bucks live quiet lives here. Though hunting is not allowed as of this writing, things haven't changed much from when it was. If human activity shows, most game simply drops down into the breaks, then appears again when the heat is off.

In my experience, an elk will not normally range far from water (an exception being during migration). Some needs are met through moist vegetation. But studies show that elk, in the absence of snow, prefer to keep within one-half to one-third mile of water. So "elk country," technically, does not require immediate water.

The Wapiti's Diet

An elk is not limited to a few palatable grasses. Wapiti get along very well with any combination of the following preferred foods, compiled with the help of big-game biologist Norman V. Hancock, Chief, Game Management, Utah Division of Wildlife Resources. (If several species exist, they are listed with the designation spp.)

Hunter wisely checks for elk in one of few clearings in heavy timber: a river canyon.

Grasses and grasslike plants (*Joint-stemmed*)

Wheatgrass	Very widespread and important; includes many native and exotic species of the genus *Agropyron.* Usually palatable.
Bromegrasses	Also widespread, but especially important on spring, summer, and fall ranges. Includes many species of the genus *Bromus,* even exotic annuals such as *B. tectorum.*
Ricegrass	Includes relatively few species of the genus *Oryzopsis,* but important on spring and winter ranges. Greens up very early in the spring.
Wildrye	Several important species of the genus *Elymus* on all seasonal ranges. Often important on winter ranges because its size protrudes above the snow.
Bluegrasses	Many exotic and native species of the genus *Poa.* Very widespread and usually quite palatable.
Fescues	Widespread, but most important in the northern and central parts of elk range on spring through fall habitats. Genus *Danthonia.*
Oatgrasses	Important in forest habitats at mid to upper elevations. Genus *Danthonia.*
Muhly Grasses	Also important in forested habitats, especially in southern part of elk range. Genus *Muhlenbergia.*
Timothy Grasses	Primarily a summer-range grass important in meadows. Genus *Phleum,* very palatable, widely cultivated.
Sedges	One of the largest and most variable genera in the world. Locally important in most elk ranges. Varies from dry to wet habitats. Generally palatable, especially in the fall.
Forbs	(Non-woody broad-leafed plants) Many genera, of which almost all are utilized at least some by elk. A most important feature for elk habitat is their variety, rather than the presence of any single species. Some representative forbs that occur on elk range and are important include:

Balsamroot (*Balsamorhiza spp.*)
Mulesears (*Wyethia spp.*)
Sweetvetch (*Hedysarum spp.*)
Peavine (*Lathyrus sp.*)
Penstemon or
  Beardtongue (*Penstemon sp.*)
Groundsel (*Senecio sp.*)
Lupine (*Lupinus sp.*)
Rockcress (*Arabis sp.*)
Aster (*Aster sp.*)
Milkvetch (*Astragalus sp.*)
Paintbrush (*Castilleja sp.*)
Thistle (*Cirsium sp.*)

Buckwheat (*Erigonum sp.*)
Gilia (*Gilia sp.*)
Helianthella (*Helianthella spp.*)
  or Little sunflower
Biscuitroot (*Lomatium sp.*)
Alfalfa (*Medicago sp.*)
Sweetclover (*Melilotus sp.*)
Bluebells (*Mertensia sp.*)
Sweetroot (*Osmorhiza sp.*)
Phacelia (*Phacelia sp.*)
Phlox (*Phlox sp.*)
Cinquefoil (*Potentilla sp.*)
Goldenrod (*Solidago sp.*)

Spring parsley (*Cymopterus sp.*)   Globemallow (*Sphaeralcea sp.*)
Droba (*Droba sp.*)   Meadowrue (*Thalictrum sp.*)
Fleabone daisy (*Erigeron sp.*)   Clover (*Trifolium sp.*)
                                              Valerian (*Valeriana sp.*)
                                              Dandelion (*Taraxacum sp.*)

Important shrubs and trees

Big Sagebrush	(*Artemisia tridentata*) A very widespread species of supreme importance on winter ranges; subspecies differ somewhat in palatability, preference, and growth habit. Probably the most abundant shrub in Rocky Mountains. The subspecies *Vaseyana* and *Wyomingensis* are the more palatable forms of *A. tridentata*.
Other Sagebrushes	(*A. arbuscula, A. cana, A. nova, A. longitola, A. tripertita*) Confined to more specialized habitats; generally less important than Big Sagebrush.
Maple	(*Acer spp.* — two species, *A. glabrum* and *A. grandidentatum* are most notable) Only moderate forage value, but often are important cover plants, especially in northern half of elk range.
Saltbush	(*Atriplex spp.*) A large genus only marginally important on winter range. Most prevalent in south part of elk range and at lower altitudes.
Birch and Alder	(*Betula spp.* and *Alnus spp.*) Marginally important forage, but very important riparian cover plants.
Buckbrush	(*Ceanothus spp.*) An important genus of evergreen or semi-evergreen shrub. Occurs at varying elevations and is most common in northern part of elk range, also more species.
Mountain Mahogany	(*Cercocarpus spp.*) Two to four species of critical importance on winter ranges. Very palatable and long lived. *C. ledifolius* is an important cover plant.
Rabbitbrush	(*Chrysothomnus spp.*) A widespread and variable genus that is low to moderate in palatability. Occurs on most elk range but is most important in winter.
Juniper	(*Juniperus spp.*) Many species of evergreen shrubs and trees. Three species are of high importance — *J. osteosperma, J. scopulorum,* and *J. communis* are important on winter ranges and often associated with pinyon pine (*P. edulis* or *P. monophylla*).
Coniferous trees	(Spruce, fir, pine, larch, hemlock, etc.) All are of great importance. One or more occur almost everywhere in elk range. Especially vital for thermal and escape cover, but also provide forage available during even the most severe conditions.

Aspen and Poplars	(*Populus spp.*) Aspen is the most well-known, widespread, and no doubt the most important for both cover and forage, wherever it can be found. Much utilized by elk in spring (especially southern range) through fall ranges. Other poplars are locally important in riparian habitats.
Cherry	(*Prunus spp.*) The most important native species is *P. virginiana* or chokecherry. Includes many exotic varieties that have escaped into the wild, or are preyed upon by elk in damage situations.
Antelope Bitterbrush	(*Purshia tridentata*) A widespread shrub on winter ranges. Generally quite palatable and very important.
Oak	(*Quercus spp.*) Most important is Gambel oak, *Q. gambelii,* a much used shrub in the south and central portions of elk range. Of moderate palatability, it is the dominant species on thousands of acres of elk spring, fall, winter, and occasionally even summer range. Where it occurs, it is usually the principal cover plant as well.
Currant	(*Ribes spp.*) Occasional shrub on elk range of moderate to good palatability.
Rose	(*Rosa spp.*) Occasional shrub on elk range of moderate to good palatability.
Raspberry	(*Rubus spp.*) Occasional shrub on elk range of moderate to good palatability.
Willow	(*Salix spp.*) Many species occur throughout elk range. An important food and cover genus in riparian habitats.
Elderberry	(*Sambucus spp.*) An occasional shrub of moderate palatability. One species, *S. racemosa,* is most important on high summer range, while *S. cerulea* is most frequent on winter ranges.
Snowberry	(*Symphoricarpos spp*) Includes three to four species that, taken together, occur throughout elk range. They are moderately palatable and occur at all elevations, but are perhaps most important on spring-fall ranges.

Hancock stresses that aspen leaves, bark, and twigs are utilized by elk, especially during the hunting seasons, in the southern climes like Colorado, Utah, Arizona, and New Mexico. In Montana, much of Wyoming and Idaho, as well as the Northwest, aspens are not as common. Browse more frequently utilized by elk there includes big sagebrush, berry plants, and the conifers, in addition to many grasses. The oft-used Gambel oak is a companion species to aspen, usually growing at slightly lower elevations. Aspen may also overlap down into a zone of junipers. Sagebrush is widespread from lower to middle elevations in all of the elk states, and is heavily used by the Rocky Mountain species.

Other foods showing up in elk stomachs include: clover, thistles, lichens, mosses, fireweed, nettleleaf mint, mescal (Southwest), flowers such as wild geraniums, and the domestic foods—alfalfa (and cured hay), wheat, oats, and other grains. According to naturalist-author Dean Krakel (*Season of the Elk,* Lowell Press), wapiti will also eat meat on occasion.

Elk dine on such a wide variety of nutrients that they are not restricted to the classic emerald-green meadows. Consult a local botanical list, perhaps from a school biology teacher, to learn more about the most abundant species in your region and where they are found. The foregoing list gives you a starting point. Concentrate on the plants most available in autumn. In general, elk prefer green plants, but some are dried out by late summer. Elk also seek out vegetation rich in proteins, much of which grows in shallow soils along ridgetops—another reason (in addition to the fact that winds sweep away snow there) elk can be found in such places from middle autumn through winter. Rocky Mountain elk will often feed on whatever is to be found when snow piles up over grasses and low-growing plants, including fireweed and bitterbrush. Roosevelt elk encounter less snow in most winters, and so remain on green feed. Many wapiti take advantage all year long of woody foods including tree bark, twigs, and many types of conifer needles. The adaptable wapiti generally can find food at almost any elevation, in absence of deep snow.

Bulls have been known to thump trees with antlers to knock down tender twigs so they can get at them. Wet aspen leaves on the ground are palatable. Elk can subsist on a fibrous diet for a time, but conifer needles tend to mat in the stomach and cause problems if no other edibles are found.

An elk, like any human gourmet, is rather constantly on the search for desired foods. But if elk cannot find precisely what they want, they may subsist on lichens and moss from wet boulders. They can also reach up as high as seven feet for tree branches and leaves. Elk will frequently do just that—deserting the lush meadow grass if danger lurks there. No wonder an elk can keep a low profile when open seasons bring swarms of venison-seekers. Elk have enough ways to satisfy hunger to remain out of harm's way for several days or longer, if necessary.

It is important to remember, however, that in cold weather an elk's calorie needs increase. He may require nearly twice as much food as in warmer temperatures. That is one reason hunting elk in cold weather can pay off. Besides, even in "bluebird" climes, if you keep at it, you just might find a bull ready to indulge himself in some special delight like cow-parsnip or bluebell.

In many places I hunt, arrowleaf balsamroot is prolific. And not surprisingly, it is chewed down to nubbins by elk. Yet in contrast, flowering plants like thistle blooms are merely "topped off." Interestingly, my horse loves to eat the entire thistle. If the stalks are eaten rather than just the tops, the animals grazing there were probably livestock rather than elk. It is indicative of an elk's "smarts" that it will not touch the poisonous and prolific larkspur. To the dismay of stockmen, domestic cattle will and do eat larkspur, frequently dying from the mistake.

Check All Edges

If all this profusion of plant life an elk finds edible becomes confusing to you, remember one thing: elk are like deer and other game animals in that they usually find the more succulent food at the "edge" of trees and meadows. They feast there because sunlight and water tend to concentrate food in such places. Game, especially the skittish type, also prefers to browse or graze head-down in such places because cover is just a leap away. Such smorgasbord "strips" may be only a few yards wide.

Waylaying a bull might be tied to what an elk prefers to eat in late fall. Then, or even earlier in alfalfa patches, you might ambush a bull nibbling on domestic crops. Elk particularly love cultivated wheat. A plan that puts you between agriculture and the nearest foothills could pay dividends.

I haven't mentioned several other possible elk haunts, including river bottom-lands (often harboring mule or whitetail deer as well), flatland forests, and man-scorned deserts. If it's cool enough in those places, elk might be present. Roosevelt elk are apt to be among the stream lowlands, Rocky Mountain elk less so. While cover and water probably exist there, midday temperatures may be too high for elk.

Since wapiti are normally a gregarious, social animal, they do not take to the limited ribbon of cover along a stream the way deer do. Hot deserts are usually out, unless winter-cooled. Elk will hide out in sizable flatland forests, but they usually prefer slanted terrain.

That leaves one more type of elk domain to mention: migration routes. A little research on traditional migration

Elk country for a good reason: man is only a visitor, not a permanent resident in remote back areas like this.

lanes can help a hunter be where he wants to be some cold and snowy dawn. Since this is transitional "elk country," timing is everything. A hunter should also remember that elk frequently migrate at night, or in dim light. They usually select migration trails which follow the longest line of cover. In the process, they may break the normal pattern of feeding on sharply sloped acreage in favor of gentler, tapering ridgelines. Here they can halt among the greatest amount of food for the most animals at critical "comfort zone" elevations.

Deep snow may send wapiti scurrying from higher elevations down the migration lanes, but the elk will halt wherever they can paw their way to food, or reach browse. If snow should recede, they may move uphill again. But chances are they will have to head down even farther as snow accumulates.

"Migration" hunting is one way a hunter can gain a valuable edge in an often difficult challenge. However, there also can be the unnatural "shooting gallery" approach to migration hunting, such as that offered on the north "entrance" to the National Elk Refuge in Jackson Hole, Wyoming. An in-depth look at this sometimes controversial method of reducing surplus elk appears in Chapter 18, "Hunting and Game Management." Suffice it to say that by "elk country" in this chapter we mean natural habitat where elk can be located. In that sense, winter feeding grounds are not wapiti terrain unless the animals traditionally migrated there without being attracted by artificial feed.

7

Tactics in Locating Elk

If we recognize general elk country, what's next in pinpointing the animals' location, and then putting a bull within the cross-hairs on our scope?

After all, simply being in the right country isn't a guarantee, just a prerequisite to success. I learned the difference once while riding through scenic alpine meadows interspersed with conifer forests—traditional wapiti habitat. But three days netted a glimpse of three bald elk. When we returned, the "lack of game" was taken to Phil Mooney, big-game biologist on Wyoming's Bridger National Forest. Since he had just spent a month with the animals, Mooney wasted no time in providing a positive answer.

"Come with me next Tuesday," he said, "and I'll show you."

It was late July, and I wasn't surprised that he aimed his four-wheel-drive high

into the mountains. On a knoll where we could look out two to three miles, he set up a 30-power spotting scope. He used the only foundation around, his pickup-truck door. Then he focused well away from any visible trails. After scanning along a line at approximately our same 9,000-foot altitude, he motioned me over. "There, north of Electric Peak. Look at this."

Between a series of ledges and broken patches of chartreuse-colored cover, I found myself gazing at dozens of elk. As dusk approached, more moved from shadowed gulleys to make 42 in all. Nearer by, on the upper edge of heavy oak brush, we counted 14 more, including two large bulls. In a different direction, 17 elk browsed in intermittent aspen, including still more bulls.

Yet I had ridden through here on horseback just a few days before—without see-

Brent Chapman with evidence of hunting prowess for oversized bulls in Idaho and Colorado. His first rule is: get way back in. Second: scout ahead. *Photo courtesy of Brent Chapman.*

ing these elk at all. Of course, casual conversation and casual searching were major reasons.

There is no substitute for meticulous scrutiny of elk from a high vantage point with a spotting scope, or at least a quality pair of binoculars. That's the way the experts, the pros, do it.

Probably no hunter has taken more big bulls in a lifetime than Idahoan Brent Chapman. He has outwitted 19 bulls with 4 points or better (per side, standard count) in both Idaho and his native state of Colorado. Several have been in the "monster" category, with six (Royal) or seven (Imperial) tines on a side. Many smaller bulls have also fallen to him. Chapman is one license-holder who can get lucky at times, but with his consistency, it's obviously far more than that. He advocates the same basic steps used by Mooney for locating elk:

1. Love what you are doing. Learn about your quarry every chance you have, and don't underestimate him. Look for elk whether you are fishing, hiking, or even driving along.

2. Concentrate on glassing from a high vantage point. Check all timber edges and small openings. When you are as familiar with the terrain as your own backyard, you can even begin to predict where elk will show.

3. Be at it dawn and dusk. If it is hunting season, check only upwind. You wouldn't be able to stalk bulls downwind from you anyway.

4. Be patient. Keep at it. Remember that even though it may be lonely or monotonous, glassing is still your best bet—much better than wandering around below, where you may blunder into something and spook it.

Is that all there is to it? No, but it is by far the fastest way in most situations to locate shootable elk.

If you aren't certain where to begin glassing, take any map of potential elk territory, then study it to find high or remote regions away from roads or civilization. Start glassing in such a place. If you can't work into it afoot or on horseback, at least check the interior of such hinterlands.

An excellent place to look for bulls: high, windswept ridges where grass is exposed. *U.S. Fish & Wildlife Service Photo.*

However, as any beginner knows, the experts—those who have done more looking—seem to do more finding. Is there a special technique for locating bull elk?

Yes. Veteran hunters and guides study all edges of cover. This is especially important if you are searching within rifle range of your position. After all, if the game is just a leap from cover, you want to see it first. If game is standing in the open, you have more shooting time.

Some ask, "What are we looking for?" If not an entire elk, then a leg, antler tip, maybe just the ears. Look for "soft" hues,

Did you look close enough? This nice bull could be overlooked by a hunter in a hurry.

or a fuzzy texture among the "harder" rocks and rims. Even from a couple of miles away, a game animal does not appear exactly like the plain brown earth. Ground color is mostly uniform, while elk have two different colors—dark about the neck and head, and a lighter rump patch. The latter is not as pronounced as on the deer, but if the animal is looking away from you (especially if feeding with its rear up), the white patch is conspicuously different from the landscape. Autumn body pelage is usually tawny to beige, almost cream-hued for most of the body on Rocky Mountain elk, dark brown on Roosevelt.

What if you're not sure the animal you see is actually an elk? The elongated muzzle and nose of an elk—cow, bull, or calf—gives it away, even when bedded. Nothing in the world looks like a trotting or running elk. In size it is much larger than a deer, and far less blocky than a domestic cow. It is never as coal black as a moose, which appears more like a horse. With some time spent afield, you can pick out elk at distances which will amaze you—up to three miles away or more. I know of one Canadian guide who can spot elk, bear, moose, or caribou when no one else can see even a speck on the horizon. But he has become so familiar with the landscape that any change is like a neon sign.

Stalking Methods

Now let's look at the best methods of stalking elk under these five possible conditions: dry-brittle ground, crusted snow, soft snow, rain-soft ground, boggy turf.

Dry-brittle—Approaching silently to within rifle range in this situation is possible but by no means a snap. Make a slight sound, and you can expect elk to be alerted up to 400 or more yards away. Step over all branches and twigs. If there are too many to avoid, at least go slowly enough that elk spooked by others might run toward you. Also, check opposite slopes as well as the one you are on.

Crusted snow—Your chances are slim within the same canyon, basin, or ridge you are in or on. Since elk can hear you up to 600 yards away in these conditions, wait for elk to come to you, or approach your target canyon or basin as stealthily as possible from a "protected" direction and peer over a rim or ridgeline.

Soft snow—Makes for good-to-excellent stalking conditions. Take advantage of them. Watch for elk within shootable ranges. However, be careful to avoid slippery branches buried under snow, especially on sidehills, which can cause you to fall noisily.

Rain-soft ground—Always an excellent time for walking in woods. Wet soil makes for silent underfooting. With any luck at all, you may approach within 50–75 yards of elk.

Boggy turf—A bowhunter and muzzleloader's dream. If the grass is thick, such as that around lake beds, and there's enough cover, it may be possible to move within 20 yards of elk. As with most stalking, wearing sneakers rather than heavy hiking boots seems to help. Of course, if the bog is really a swamp with intermittent mud holes and tule clumps, silence is usually destroyed. Lift the feet slowly anytime water is encountered.

In addition, locating elk can depend on many weather factors. If wind blows from the west, check the east (lee) side of mountains or tree groves.

However, it also pays to do what any football offense does—take whatever the "defense" gives you. If the terrain does not lend itself to lengthy glassing, focus on the farthest huntable places you can view before you get there. You want to locate the quarry without alerting it. Both the finding and the shooting are better with such a stalking advantage.

In 1984 I listened to Rocky Vandersteen, veteran taxidermist and trophy elk hunter from Rock Springs, Wyoming, explain about the big bulls he has taken nearly every year for a decade from the Wyoming Range. Some of Rocky's taxidermy clients also take outsized elk here between Alpine and LaBarge. Yet it would be possible to trek through the entire 80-mile length of this roadless hinterland without seeing a single bull. Many have done so.

Vandersteen advised me: "The entire region has a multitude of trails, but mostly on creek bottoms and a few passes. Use them as access only. Then use a horse to gain about 8,500 feet in altitude. Tie up well away from the little highland meadows. The elk won't be in them, but they will be in nearby cover, often a tilted spruce patch not even visible from the trails. If your first impression of a place is that it's too rough and harsh for you, be sure to check it out. And keep looking. You'll find elk others haven't."

With that precise strategy, Vandersteen has bagged bulls scoring up to 360 Boone and Crockett points, just shy of the minimum for record-book entry.

I didn't find a bull that big, but I found conditions as Rocky described them: plenty of tracks from the trailhead to Roosevelt Meadows and into the upper Hoback. But they were not made by elk. Those human and horse prints spelled an array of cowboys, prospectors, fishermen, and, of course, hunters who had been there before me.

Camp was pitched by a meadow near water, with a splendid view. But hunting was done well away from camp or trails. That's where we found wapiti. I also found oversized muley bucks in a rocky gorge where no trail could possibly get through. Feed was too scarce for many elk, but it was a place where a solitary old bull might hole up for a few days if hunting pressure mounted.

Slopes like this in Wyoming's North Shoshone Wilderness are not too steep for wary bulls. In fact, author took one right on this slope.

Many times, when heading for a particular elk hotspot, I've passed up terrain where other hunters (many of them guided) sat beside fires "waiting for something to happen," perhaps a suicidal elk leaving the timber to run across a wide meadow or heavily used trail. I've also observed orange-vesters driving up and down highways, hoping for a bewildered wapiti to run across the road. The first hypothetical situation provides the hunter a slim chance, the second practically none at all. Even if an elk did venture across the pavement — a 30-yard opening between trees — he'd be gone in a few seconds. I doubt any nimrod could stop a vehicle in time to shoulder a rifle and take aim.

Seven Special Challenges

Let's look at seven possible situations you could find yourself in during an elk hunt, and examine the best strategy for each. All the situations actually occurred and had happy hunter endings. The challenges are presented in order ranging from the easiest to the most difficult, the first two being "plain vanilla" types with relatively similar solutions.

Situation One: You and your hunting party ride to the crest of a hill. All tie your mounts to low-growing bushes below the rim, peer over carefully, and make out the forms of several dozen wapiti on a higher slope about 600 yards ahead. You keep your outlines low. The elk remain bedded, but one "sentry" cow feeding at the edge of aspens will detect any straight-ahead stalk.

What do you do?

Years ago, as a hunter with only a deer permit, tagging along for a look at how the professionals do it, I listened intently as outfitter-guide Sharon Dayton of Coke-

ville, Wyoming, outlined strategy to his Midwest hunters. Most had never hunted wapiti before. Here was Dayton's solution:

"We'll make a wide circle to skirt them," he told his wide-eyed clients. "Then we'll tie up about 250 yards south from the canyon rim, and sneak quietly over at the same elevation as the lowest elk. That'll make the shooting range about 300 yards. Ready?"

Then he led the hunters by hand signals to the canyon's edge. So far, so good. The elk remained bedded. Dayton distinguished the form of one bull, and an eager hunter prepared to touch off a shot. But as he wiggled into a sitting position, he stood up a little too high. The entire band was alerted. We did nail a large bull, but the rest were in flight even as the hunter fired. Yet Dayton predicted which uphill pass they would exit, and he hurriedly got another hunter to his horse and upslope in time to dispatch a 6-point bull as it reached the pass. Two bulls sighted, two bagged. Not bad for a morning's work.

Situation Two: Elk were sighted in this region several days before. Even now tracks are scattered throughout the forest fringes. Hunters are converging from all sides, with four-wheel-drive vehicles plying the roads. Some hunters have branched out on foot. It is difficult to know where the elk, which have to be there, might show. Some nimrods return to camp with tales of hearing elk in the woods, but no one can get close enough for even a glimpse of game.

Solution: Two hunters decide to work together. They walk parallel ridges, keeping fairly even by checking the other's progress and by hand-signalling. Neither bothers to watch the same ridge he is on, concentrating instead on the area a few hundred yards ahead of the hunter on the other side of the canyon. Each tries to keep in mind the location of any other rifle-toters plus their position and approach. Thus, they hunt elk put up by others. The second day, O. E. "Moe" Neuman, a valuable tutor in my younger years on the finer points of all big-game hunting, scores with a bull put up by his companion.

Situation Three: There are elk about. After two hours in the saddle, you are making your first on-ground inspection of elk sign in six inches of snow. You find fairly fresh droppings and beds. The pellets are still moist-looking, not faded or crumbling. The beds are in matted snow, with some bent June grass now reaching back toward the sky. Tracks are difficult to read at first in the six-inch-deep white mantle. But you get down on your knees and make out some larger prints, which should be bulls. The edges seem still to be sharply etched — the "roundness" connected with time has not begun to show appreciably.

Solution: As a guide, that recently happened to me. Our two hunters bagged two nice bulls within two hours. Here is how the guides planned it:

First, guides and hunters sat down to eat lunch and map out strategy. We determined where the elk might have gone. It did not appear our party had put them up, for the spacing between the tracks wasn't wide enough to indicate they had departed hurriedly. But they had moved — where and why? The weather was not likely a factor, since it hadn't changed much in the past few days. We noted horse and hunter tracks toward the southwest, down-canyon where access was easiest. But horse tracks grew scarcer as we continued up the drainage. Our guess was that the elk were a couple or three canyons to the northeast,

away from down-canyon hunting pressure, at about the same elevation, where access was most limited.

After lunch, one guide took two hunters up to the top and crossed over it to eliminate human noise or scent within the same canyon. Then they tied up their horses and crawled slowly to the rim where they could command a view of the aforementioned northeast terrain 2½ canyons away. We remaining guides allowed an hour for them to get into position. Then we rode mounts northeasterly. One driver pushed low, and one moved at the same elevation as the elk sign. Two bulls were among several dozen cows bedded two canyons away. Our hunters felled both at a range of about 200 yards.

Situation Four: Elk are in the region, but you have seen none in the meadows or other openings. Tracks indicate they are using these openings, but you can't seem to get there when they do. You and your companion are too few for an "organized" drive. Elk would just remain in the timber ahead of you anyway, if you start making too much noise.

Solution: Your best bet is to wait them out. Since there are fairly fresh tracks in some of the meadows, the odds favor being patient. Sooner or later, at dawn or dusk in particular, they should show again.

On one wapiti quest, my guide, Roy Sanders of Cabin Creek Outfitters, Powell, Wyoming — as elk-savvy a man as a hunter could meet — suggested we take turns napping on a rock outcropping overlooking small patches of greenery, high and deep within the Shoshone National Forest. One pair of eyes crisscrossed that region for several hours. Well before dusk, at about 4 p.m., Roy gently nudged my arm. I looked down at a respectable bull grazing from lodgepole pine. When we decided he would step forth no more boldly, I supported my elbows against some rocks, then held my Weaver 2-7X variable scope's crosshairs just above his shoulder. It was a far easier way to find and dispatch the animal than trying to "jump" him in the trees and get off a snap shot.

Situation Five: Elk are not showing at all in the openings. If they do put a hoof there, it must be by moonlight. (Research shows wapiti do feed by moonlight, and in fact can be observed doing so on natural grass in winter elk refuges.) Hunting pressure is heavy, and elk must be feeding on little hidden patches of moss or on tree twigs within the forest. You are going to have to sneak in after them, or amass the manpower for a drive. In the absence of drivers, you'll need to be quiet indeed, since the elk you locate will probably be your only target.

Solution: Roy Abbott, a dedicated hunter from Minneapolis, has succeeded frequently under these conditions. He selects ridgelines to pussyfoot along, looking for elk bedded down at midday. He prefers snowfall periods, when most other nimrods hate to be out. He knows that falling snow, minus winds, usually means uncrusted underfooting. Oversized bulls are less likely to hear your approach then, as snow muffles many human sounds.

I helped load one of Roy's 6-point giants on a snowy October day, and the hunter showed me the exact spot—42 paces away—where he stood as he shot the bull. "As I crept up," he said, "the bull was bedded here against the ridgeline, facing down the slope toward possible danger. As he leaped to his front feet, I nailed him."

If it hadn't snowed, Roy just might have scored anyway. The bull would likely have been there where he had a chance to slip down either side of a long crest, away from danger. But without the storm, the hunter probably wouldn't have been able to approach as close as he did.

Situation Six: There are no openings, so a drive of any sort wouldn't be profitable. Any elk pushed would just continue to remain in cover. As a matter of fact, you're not even sure any elk are around. They should be. They have been in the past. But they seem mighty scarce now.

Solution: Avoid hunting the flatlands. There may be elk there, but with the extremely thick cover, you won't likely see any shootable specimens. Get high enough to look down into the cover from above. You will see more from there, and game will least expect danger in that direction. Look within shooting range for anything at all that seems out of kilter with the landscape.

On one occasion when I had no elk permit, I went along to learn the area. I happened to peer down into a small pocket with dark stumps and deadfall timber. At first I saw nothing. Then I sat down and peered more intensely. Finally, I made out a white antler tip, blending perfectly with patches of sunlight filtering onto the forest floor. Next I located the base of those antlers and a pair of eyes staring back at me from no more than 60 yards. It was late in the season, and hunters had been through here a number of times. In fact, I was but a short distance from camp.

After memorizing the exact location of the bull's lair, I left an orange vest to mark the spot, walked out, topped the ravine, and went down the other side to locate a hunter with a tag. Then we walked back in just as I had before. The bull grew edgy, wheeling up to exit downhill, but the shooter was ready. An extremely heavy-beamed bull, it had apparently made a habit of hiding in timber when hunters loomed everywhere.

While some luck was involved here, it is often best to search for hiding bulls when you suspect elk are about but they won't show. To locate bulls that are staying put, you have to study the terrain thoroughly — more so than hunters who were there before you.

Situation Seven: You don't have the slightest idea where elk are, and what's more, you have searched for several days without locating the slightest sign.

Solution: I would continue to drive, ride, or hike until I found sign. I once spent the first day of a hunt driving a Jeep along rim roads, checking for tracks in all soft-mud areas. Finally I located a brook where it appeared elk had been recently. A few young saplings had been rubbed, and elk tracks showed on the bank. The first day was thus spent just locating elk country.

On the second day I was to have the help of a guide, but he became ill and could scarcely even sit up in the seat of the Jeep. By all rights we should have given up and returned to camp. But I was too eager for the hunt to sit around. I drove around, found nothing, and then headed for camp. At dusk, I drove past the brook, "just in case." It paid off. Fresh elk tracks were there — so fresh, in fact, that the elk were still in them. At the sight of the Jeep they fled across a small meadow and then up into oak brush. I sat down with my sporterized Springfield 30-06 to wait until the first cow's head bobbed into a small opening between oak and aspen. Then I trained the Weaver scope on that point some 250 yards away until I saw antlers.

The bull proved a good one, with high, thick tines. There had seemed no chance at first, with little elk sign and a sick guide

to boot. But it proved something about locating elk: you always have a chance as long as you don't quit.

One hunter I know scored because he didn't stop looking even after his hunt in the highlands was over. Maintaining vigilance in the foothills, he found a wounded bull which had apparently found it painful to go anywhere but downhill. The bull had stopped at a ranch fence. The hunter finished off the animal and tagged it.

Roosevelt Pursuit

Challenges within various elk regions vary greatly. For example, as an adventurer in western Canada some 40 years ago, previously mentioned Jim Bond found plenty of oversized bulls just by getting way back into known game country. He writes of Alberta's Brazeau River district when heavy snows bunched bulls in a valley bottom. They crashed around him on all sides. Bond finally tagged the "Boss of the Brazeau." Even after he had dispatched this old sultan, many bulls still stood around. The veteran hunter has taken many other monarchs in Montana and Idaho after packing his way back in.

Recently Bond wrote me about a much tougher hunt, one he participated in more recently on the Oregon Coast, not far from his home city of Portland.

Said Bond: "I had a piece of 'inside' information about an area not 100 miles from home, down on the coast. Not another soul was supposed to know about it. I was informed the big Roosevelt bulls were coming back into a certain logged-off area in great numbers, at least by modern standards. All Oregon and Washington coastal elk hunting grounds are in logged-off areas, although some are more logged-off than others.

"In any event, we scouted around before the season opened, and then as soon as we got our tent pitched, four-wheelers, trucks, and cars began converging. The only elk we ever saw were running away from hunters across timber cuts or back roads."

He concludes: "I would hate to give the impression that getting a Roosevelt elk in Oregon is an impossibility. Many local hunters who know the specifics of an area have a good chance."

But Bond makes it clear that hunters had better know where the timber-cut openings are, because seeing shootable elk where 90 percent of the terrain is heavy cover can be extremely difficult.

Bond has another tip: "If that type of hunting for Roosevelt elk in the coastal thickets isn't for you, head for eastern Oregon. There are actually more Rocky Mountain elk in Oregon than the Roosevelt species."

Research indicates most Rocky Mountain wapiti seem to feel comfortable with a cover-to-opening ratio of 60-40. But if they have been continually pressured, they may seek an 80-20 ratio or even 100 percent forest canopy. For these skulkers— perhaps one of the greatest elk challenges of all—you will want to try the solution to Situation Four, covered earlier.

With some heady thinking, you can do something else to get shooting in that situation. One of my favorite ploys in extremely thick cover is to start noisily one way as if I'm going straight on through, then extract myself to check on the fringes off to one side. Mule deer hunters call a circular adaptation of this idea a "fish-hook pattern." With elk, I use it when I think tough, noisy hunter progress might have spooked something out a side exit. If it departs out the far end, so be it. If alone, I won't see that one anyway.

In addition to fish-hooking, I like to just stop walking occasionally. It works to flush hidden rabbits and pheasants. And it works on elk. When you are walking, they sit tight. When you stop, they are frequently fearful they've been spotted, and may show for a shot.

Reading a Mountain

While elk reside in many different types of cover, they are easier to locate in some than in others. I would rate the following as toughest, even though elk may be there in numbers: juniper, oak brush (Gambel oak), chokecherry, conifers. Easier: mountain mahogany, conifers mixed with deciduous (leaf-shedding) trees, berry bushes, other thick browse. Easiest of all (except for sage or open grass) is aspen.

Fortunately, elk haunt the 7,000 to 9,500-foot-high "quakie" belt almost as frequently as mule deer do. An elk's horizontal shape is readily seen among the vertical aspen trunks if you take the time to look closely. The manes, necks, and heads of a wapiti band are darker than the whitish-to-beige hue of aspen trunks. And if frost has stolen the gold from a patch of aspens, you can peer into them readily, not only from an equal elevation but from higher up the slope, especially looking straight down. Wapiti not only bed and rest in quakies but also feed there on the wet leaves, trunks, and twigs. The surprising thing is that elk take cover in them despite being so readily visible, especially from higher ground.

Thus it is that wise hunters will sit down first to read a mountain. If they are not certain where a respectable bull might be, the aspens are a good place to start looking. Besides, quakies rarely grow as continuously as conifers. Sometime, somewhere, an elk in aspens will have to pass across open ground to hightail it away from you. This is less likely to happen in other cover, especially those kinds which grow thick and have branches low to the ground like oak brush and juniper.

All else being equal, select the type of terrain and vegetation where you have the best chance of locating a shootable elk. You may later have to duel the elk on its own terms; but you might as well try it first on yours!

Strategy for Migrating Elk

As mentioned earlier, elk can be vulnerable during lengthy migrations. And some are very lengthy. One cow neck-banded in Colorado's Rio Grande drainage was observed 2½ months later no less than 110 miles away. Other studies in New Mexico measured migrations of two cows at 84 and 150 miles. On Montana's Sun River, a study showed that 33 of 49 tagged elk were bagged by hunters during lengthy migrations. By contrast, the Roosevelt elk of Washington's Olympic Peninsula—relatively low terrain where there is ample feed both winter and summer—migrate little. The 70-mile annual migration of Yellowstone wapiti to Teton County, through the Pacific Creek drainage and into the National Elk Refuge, offers several opportunities to ambush an oversized migrant on public hunting grounds. Many other wapiti move 30-40 miles when snow piles so high that even browse is reached only with strain.

However, in my opinion the "ease" in bushwhacking a big bull during migrations has been overstated. You still have to locate the exact route used. And merely walking the woods, hoping to stumble into a target, is seldom profitable. Most of the animals are bunched. It is all or nothing. That likely means monitoring move-

ments for several years—or hunting with a veteran nimrod or guide who has done so.

Elevation is the key. Find the altitude where feed is most readily attainable. Keep checking a particular rim to see if elk have crossed it. Note the direction they move. For years people talked of elk migrating from Jackson Hole to the upper Green River and Salt River valleys, but old-timers say it never happened. "The elk would have had to cross down into one valley and up over a mountain to reach another valley," a Jackson rancher explained. "That isn't likely. I don't think such a migration ever happened."

A serious hunter can hear many rumors of the "herd that stretched to the horizon—I could pick any bull I wanted. . . ." Maybe. But while elk do migrate through small openings, or even occasionally large ones when desperately hungry, they will also follow north-slope conifers when possible, ducking into cover at the slightest danger. Much depends on the intensity of storms, elevation, and previous range condition.

Chapman states that "elk do not necessarily head downhill with the first major snowfall." He has witnessed a few large bulls remaining on so-called summer range until snow was three or four feet deep. Four feet of snow is about all any bull will tolerate, he advises. "Obviously, a permit-holder had better be prepared to hunt in snow up to his knees, or even his thighs." All of the above is vital in deciding on hunting tactics for high-elevation elk which might soon head downhill.

One of the toughest challenges is getting within rifle range when elk are bedded or feeding in large open tracts with no cover in sight, as may occur during migration. I found one ploy which works often enough to be worth a try. You'll feel foolish doing it, but hunch into a bulky shape with hands near the ground, as a range cow would appear. Sure, the elk might mistake you for a predator such as a bear, but bears are less feared than the dreaded human form. Cradling your rifle won't be easy as you walk slowly forward in that posture. But it can buy you time and distance, often letting you lumber within the maximum shooting range of your rifle, from 350 to 400 yards. Chances are the game will watch you closely. Always approach at an angle so that you don't directly "confront" the quarry. Select a spot where you can shoot, and be ready to do so. I've used the "range cow" approach to get within shooting distance of both deer and elk.

More Elusive Bulls

I've run into some interesting moments when searching for elk which "have to be here somewhere." One of them involved a fish-and-game department regional director who tried to show several outdoor writers some elk a few weeks before the Utah hunting season. After a day and a half he was about to give up. Then local conservation officer Ken Tuttle returned from out of town.

"You were close," he told the director. "You should have walked a few hundred yards beyond the end of the road where you can see a little escarpment hidden from road hunters." He took us there and set up a spotting scope. Half an hour later we observed a single elk's head looking over the shelf edge. After climbing higher and setting up the scope a second time, we counted 14 elk. Making a stalk over wet ground, I came within 75 yards of a giant bull. I sat down and admired the majesty of his lordship. The animal knew danger lurked about, but wasn't certain where

to go next. Several minutes later, he "guessed" correctly, stepping lightly into the only unpeopled timber around.

Once again, a spotting scope and patience, plus a few more steps where others hadn't recently trod, located elk when many would have said, "They aren't there."

Another time, in northern New Mexico's Vermejo Ranch among the beautiful Sangre de Cristo Mountains, elk couldn't be located as a hunting manager and I toured lonely canyons at dusk. We saw brown bears and mule deer, and caught myriad trout, but the elk proved elusive. Then the manager said, "We're moving around too much. We'll just sit down right here in the heart of elk country until we see elk." Within a few minutes, elk began to show. Watching carefully, we saw the forms of 5, 6, and finally 7-point bulls step slowly out of cover. In a short time five bulls graced a single meadow in the deep shadows of a snow-crowned peak.

If near a feeding refuge, elk will often make a beeline to it well ahead of heavy hunting. The first influx of hunters may send them scurrying to what they know is complete safety. In northern Utah I once asked a Forest Service employee if he had seen any elk lately.

"Sure. Down in the refuge. Hundreds of them."

It was early October, well before any snows might have made feed tough to come by in the mountains. Yet when I glassed into the valley from an overlook, there they were—some 600 wapiti grazing where no hunter could touch them, on the wintering grounds in the same numbers as they would be in January. No wonder finding elk had been so difficult. That's a major problem where sanctuaries are around—at least when the animals are allowed to remain on the refuges. But how do you get a normal harvest that way?

Another time near Telluride-Sawpit in Colorado, elk permittees complained that they couldn't find any wapiti. While hunting deer, I found plenty of elk hiding out in a long coulee *below* ranches, instead of above them. Normally, they wouldn't have been there. But who can argue with the facts? Hunters didn't expect to find elk there, and didn't look, even though it was public property administered by the Bureau of Land Management where anyone could have gone after them.

Still another time, I witnessed a bull elude hunters who glanced at cows in the open, saw no immediate antlers, and departed. However, a guide hung around long enough to see the bull try to sneak away opposite the cows. The huge 6-pointer fell victim to a suspicious rifle-toter who wouldn't give up easily.

But the champion hunter-eluder I have seen was a particularly goldish-hued mosshorn bull which "wasn't there." Four deer hunters and I, the guide, spent two days zeroing in on a series of rockslides and spruce clumps which had always yielded a buck or two. We found no game at all this time, except scattered doe deer. We rode out at dusk the second day, hesitated a minute to glass far country, then mounted horses again. I happened to look back over my shoulder—a bull elk had emerged from the same rock-spruce slope we had just worked. He had been holed up, but now was headed for a downhill stream. It was not possible he could have been there. But he was. And we all learned something about looking harder for elk.

8

Meeting the Challenge

No matter what challenge you face in life, you'll want to correctly size up the opposition's strengths and weaknesses. Let's look first at the strengths of a bull elk:

Superior nose and ears.

Good eyes.

Speedy legs.

Lives in remote and rugged habitat.

Intolerant of man and his artificialities.

Camouflage.

Knows terrain intimately.

Strength in numbers—a band has many watchful eyes.

Excellent memory and savvy (pattern learning).

Magnificence of trophy can cause buck or bull fever in shooter.

Now, let's make a list of the weaknesses: all of the above. That's right. Everything that works so favorably for *Cervus canadensis* can, if you know what you're doing

as a hunter, also be used against him. Realizing this fact helps the hunter avoid discouragement. You want to know a male wapiti's strengths so you can limit or prevent mistakes. But you're not hunting the strengths. You should concentrate instead on exploitable weaknesses. Your quarry is going to make a mistake sooner or later, and you are going to make the most of it.

Rather than taking the weaknesses in order, let's look at some of the more obvious ones first. Take camouflage. It certainly does at times help the animal hide from a rifle-toter, especially one who does more hiking than looking. However, for the hunter with patience and determination, the elk's camouflage is an asset. If the creature feels camouflaged, it is going to just sit or stand there. You simply need to make out the chest-shoulder area of that tawny-to-dark body with the ivory-tipped antlers—quite likely the only horizontal shape among a stand of vertical tree trunks.

But suppose he doesn't attempt camouflage, and instead uses his speedy legs. They can take him into trouble as much as out—especially if he flees another and enters your sights. Of course, you will have to develop the hunting habit of ambling along quietly enough to hear his approach and be ready to take full advantage of it. There again, size often works against the wapiti. With his nine-foot length and bulky weight, he rarely slips through the woods as silently as a deer, which may scuffle a leaf or branch, then melt away forever. A bull elk, twisting his massive antlers through tree limbs and flattening brush and branches with his large hooves, seldom goes far without creating a ruckus.

Strength in numbers, many pairs of vigilant eyes? More bodies for you to see.

Even an elk's intolerance of man comes into play. Frequently eager to get away from you quickly, he could well thunder through the forest with sufficient noise for you to determine direction. You may then be able to train your sights on an opening he will cross through.

On the surface, it would seem his superior nose and ears are wapiti benefits with little value to the hunter. But wait a minute! If you sneak along quietly into the wind, you may locate a bull with an overdeveloped sense of security, probably from depending wholly on those ears or nose. He may even be bedded comfortably and feel it unnecessary to stand up and look around.

Eyes? An elk can see almost any slight movement below his position. But you aren't approaching from below, where most of the man danger appears. You have gained altitude on a brushy ridgeline away from the target area, climbing along just under the top to avoid being skylined. You made sure with binoculars that no other elk were there to spook and warn your target. Then you crept along slowly until you reached a rim, where you caught your breath, placed finger near trigger, and peered over, ready to shoot. And if you had glassed from a vantage point through spotting scope or binoculars, you had more magnification than an elk's eye possesses. While their eyes are good, they can't simulate the 7X or 8X power of your "artificial" eye.

Rugged and remote habitat? To be sure. But that too can work in your behalf. If hunting elk was easy, wouldn't they all be gone? It's like your job security. If you're willing to take special training on a machine or new technique others don't have, you gain an advantage. When you are willing to pay the price to go where elk go—likely harsh or difficult terrain for man—you are also one up on the human competition, which mills around by road's end or in the first canyon. You are also one up on the elk, for they have become accustomed to enjoying some security from knowing they are where man rarely goes. Work at it hard, as my sales manager used to tell me, and success can come easy.

The elk's special savvy or pattern learning, plus memory to repeat whatever behavior ensured survival previously, can admittedly be a tough nut to crack. But it too can play into your hands. A giant bull grew old by doing something that foiled hunters. When it works, it is repeated and becomes a habit. If you "crack" that pattern, you're home free. Imagine—a trophy animal doing something the very same way season after season! All you have to do is learn the particular stratagem, and intercede.

Is he bedding like a big muley below the crest of a ridge, then bounding over in one leap if danger approaches from the same side — with an option to move laterally out of the way if danger approaches from the other side? Such a savvy creature, sensing your approach, will figure you to be just another hunter, doing what all the others have done before you. He could grow a little ho-hum careless in figuring he can easily elude you. But this time you are going to fool him. Do most of the hunters climbing this ravine approach on the obvious trail along the bottom? He has all his senses tuned in there. If you walk along at a rapid pace, he will do nothing as you race by. If you pause long to make him nervous, he will probably just sneak south as you go north. If you stop frequently, he may get up and run. But there is a better way. You "troubleshoot" where most people don't go. You skip the well-worn trail to circle or fish-hook (mentioned earlier — looking over your back trail to see what is moving behind your path) up the mountain. You gain altitude first, then creep along just under the rim, checking meticu-lously for anything below you which could possibly resemble an elk.

Poison-Ivy Bulls

You also pay particular attention to any blowdown timber, jungled pockets, or tops of little arroyos which could lead to escape exits. You try to locate places out of the way where an elk could get "lost" year after year. As a youngster fishing a small creek within the city limits of a large metropolis, I always avoided one place within 100 yards of a highway bridge. Everyone else did too, and for a good reason: it was thick with poison ivy. But I decided to break my routine, rolled down my sleeves, and threaded through the forbidding stuff to the virgin, gurgling stream on the other side. It wasn't surprising that the grasshopper I impaled on my hook was rapidly snapped up by the largest trout taken in that heavily pressured water in a long time.

Bull elk like to get behind their own poison-ivy patches. Usually they come in the form of chokecherries, spruces, oak

Meeting the challenge is easier with a seasoned packstring. This scene is on Wyoming's Gros Ventre River, heading for the Gros Ventre Wilderness.

brush, etc. One veteran nimrod I know told of a bull outwitting him in heavily hunted terrain by moving around to where he had been. The bull even bugled incessantly throughout the early morning, seeking out a harem. The single hunter bothered him little, since the bull had become accustomed to man in the region. He knew he could not elude hunters with his legs alone, and so resorted to the cat-and-mouse business. But a bull in the wilderness would be much more prone to use distance for escape. How to cope with both sophisticated and wildlands bulls will be probed later. For now, suffice it to say that the wilderness animal will soon "catch on." Before long you'll have to do your homework to keep up with him too. Elk prefer to live a secret life whenever lazy hunters allow it. However, if continually pressed, wapiti will make adjustments to avoid man contact.

A bull's regal and grandiose bearing certainly can send shock waves through any nimrod, particularly a novice. Overcoming buck or bull fever, or at least putting it to work for you, should start on the rifle range. But remember that a bull's great size has its liabilities to the animal. For instance, tracks and beds are much easier to locate and read than with deer or smaller game. Prints of even large bucks might barely bend grass or show in snow, but elk prints are there for all to easily distinguish, even from horseback. Size, number of animals, speed of flight and other factors can be readily determined. Elk sign can make an entire story unfold before your eyes.

One day in the off-season, camera in hand, I followed elk tracks through snow across an open grainfield. The prints stopped abruptly at a fence line, not because the elk couldn't jump the barbed wire—they had leaped higher ones enroute—but because a highway paralleled the fence. The tracks showed that the elk had milled about, regrouped, and then retreated across the field back upslope toward a certain canyon. Tracks were evenly spaced, with no panic in their movement—the elk just refused to cross the road. They had grazed in the grain at night, then sought cover with advent of dawn.

I knew the elk were probably in the first cover in the canyon where tracks led, but I also knew I couldn't just follow them up there. The elk could run faster than I. I'd be lucky to catch a glimpse of them half a mile away as they topped out. But if I reconnoitered up a side canyon and then crossed over above them, I would be within camera (or rifle) range, with the elk at least temporarily pinned below me. They were "trapped" because they wouldn't want to recross the open grainfield again in daylight toward the road they refused to cross. It worked out perfectly. I got the pictures I wanted when the elk attempted to flee uphill within 100 yards of my telephoto lens.

One thing about elk tracks which is more advantageous than finding deer tracks is this: save for late in the post-rut fall, if you find cow prints, odds of a bull being somewhere around are very good. Old tracks don't prove much, since elk move around so much. But with the weight of an elk, prints are deep and easy to interpret for freshness (see chapter titled Elk Country), especially in any mud or stream bank. When you feel you know the specific direction of the animals' travel, check 300 to 600 yards ahead. If the tracks lead over a ridge, don't follow directly; rather, angle obliquely so you can avoid direct confrontations with the ani-

Assume you glass this bedded bull (hypothetical situation) in typical highland elk country at point A in the accompanying photo. How do you approach him?

mals. Interestingly, most elk also cross over a rim at other than right angles to avoid running smack into danger.

Mental Challenge

Throughout the entire elk hunting challenge, you will (if you're normal) occasionally tell yourself this entire process is like looking for a pin in a hayloft. Yet, try to maintain a positive attitude. After all, does a coach tell you your challenger is better than you? Would you compete for long if you thought so? Tell yourself you are prepared, and that you deserve to score.

The importance of mental attitude cannot be overstated. I've seen rifle-toters disguised as hunters putting in their time by walking perfunctorily around the woods. They might as well sit down and tune in a ball game on the radio. One day I witnessed two nimrods in a perfect mountain pass where a a bull might indeed show.

Avoid normal, average ascent directly up canyon from B. Elk would likely escape uphill on line E to F, without giving you the opportunity for a shot. Instead, make stalk along line C-D to top of ridge. There you are above bull and enjoy aiming opportunity downward toward elk. If elk spooks, you still get a shot.

But I could hear their transistor radio 200 yards away, and I'm sure any normal elk could have done so from five times that distance. Elk have a few liabilities, but deafness is seldom one of them. Even at elk-checking stations you can sometimes see that defeatist look in a hunter's eye. You aren't beaten on an elk hunt until you admit you are.

As a guide, I've seen both kinds. There are two California hunters I know who will always find elk if there are any about. They simply assume elk are there, and since they are, "We'll locate them." Yet other nimrods in the same circumstances will return (usually two hours before dark) with the lament that there are no elk to be found. They're correct, of course.

Hunter checks for bulls that might be feeding to beat the cold, wet storm that's moving in.

This hunter, rifle at the ready, pauses before entering a new canyon.

Several years ago a noted brown-trout fisherman and I camped on a reservoir sandbar for three weeks, and one night heard a tapping at the tent door just after midnight. It was two frustrated fishermen complaining they had dragged a popular lure around the lake for three days without a strike.

"What else do we need to do?" they asked plaintively.

"Simple," the angling expert said. "Drag it around until you get it in front of a hungry brown trout."

In hunting, of course, the pursuer has an advantage. He doesn't have to wait for a cooperative quarry to come hungrily to him. He can go to the prey—and take him with or without his full cooperation. But you need to *actually hunt* to enjoy such an advantage.

Games Bulls Play

You must also be aware of the many outright sneaky tactics used by beleaguered elk. Bulls don't always step proudly into high gear. One time I placed a hunter on a knoll above a known location of a band of elk. I made a little drive to push them into the area's only opening. When I arrived at the hunter's position, he had seen nothing. However, on the back side of that knoll, where he had not kept vigil, we saw the inevitable story in the snow: the animals had crossed a sector of the opening, all right. But they had sneaked by him on one side of the knoll while he had apparently been looking on the other.

Another time, we glassed wapiti on a hill as we were making a push from the side opposite to two waiting hunters. The elk attempted to slither through scattered timber with their backs held low toward the ground. With this strategy, they almost eluded us. However, an alert hunter on foot, ready for such antics, filled his license there with a respectable bull.

One of my favorite methods is simply to gain altitude (with horse or otherwise), then filter slowly down, watching for hiding game. This process cannot be hurried. Better to take half a day to go half a mile than just hike haphazardly through the pines.

Your strategy must often encompass a multitude of other hunters and their intentions, especially where an unlimited number of permits have been issued. Remember that you have yet another advantage over fishermen—there isn't any way they can spook targets to their hook, but other hunters can put game into your net. When you see competition, try to determine where you would go to elude them if you were an elk. Often it is up-canyon, over a pass or "saddle," and into another canyon. So get to the pass first. Especially valuable is a connecting ridge or saddle "fed" by several converging ravines.

Timing is also important in order to benefit from the competition. On one occasion, noting several parties headed toward a knoll south of me, I got there just in time to see the heads of several cows bobbing my way. The fourth animal was a nice "eating"-sized bull. My shot was the only one I heard that day. I doubt any other nimrod hauled an elk out of that area during the period. The point is, those elk-seekers helped me—I might not have spotted a bull at all that day without their unknowing assistance.

Another time, I spotted several horsemen some three-quarters of a mile away, working in my general direction. I stopped walking. It might have been Lady Luck who sent those antlers into a hole in the spruces less than 15 yards away. But when she was ready with her gift, so was I—in a sitting position with my finger near the safety.

Elk in Perspective

But let's talk about the elk which could be right under your nose without your realizing it. It happens more times than

most hunters ever imagine. A highly successful hunting acquaintance of mine, Robert Irvine, who didn't even take up big-game hunting seriously until he was some 30 years of age, has taken specimens over several continents, including leopards, cape buffalo, bears, deer, antelope, moose, and wapiti. He set out to accomplish the Grand Slam of sheep (Rocky Mountain, desert, Dall, and Stone) and completed it. His Stone ram, with 41-inch-plus curl on a broad base, is in line for the Boone and Crockett record book.

How does the elk stack up with Robert Irvine? And how does he suggest outwitting an oversized bull? Irvine views his big bull elk as one of his most memorable trophies. He also tells of the time he and several companions were hunting elk in Wyoming's north-central Bighorn Mountains. After searching in vain for several days, his cohorts gave up and headed for the vehicle. He remained to glass just a little longer. He located several ledges he hadn't seen before, then glassed into the foliage below at a different angle than he had before. He saw a "tawny" form there, then another, and more. Before long, he had looked at some 250 elk filing through trees and brush below. "I remained there so long the guide and other hunters came looking for me. When they did, all were as amazed as I. The guide said he knew how to get on a road on the slope where we could get a better look at antlers. But before we could get back to the vehicle, we located other elk, until the entire mountain seemed to be on the move! I took a nice bull. I also realized that only an hour before, we had been convinced there were no elk in this area at all."

But Irvine's best bull came from British Columbia. He and a guide hiked for 11 hours up a steep, long mountain just to reach the slopes where the search for a massive wapiti rack was to begin. "He was sure of what he was doing," Irvine told me, "so I just kept putting one foot after another like the guide did. When we arrived at this long-awaited hotspot, we saw nothing. Then, just before dark, the bull my guide expected stepped from the spruces. By the time I dropped the monarch and we cleaned him out, it was well after dark. Return by flashlight required four hours. My most memorable trophy among hundreds of memorable hunts was probably that elk."

Respect for the wapiti? Irvine tells of an unsuccessful quest. He and a guide had watched elk via spotting scope from a mile away. Then they spooked them while creeping away, well off the skyline, across a patch of snow which apparently silhouetted them and signaled their presence to the elk eyes some 1,500 yards away. He recommends that deer hunters not "handle" elk the same way they hunt muley or whitetail. "The difference—with all due respect to the deer—is like the difference between hunting ducks and geese. Deer suspect that a noise could be danger; a bull elk *knows* it is until proven otherwise. That's one reason you might stumble into deer, like you do ducks; but with geese and elk, you'd better have a plan."

I know of other hunters who have located elk at a distance, then studied something else as important: wind currents between stalker and stalkee. If the wind is blowing from you to them, forget a stalk from your present position. If there is no way to "move with the breezes," come back another day. In a wilderness setting, elk are likely to remain where they are for at least a day or two when undisturbed.

Many nimrods do not comprehend the full importance of hunting at dawn and dusk. During much of the rest of the day,

elk are tougher to locate because they are ruminating, and bedded, usually in cover. At the extremes of daylight, they are on their feet, usually moving, and visible. On several occasions as a guide, I have encountered situations where an established hunting camp/lodge hierarchy hold to a rigid, impractical schedule. Some cooks and even outfitters wanted to put supper on when most of the licensees returned to camp, which often was at 5 p.m., with another hour of hunting to be wrested from the day—but not just any hour. Evening's magic hour is when things happen, even if they haven't so far.

When that situation occurs, you may have to take the bull by the horn, so to speak. I tell the cook to put my plate of food in the refrigerator, and I'll eat when I return. If you get a heavy argument, you as a hunter can simply remind the outfitter why you chose him—to seriously hunt elk. A guide, an employee of the outfitter, has less to say about it; but more than once I have announced that my contingent of hunters wouldn't return until at least a full hour after dark.

Seven Hunters

As a guide during the 1984 wapiti season, I witnessed an interesting challenge: seven hunters arrived with both mule deer and elk licenses. They selected our upper camp, a less luxurious one but one with more opportunity for oversized bulls. Four hunters nailed both deer and elk. A fifth took a deer and had a bull elk in his sights but missed him due to a rifle malfunction (firing pin froze up, possibly due to congealed grease or oil).

I believe there were two reasons these five men put their scopes on both game species. One: they utilized to the fullest every moment of hunting time they had. Even when looking for deer before the elk opener, they kept a vigil in the higher openings for wapiti. When the elk opener arrived, they had already tagged bucks to be hauled out, and they had their mental sights on elk ledges and terraces just beneath the higher rims. Also, we had a policy in that camp which required the cook to prepare supper for each and every hunter whenever he returned. This placed extra burden on the cook, but he responded to the hunters' schedules, not they to his. This policy may cause chaos in some elk camps, but there is no reason permit-holders returning to camp in mid-afternoon can't wait for the return of the other hunters before they eat.

Six Specific Methods

Now let's look at six possible ways in which you might go after elk. They are: (1) glassing with scope or binoculars from a high vantage point (in the meantime remaining vigilant for any elk which might walk within rifle range); (2) walking while looking; (3) a combination of one and two; (4) searching from horseback or in a vehicle; (5) hiking quickly to a specific point where you expect to find elk through deduction or previous scouting; (6) organized drive.

Plan No. 1 is tops in any law of averages, especially if you can glass a multitude of likely haunts. Checking five meadows carries five times better odds than glassing just one. However, after spending hours at it in vain, a hunter may choose some alternate modus operandi. On occasion I like to walk slowly, stopping often to listen and look (No. 3), then sitting down to glass on points and overlooks along a ridge. I would not recommend

No. 4, except when going to and returning from the prime hunting area. You might see elk along the routes, but it is not, in most cases, the best way to spend your day. A possible exception is a hunt on a private ranch with many but little-used back roads. Hunting via horse or vehicle is a method favored by elk guides in New Mexico's vast Vermejo Park, but even there, guides report much more success when hunters are willing to get out of the vehicle for the bulk of their looking.

Another factor regarding a 4 x 4: extra drive power by itself is often not enough. Traction is as least equally important. That means tires with good tread and chains that fit, plus stretch rope fasteners such as backpackers use. However, I've also seen many a rancher-guide utilize baling wire or just durable old hay-bale twine to keep chains tight. If bogged deep in the mud, you may lose the chains themselves as well as the traction. Practice applying the chains at home on dry terrain, with the flatter side against the tire. Fasten the more difficult inside loop first. Keep taking up slack until it's completely tight. Remember that if you have only two chains, they will do the most good if applied to the pulling, or front, tires on a 4 x 4.

The organized drive can be a most successful way to hunt wapiti because, unlike deer, elk rarely have a staked-out bailiwick which they refuse to leave. However, for best success you will need to place the waiting shooters well out in front, since wapiti can take flight 500 to 600 yards away from the drivers. Some guides don't like this method, because it spooks elk out of the country, but others hunting mostly migratory elk don't hesitate to use it. They know the elk in their territory might well be gone the next day anyway. If you are hunting without a guide, try to get the drivers on the uphill side, brushing or dog-ging downhill. Although driving uphill can work, elk escape more easily if you press from the bottom, and may spook before you even get into position. Drivers, of course, have to go up a different slope than the one they'll push. Be sure to post along the sides, for wapiti, like deer, won't always exit in a straight line.

You can do some successful driving with only two or three hunters by tossing rocks (or shooting marbles with a sling-shot) to spook the animals. This is best with at least one downslope hunter and one or more rifle-toters guarding the sides of a given cover pocket.

Hanging in There

One beginner at elk hunting, Utahn Jeff Pierson, tried No. 1 for several days with-out success. The elk just wouldn't show again where he had observed them earlier. Finally, after several days of glassing from one spot, he headed back for camp. But, wisely, he did not just quickly hike back down open terrain. Instead, he chose a fence line near timber which would allow him to walk quietly while searching aspen and spruce. Moving at a pace slow enough that he couldn't hear his own footsteps, he figured that elk on the move or pushed toward him, and making noise of their own, wouldn't hear him. Every few steps he stopped to listen. Eventually, he heard something 100 yards into cover. Sitting down immediately against a fence post to break up his outline, he waited for game to show. It did—first several cows, then a broad-beamed 5-point bull. The bull trot-ted to the fence, lifted its front legs to jump across, and in mid-leap, at a dis-tance of no more than 30 yards from Pier-

son, sensed his presence. But by then it was too late. When the bull had all four hooves on earth again, Jeff had the scope on his front shoulder.

Pierson may never have bagged that bull if he'd spent the season just waiting and watching. Sometimes you have to go after them. But in Jeff's case, it was a les-son in how alertness, even when headed for camp, can pay off. And it all happened in several seconds, a typical elk-hunting occurrence.

Another hunter, Dee Smith, describes a slightly different waiting-watching combi-nation: "We spent the first half day in camp—we had gone up high due to warm weather—checking for elk sign and found rubs on spindly aspens. I hadn't seen any bulls by 4 p.m., but knew they were in the general area. Then, on a ridge overlooking the aspens and several meadows, I began setting up a spotting scope to maintain a watch until dark. I'd scarcely begun brac-ing the scope legs when I found myself looking down on two cow elk. Several more cows appeared, then a huge bull! They were too far away for a shot, so I checked to make certain I had a 130-grain Nosler in the firing chamber. Then I tried to figure where they were going. I felt anxi-ety gripping at me, but I told myself I was doing everything I could possibly do to meet the challenge.

"Earlier, I had seen a small pond in the direction the elk were going, and as they disappeared, I figured they were headed there. I hurried around toward the pond so I could arrive on the far side as soon as possible. I left my scope and daypack right where they were. Five minutes later I ar-rived at a point where I could quietly over-look the pond. When I did, it was some-thing of a comical sight. Several elk were already in the water. The bull was annoying the cows by thrashing and hooking his antlers at them. The cows eventually walked to the bank and shook off the accumulated water. The bull remained there belly deep, grunting threats at the cows. In a sitting position, I rested my .270 over my left knee, then slowly melted my finger into the trigger. Rifle and pond seemed to explode simultaneously.

"I had aimed at the best target I had, the lower neck. But when he stepped forward with the shot, his front shoulder was visible. I touched off a second round. Spray went flying, but from the bull, not the water. The cows trotted quickly off, but the bull didn't move. Then he turned his great rack toward the cows and stumbled after them. Just as I was chambering a third cartridge, he sat down in the water just like my Australian shepherd as he waits for me to open a can of dogfood. He rolled over and then, incredibly, got up and staggered toward north-slope timber. I sent two more shots his way, and this time he fell for good 40 yards from the pond. I had hit him in the lungs with the second, and possibly the first shot as well."

Only then did Smith realize the bull had been taken a short distance from where he'd felled a giant muley buck several seasons before.

Smith's past deer hunting skills had paid off, but he had gone a step or two beyond them. In a number of deer-hunting expeditions with him, I had never known Dee to take along a spotting scope. He had one on this hunt. He further prepared for elk by practicing at longer distances than for deer hunting only. But the main reason he scored was that he had a plan: locate elk, then figure where they will go and how to get within shooting range quietly.

Welcome Luck

As a hunter works his plan, he must also be ready for that rarest of happenings: the "gift" bull. It's akin to a salesman driving across Los Angeles or Chicago or New York to a possible appointment for a small sale, and finding someone along the way who wants to buy big, here and now. It can happen, and it helps to be mentally prepared for such an unforeseen windfall. I realized that fact while interviewing thousands of hunters at check stations. It was clear that a small percentage — say, 10 percent — of any wild quarry is more vulnerable than the rest, possibly because it takes up residence in a certain area, pursues food in a certain way, or because of its "education." Certainly, if a new road opens up a previously inaccessible region, sportsmen will funnel in there and may find unsophisticated, neglected trophies. The elk aren't less "bright," just less man-experienced.

Although it happens less often with elk than with perhaps any other game animal, a totally unforeseen break could come your way. You can't expect it, but you won't turn your back on it, either. One of my best elk racks seemed somewhat handed to me: a bull coming to water in a meadow at dusk. Of course, without having spent hours on the practice range shooting at rolling tires, I wouldn't have dropped him as he fled at a full run. I believe the bull had watered there repeatedly at evening; I happened to locate him simply by going home on a different route than usual.

I can't forget one hunter who left the highlands disappointed. Then, while driving home, he decided to probe a few back roads in the foothills. He found a 4-point bull which had been wounded, stopped by a canal it couldn't get across. The hunter went home with meat for the freezer, and a smile.

Tougher Times

It is possible that terrain which held elk in the previous several years doesn't have any now. That's often due to human disturbances. After a busy opening day, elk just don't remain around. One outfitter-guide, Gap Puche of Jackson Hole, Wyoming, keeps an eye to the future in the hunting tactics he employs. He never drives, pushes, or brushes for wapiti, because such tactics spook them away. He has developed a technique of picking off bulls in certain fringe areas where there's little human intrusion, so other elk won't be disturbed and chased off. Consequently, he can locate elk with fair consistency. Most of his elk are residents rather than migrants; to keep them around, he stresses minimizing noise at all times, even in camp.

Maybe the area you have relied on for elk in the past suddenly doesn't have any, for no reason you can fathom. Drought, deterioration of food, or other natural causes are more likely to trigger wanderlust in gregarious animals with combined needs, like caribou and elk, than in more individualistic creatures like deer. In any event, what do you do in midseason when elk are not where they were?

Toughest of All

Let's suppose you are not guided, are hunting unfamiliar terrain, have plunked down good money for a permit you may not be able to duplicate next year, and that you desperately want to find elk before the season ends in a week. You approach a mountain range, having been told that it

has yielded a few bulls in the current season, or has some to offer, but you haven't the foggiest notion where they might dwell. Let's make it even worse and say you tried to arrive the night before for a look around but weren't able to do so for one reason or another. Now it's a moonless night. You can't even get an idea of what the projected hunting territory looks like. How do you get started the next morning?

You could wait for full daylight, hike to the top of a knoll, and get oriented, and/or glass for elk. But that would waste a precious morning of potential hunting time. If you can decide which way is north the next day before sunup, you needn't despair. (At night check the Big Dipper— its lower or "pouring" end points to the North Star.) You decide to proceed by flashlight two hours before dawn. But you don't want to get brushed up where you can't use your binoculars or where you can't make headway without making noise. Here is what you do:

If the mountain range or other likely hunting grounds run north-south, let's say you enter a canyon heading east. Slopes on your right (shaded, water-retaining north-facing slopes) will have the heaviest brush. You want to avoid them in the morning, not only because you would thrash around through them in the dark but also because elk aren't there anyway. Elk are almost certainly on the south-facing slopes (to your left from the canyon bottom), where sunlight grows more grass and browse that attract feeding elk and where you can check well ahead. If you are on the other side of the main range, heading west into the inky blackness, you can be sure the thickest vegetation is on your left. Slopes to the right will be more open.

If facing south while walking in, the

densest cover will be on your right (east-facing slope) and the more open terrain on your left (west-facing slope with less water and more warm afternoon sunlight). Reverse that if you approach facing north.

However, things switch around 180 degrees in midday. The elk are finished filling their stomachs and are more interested in a combination of rumination, resting, and security. They are more likely to be in the heavier cover on north and east slopes. It's cooler too, another reason for elk to move there as the sun climbs. Glass carefully at all times. Do not attempt to stalk elk directly out of canyon bottoms. Circle around if possible to higher ridgelines where you can be above game, and do not forget to remain off the skyline itself. Warm air currents, usually rising in the morning, are in your favor if you stay high. When glassing for elk, also check for dead-end ridges which may stop you. Retracing your way around such spots costs altitude (energy) and time. Keep to the ridges which offer an avenue into the farthest back country. Your chances definitely improve with every mile you can remain on these high ridges away from well-traveled roads or other signs of civilization. It is not always practical to flee from every primitive back road you encounter, but try to get off rims or points where tire or boot tracks reveal human activity.

On the West Coast Roosevelt elk ranges the same holds true, except that in the rainforests you may have to stick to roads or logging clearings in order to see elk at all. Your chances of creeping up on a languishing bull in thick timber are about as good as finding a weasel asleep, so concentrate on moving slowly near openings through which hunters might push something shootable to you.

Now, let us suppose that after a time you think you see something resembling an elk on the same or an opposite slope, almost within rifle range. You slowly creep forward until you can make out an antler tip. It proves to be a bull all right, but is in the shadows, one leap from escape, and still just out of best rifle range—about 400 yards away by your best estimate. As long as he does not sense you and show sign of alarm, there is no real need to hurry. Both elk and deer, unlike people, are seldom eager to flee if they have not been frightened. Even when they do sense danger, I have witnessed bulls standing statue-still for long periods to pinpoint its exact source. You must decide if the animal will move in your direction or, if not, which arroyo or other cover might allow you to quietly approach at least 50 yards closer. You want to get within at least 325 yards and be able to hold on the bull's upper front shoulder. Allow for bullet drop (see the chapter on ballistics to get figures for your particular firearm).

If you can't get close enough to place the scope's crosshairs on a vital area from a solid shooting position, consider waiting for such an opportunity. Snapping off a "hope" shot at long range from a standing position may be better than nothing if you feel you'll never see the game target again. But it is a very poor habit to get into or rely on. The odds are stacked against you.

Bull in Your Sights

When you feel you can visualize that elk's front shoulder as you did the target on the rifle range, squeeze off a shot. If any other hunter is with you, be sure he understands ahead of time you want him to glass the animal as you shoot. (A guide should do this automatically.) After your rifle discharges, he should be close enough to whisper to you any unusual reaction by the game. Did the bull try to walk, then falter slightly? Did he leap up? Or did you miss altogether, and if so, where did the puff of dirt kick up? It is extremely important to know if you hit the animal. Hit or miss, hold on him and shoot another round if the animal is still on his feet. If he falls, watch him closely to see if he stirs. You might have merely "shocked" him with a slug to the base of an antler. I've seen such game get back up, shake it off, and run away as if nothing had happened. But always be ready to shoot a second time, even if you see the game drop like a dynamited pile of bricks. One thing you do not want is a wounded animal crawling away to hide, die, and be wasted.

Do not rush up unless there is some clear reason for so doing—for example, if the animal is about to disappear over a rim. An elk which has been wounded in the front shoulder, especially in the lungs, will likely die within an hour or so, and certainly can't make many tracks after minutes of internal bleeding. At all costs, avoid pumping him up with enough adrenaline so he'll go where you can't find him. If you can't see where he went down, have a partner remain at the shooting site to direct you to the last place you saw the game. Terrain can look much different close up than it does from a few hundred yards away. If tracking is required, you'll want to have a beginning point!

I once hit a nice bull with two slugs at long range, and the guide recommended waiting for at least 45 minutes. His reason was a good one. The bull had slumped at the second shot (we later found two slugs in the lungs), then "looked sick," according to the watching guide. It then walked a dozen yards to lie down in a clump of low spruce. After 45 minutes it still managed to get to its feet, but couldn't by then make them do much but wobble downhill.

We moved in quickly to finish the job, although the bull still refused to quit without a close range coup de grace.

Gap Puche says he has seen elk go long distances even with vitals ruptured—if hunters are in hot and noisy pursuit. On the other hand, he also witnessed a bull that had been barely nicked in the shin lie down to nurse the wound. Trailed meticulously but not hurriedly, that bull succumbed to a sure second shot.

Obviously, if darkness is closing in, you will want to waste no time. But it is most important to know the precise route the quarry has taken, rather than guessing wrong. You will want, of course, also to keep an eye on openings or ridges ahead that may help you catch sight of the game. A good look can speed up the "chase" and tell you how badly hurt the animal is. If he is headed rapidly uphill without a stumble, you may not have a "chase" at all. But if he shows a propensity to head downhill and has an obvious hitch in the rhythm of hoof placement, keep at it even if you have to return the next day. Watch for more than blood: broken branches or logs lurched into, skin or hair on both ground and "tight" cover can be revealing. It is possible for an elk to continually get up after resting, so be alert for the sight or sound of same just ahead.

Hit-Game Checklist

After watching hunters recover wounded game over the years, Puche recommends following these basic steps.

1. Mark the spot where you last saw the game. Let a companion help direct you to it. If alone, make certain you can later locate the exact sage, bush, or tree nearest the downed animal.

2. Proceed slowly. Any wound can

cause an elk to lie down, and when this happens, time is usually on your side. As long as an ailing elk feels secure, there is no reason for him to get back on his legs.

3. Check for blood in ever-widening circles. Speed is not as important, if the elk is out of sight, as accurate searching.

4. Don't overlook the obvious. The elk could be hiding, or even dead, within a dozen yards. Downhill—the direction of least resistance—is where a badly wounded animal is most likely to go.

5. If not pressed too hard, even a slightly nicked elk could be looking for a safe place to lie down. Let him. If you don't, you could push for miles on a bull going mostly on adrenaline. He may well die, but in a place where you can't find him.

Puche has seen elk with mere flesh wounds overtaken by patient nimrods, and other elk that led too-anxious hunters up to 11,000 feet.

If you are bowhunting and must approach within 30 yards to make a clean kill, it is assumed you have taken advantage of camouflage clothing, scents to mask human odor, darkened face to reduce sun glare, cloth to dull glare on bow, etc. It is also assumed you avoid stalking over rockslides, limb-littered turf and such in favor of soft snow or wet ground to muffle your approach. You should also join bowhunters' organizations to discuss techniques. Check on special schools or archery lanes for bowshooters. One I can vouch for is the Dwight Schuh School of Bowhunting (see address in Chapter 21), where students examine such things as tree stands and pussyfooting tactics—everything to get you within bow range. Schuh, incidentally, has proven his methods sound by taking a number of trophy game animals, some entered in the Pope and Young Club's record books.

Ten Deadly Sins

Recently, I asked a wide range of guides what factors most often cost hunters a bull after the game is sighted. They listed these 10 "little" but deadly sins:

1. Scope covers that are either unfamiliar to the hunter or awkward or noisy to remove.

2. Ditto for the rifle's safety latch.

3. Colds, coughs, or sniffles which can spook game. Several guides, including Puche, carry cough drops for ailing clients.

4. Scopes knocked out of action by mishap, with no peep or iron sights or a second rifle available.

5. "Hopped-up" guns unfamiliar to the hunters. Some fail at the moment of truth because a handload won't fire. The cause for this failure is usually traceable back to the rifle range—the hunter didn't go there enough.

6. Hunters not certain about what they will do when game is sighted. Once I witnessed a client almost shoot the hunter next to him when a Boone and Crockett-candidate bull loomed 600 yards ahead. The hunter fumbled for his firearm with heavily gloved hands (the safety not on) that took away any sensitive feel for the trigger. He should have used a glove with the trigger finger out, or shed the glove on his shooting hand. If you insist on using a glove, practice shooting with it.

7. Shells clinking in a pocket, giving away the hunter's location, particularly when hurrying into a shooting position. Likewise, clothing which rustles, shoes which squeak, and a vehicle's rattling tailgate.

8. Overuse of horses to closely approach sighted game (covered in another chapter.) Also, noisy mistakes with stirrups, dismounting, etc.

Hunter Dee Smith took this Utah bull from sage and brush.

Roy Abbott took this bull in heavy Wyoming timber.

This Roosevelt bull is from coastal British Columbia.

9. Hunters who give up or lose patience during drives, including loss of alertness during a long ride.

10. The mental aspects of seeing an awesome trophy. Several guides reiterated the story of the orange-vester who forgets to shoot or pumps shells out onto the ground. A hunter must be prepared, and he does so via time on the practice range, scouting, and visualizing ahead what he'll do.

Here's an example of how a nimrod can benefit from being ready. Olympic skier Bill Johnson, winner of the men's downhill event, said after his triumph at Sarajevo, Yugoslavia: "Relaxed and confident? Sure, but only because I didn't dwell on the importance of what I was about to attempt—there was no glory until afterward. During the time it happened, I just concentrated on the task at hand. I thought of it, regarding mechanical execution, as just another practice race."

9

Scouting and Success

When veteran elk slayer Don Cozzens goes after elk, he usually knows about where to find one. No. 50 will be sought close to where he found the 49 others. But now, at age 80, he prefers to use his head rather than his feet. Such advice is helpful to anyone at any age.

Of course, we will also have to do some walking to locate game. But it can be kept to a minimum if we do our scouting in other ways. For example, the other day while driving back roads to see where elk tracks or other sign might be located within a day's travel of roads, I came across a sheepherder who barely spoke English. In language sprinkled with Spanish and gesticulation, he told me, "Not here, Señor. But over in Devil's Hole, two, maybe three day ago, I see, oh, 75 elk." I made plans to backpack into Devil's Hole. I wasn't too surprised to discover it has

only a few entrances, none of them easy. All require hiking through steep cliffs. But that's elk hunting.

Cozzens has been making mental note of such places all his life. "They're where people generally don't like to go," he says in mild understatement. "Those are the places I try first. It's taken years, though, to learn exactly where they are."

Even Cozzens has to update his program occasionally. Conditions can change. That roadless basin of two years ago may have a road bisecting it now. Or an entire hunting camp may have discovered it yesterday. You have to keep up on things. Here are some ways you can keep your scouting current:

1. Subscribe to a newspaper in a small town near your intended hunting area.

2. When fishing, gathering wood, or vacationing in potential wapiti country,

Best way to scout for elk: glass at dusk from high ground.

talk to everyone—gas-station attendants, sheepherders, forest rangers.

3. Telephone experts such as fish-and-game personnel, especially biologists. They will likely tell you more if you can distinguish yourself from the thousands who call for such information. One way to do that is to know something about the "hotspot" before you pick up the phone. Tell them, for example, that you know there are elk in upper Whatever Ridge, but is there an access road probing farther than the dead-end route up the canyon bottom? If he can't talk to you now, make an appointment to talk later.

4. Attend seminars and big-game discussions. Ask pointed questions of the speakers, such as: "You showed 65 percent success on the White River unit last year adjacent to that reseeding project. Have you seen any big bulls in there?" Also ask how long he figures it will take for the reseeding to establish itself. And exactly how do you reach the reseeded area? New and tender unbrowsed grass, bitterbrush,

etc. will almost certainly be a magnet to elk.

5. Interview hunters at game-check stations. Sometimes you'll learn more there about what *not* to do, but the main thing is to learn all you can. Listen carefully to all success stories. Note the reasons for the failures.

6. Take your binoculars and glass, glass, glass, particularly at dusk. I've taken many friends into proven big-bull terrain, only to have them say something like, "Didn't see an elk all day. Must not be many around." The last time a friend said that, we were in country where I had helped guide hunters to five branch-antlered bulls. Don't make judgments until you've meticulously studied the real estate at dawn and dusk with good optics.

7. Lastly, there is no substitute for walking the access fringes of your intended hunt area. Recently I figured on riding into a certain creek drainage where I had glassed elk from a distance. But after walking only one-quarter mile into

the edge of it, I discovered far too much blowdown timber and steep ledges to safely get a mount into it. However, scrutinizing a nearby ridgeline at close range indicated a possible course to the canyon bottom and up the other side. I'd never have "felt" this inspiration without actually having probed into the place on foot beforehand. Of course, I would have recognized the same on the elk opener, but then it would have cost me valuable hours. By the time I got in there, I'd have missed the best morning hunting. Some competitor who had done his scouting a little better might also have beaten me to the target.

An excellent way to scout potential wapiti territory ahead of time is to put a pack on your back and strike out for several days. In horse country, many hopefuls remain in the saddle while doing their looking, but they simply won't see as many wary wapiti that way. In the off-season you have plenty of time, so sit down in the outback, relax, and do nothing for a while. When your presence is no longer known or becomes accepted, it is amazing what you might see: a ruffed grouse stirring which previously had blended in with the spruce needles, a weasel chasing a squirrel, even a cow elk whose legs first seemed to be nothing more than spindly tree trunks.

In order to avoid hurrying—always a no-no—take along a flashlight, a poncho to help you wait out storms, dry socks, anything to let you become part of the landscape, no matter what mood nature is in. See what is really there. *Act as if you were hunting*, even though you don't have a license or rifle with you. Decide what you will do in any given situation later. Does the rim westward take you to more good aspen and pine elk country, or lead

to a thousand-foot dropoff? Now, not during the season, is the time to learn.

Check Closely

How thoroughly are you scouting? Once I searched along a stream for hours without locating any tracks or droppings. Yet I was certain a big bull I'd seen the preceding season must have been headed here for water. I figured there could be no other reason he would depart heavy cover (with grass nearby) at dusk to move through an open, rather barren ravine. Surely he was heading for water after a warm day.

Later on, with additional scrutiny, I found the answer. A hidden spring halfway from timber to stream was quite likely the bull's destination. A little bog on a small plateau there was deeply imprinted with elk tracks. Without that information, on the next elk opener I would have waited in vain for bulls to show in the stream bottom, a conspicuous place not attractive to hunted wapiti. Only terrible thirst would have driven a bull there with hunters milling around. I now have a hidden place in mind where, come next elk season, I can wait out a wily bull headed for this secret spring.

Many times a nimrod is unknowingly but one canyon away from his would-be target. While fishing in a roadless canyon one day, a companion and I saw no elk, nor any tracks. The logical assumption would be that an elk camp in this territory would be a total waste of time. However, I knew better. Within a half mile of there the year before, I had helped guide several hunters to branch-antlered wapiti. The following season, too, we saw numerous elk on the ridgeline above that fishing canyon. They simply bedded, fed, and

Are you looking closely enough to locate elk in cover? How many can you spot in this scene?

watered on the upper fringes of the mountain cut while we had only walked the bottom.

Another time, I didn't find elk while scouting a certain canyon, or in the one tributary to that. But a smaller side ravine held several dozen wapiti, including a nice bull. Blundering into him during the hunting season would likely have resulted in nothing more than a glimpse as he exited in the opposite direction. Knowing his location ahead of time, I could devise strategy to get him in my rifle scope within reasonable shooting range.

A methodical approach, checking the escape routes, then maneuvering into position to take advantage, carries no absolute guarantee. But the odds are much better that way than barging in without knowing what's there. Make certain, anytime you spook elk, that you note which direction they go. Big bulls are creatures of habit. The ploy they use this time may well be repeated again.

Before the season opens, you can pon-

der strategy without hurry. Can you get up this road in your vehicle – even if it rains? Do you need to buy better tread for your rig, four-wheel drive or otherwise? Will you need chains (always a good thing to have on hand anyway)? If so, do you have chain tighteners? Now is the time to prepare.

To Study Contour Maps

To help you make decisions, buy a contour map of the area. Check out the U.S. Geological Survey office in the nearest town of size. Such map treasurehouses are usually located in a post office or other federal building. Look for a large "identification" or index map of a county or state. Such a general map will be numbered or lettered to identify more detailed maps of smaller areas that will likely show your target canyon, ridge, or mountain. These valuable topographic maps show changes in elevation with meandering brown contour lines (usually representing altitudes 200 feet apart). They help you decide where you must rely on your own two feet, where you can take a horse, and where not to try either of the above. Sometimes you must make a wide detour to get above cliffs (where the brown lines nearly touch each other) and then be ready to glass meadows or treeless slopes, indicated by wider-apart contour lines. The maps even show heavy green areas, where you can expect to find timber or other cover. White denotes open ground. Trails and roads are also shown.

In the off-season, particularly in winter when you can't actually get on a suspected elk slope, study these contour maps meticulously. Let's suppose you want to locate new elk country. Maybe you don't have horses right now, and you want access near a road. Admittedly, this is not as good as riding a mount far back into remote terrain. But it is often possible to locate by map potential elk hotspots within a few miles of roads or valley trails. Best of all, this can be done in the off-season.

Seek out plateaus or rims above cliffs, especially if they are timberless. Grass generally grows in such places. If cover (timber shown in green) is nearby, so much the better. Check closely for open south-facing slopes, shown on map as the north side of a stream (blue line), in mountainous terrain as they frequently have grass and other elk-preferred foods. The north slopes carry little food but plenty of cover, because moisture-retention is high away from the sun. Ditto for west-facing slopes—the east side of the map's blue lines.

Maps of national parks, monuments, private ranches, and Indian reservations have also given me some better-than-average hunting by pointing me toward boundary lines. I've taken game by hunting the legal (public-land) edges of posted lands on a number of occasions, but you have to be certain of precise, accurate access into open hunting domain. At one time, I was certain there was no way to get to the edge of a certain Indian reservation, but tribal authorities themselves helped me get onto access roads adjacent to Bureau of Land Management terrain. I'll give one prime example: the Wind River Indian Reservation in central Wyoming. There are trophy bulls there, and they don't read border signs. You can find them on the reservation, and also within a few miles of it. It's possible to literally map out a hunt there.

Maps and a magnifying glass on a winter's night before the fireplace can help you scout out any new elk spot. Go there in person the first chance you get.

Several days of storms might push surplus elk off a national park like Yellowstone. Since park rangers are almost certain to kill elk which multiply too rapidly for the winter range to handle, you need have no qualms whatsoever about taking advantage of migration opportunities. I feel it is more sporting to take migrating elk just off park boundaries in wilderness-type settings than to wait for them to show up hungry and desperate on the edge of winter feeding grounds. That subject will be treated in the chapter on elk management; but again, such near-park hunting should be preceded by mapping out your hunt.

Such planning shakes down to a motto an old guide once told me: "Do everything you can in the off-season except actually shoot your elk."

Sensitive Scouting

Another thing: do your scouting sensitively, in a way that won't drive the animals away. It may not be so important with mule deer or other game, even antelope. They will likely return to familiar haunts. Elk are frequently homeless, wandering creatures, especially if provoked. No one spot on earth is so sacrosanct that an elk won't vacate it.

So do your glassing and especially any on-site inspection slowly and carefully. When elk are located, remain at a distance. During recent scouting expeditions in Wyoming's Bridger National Forest, I located several herds of elk a few weeks before the season opened. I had three or four large bulls catalogued as to ridge and arroyo. They remained there in a lush meadow above the steep ledges within a mile of a well-used trail, almost to opening day. But, with no change in weather, they vanished within a day or two of the opener. Human footprints in the snow led directly into their lair. Sadly, I had studied them day after day, tying my mount well away from their bedding grounds, looking over several admirable racks, and, indeed, doing everything but shooting one particular royal rack. But they were all spooked off by what can only be called careless scouting.

Don't overdo a good thing. After finding elk, check on them from half a mile or more away if possible. Then forget them until the season opens.

I do not advocate looking merely for tracks, wallows, or other sign. In my opinion, it does a hunter a world of good to behold those regal antlers themselves. It provides incentive for later, because you know they are in there somewhere. It is also helpful in combatting "buck" or bull fever. You are simply not as likely to be overwhelmed at the critical moment of truth if you've beheld this magnificent scene of antlers before.

Another thing that sighting elk in the wild does for you is teach you how to find them. You no longer search for an entire animal, but rather an ear, an ivory antler tip, or a partly shaded leg. You know from experience how to begin looking. With a sweep of a mountainside with glasses, you can determine if something is out of kilter and worth a second look. You also gain experience in where to begin searching — just below ridgetops, at the edges of cover, etc. Especially important is recognizing how easy it is for a russet, tawny, or dark brown form (elk at various times of year can be any of those colors) to escape your scrutiny when viewed against a similar background. That knowledge helps you slow down when seriously searching.

Then, too, patient scouting teaches you much about elk behavior in general.

Even observing the animals on winter feeding grounds can help. You see the ones which got away — proof that many elk outwit the hunting brigade. Even if you can't get to a winter elk refuge, you can probably observe foothills elk anywhere in the West from December to April.

As for bull fever, my own analysis of why it happens is this: desire overwhelms performance. If you can't earn the trophy with steady shooting, the kind you do on the rifle range, tell yourself you don't deserve the trophy. And while you are looking at off-season elk, there's nothing wrong with mentally sizing up that vital zone just behind the front shoulder. Do that a few times, and it seems more routine when you do it during the season.

I've looked at numerous old bulls in the National Elk Rufuge in Jackson Hole, and the amazing thing about them is this: when the wapiti season opens to reduce elk numbers in nearby Grand Teton National Park (and the upper part of the refuge), those monster bulls vanish overnight. They reappear in the heart of the lower refuge, the only place around where absolutely no hunting is ever allowed at any time! That area is also relatively close to heavy auto traffic on U.S. 191. How do these elk know they are safe there?

No one can be sure. But they graze there, scarcely lifting a head at traffic 250 yards away. I've photographed them through a wire fence which noisily heralds my presence when touched. Still, it is a familiar sound to them, and they go on about their business with little concern. Just being there when this occurs tell me something about elk: if their brains are not "computerized" with the details of meaningful past experience, then computers ought to be more like seasoned old bull elk.

Tracks, Wallows, Rubs

None of the foregoing is meant to suggest you should ignore elk sign of any sort whatsoever. Tracks, wallows, rubs, and so on, can lead you to off-season sightings and, of course, to haunts where elk might be found during the season. But you need to know how to interpret what you see. Granted that you can recognize a hoofprint four inches long or larger as that of an elk (mule deer prints almost never exceed four inches, and a much larger moose track is nearly identical to that of an unshod horse). But can you tell just how fresh it is? Ditto with droppings, rubs, et al?

Kneel down to examine all tracks closely. If tracks are sharply "etched" with thin ridges between the imprint and the surrounding mud or snow, they're fresh. An elk could have passed through within the previous 24 hours. In tracks that are a few days old, the effects of weathering tend to "round" those edges and dull

them. New prints will stand out in contrast with the background, while older ones begin to blend in.

The same is true of beds. If you are lucky enough to have new snow, an elk bed will be conspicuous by not containing as much snow as its surroundings. If the elk just vacated that bed in a snowstorm, you may not see any snow there at all, since body heat would have melted it. All of this is often overlooked by hunters who think the only thing to watch for is *Cervus* itself. Yet, I've seen many an elk quest turned into a tag-tying ceremony by hunters who took time to read the story on the ground.

In one instance, I had searched a mountain in vain for elk. Then I located some sharply delineated elk prints. They led to a patch of nearby spruces. I entered them with my rifle ready. The elk were standing there less than 50 yards away. In time I might have entered those conifers anyway, but would not have been so watchful and ready.

As for pellets (or manure if the animal has been on green food), they will appear moist and dark when fresh. When crushed slightly with your foot, they mash rather than crumble. After several days, they tend to grow dull black and hard-crusted, and will crumble when pressure is applied.

There are other ways to ascertain freshness. You can pry droppings apart with a knife to make an "acid test," but the appearance is usually enough. If there is snow on the ground, body heat carried by the pellet will melt a wide ring around the droppings. If it's still snowing but there's little around the pellet, you know the sign is relatively fresh.

Droppings which have a manure-like appearance are often incorrectly labeled as being from domestic livestock or moose. However, an elk on "soft" feed may pass along a "soft" signal: the animal has been feeding on rich, lush grass as opposed to brush or dried sedge. If you know where a grassy meadow is located, it is an excellent idea to ease carefully to its edge for a look.

When scouting, it is also wise to check among the elk messages for human footprints and other predator sign. Elk were here, but they departed. Why? Are the tracks close together, indicating an undisturbed animal merely moving about? Or are the hoofprints farther apart, with dirt kicked over the snow, showing a spooked creature?

As for rubs and wallows, I don't pay much attention to them unless they've been made in the past few weeks. The bull in rut which used the wallow or rubbed his antler velvet on a tree could be some distance away by now. Such signs do show that you are at least on the fringes of elk country, however, and tell you to be increasingly vigilant. Here, too, you can tell freshness of the sign by looking for the effects of weathering. If a thin strip of bark is blowing in the breeze on that sapling, it was probably stripped recently from the tree. New rubs have a look of wet brightness, either yellow or almost white. Old rubs will quickly turn dark brown or appear dry and stained. A bull that wants to rub velvet from antlers or do battle with something during the heat of the rut will commonly select a young tree about two or three inches in diameter. It is almost always one with pliable bark—soft rather than dry or hard.

Regarding wallows, the best clue to recent use is mud which is not hard or dried. At fresh wallows the banks and nearby vegetation will have a wetter look. A dried-up, dark-appearing mud bath simply means a bull was likely there during the late September, early October rut, and is of only token value. If you discover a wallow during the rut itself, the bull which used it is, of course, more likely to be somewhere nearby.

High Bull Ratios

Another thing to look for while scouting is a high bull-to-cow ratio. Even if you don't see the elk themselves, wallows, rubs, and the deeper and slightly larger tracks of heavier animals are indications of good bull populations. Ideally, you want to locate places where bulls comprise about 15 percent or more of the total elk herd. With deer, some areas seem to be frequented mostly by females of the species. But cow elk are warier than most doe deer, and anytime you find cow elk sign, you can strongly suspect the presence of antlered counterparts. For one thing, bulls often depend on cow sentinels.

Almost anywhere in elk country, you may occasionally run across shed bull antlers. Since they are lost in spring, however, the antlers only indicate that you are in a foothills wintering area (in many western mountains, winter lasts from late October to May); but it may also mean that in the fall wapiti might inhabit surrounding higher terrain. High-elevation antlers should be a definite alert. Just last hunting season I found a 5-point antler on a high, steep sage slope. The elk themselves were 400 yards up-trail in the nearest timber.

In all your looking, your primary goal should be to locate what some veteran hunters call "elk nests." These are the Mother Lode, preferred places to which elk are almost sure to return. Recently I found such a place. Even though elk were periodically moved away by hunters, they always returned within a few days. It was the type of place where elk find food and feel secure whether they actually are or not. Such a place might be spotted easily from some distance, even from a valley trail or road. Yet the elk feel comfortable in the lair, possibly because they can also see you or any movement from far away.

Such places often exist in quaking aspens. The animals' coloration approximates the tan tree trunks, but the careful scouter searches for horizontal forms against the vertical aspen trees. After the aspens have lost their crowning autumn foliage, peering into them, especially from above, is like looking into a bay window.

However, during scouting trips in summer or prior to hunting season, the quakies usually haven't yet shed their leaves. You will have to check the edges of those aspens morning and evening, or get in some looking later through bare branches if enough cold weather precedes the hunt.

Searching the aspens for "conspicuous" elk works best in the central and more southerly Rocky Mountain states; much of northern Wyoming, western Montana, eastern Idaho and mountains extending into Canada have few deciduous trees. Habitat here is sage and conifers. Let's examine some ways of probing this northern evergreen habitat. First, search for high, hidden pockets rather than large expanses of solid timber. In addition, difficult-to-reach conifers are less likely to have been bothered by people movement of any kind. Try to glass such isolated patches from a distance. Any elk pushed there from worked-over terrain are probably apprehensive, and can be prone to move again in a hurry. It is also true that peering into conifers is much more difficult than searching aspens. In fact, the only way you will know for certain what is in pine-fur-spruce timber is to penetrate it.

Ease in Gently

However, there is a special technique. First, never just begin walking in. Elk could be bedded or hiding there. They may tolerate a gentle approach, but bust in, and the elk won't look back over their shoulders at you—they will leap directly into flight. Take it easy! Peer in first.

I know one little patch of firs which always seems to have wapiti. The area is only several hundred yards square, yet even the most well-organized drives seem incapable of forcing game from this little Valhalla. Grass and browse grow profusely in much of this cover, and there's little reason for elk to leave it. Several guides and myself worked this fir slope for several years without getting anything out to waiting guns. We falsely concluded nothing was there.

Then one leisurely day I happened to be hunting it myself. I sat down. In time I noticed a badger I hadn't seen previously, and a couple of nut-gathering chipmunks. After eating a silent lunch, I thought I noticed antlers bobbing slightly where oak brush crowded the greenery behind. It was a nice muley buck with a delicately tined, symmetrical rack. This was a start. I hadn't noticed any deer here before. Finally, while glassing from a prone position beneath the firs, I made out the dark brown legs of elk. When I was able to move to a lower vantage point on the ridge, I realized these animals all fed as if the rest of the world wasn't there. For them, in effect, it wasn't.

I haven't yet located the bull in this forgotten pocket. But I know one is in there, for the cows were there during the late September rut. It's only a matter of time, and more unhurried scouting, before I find the bull. It's not just a matter of scoring, though. I want to figure out how all those elk, and the deer as well, managed to elude our every drive over the years. The knowledge might also pay off elsewhere—maybe in some arroyo or depression where the game lies low with steel-nerved confidence as hurried hunters pass by within a dozen yards or less. Why shouldn't elk get to like places like this? What about those lowland junipers no one hunts? Could there be bulls hiding in there?

Scouting builds confidence in many ways. A few years ago a friend of mine was hunting Montana's Bitterroot Mountains west of Superior. He didn't find elk at first. But he was absolutely certain he would. He had looked over this terrain from Missoula to the Idaho border; he knew where the elk had been previously. It was so bitter cold on this November day that many other nimrods had given up and headed for the indoor fireplace. My friend and his buddy felt like it, too. But they had in mind a certain little canyon where they had glassed elk on a previous visit. Knowing precisely where the game should be, they eased over a ridgeline on foot. Sure enough: after a few minutes of scrutiny, they spotted the forms of cow elk against the timber.

As the hunters attempted to approach more closely, a cow sensed their presence, barking an alarm. Head held typically high (some label it a super-alert posture), the sentinel cow trotted toward the heaviest timber. A bull not seen earlier then stood from his bed. The hunters were ready. There was time for only one shot, but it was enough.

When my friend returned with the thick-antlered 5-pointer, a few well-warmed licensees had the audacity to call it "luck." But luck has a way of joining those who scout for it.

In southern Utah, there's a persistent hunter and guide, Val Robb of Paragonah, who wouldn't take it at face value when many people said that elk transplanted near there "didn't take." No, he didn't find elk in the usual places, but he did find them in the vast juniper forests. In time, he led family members and others into some nice bulls. Of course, such places are not easy to hunt. But via extensive scouting, Robb knew when the season opened where the wapiti were.

Best Hunting Times

Some days are definitely better for hunting than others. My favorite weather situation is a cold day after a lengthy storm. Too often, hunters fail to take advantage of that condition. But you can prove its value to yourself in the off-season. Get out right after winds and uncomfortable drizzle cease. I know of instances in which the cook has ambled half a mile from camp to take elk that were suddenly on the move to overcome their empty bellies and cramped legs. You can also learn this lesson during the season itself, but your time is far too valuable then. There is no doubt in my mind that the best time for sighting game is any morning or evening following inclement weather, no matter how cold the temperature. The cold front that often follows a period of bad weather is frequently enough to keep most hunters in bed. But it is a glorious and usually fruitful time to be out.

This isn't to say that a licensee should hunt only on those ideal days. Sometimes perfect conditions don't occur during an entire week of hunting. But scouting long ago convinced me to sit out the windy or rainy days and be ready the second clearing begins. I've found elk likely to lay low during those times, too, seemingly as uncomfortable as man. They also lie low during heavy snowfall; but that's an excellent time to be hunting, because human sounds are muffled, and visibility isn't too bad unless the snow is quite heavy or the wind is blowing hard. More about that elsewhere.

Look for Water

You will want to know some other things ahead of time: Where are the waterholes elk might hie to in dry weather? With snow on the ground, or in a humid climate, elk can often go long periods without seeking open water. And if you are going to be hunting alone, try to discover where the elk will exit once you enter a patch of thick brush or timber. You'll hear the unmistakable crashing noise of panicked elk. Take note of their direction, and make adjustments come autumn. As elk flee, how can you get to the right ambush spot without making an elphantine racket yourself? Seek out the silent game trails, uncluttered slopes, and open areas that will let you get into shooting position.

An extremely wet summer will have a decided effect on elk come autumn. They won't need to move as far to find succulent grass or browse. The food may be actually inside cover. Elk will not venture into open meadows for a morning or evening fill. A few years ago a western state held a "game hearing" to determine where all the deer and elk went when hunts opened. After game biologists provided proof of numerous sightings of animals in cover from helicopters following the much-lamented fall, it was officially decided the game was there all the time. The animals just didn't have to leave cover as they had in past years.

One wonderful way to scout for elk is with a fish-and-game department hunting summary in your hands. Total harvest figures for a given area are not as important as hunter-success ratios. Total harvest can be increased by more hunting pressure, scarcely an elk hunter's goal. But if a unit which had only 10 percent success several years ago suddenly shoots up to 30 percent, you'll want to know the reasons. Was it the weather? Other factors can cause elk-hunting success to improve in any given spot—maybe an underharvest of available game, the very thing you are looking for.

Discussions with conservation officers and game wardens who are first-hand familiar with a "beat" are nearly as good as seeing the game with your own eyes. I can remember several wardens who could almost predict, under any given set of circumstances, which canyon or ridge would harbor elk at this very minute. Rather than calling such sources for a brief chat, try to meet them in person. They usually patrol large territories, and may welcome your going along with them on routine patrol. I've had many say they would "benefit from an extra pair of eyes," especially on assignments like sex-ratio counts, where elk seen are divided into bull, cow, and calf statistics. Such observations can be of great benefit to you later as a hunter.

Sporting-goods dealers, like chambers of commerce, may be "over-optimistic" about your elk-hunting chances or best places to try. Yet I've found them to be a melting pot of information, especially those who hunt avidly. I've found a few who are gold mines of information, having distilled gems of wisdom from their customers. It doesn't take long to determine if a dealer knows his stuff.

I avoid the guy who doesn't participate himself, not because he doesn't pick up some vital tidbits but because he doesn't know what to ask other hunters and probably doesn't remember the more important details.

Private-ranch "game managers" may also have a hotspot in mind for you, if you are willing to pay the price. Yet it is doubtful any would charge you to take a look around in the off-season to see just what type of sport they have to offer. Then you can decide if the cost is worth it.

Sheepherders seldom have any ax to grind. They just tell it like it is—if you can get them to talk at all. I remember one Basque, deep in elk country, who said nothing for a long time. When we had chatted idly, he suddenly offered more insight into his work.

"I love it here," he said. "Don't like to leave a beautiful place like this."

"Don't you ever get lonely for the city?" I asked.

"Went last week when I had three days off," he offered.

"And . . ."

"Stayed one," he answered.

"Well, why do you like it so much here? Do you see a lot of game, like elk maybe?" I ventured.

"All the time."

We were warming up.

"Where?" I pushed my luck.

He laughed, hesitated, then pointed at a small ridge several miles distant.

"Up there." He said that when he moved his sheep to and from the summer range, he always saw elk there. At the end of the conversation, he asked my partner and me if we would "put in a good word for him" with his employer, who lived in the same city we did. I told him we certainly would.

Such treasured tidbits save hours—nay, days—of searching in vain for restless elk. In addition, I don't merely "pump" for information. I made certain I did put in a good word for that sheepherder. And I know I can go back to him anytime for more clues on finding elk in his locality.

One sheepherder I became well acquainted with over several years, Wyoming and Utah's George Chournos, called me over one day to show elk movies he had made "on location." My spirits soared when George showed me mosshorn bulls he had photographed while tending sheep on a certain mountain range. I didn't have to hustle out there to check—he had done my scouting for me. He also opened my eyes to what coyotes and other predators can do to both lambs and elk calves in some areas.

Among my best sources of information, particularly for trophy heads, are veteran taxidermists. They know where the trophies are being taken. Rocky Vandersteen of Rock Springs, Wyoming, fits that category, and he is an avid trophy hunter himself. In my first conversation with him, he told of recently taking bulls scoring over 350 Boone and Crockett points almost beneath my nose. But since his hotspot was a continuous strip of high country 80 miles long and 20 wide, the name of the range alone did not do me much good. At first he wouldn't tell me any more details. Then I took an exploratory trip into those mountains, but did not locate the trophy-sized elk he spoke of. Thereafter, Vandersteen opened up considerably, talking of big bulls with some specificity. The reason, I believe, is that I had made an effort on my own—I had learned much of the country sufficiently to converse intelligently with him about it. I could ask the right questions.

One person who knows how to scout efficiently is Brent Chapman. He loves the wildernesses of his native Colorado and new home state, Idaho, and rides in occasionally just for another look at their grandeur and size. Most city dwellers have no concept of the depth and breadth of wildernesses like Idaho's River of No Return, Montana's Bob Marshall, Colorado's San Juan. But if you visit them as often as Chapman does, you come to realize a huge herd of African wildebeest could easily hide in one small corner. You begin to comprehend the magnitude of potential elk habitat in much of the West.

Here's Chapman's advice on how to scout for trophies: "The first thing is to get away from any sign of civilization. Do not make a thorough inspection for trophy bulls until you have accomplished this." Right there he has already weeded out the casual license-holder. "If you expect success in the fall, you will want to be busy in the summer." Chapman isn't talking idly—he has to his credit 19 bulls of four points per side or better, all taken in remote terrain.

Ranchers are a most valuable source of information. One in Idaho told me of a certain giant muley buck which continually avoided being sighted by hunters by using one stratagem repeatedly. The deer put his chin on the ground whenever danger approached.

"Have you seen elk in that area—and did they pull the same escape trick?" I asked him.

"Interesting you asked. I've seen elk in there at times, but the hunters who go into that canyon say they never do. However, they didn't see the buck either."

Now, I've got to see if the elk there are using the old buck's ploy. It died of old age last year, the rancher told me. One thing I'm sure of is that any hunter-wise bull is capable of "pattern-learning" whatever it takes to elude the masses. If such a bull isn't lying flat on the ground, he could be bedded in the heaviest oak or chokecherry bush. These are traits you'll want to know about ahead of rifle-toting time.

During the 1985 Wyoming hunting seasons I helped connect several deer hunters with bucks having antler spreads of more than 30 inches. Interestingly, elk were located in the same vicinity. After one huge buck was glassed across a canyon, the hunter and I devised a stalk designed to put him in shooting range above that deer. The stalk had one problem: it would put him near or into a herd of several hundred elk. Surely they would flee directly away from the hunter into the browsing deer. The wapiti were bedded on a rim overlooking a meadow, with the bottom of a glacial cirque behind them. The rim offered this hunter the only means of getting across the canyon and being above the quarry with any view at all.

My job was to circle the horses around to the south side of the mountain. There the nimrod would meet me at dusk. But since I had plenty of time to get there, I stayed put long enough to see what the elk would do at his approach. To my amazement, a cow which alerted the entire herd did not run away from the hunter. The other animals stood from their beds, milled and sniffed, then streamed directly toward an uphill gap . . . straight toward the would-be danger! This was fine for the hunter—the elk wouldn't spook his mule-deer target. But as he told me later, several huge bulls walked to within about a dozen yards of him.

At the time, we chalked it up to whimsical wind currents. Yet the hunter had made a great deal of noise in crunchy snow where he neared their ridgeline beds. I felt the elk must certainly have heard him. Apparently, the buck must have also, for it was not there when he arrived. So we returned next day to try once more. The elk were there a second time, and so was another band which had moved in from an eastern ridge. The hunter and I decided on the same course of action.

The elk repeated their flight toward the hunter just as they had done the day before! This day was calm and still, with no shifting air currents. A cow at the edge of the meadow traipsed ahead of the hunter into the bottom of the cirque. Elk stood nervously. And again they trotted toward the same upper gap, even though the hunter was in it. My only explanation is that the elk had entered this cirque through that gap, it was the pathway into more rough, remote terrain, and that's where they were predetermined to exit when any danger arrived. In any event, I made a mental note always to approach future elk from the direction of any uphill gap.

I didn't check those elk a third day. The hunter got his buck.

While this chapter has emphasized the importance of looking for elk in remote terrain, it shouldn't be assumed they can't ever be found near roads and easy trails. Sometimes they can. (No one loves that fact more than guides who have to haul out 700 to 1,000-pound bulls.) Locating elk near man's contrivances is seldom easy, but it's worth a shot. One day a skier I'd talked to about elk hunting told me that from the top of a certain ski lift he looked out over more than 100 elk. The fact that they were wintering there didn't pinpoint their autumn location, but the information proved useful. Next hunting

season a nice bull was taken in the first patch of heavy timber uphill from that ski terminal. It pays to never stop scouting.

Once during the off-season, I conducted an experiment to determine in my own mind whether elk see bright hues like fluorescent orange. I'm convinced they don't — under most circumstances. In this case my solid orange snowmobile suit against an open snowfield seemed to blend in. The elk detected my presence only when I moved. A cow let me walk within 60 yards and a 6-point bull let me get within 75 if I remained completely motionless in the snow every time they looked up from feeding. Yes, I was fortunate that no wind wafted about and no snow crunched beneath my feet. When the elk finally fled, it was because I walked in their direction while they stared directly at me.

I know of many elk guides who ask hunters to remove orange caps or vests when making a stalk. Some hunters insist on wearing checkered hunter orange or something else to break up the human outline. In timber this might work out very well, but in solid-background situations like open snow, I'll go with the coloration which works for me. I see no reason to shun the bright colors, which are now required by the game laws of most states. I believe the important thing is how and where the colors are deployed. You can do your own experimenting, but I have no qualms at all about wearing fluorescent orange while elk hunting.

If you're a serious elk hunter, scouting doesn't cease even when you're enjoying a day in camp. In one camp, a spotting scope was set up near the kitchen door. Everyone took an occasional look. One morning after a new snowstorm, a hunter happened to check the scope. In it a high-racked bull stood silhouetted atop a ridgeline three-quarters of a mile away. The following day, two small bulls could be seen browsing toward the bottom of the mountain. The wapiti season opened a few days later. By then we had a bead on our quarry.

Another time, while fishing on a summer day, I was struck by the thought that elk ought to reside somewhere on the upper end of that mountain lake. I strolled off the beaten lakeside trail to check a few nearby slopes. Nothing. But one bluff looked promising. I started off a point directly into the thickest cover. Suddenly, it exploded with elk. Noting which way all exited, I learned what to expect here the following hunting season.

That's scouting: knowing what to expect, when it counts the most. It's the key to success. It's simply hunting without toting your rifle.

10

Scoring on the Practice Range

An elk hunt, like most other hunts, begins on the practice range. All the preparations, money, licenses, guides, time, hard work, and patience do little good if you can't shoot. While this may seem obvious, it is surprising how many sportsmen leave marksmanship at least partly to luck.

Yet it is the one and only non-variable. If you stop to think about it, everything other than shooting accuracy depends in some way on an unknown—from game movement to weather visibility. But when it comes to your rifle, you control your own destiny.

At least you *can*, with the right approach. Think of the hours with the paper target as part of the hunt itself. It is. Do everything here as you will on the hunt. And when do you start preparing for next fall's quest? The day after your last hunt ends.

Storing your rifle in the right place, for example, can be one of the most important things you will do for shooting accuracy. In nearly 40 years of big-game hunting, I've had my scoped rifle not shoot where I aimed it on only two occasions. One was when my horse somersaulted down a mountain, tossing the rifle out of its scabbard. The other was when I stored my rifle in an unheated camper. Each time, I had to make a trip to a gunsmith, then spend time on the practice range to recover accuracy. In one instance I did, in time to bag a bull elk. In the other, I missed a massive 6-pointer at 350 yards that I might have had.

Avoid storing a rifle in any place which could sustain excessive changes of temperature. Keep it in a dry place to avoid moisture and possible corrosion.

If you do this, can you be certain your

firearm will shoot with precision? It should. But don't bank on it. If you did not continually check accuracy through the winter via rabbit, varmint, or predator hunting, do not wait for late summer or early autumn to get on the practice range. Do so early enough that if any problems have developed, you can work them out. In addition, gunsmiths don't want to see you in September nearly as much as in June or July.

Before heading for the rifle range, gather the following, in addition to rifle and ammo: lubricating oil, a target large enough to see at long ranges up to maximum flat trajectory of your particular rifle, masking tape to cover bullet holes (even a pencil to "eyebrow" the holes is better than nothing), some of the padded clothing you will wear on the actual hunt, cap, cotton or earplugs, and most important, an open mind.

Now let's take a look at what you do with the above. Make certain the rifle breech and bolt (or action) are lubricated with oil. (Avoid putting any grease on the firing pin, however, as it could jam or slow the pin in cold weather.) It is uncanny how a cartridge can stick if not loaded uniformly tight, yet a film of oil will always assist in feeding ammunition through smoothly.

Before setting out your target, estimate the distance to the spot where you will place it. This doesn't take any extra time, and will help you later in calculating distance to game. Estimate in multiples or parts of a 100-yard football field. After you have guessed distance to the paper target, pace it off. Estimating accuracy can be helped by walking an empty football field, or noting markers when playing golf.

Before shooting, make sure the range is a safe one. You could be here for a while,

and you don't want to quit partway through. It can spoil your concentration. Don't settle, either, for the local 100-yard small-bore range. You'll need at least 350 yards. So if necessary, take half a day and drive into the country.

Also make certain you have covered any previous holes in the target before placing it out. You want no guesswork about where you are hitting right now.

Sitting Is Most Practical

Practice getting into the same shooting position you will use later on the hunt. Drilling over sandbags from the prone posture is wonderful for fine-tuning your rifle. But you will find that prone doesn't allow you to see even over average sagebrush. So work out a comfortable and stable sitting position, for the very good reason that it is the most practical posture of all.

Here is how I acquire mine. After dropping into a "quick sit" with feet pointed slightly to the right of my target, I face the target itself. I brace my left elbow on the inside of my left knee. My right elbow is just below my right knee. My elbows are not locked, but they are firmly wedged into a solid foundation for my rifle. As I lean slightly forward, my rifle butt is braced well into my shoulder. Infantry rifle training outlines such procedure, but you should squirm into your own most comfortable and stable position.

All this time, of course, the rifle remains on safety. You must, however, be able to locate the safety quickly. Since the day fumbling cost me a massive 4-point buck, my thumb knows where the safety is. I've never fumbled for it since.

Frequent shooting can be hard on your hearing, so bring earplugs or cotton (or wear your cap with ear flaps down).

The importance of the last item on the list, an open mind, cannot be overemphasized. A few years ago I fired a certain airgun at a three-day county-fair shooting contest sponsored by the National Guard. I was happy to learn on the final day that my score was tops in a category with elk guides, varmint shooters, and "mountain men." But up strode a man who fired the same airgun several times, looked at his score, and tossed the gun down in disgust. "Damned thing shoots high!" he roared, and stalked off. As a matter of fact, if held steadily at the bottom of the bull, it printed right in the 10-point target center.

There have been times when I, too, would have liked to blame the rifle. But if we possess an open mind, and the courage to believe what the print marks on the target tell us, we know when we must do better. Even if the rifle adjustment is off, it is we, not the firearm, who are temporarily at fault. It can't make adjustments on its own, so we must.

I've seen rifle-toters explode a magpie in the field and take it as proof they are "right on." But the target is often no more than 50 yards away. Can we cut a group no more than several inches apart at distances up to 300 or 350 yards, maximum "reach-out" range of our rifle?

If your target is a military or police type with point-value circles (10 for bull, 9 for closest ring, 8 next, etc.), so much the better. As you check the point of impact on target, you can measure it as on a vertical clock — say, No. 9 at 2 o'clock, and so on.

Sighting-in Methods

Now let's talk about the actual sighting-in process. Some say shoot at 25 yards and you'll know where you are shooting at 225. That is roughly true, as the line of sight (above the rifle muzzle) and the line of fire (through the muzzle itself) first intersect at about 25 yards, and do so again at 225. Browning's traditional explanation is: "A bullet leaving a slightly upward-pointing barrel must pass through the line of sight twice. The first is while traveling up, the other as gravity pulls it down. This second time is the point at which it is zeroed in or sighted in." However, there is one asterisk on the matter. If you are slightly low and left on the bull's-eye at 25 yards, the error is multiplied by nine times at 225 (9 x 25 = 225). You'll also want to shoot at the longer ranges to make absolutely certain of accuracy. And if you miss at 25? Warn your wife or mother you could be late for supper.

You will also want to shoot more than one round per sitting, at least over the greater distances. I like to shoot two, giving me a pattern. After all, a slight flinch on one shot could lead you astray in making sight adjustments. Ballistics experts point out that if you aim right at the bull at 25 yards, and hit it, you should be about three inches high at 100 yards in order to be right on at 225. It's not that the slug "rabbit hops" up and down; it simply lines out straight until gravitational pull brings it down sufficiently at about 225 yards to intersect with your aim through the sights. Thus, zeroing in for 225 makes much sense. It is also an excellent compromise range for deer which you might see at, say, 150 yards and elk at 300. After all, there's no use sighting in differently every time you hunt a different species when the trajectory (bullet path) is relatively flat up to the 225-yard sighting-in range.

How to adjust your sights for, say, a No. 6 ring at 10 o'clock? The rule is that you always move the rear sight, or scope sight adjustments, in the direction you want to shoot. With the No. 6 ring at 10 o'clock, let's say you are four inches left and two inches high. You must move the windage (left-right) knob on your scope enough clicks to the right to bring you home again. If you are calibrated at one-half inch per click (listen carefully with each slight twist of the knob), you will need eight of them. Then you will need four clicks down on the elevation knob. That should do it. Shoot two more times at the same range to make sure. When you see the bullets print where they should, try two at longer ranges. This may seem superfluous, but it will bolster your shooting confidence to see the print marks where they should be. Incidentally, always remember your sight picture — where you were holding when the gun fired — and compare it with your shot. The reasons will be fully explained later.

There is another, simpler way to sight in, a one-shot technique. Aim carefully for the bull, and when checking the print mark, circle it in heavy pen or bright crayon. Return to your station, and hold the scope exactly on the bull just as you did before. No matter where you shot, do the following: *While still holding the scope on the bull's-eye*, adjust the windage and elevation knobs to the point where you *actually* printed. Thus you have moved from where you aimed to where your rifle is, in reality, shooting.

Longer Distances

Now let's suppose you are a practical elk hunter, and you want to shoot accurately beyond the range at which you zeroed in — i.e., past 225 up to the maximum shooting efficiency of your rifle. By this, I mean the distance at which you can shoot your specific rifle, plus ammo (both grain weight and shape of slug), and expect a hit

without holding over the target. For example, the accepted standard depth of a deer's chest is 18 inches. For elk it is more like 24 inches. If you held on the backbone of a big bull with your 270 Winchester or 7 mm. Remington Magnum at, say, 400 yards with a 150-grain slug, with the rifle sighted in for 200 yards, would you have a hit?

Let's check a Remington Arms ballistics table for the above and find out. The 270 drops 29.2 inches over that range, so the answer is "no." With the 7 mm. Remington Magnum it's "yes": the cartridge has a flatter trajectory, falling 22.7 inches. By comparison, the Springfield 30-06 dips 25.0 inches. As you can see, the average gunner is not going to connect at that range with the first and third rifles, but the 7 mm. is in the ballpark. So why doesn't every hunter use a 7 mm. Remington Magnum? For me the answer is: I know my 30-06 much better.

The point is, a bullet plummets so rapidly after 350 yards that ballistics experts advocate shooting only up to that range. A shooter with the right rifle who really knows what he is doing might connect at longer distances — by holding steadily in the air space over an elk's back. But basically, anyone sighting game beyond 350 should seriously consider stalking closer, or returning the next day. A special shooter — one who spends many hours on the practice range — could with the 270 or 30-06 strike the lower portion of an elk's chest from 400 yards with a shot held about seven inches over the back; but since the vital heart-lungs area is not found at the very bottom of the chest, make it 10 inches over to be sure. Without that, the 270 would strike 5.2 inches below the target (29.2-inch bullet drop on a 24-inch target means 5.2 inches under). Moving 10 inches higher would allow hitting 4.8 inches above the bottom of the chest. However, it should be remembered there isn't much room for error, considering an elk's heart-lung area measures little more than 10 x 10 inches.

Obviously, just shooting somewhere "way over the animal," as some nimrods boast around the campfire, is not specific enough to get the job done. Heart shots at 600 yards are myths or, at the very least, far more luck than shooting savvy. As for the worry of "wind deflection," it is mostly an idle worry. If wind is gusting heavily, forget about shooting entirely because it will probably unsteady your aim and your concentration. Most mountain breezes won't affect bullet placement. One chart (in Jack O'Connor's "Complete Book of Hunting") shows that a 180-grain 30-06 slug will "drift" a grand total of .52 of an inch at 100 yards with a 10-mile-per-hour wind. Of course, this figure varies with various muzzle velocities, but amounts to only a few inches even at 300 yards with any elk rifle. The main thing is, if you compensate for wind, don't overdo it. Aiming accurately with confidence is far more important.

What about best grain weights? Many hunters swear by 180 for elk. Since I like to stay with one bullet weight from the practice range to the hunting field, I use 150-grain for everything from antelope to elk and moose. That way I don't have to worry about trajectory differences on each. The 150-grain also possesses an advantage in that it shoots a slightly flatter trajectory than the 180. In 30-06 it isn't much difference: the 180 drops 9.5 inches more than the 150 at 400 yards. But if that is added to the aforementioned 25-inch drop (making 34.4 inches in all), it can be a significant difference! But won't you get more "shock" power in the heavier slug? A little. Plus more recoil. But I don't put much stock in shock power if I can't hit the game.

Many debates are sparked about where to aim. An elk is big enough so that at close range you might go for the neck or even the head. However, on a trophy, a head shot can splinter an antler. I've felled elk, and witnessed them downed with shots to the neck and the backbone. But the surest shot is to the chest or shoulder (just behind the front leg) where heart-lungs is located. When hit there, an elk will sometimes move on, but rarely very far or fast. As mentioned, the heart-lungs target area is a relatively large 100 square inches. Even if hit near there, the animal's blown-up arteries and vital organs will slow him down. Hitting aft of the shoulder usually means a long day ahead, since elk are creatures of stamina and determination. More about tracking them later.

Best Elk Rifles

Now we enter one of the most sacrosanct arenas of all, the perfect elk rifle. To me, it is the one you shoot accurately. Obviously, the 7 mm. Remington Magnum and the 270 so popularized by *Outdoor Life* magazine's late shooting editor Jack O'Connor have solid advocates. Some lengthy pieces have been penned about which is best. I have used the 30-06 (30 caliber, introduced in 1903 and redesigned in '06) long enough and happily enough to have full faith in it. Use the caliber and model you are most familiar and successful with. End of debate.

As for some of the old-time, oft-championed (and often romanticized) firearms like the 30-30, chances are the ballistics charts will rule them out for elk at longer

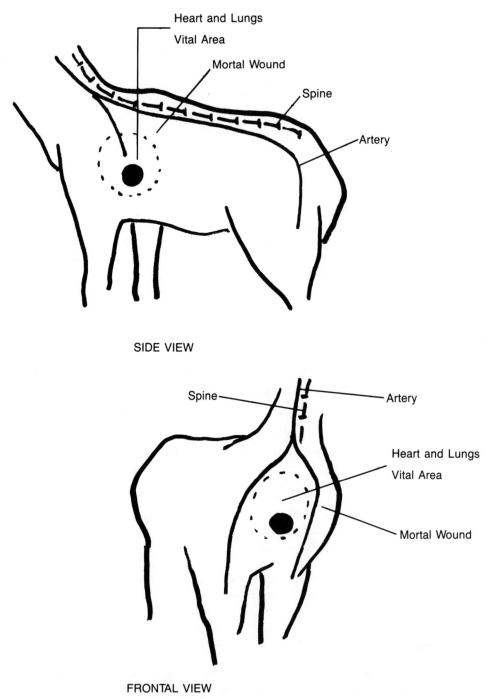

Heart and Lungs
Vital Area
Mortal Wound
Spine
Artery

SIDE VIEW

Spine
Artery
Heart and Lungs
Vital Area
Mortal Wound

FRONTAL VIEW

Where to aim, side and front, to hit vital areas on elk.

ranges. Ditto the 30-40 Krag, one of the big-game rifles most utilized years ago. A check of the trajectory tables shows clearly it won't hold up beyond 250 yards.

On choosing any rifle, consider weight. Anything weighing over 7½ pounds can get unduly heavy by the third mile.

Style is up to you. Lever actions are "macho" Old West, but bolt action is considered a trifle more accurate than any of the others.

Then there are the velocity figures, in feet the bullet travels per second. But again, even an elephant gun cannot outdo the one you have practically slept with on the rifle range. I don't recommend doing so, but a friend recently pole-axed a mountain lion with his trusty 22 with one well-placed shot behind the ear. Many ranchers I know dispatch cows with nothing but a 22.

Sooner or later you'll come up against the handloader who says his personalized ammo is superior to your factory loads. After shooting both types, I would have to agree with him. But if you are not into handloading expertise, modern commercial ammunition is certainly accurate enough—if you are. I also used to practice with the GI (Korean, Vietnam, war surplus) ammo, and still use it on rabbits. It was cheap. It is now very hard to get. If you ever get your hands on it, however, be sure also to practice with regular loads just prior to the hunt. The light, army "practice" ammo doesn't shoot precisely where your elk loads do.

Scope Accuracy

Let's suppose you have never fired your scoped rifle. How do you get the most from this hunting tool? Is the scope better than iron sights?

Browning Company's firearms catalogue includes the following elements of scope superiority: more detailed view of the target with greater magnification, a reticle superimposed over the target instead of covering it, focus is faster on one object (rather than having to align rear and front sights plus target), light-gathering properties, and safer to use because it magnifies the background beyond the target.

If you're buying a scope, favor one with a fine reticle made by an established firm.

When it comes to shooting a scoped rifle, I like to snuggle my right (shooting) eye up to the eyepiece (some texts say keep both eyes open—take your choice), turning my variable 2-7X scope to five power. (We assume your scope is properly mounted and won't cause a headache or, worse, a cut eye as you pull in close and fire.) Four power is also a practical setting. A popularity poll conducted by one outdoor magazine indicated that 4X setting is most preferred. I started with 5X on the range, so I stay with it. I don't recommend that beginners go with 12 to 18X, since the field of view is so limited that they will have difficulty locating the target itself. I'd save such high settings for distant, small targets like chucks and other varmints that will sit still for the shooter. Whatever you shoot in practice, remember the sight picture on shots that punch the paper properly. You'll want to repeat it later when the paper is replaced by game.

Iron sights? I'll leave them to the old-timers who think they are too far past prime to change. After obliterating the target way out there with the front bead a few times, and squinting in the dusk to merely see, I'll take the delicate crosshairs of a good scope anytime. Yet I'll admit that I switched reluctantly. For the first two years I owned a scope, I left it in my gun closet. One reason was the so-called inability of a scope to pick up close targets, like game coursing directly toward you. That happens infrequently; but it can be cured with a few sessions on close-range rabbits. Of course, when you're expecting nearby game—perhaps a wounded animal—turn your scope down to 2X to get a wider field of vision.

Far or near, practice focusing your scope upon various objects like a rock or clump of dark sage. While you wait for an elk to show is a great time to practice "finding" objects in a hurry. At first you may have a tendency to "throw your eyes" too far left or right, up or down, but again, practice makes perfect. Then, when the biggest bull you ever saw shows, you can find him in the crosshairs without delay.

The Shooting Touch

Shooting confidence at any range comes only with seeing, time after time, your cartridge hole out in or near the bull's-eye. In time, you will have firmly in mind an expectation of positive results even as you take up a shooting position. As you line up the crosswires on a target, do this: take in a full breath, and release part of it; flip off the safety, and place the finger gently on the trigger so as to take up slack. Begin a steady squeeze.

Experts realize the importance of gentle trigger pressure, and practice it in the off-season by "dry firing." Rifle manufacturers agree it won't hurt your rifle.

Before shooting, make certain you have done everything to stabilize aim. Utilize your rifle sling if desired (make this decision ahead of the hunt, and learn to engage the sling quickly); or brace the rifle against a tree stump, rock, fence, etc., but cushion the hard object with coat, cap or

something similar. Some hunters mount a folding tripod under the rifle muzzle.

As you seek out the best sight picture, avoid canting or "tipping" the view. Try to obtain the same, square sight picture on every shot you take.

Should you use a rangefinder, which "calibrates" where to hold on the game? I've never used one, so I can't very well advise. But I will say this: I've never found any need for one. Satisfactory range estimates can be quick, given practice. If a range-estimator works for you, fine.

Mental Approach

Up until now, most of your actions have been mechanical. But sharp shooting is as much psychological as physical. I always envision myself "slipping" the slug into an animal, never "blasting" it. The former gives me more of a delicate touch. I want to release the trigger, not slam it. The mind picture also helps me maintain concentration on holding the crosshairs steady. I don't want to think of myself as firing a cannon. I might flinch at the recoil. Instead, I want to think of the "kick" as merely a prod against the shoulder. Try to visualize such a nudge, even if the rifle does indeed kick hard.

The foregoing also helps with follow-through. Even though the slug has left the muzzle by the time you feel the rifle discharge, follow-through is as necessary in shooting as it is in golf and other sports. Keep an eye on the target until it is no longer possible to do so. That way you don't look up too quickly "to see where you hit." More times than not, you can see an animal a lot better when it is down than when it is running off untouched. One or two cartridges is likely all you'll actually need, if you know what to do with them.

In time, you may learn to shoot with the speed (well, almost) of an Olympic biathlon champ. You steady the hold and squeeze almost simultaneously. Tell yourself that if you do your stuff, the rifle and ammo will do theirs. When the hunt arrives, you have a deadly combination.

If you need personalized assistance, join your local gun club. Publications such as those of the National Rifle Association can also help you. Whatever it takes, make accurate shooting as much an automatic reaction as possible.

More Difficult Shots

To be sure, some shots are more difficult than others. I would rather shoot at an elk standing broadside at 300 yards against a snowy backdrop than one on the lam at a fourth that distance. Some shooting texts say never fire at a running animal. Balderdash! You can learn to hit running game, but it won't happen by accident. It will happen on the practice range. Get a friend to find a safe place where he can roll a tire surrounding a cardboard target down an incline and then step safely behind a ridge.

Incidentally, make certain you include the cardboard. The tire's rubber itself will close around your slug, and you won't find the hole. As you see the tire bounce downhill, you will have a strong inclination to hurriedly snap off a shot. Resist the temptation. It is a waste of energy, time, and money! You must move the muzzle *with* the target as you aim, and follow through.

Moving your scope at the same speed as the target requires practice. Pretend you are merely observing through binoculars, and slip off the trigger when aligned on target. Keep the scope moving until you can no longer see the tire due to rifle discharge. Later, when you are shooting at moving game, avoid tension by emphasizing the same skills learned on the rifle range. Concentrate on the technique rather than the prize to be won.

I remember once missing a shot I felt I should have had. With my first antelope hunt coming up, I geared for hours to the speedier challenge—the pronghorn runs much faster than a deer. Only after gaining confidence on rolling tires did I go antelope hunting. Several respectable pronghorn bucks wheeled off a mesa into the prairie nearby. I followed the lead buck carefully, not wanting to hit a lesser animal behind him. At 150 yards, with the target speed an estimated 40 miles an hour, I "slipped" off a 150-grain 30-06 slug. I couldn't tell where it landed until the dust cleared. It landed in the pronghorn's heart, thanks to the long bout with rolling tires. The story of that hunt and its preparation ran in *Field & Stream* a decade ago.

While elk rarely run as rapidly as antelope, elk do tend to lunge or jump like pogo sticks, often making a tougher target than the roller-skates-smooth antelope. A wise old bull will also head for the nearest cover, so you haven't got as long to shoot. But there again, tires released on steep, rocky terrain giving way to brush will provide needed practice.

How much lead do you need to give the moving target? Well, a 30-06 has a muzzle velocity of about 2,700 feet per second in the oft-used 180-grain cartridge. Suppose the elk is running left to right 200 yards away at nearly top speed, 30 miles an hour. This is the same as 44 feet per second. According to ballistics charts, one-fourth second is required for our slug to travel 200 yards. And in that one-fourth second, the elk will have moved one fourth of 44 feet, or 11 feet. Since a bull elk is about nine feet long, it is obvious we must aim a little more than one body length ahead to score. However, we must also be certain we swing the muzzle with the animal's flow.

If we have accurately estimated the animal's range, the rest is physics.

No, there isn't any quicker or easier formula. But drilling on tires (then perhaps graduating to jackrabbits) can make it happen. Stay with it, and you'll make some shots you never thought possible at first.

There are other difficult shots, including steep uphill and downhill (gravitational pull on a vertical plane is not the same as on a horizontal one). Trajectory is flatter when you shoot up or down, so bullet drop will be less. And if your previous shooting has been over relatively flat terrain, the more vertical angles will tend to encourage shooting high.

The rifle range will tell a hunter what he can and cannot do. After a few tries at long ranges from the standing position, he learns never to stand if he can kneel, and never to kneel if he can sit. You come to know so well what you can do that instant decisions on the hunt come much easier. Rather than tossing lead after a fleeing elk from an awkward non-sitting position, it's better to tell the buddies at camp you had no shooting at all. As a guide, I've heard enough bragging that I now listen politely . . . yet pay no attention to anything much beyond results. A man who admits to problems when he has them will also get some help, while the one who thinks he is Daniel Boone and Jim Bridger combined will probably get none until it's too late in the hunt to do anything about it.

Confidence and Sights

Many hunters lose confidence in their rifles and scopes with the slightest jar dur-ing the horse trip in, or after a slip afoot on a snowy hill. Did the bump knock their scope off zero? Should they re-sight to make sure?

I've seen scoped rifles fall from camper beds four feet onto the floor and still hold their zero. (Of course, the padded gun cases undoubtedly helped.) I've witnessed a scope with so much cracked glass in it (from a hunter's fall on an icy slope) that he could scarcely see the crosshairs, yet it continued to fire true. Scopes are jostled and scraped while in scabbards on horses. Naturally, you try to prevent such mis-cues. But they are not as serious as, for example, extreme fluctuations of temperature. If you have misgivings which could undermine your confidence, re-check zero if at all possible.

If absolutely necessary, shoot at a natural feature on the hunt itself "just to be sure." But try to avoid spooking game by shooting on the eve of the hunt or during periods when there is no other rifle fire.

There are times, though, when you have a major disaster, such as having a rifle thrown from a horse. Once, when that happened to me, I shot the rifle at a fry-ing-pan-sized depression of water, noted the welcome splash, hiked another mile, and dispatched a nice bull with a long shot. It wouldn't likely have happened if I hadn't convinced myself on a makeshift "rifle range" that the rig was still shooting as accurately as before.

Role of the Gunsmith

One day on the drill range I discovered my rifle shooting high. Fortunately, there was time to get to a gunsmith before the hunting rush began. While shooting, I also decided my trigger had too much slack in it. I had to hold too long before getting the shot off smoothly. Frank Mitchell of Montpelier, Idaho, didn't have what he needed on hand to make a replacement, but he ordered for me. Getting the part took nearly a month, so it was a good thing I hadn't left this matter until August. But between the gunsmith and myself we got the rifle shooting where it once did—with trigger slack to my individual taste.

Another time, I had to take my rifle to the gunsmith three days before the elk season opened. As previously mentioned, I was out deer hunting when my horse slid down a snowy slope, the rifle catapulting out of the scabbard. There seemed to be no visible damage, but the piece was soon discovered to shoot high. However, the major question was: had the barrel been pushed out of alignment? After lengthy examination, Mitchell didn't think so. Yet the only way I could be certain it would not "cartwheel" slugs was to shoot it. The scope was altered to reach zero as before. Then I went to the range again. After more than a box of cartridges printed as they had prior to the mishap, I was convinced. With this assurance in mind, I bushwhacked a nice bull which hesitated for a second at 275 yards. I doubt he would have been mine if I hadn't regained confidence in the scope and rifle.

Mitchell's philosophy as a gunsmith is similar to that of a good guide: "It's your shooting program. Tell me what you want. I'll do whatever I can to get it for you. It is your money. You're entitled to get things the way you want them."

Overcoming the "Fever"

Before we leave the rifle range, let's take a look at so-called "buck fever." The best cure for it is shooting practice. It also helps to look at enough elk racks during the year so you are not overawed by them on the hunt. But you must rely on previous rehearsal. If you are confident that you drilled well enough during the week, you'll think of that as you shoot, not the terrible importance of making the kill. No basketball coach has a player do layups under the basket all week, then instruct him during the game to shoot only three-point attempts from way out. Drill on the range for what could be required later—then repeat when it counts. The physical process is no different in the field than it was in the practice arena. You just sit down, take a deep breath, push off the safety, take up the slack in the trigger . . . and respond automatically rather than think about the trophy.

Buck fever is a big enough subject that we'll look at the malady again in this book from time to time. But remember this: there is seldom any shame in it. If the time arrives when you don't grow excited at seeing a high rack of elk antlers, it is time to take up something more tranquil—like dominoes.

Summing up, the practice range is not always warmly embraced, possibly because the work done there is rarely translated into immediate reward. Yet it is a key to all future success. Whether your gun is fancy or plain, you must prove you can use it when it counts.

11

Are You Really Ready?

Recently I asked a man who had killed more than 40 elk what he considered the most important tip he could give a newcomer about hunting elk. He told me: "Make sure you are dressed properly."

"Why?"

"Because you rarely find elk in a few minutes. And if you aren't dressed right, you won't stay at it long enough to succeed."

I didn't argue. In three consecutive years of guiding and hunting for elk, I ran the full gauntlet of weather conditions. In the first year, we hunted out of a middle-elevation cabin where a large barrel stove could remain burning most of the night. Add a log or two in the morning, and the one-room cabin warmed hurriedly. After a hot breakfast, we were on the trail. If it rained or blew, hunters could return anytime they wanted to instant rustic luxury.

Things were not like that the following

year. Our outfitter told the guides to prepare well, for we were to open a new tent camp 2,500 feet higher and eight miles from the nearest road. It was a pleasant enough place — in the summer. But in the shadow of a 10,100-foot mountain, which blocked out morning sunshine, even the days were cold during hunting season. Nights fell below zero. We would have to build a horse enclosure and a wooden latrine to satisfy the U.S. Forest Service. We had to do many other things to ensure the comfort of our hunters as well as ourselves.

Our outfitter told incoming clientele of the great game country they would be hunting, but "to come completely ready for harsh weather conditions."

I had just spent two nights in very wet weather. But now we would be spending two weeks away from civilization, and I made doubly certain I was ready for the worst that nature could offer. It was a good thing I did. Nature threw everything imaginable at that elk hunt. Temperatures fell to more than 30 below zero at night, and by day, rain, fog, and eventually two feet of snow challenged our preparation. Yet I was never uncomfortable for any length of time.

There were restrictions, however, on what we could carry in via horse pack. Below is listed, item by item, valued paraphernalia I take along on such trips.

Clothing

Elk hunters are well advised to dress in layers. The idea is that clothes can be peeled off as a cold day grows warmer. And layered clothing traps warm air inside. Of course, riding a horse (or sitting on a high ridge) can be much, much colder than any hiking anywhere. If you'll be riding to far destinations and then waiting for game, there is only one way to go: inside layers covered with a padded or quilted snowmobile suit.

I have one in blaze ("hunter") orange. The zippers work. It keeps body heat in (even at midwaist, where two-piece clothing does not) and the wind out. Even with that, I may wear a pair of extra pants, with North Woods-type wool shirt (wool is warm even when wet or moist) and a sweater. I like a shirt with a collar which can keep wind and sunburn off my neck. A scarf or muffler can also do a wonderful job. I do care how I look, but not at the expense of being cold. I also like a vest (mine is a hunter-special Ten-X brand), which keeps the torso warm. It is orange on one side, so I can also wear it as an outer garment. Where the law allows, as in bowhunting, I can turn the camouflage side out to aid in stalking. I also buy checkerboard orange clothing. There is no

doubt in my mind that elk and deer in timber are less likely to notice a mottled pattern than a solid color.

If it is not brutally cold in the morning, I wear the foregoing with a down-filled windbreaker outside instead of the snowmo outfit. As I shed layers at midday, I can place them near the return trail or tie them around my waist. I can also put them in a saddlebag or vehicle if available. I always keep a rain poncho in either of those places or, if hiking, in my coat pocket. I never use a nylon ski parka, even though it is perfect for inclement weather. The reason? Too much rustle against whatever it touches. Shake any potential clothing to determine if it is quiet before buying or wearing. Also check zippers and snaps. Their noise isn't necessarily fatal — if you keep your hands away from them while hunting.

If I'm going to be hiking most of the day, I know I can sacrifice some warmth while on the move. However, I must be prepared for the full impact of cold temperatures and/or wind when I stop. If rain (snow is not as much of a problem) is a possibility in early fall when temperatures are well above freezing, wool is an excellent garment. According to the American Wool Council, when a dry article of wool clothing is worn in a wet or even moist outdoor atmosphere, the material absorbs water vapor from the air, "and in a physiochemical process, heat is produced. The heat prevents the surface of the wool garment from cooling too rapidly, and thus helps maintain body warmth." In addition, "wool sections are spirally twisted around each other . . . so each fiber stands away from the others. Air trying to move through the fabric clings to fiber surfaces, and the air becomes trapped. . . . The dead air in the fabric acts as an insulator."

Wool's absorbency is also a factor in the

warmth of the fiber. The human body is constantly exuding moisture vapor and heat. Water in fabric is a high conductor of heat; wool not only helps keep cold out, but body heat in. Wool can soak up as much as 30 percent of its weight in moisture before it begins to feel damp. Even then, it does not feel clammy. Conclusion: you can't go far wrong by bundling up against the cold in traditional wool clothing.

This advice isn't meant to rule out modern super synthetics. Gore-Tex is the trade name of a "wonder fabric" that cold-weather experts are championing these days. Gore-Tex is waterproof and windproof, thus keeping the wearer dry and warm in even the most inclement elk-hunting weather. The fabric contains a type of membrane that "has nine million pores per square inch," according to manufacturers. Water and wind can't get through pores that small, but your perspiration can get out to let the skin "breathe." No wonder magazine articles have extolled Gore-Tex to the skies.

Nonetheless, I'm going to let you in on a concern of many elk guides. They say that Gore-Tex in an outer garment during an actual elk stalk isn't totally noiseless and that the same wonderful research that went into this synthetic fabric needs to be duplicated in the "quiet department." Many retailers say the same.

Always check out each individual garment for your own elk-hunting requirements. Before using any material, rub it against your arm or other clothing to see if it rustles noticeably. If you hear it, elk certainly will. Further improvements, of course, may make Gore-Tex even more "elk proof," so check it out to your personal satisfaction.

Gore-Tex is also used to make lightweight, waterproof footwear, headgear,

and gloves. All are popular with hunters because they are warm and dry, with less problem of noise than a coat or vest. I heartily recommend Gore-Tex snow-pack-type footwear. Whatever the material used, you will want to pay special attention to body extremities in extremely cold weather, even if you must pay extra for the protection.

Many other fabrics are light and warm when dry. But some won't let perspiration escape (you are likely to sweat profusely at some time during an elk hunt). Some down-fills lose loft and insulating abilities when wet, although it would take a pretty consistent downpour to completely affect the fluff. The worst part of down-filled clothing for hunting can be the noisy outer fabrics.

There are several ways to go. DuPont has a new product known as "Hollofil," which insulates well in light, thin clothing and isn't a "soaked duck" when wet. Another recent innovation is "Thinsulate," a filler of tightly compacted fibers that have many advantages skiers are utilizing on high slopes. It is as warm as goose down, but without its bulk.

If weather is particularly wet, I keep tied on my saddle what is called a "stockman's" outfit. It consists of a two-piece rubberized rain slicker with hood and a pair of pants which can be donned or shed easily. They are dry and warm — but too heavy and hot for long-distance hiking. The "rain suit" doesn't hinder reining in a horse, but it is a little bulky and cumbersome to wear while shooting an elk.

These outfits come in colorful yellow or orange hues, so you can legally hunt with them in most states. Their main duty is to help you survive a monsoon or thunderstorm. I don't care as much about getting wet while coming in to camp as going out. I absolutely do not want to arrive at any elk hunting hotspot too cold and wet to concentrate on the challenge at hand. Therefore, I keep adequate gear on hand for mean and nasty weather.

Likewise, I want a different pair of footgear for riding than if I'm mostly walking. If I'm riding, I'll go with a pair of insulated, waterproof snow pacs. These boots are not light, so I do not prefer them for hiking. Under no circumstances do I want cowboy boots. They are neither particularly warm nor easy to walk in. One western outfitter told me he wouldn't even hire a guide who wore cowboy boots, because it was a sure indication he didn't know what he was doing. The snowpacks are excellent for sloshing around in the water, mud, and snow usually encountered during the fall at higher elevations. I would wear them if I were hunting only downhill. But if hiking uphill, I would wear a pair of sturdy, broken-in hiking boots with tightly stitched seams and a tight-fitting heel. Such a pair of boots may cost more than you planned on, but they can last a decade or more with proper care. (Regular leather "hiking" boots are not only cold, but eventually let moisture in.) One thing's for sure: you aren't warm unless your feet are.

One time years ago, after three weeks of unusually wet autumn weather, I would likely have stopped hunting without a borrowed pair of waterproof snowpacks. Standing water reached my upper ankles along the horse trail. Luckily, a sympathetic guide had such a pair of boots to loan out. It's much better to take your own along.

One thing all my boots must have is grip-type (not smooth) soles. Vibram is ideal. You'll need the tread on snow and steep slopes.

As for socks, the standard rule is to wear a pair of wool socks over cotton ones. Gym teachers tell you this reduces friction. But you are also warmer when your feet are not cramped. Allow an extra size when purchasing a pair of hiking boots. With the insulated footgear, I've found that two socks are often not necessary. Keep the second pair in reserve in case you perspire heavily or have to walk in deep snow. You can often prevent water from getting into your boots by tightly fitting two ordinary plastic bread sacks over your socks with rubber bands. Then fit another band over each pant leg to keep it fitted tightly over your upper boot. Putting the pants legs inside your boots just invites more snow and water inside. Always make certain nothing inside the boots is too tight. Tightness is likely to hinder blood circulation; it is an enemy to warm feet.

My warm-weather headgear is a simple orange cap. But in my saddle bag or nearby at all times is an orange pull-over stocking cap for colder days. It is true that such a cap pulled warmly around your ears tends to "insulate" against sounds, like those made by an elk rushing toward you over deadfall. But I keep my head warm to and from prime hunting terrain, and uncover the ears when I reach it. Make certain you can hear what goes on in prime elk terrain. Parkas or snowmobile suits with hoods keep necks warm, but insulate ears as well.

At night I wear the stocking cap to prevent loss of body heat through the top of my head. Arctic explorers discovered years ago that much heat is lost there.

When I leave in the morning, I take lunch and clothing for the entire day. It is foolish indeed to keep coming to and going from camp when, more times than not, the farther you are from camp and the longer you stay out there, the more game you'll find.

Warm hands are extremely important. Yet it is just short of incredible how much time hunters (and sometimes guides) spend sitting around fires to warm their hands, even in the best hunting areas. I have certainly participated in this ceremony. But the less often you do so, the better your hunting success will be.

Be sure your gloves are warm and waterproof. However, you cannot shoot with a pair of ski gloves on. I compromise in below-freezing temperatures and carry both an "en-route" pair of big gloves and a "working" cotton pair I change to when I near the best hunting grounds. On the lighter pair, the tip of the shooting finger is cut out for more sensitive feel of the trigger. If conditions are not brutally cold, I take off my right glove (left glove for southpaws) while in the heat of the hunt.

If packing for limited space, especially by air travel, you may have to choose carefully what you'll take. Horse packers always have limits on what they can transport. But I would select the basic items mentioned over any others.

Backpack Hunting

If you can make arrangements to horse-pack your elk out, backpack hunting isn't a bad way to go. You can get away from roads and other hunters. But if you'll be making a light camp in upper elk terrain, remember that silence is golden. The best fire is a small one, and a better idea is a backpacker stove. I use a 2½-pound Coleman Company model that has a tank for one quart of fuel.

Sleeping Bags

Reams of information have been written on this subject. But the main criterion is this: will your sleeping bag keep you warm on even a *very cold* night? I have settled on a Coleman mummy bag (DuPont Dacron Hollofil II) that allows me to forget about the elements and get a good night's sleep. If in doubt, buy one on the warm side, even if it costs more. This is one item of equipment you must not take lightly. In elk hunting above 9,000 feet, you can count on temperatures dropping well below freezing, frequently well below zero.

In the absence of a good sleeping bag, you can get through in a pinch for a night with two poor ones, one stuffed inside the other. Add a blanket to insulate the colder (zipper) side. Also turn the zipper side to the tent's center, where the air is warmer. The bulky sleeping bag is no particular problem if you're horse-packing, but for a backpacker it is a poor substitute for a lightweight (say, 3½ to 4½-pound) sleeping bag.

Of course, you will want a ground cloth of some kind under your bag. I also like a foam pad (you may prefer an air mattress, but make sure it doesn't leak) to insulate against cold and damp ground. If you find the ground extremely wet, place the foam pad *under* the ground cloth. You'll absorb less moisture into the bag that way. Foam pads are difficult to convey on horseback unless you have them tied in a tight roll. Don't expect an outfitter to pack yours in unless it's so compacted. Tie the roll at two ends with cord. You'll want it rolled the same way if backpacking.

Sleeping Cots

For a reason I'll personally never fathom, some hunters do not cotton to cots. They prefer to sleep on the ground itself. I don't argue with such an arrangement on a warm, dry night, especially with a thick pad as a cushion. But after hundreds of nights spent sleeping on the ground, I have no burning crusade to prove anything macho. I'll sleep on a cot anytime, but especially during inclement weather. Rain or melting snow can get through any tent floor ever made. I've spent nights in standing water. I won't invite it again. A camp cot of some sort allows air, including cold air, to circulate beneath your bag, but it is worth its weight in diamonds any time inclement weather threatens. Water doesn't have to actually creep upon you to destroy a night's sleep. It only has to threaten—anxiety alone may well keep you awake.

Tents

My favorite tent for a few people is a springbar type that has a minimum of support poles to get in the way. It is supported primarily by "tension bars" which keep the tent tight with ground pegs. It goes up quickly and holds in wind and rain.

Many western outfitters still go with the canvas wall tents for large groups. These tents work fine, although they can be easily ripped or gouged if the support poles are not properly trimmed before being used. After pitching and removing a number of these wall tents, I strongly recommend taking along a hammer and stout nails to connect the ridge post (the one running the length of tent) with the vertical support posts. If you nail them together, the resulting U-arch offers greater strength in wind or storm. Outfitters who use such tents every fall also notch the top pole to fit snugly against the two end supports before nailing them in firmly. A large wall tent is rarely put in place by one

person. But then it generally houses five to seven hunters. One person can hold up the limp canvas while others hoist up the end posts. A teamwork effort puts the whole thing in place. I also like to dig a small hole for each end post in order to further stabilize the structure, replacing the dirt. But be sure to allow for the hole when measuring and cutting the two end support poles. Trim off all branches that could puncture the tent in a wind. You can, of course, use the same poles each year.

The heavy canvas is usually best held in place when the corners are roped to trees, if available. Middle loops can be anchored to the ground. However, ropes in the wrong place can trip the unwary, especially at night. Place them out of the way. Also decorate with bright ribbons. Keep ropes taut for maximum structural strength.

Camp Preparations

Much has been written about where to place your camp. If you do not plan ahead so that, for example, the source of drinking water is upstream of the latrine (possibly only a hole in the ground), you could suffer some dire consequences. No one has to show you where the most protected and level ground is, but I have been on expeditions where there was little level ground. Once we almost had to keep an arm wrapped around a pine all night to keep from sliding downhill. But a night or two of that is worth a thousand lectures. Somehow, some way, you'll find the right spot next time.

There is one aspect often overlooked by newcomers to elk hunting. Remember, when you get away from camp, all those scenic meadow edges in the wilderness look very much alike. If you position the camp alongside a certain canyon stream or jutting ledge landmark, you'll be glad you did when you return after dark, drenched from top to bottom. You want a camp you can find. Commercial outfitters on public land have certain restrictions they have to follow to retain their licenses. But there are few such stipulations with private hunting parties, other than keeping the site relatively small to minimize the impact on the landscape. It goes without saying that any camper will find even his hunting success improved if he develops disciplined habits, which include picking up litter, being careful with fires, and not polluting streams or lakes with latrines, livestock, or careless kitchen practices.

If your camp is near a road, you can enjoy some additional conveniences. At one of ours, we lowered an old refrigerator into the ground like a coffin. Its cooling effects kept meat, milk, eggs, and butter from spoiling in a place animals could not reach. You can also use a picnic cooler or a wooden box inside a ground hole.

If you install one, place the handle toward your kitchen tent. It will save you many steps. If you construct a small platform near the cooler door, it will allow you to put food down temporarily while deciding what goes into which compartment. Of course, soda pop or beer cans, watermelon, etc., can go in the traditional place—a spring or creek.

An elk camp takes advance planning. The tack or saddle tent should be near the corral, where guides can get to it easily. Clients need not bother with it, except when loading gear into saddle bags. Sitting around a well-planned elk camp each evening is a joy in itself, and one worth all the work involved.

For best elk hunting, a camp should not be in the heart of the best hunting territory, where camp banter can spook game. It should also not be so far from it that you have to ride six or eight miles a day to get there. Ideally, it should be about 1½ to two miles from the anticipated hunting. Even then, you should be careful about unnecessary noises. Tent pegs must be "pounded" in, yet firm tapping can do it as well as carnival-type sledgehammering. Cutting wood is a different challenge. A hard, sharp blow is best for splitting logs. A saw works well to get that large, dead limb on the ground, but is not as good as a hatchet or an ax for quartering wood into stove-sized logs. But when you begin, have the logs firmly in place and on level but soft ground. Best of all, have some wood cut before opening day. I have found that elk are spooked by log splitting up to a mile away. But if it's the only way you can lay up a few days' firewood, it is a necessity.

Occasionally, a metal fence post might be hammered into the ground to hold wiring for a horse enclosure. Such pounding, especially if it's in rocky ground, carries much farther than any woodcutting chores. If possible, go with ropes strung around trees near a grassy spot where the horses can subsist for a day or two. Then move the fence. Vehicles and tailgates can also be utilized to help keep horses inside an enclosure.

Drinking Water

Do we worry about treating our drinking water? I never have while out hunting, because sooner or later I can locate a small spring or stream bubbling directly and cleanly from the ground. In over 40 years of hunting and fishing in high country, I have never had much difficulty in finding pure-water sources. The challenge comes at camp where the air-clear creek rushing by may be inhabited by beaver, or have a dead elk damming it upstream. What then?

I know of one hunting camp which ignored such a situation for a decade. No problems. But one autumn a family of beavers moved into the canyon above camp, and hunters suddenly came down with stomach cramps, diarrhea, headaches, and general nausea. The problem is not solved with halazone tablets or a few drops of chlorine bleach or iodine. *Giardia lamblia*, an invisible protozoan carried in droppings, is neutralized only by boiling the water. If you do so with your coffee or hot chocolate, no problem. But with "fresh" cold water (even for brushing your teeth), boiling is the only way to be absolutely safe.

Possibles Bag

There are other things you will need in elk camp. My "possibles" bag, like the mountain men of old carried, has everything I could need in a hurry for elk hunting. The container itself is nothing special, just a gym bag. But what goes into it is:

Binoculars, ammo, hunting knife in sheath with whetstone, oil for lubricating the rifle, waterproof vial of matches, candle, cigarette lighter for insurance against wet matches, contour maps of the region to be hunted, ropes to tie game, small saw for cutting through bones, all necessary licenses, and cotton for wiping off water. Also: an orange, wrap-around plastic vest in case I've shed any outer orange clothing (for very warm days), foot powder, first-aid kit, elk bugle, pocket flashlight (always carried with me when I leave camp to hunt), alarm clock, eating utensils, drinking cup, shoe polish and mink oil for waterproofing boots, block and tackle for hanging up game, game bag, pine oil for masking human scent, vehicle tire-chain stretches (which seem always to get lost otherwise), and last but not least, toilet paper. Other items, like tire chains for slippery roads, should be kept in a vehicle.

Now let's take a closer look at the above items and their uses in elk hunting.

Binoculars

Indispensable. I keep a pair about my neck whenever I'm hunting. Mine are 8 x 40 mm. Bushnell. I like at least 7 power. As with a rifle scope, too much magnification can narrowly limit your field of vision. Make sure the glasses are easily and quickly adjustable to various ranges. Equally important is that they be watertight. If not, on a cold, wet morning it may be hours or even days before you can focus on elk habitat. Make sure you check with the salesperson about what you are getting, and know what the warranty provides. You've got to have good, if not great, binoculars.

I keep a piece of cotton swab in my pocket to gently wipe away any dirt or moisture from outside lenses. Only a trained technician should attempt to clean or alter the inside.

Knife and Whetstone

My hunting knife is custom made, with a bleached elk-antler handle and four-inch tip-up curved blade of carbon steel. Veteran knife-maker Delbert Rentfro, also an elk guide and hunter in Wyoming for 40 years, explains why he prefers this model.

"Being a knife-maker doesn't qualify

me to tell you what knife to use, any more than being an elk hunter qualifies me to tell you what rifle to use. Blade design and length are a matter of personal taste. But I like this model knife because of its versatility. A blade of only four inches can dress out, skin, and cape the largest game animal on the North American continent.

"A larger blade is not as easily controlled when cutting around the intestines and diaphragm area. A six-inch knife is almost totally impossible when caping out a head. Of course, you can always carry several knives for each separate function. But if I had only one, it would be the shorter blade."

Why the tip-up curve? "It provides greater control when skinning and caping." And the carbon steel? "The average hunter can get a good edge on a carbon-steel blade much more readily than a stainless-steel type.

"When you buy a custom-made knife, be sure to tell the maker precisely what you want it for. Ask questions if you don't understand. It's your money. Even in a factory-produced knife, you will get what you pay for."

As for sharpening an edge, Rentfro uses two Arkansas stones—one medium, another fine. "I start with the medium to take out any nicks and rough spots. Then I put on the finished edge with the finer stone. If your blade is in very bad shape, start with a Washita stone. It has an extremely coarse texture.

"Just as important as the stones is the right oil. All oils are not alike. I feel the Smith stone and oil are by far the best. This oil is also good to rub a thin film on your blade for off-season storage. If you have an antler-handle knife, a light film of baby oil will keep the handle from shrinkage."

"Never deliberately immerse your bone or antler handle in water. If it gets wet, wipe it off with a barely damp cloth. If it gets dirty, wash it first with warm, soapy water before drying. Remember that how you use your knife could someday make the difference between a valuable wall mount and a throwaway piece of junk."

Sharpening a knife: tilt the blade at an angle on the whetstone, and make a cutting motion in the direction away from the sharp edge. After sharpening one side, turn the blade over and repeat. Tilting the blade slightly will help focus friction on the cutting edge itself.

Saws and Hatchets

Some guides prefer to work only with a hatchet (or two) when cutting up game meat to load into a horse or vehicle. I personally like a small saw and the two hatchets. The saw helps me field-dress a carcass sufficiently for loading and hauling back to camp. There, with better conditions, I can finish the job.

Fire Building

Let's look at the fire-building components you brought along. I've built thousand of fires in the woods. I also live in an extremely cold climate, and my living-room fireplace is active all winter long. But I admit to learning something new even now about the best way to kindle a flame when half frozen in hunting terrain. Here are some points to ponder:

Slick magazine pages and toilet paper make poor fire starter. The magazine pages aren't soft enough to "tinder up," and the toilet paper is so soft it singes through rather than bursting into flame.

Best are dry newspapers, or the paper bags your lunch is carried in.

Pine gum makes excellent fire starter when paper is wet or you are attempting to get a flame in snow.

Lifting up a "smolder" of small twigs provides oxygen sufficient in most cases to "orange" it up.

If possible, start with very small twigs, gradually building to larger ones. Too many big ones too soon can kill a fire.

Even in wet weather you can usually locate dry wood on the underside of a log, inside a patch of brush, and especially below a canopy of conifer boughs.

If you're low on dry matches, light a candle and use it to kindle wood.

Always build a fire out of wind. If you're on a ridgeline where this is impossible, shield the fire with your body. The wind will be your ally once you get it started. Add wood to the side where wind is blowing the flames.

Avoid building a fire when you are actually hunting, or waiting for a drive to push game your way. Use it as needed *between* hunting grounds, rather than quitting and heading to camp. The longer you can remain out in elk country, the better your chances of using your rifle. A fire can be "inspirational" also when you are packing game out or supplies in, dressing game, etc.

Physical Conditioning

The most important possession you have on any elk hunt — perhaps something you might have overlooked — is your own body. You'll want to be certain it is ready for the rigors of a week or more of elk hunting. There are many routines to follow in shaping up. But here is something which has helped me without any weights or special equipment: for half an hour every other day I do three sets of eight repetitions each to exercise muscles in legs, waist, chest, shoulders, and arms. Procedure:

Legs — move from standing to crouched position and up again;

Waist — situps with arms behind head, on the forward motion touching elbows to knees while keeping legs flat;

Chest — pushups with back straight, touching chin to floor;

Shoulders — rotate arms in circular motion with movement entirely from shoulder;

Arms — lift arms high over head, then bring them down to waist, repeating with bent elbows.

Some may wonder why I exercise other than leg muscles. The truth is, you will be riding, loading supplies and game, carrying a rifle, and doing many things which require your entire body to be well toned. If you are backpacking, or making camp without a guide, you will want to be in even better shape. Your present health permitting (check this with a physician) you will also improve your wind and stamina by running or jogging. How far you run isn't as important as pushing hard enough to get your heart working. Perspire a little. Every bit of grit you put forth now will make the hunt that much easier.

Other things being more or less equal, the physically conditioned hunter will be the one who most often scores. I have seen it as a guide many times. Frequently, I'll advance up a ridge at what I consider to be a modest pace, then check with the hunter to make sure he is near my elbow before we peer over a rim. Sometimes I discover he didn't move at all from our last rest stop.

You don't have to be as agile as a teenaged athlete or an NFL quarterback to hunt elk. But you should be able to hike at a reasonable speed for half a mile up a moderate grade. You can rarely take a horse right to the best elk hunting. You are going to find it necessary to walk.

What's more, though a guide or companion who knows the area should treat everyone alike, he may not. The hunter who is more eager to succeed — measured by the effort he puts forth — is likely to draw the most attention. A guide's job is to give you what you want. If you want to hike to another rim at, say, 4:30 p.m., a good guide will lead you. However, if you are completely bushed and want only to head for camp, your guide will give you what you want then, too. In fact, guides are always concerned about heart attacks — about working a hunter harder than he really wants. If the hunter is in good condition, he'll get more from his hunt and more from his guide as well.

It can't be overemphasized that if you lead a sedentary life, you will need to prepare your body several months ahead for that extra energy to consistently hunt hard, early and late. The law of averages is on your side if you can. If any of the above seems too challenging to you, or you have a history of poor health, see a doctor before doing any of the above.

Be patient. Remember, it took you months, maybe even years, to get out of condition. You cannot expect to get into top shape overnight. Remember, too, that elk usually live at an elevation where the air is thinner and the stress greater on a man who makes his home in a sea-level suburb. Take this into consideration when you open the mail to find you've finally drawn out on that special wapiti quest. Begin right now to build up muscle and wind. Even if you do only a little exercis-

ing every other day, it can mean much by October — in camp you will have the confidence and stamina to answer the bell today . . . and tomorrow, too.

Getting About

Now let's talk about another very important aspect of your outdoor education: finding your way around. Not just relocating camp. I mean what many outdoorsmen consider one of the most important skills in the outdoors: orientation. Can you relocate that great little patch of bluegrass on the other side of the mountain where a friend showed you some elk one day? And the canyon beyond that? How about in the pre-dawn dark?

Did you bring a compass with you? Can you line it up with north on your map, and take readings in camp so you know which direction important landmarks around camp are located?

Get in the habit of always noticing where you are going. Never just ride along, thinking about how gifted your guide or friend is to be able to find his way. You might have to duplicate that skill someday soon.

Enjoy that red-tailed hawk circling in the sky, sure, and the turquoise lake at the other end of the basin. But where is that lake in relation to camp, or to the particular bluegrass meadow you seek? Don't count on the trees or brush, all lookalikes. Check for distinguishing cliffs or other landmarks.

If you should follow a bull, trailing it down that long ravine and over a ridge, would you know how to find your way back? I've known even some highly experienced guides who have trouble finding their horses tied a quarter mile back into the timber. It is amazing how distinctive it

What about your vehicle — is it ready with chains and other gear to get you where you want to go?

can all look now, yet how similar later. That factor is an excellent reason to take along some red twine or ribbon. Pick it up on your return, of course, but note how much security and peace of mind it engenders at dusk to know this is indeed the exact patch of spruces you came through that morning. Of particular worth is memorizing the scene as you will see it on your return — turn around and look backward. Is that the precise place where you should enter the wall of trees — or the very spot you should climb the ridge to avoid the steep dropoff directly on the other side?

In addition, get into the habit of selecting a distinctive spot — say, the edge of something — to tie your horse or depart into a heavily timbered canyon. Don't tie up inside the trees; tie on the outside so you have a "line" to follow. This way you can be off a few hundred yards on your return and eventually find horses, camp, or hunting area. The same holds true for remembering a natural line such as a creek or base of a mountain — but be careful, they can all look alike later! One of the most confusing features of all, incredibly,

can be a lacework of roads. Is this the one you left in the morning to probe into timber cover? And if so, is the truck to the left from here or to the right? The right answers can be very important when you are so tired it feels every step is weighted with anvils. NOTE: if you're lost on a guided hunt, sit down and wait the second you realize you don't know which way to go. Your guide will find you easier that way.

Another matter is locating the game after you've shot it. The animal may be much more difficult to relocate dead than it was to find alive. There, over that little arroyo? Or beyond the dozen others which now resemble each other? Again, you can tie a string to mark where to cut back into the timber or depart a trail. Even while you are hunting, always take note of where you are and where you have been. If your hunt is successful, you or a guide will most likely have to return by this same route. And there is nothing more lamentable in all the hunting world than a downed trophy animal someone cannot relocate.

12

Bugling — Pro and Con

It didn't look very promising. The guide and his hunter — I was along to observe — had spent the day before and most of this one without getting into rifle range of an antlered bull.

Gaspar "Gap" Puche looked at his watch. "Just about 4:30 p.m. It wouldn't be too early now to try the bugle." Puche had blown on the three-foot rubber-tubing amplifier (the sound emanated from his own throat) much of the previous two days, without response. Now he decided to bugle again. Puche is always careful not to sound the "horn" between 10:30 a.m. and 4:30 p.m. "because bulls rarely bugle at such times, and it could actually scare away any intelligent elk in the countryside."

Puche knelt down, sucked in a deep breath, and held the rubber tubing high in the air. His lips and chest quivered.

"EEEOOONNNGGGKKK!" Puche's "elk music" was so realistic that the hair rose on my arm.

Almost instantly an answer blared across the little canyon. The elk sounded less than a quarter-mile away!

Ironically, it came from the direction we had just trod. Wisely, we had crossed the area with little noise, resisting the temptation to talk. Gap bugled back. Five seconds later the bull answered. Gap waited five seconds and responded in equal volume and intensity. Then we heard a crashing in the timber. A golden form stepped into sunlight between two firs. It might have stepped even closer, but Bill Franz of Wheaton, Illinois, had seen enough. At a distance of 161 paces, his 7 mm. Remington Magnum roared. The bull lunged to the right, and then we saw four hooves roll into the air. It was over.

A master at artificial elk bugling, outfitter Gaspar (Gap) Puche shows how: blow from lungs to mouth, with rubber tubing to amplify it all.

In cleaning his 5-point (per side) trophy, we discovered Franz's 180-grain slug had torn off the top of the animal's heart. The elk never moved again after hitting the ground. I pondered the total time from no prospects to a beautiful bull on the ground—it couldn't have been more than a minute.

Does bugling pay off? This was the third respectable bull Gap had called in within five days. Hunters saw few other elk during the week. But it didn't matter.

It only takes one bull to score! Bugling offers another advantage: Franz had advance notice of his bull's approach and had time to take solid aim for a killing shot. Your chances are obviously much better when you're ready.

But there are also some misconceptions about bugling. It doesn't always work. It can even spook game away. A licensee or guide must know when, how, and where to bugle properly. First of all, we should know what prompts a bull wapiti to bellow forth its calliope-like call. From personal experience, hunter and guide interviews, and research, I would list six distinct reasons a bull elk bugles:

1. To issue a challenge to other bulls seeking cows.

2. To accept another bull's challenge to fight.

3. To warn other bulls to stay away.

4. To merely issue a declaration of bullhood, as on a winter refuge. In this instance, there appears to be no attempt to challenge any other bull.

5. To entice a cow to mate.

6. As a reinforcement after mating.

Cows may also "bugle," but the sound is more shrill, weaker, and minus the deep-chested, guttural qualities of a bull's bugle. More likely, cows will merely squeal or bark, in or out of rut.

While a bugle for any of the six reasons can give away the location of a bull elk, only in No. 1 and 2 is a bull likely to come charging toward a hunter a la those popular magazine thrillers. Such a bull may be fully geared for battle, his natural wariness sacrificed on an altar of belligerence. Such a charge can be exhilarating, if not frightening. Hunters have been known to drop their weapons and run from such drama. Certainly, there is danger here.

Yet, there are also times, as in situations 3, 4, 5, and 6, when a bull won't locomote to your challenge. He will indeed have disclosed his general whereabouts. But since he won't move to within rifle range, what do you do?

I've personally watched 6-point bulls trot across sage flats almost to my tent door with only a lip whistle from me. I've also had them answer, but refuse to show, after a "sophisticated" call sounded from metal conduit or rubber hose. Much depends on the bull you're talking to. One morning I repeatedly conversed with a bull in aspens about 500 yards below me. Undoubtedly, he had what he wanted at his side. Why go elsewhere? He held his ground. Another time I received answers from a number of young bulls seeking the start of a harem, while deep in the nearby timber a guttural announcement from what had to be a heavy-chested bull threatened all the world to stay away. There was no way to move either of these two stubborn bulls. Several "hangers-on" and hopefuls, 2 to 4-tined males, milled around in confusion, perhaps unsuccessful in gathering courage to actually spar with the monarch. Or me.

But it would be a mistake to think every harem-guarding bull is going to lose his cool just because you attempt to entice him away with frequent bugling. Bulls rarely bugle repeatedly, and neither should you. Wait to see if one shows after each bugling attempt. Be particularly patient if the bull sounds as if he may come in without further noise from you.

The aforementioned 6-pointer, which came within 25 feet of my tent, was first heard a mile away. I called back. I heard him again five minutes later half a mile away. My third call, the last, was met with silence. I waited 10 minutes. Then he appeared at timber's edge. With little hesitation he entered the meadow where we had camped near a spring. Then he half-wallowed around in a soft bog along the spring, seemingly to cool off physically and emotionally. He appeared ready to remain for a time until my horse stamped a hoof. The bull left the way he had come. He was safe for now—the elk season was still 10 days away.

As for my whistle, there was nothing particularly fetching about it. And it occurred in midmorning, whereas the general rule is to call at the elk's most active times, dawn and dusk. Yet there is no arguing with results. The timing was right. For some reason, despite his size, this bull had enticed no cows to follow, and was on the search. By contrast, the bulls which would not budge left me with only two alternatives to get within shooting range: 1) try to sneak in after them in spite of thick aspens surrounding them, and 2) wait for them to show later. The latter is prob-

ably the smartest strategy, but it requires almost superhuman patience for a licensee to just sit still while listening to what may be a wall-mount bellowing his rage within stalking distance. I attempted to reconnoiter around that first stubborn bull unsuccessfully. I heard no more sound from him, but discovered where the sultan and his harem had dug their hooves into the soft ground below me to begin their exodus. An errant breeze might have warned him. But he didn't remain around for long.

If you can't sneak up on a bull guarding his harem, the kind that refuses to come to you, one strategem is to proceed as noisily as an enraged bull might. Rattle, scrape, and thump vegetation as you go, trying to appeal to your opponent's emotion during the rut, not his intelligence. When bowhunter Ken Adamson of Estacada, Oregon, "rattled" out a no-show bull, it was his only chance of seeing it at all in

Two bulls battle for supremacy during rut. At stake could be mating rights to cows.

the dense alders. The animal was good enough to field measure No. 1 in the Pope-Young records. (More about it in Chapter 17 on recognizing a trophy.)

The main point is, not all bugling elk have the same thing in mind. But every one of them reveals to the hunter his general, if not specific, location. The rifle-toter may otherwise have no idea there are wapiti in the woods he is walking. Like the honking of geese, cackling of a rooster pheasant, or repeated "chukar" of an Asian partridge, the bull elk is one of nature's noisy natives. Silence may be golden, but silent they are not. I've known many bulls to unaccountably "blow their cover" by pouring out their feelings. It is as if during the mating season they just can't hold it all in. Wise is the nimrod who listens carefully for this bugled message, even if he didn't bring an elk call of his own.

How To Bugle

When it comes to imitating the symphony of a rutting bull, Puche gives this advice: learn to call from your own vocal chords, using a piece of pipe (he prefers rubber tubing) for amplification. He also recommends learning the right pitches and tones from the animal itself, or a recording thereof. Many successful hunters have used the instructional cassettes marketed by Johnny Stewart Game Calls, Waco, TX 76710.

Begin on a low note, gradually rising to a crescendo of volume. Hold the high, shrill climax, pouring out an anguished soul! Finish up with an "everything goes," gradually decreasing tone and pitch to a grunting conclusion. Many game wardens and conservation officers have heard this sound often enough to simulate it quite

well. Most are happy to help newcomers learn without any fee charged. Such a person is good to know.

Puche suggests blowing into the open end of an elk call, with the other end partly plugged, varying the amount of air that escapes until you achieve the desired sound. How hard you blow is another factor to practice on. If you buy a call, check the instructions, but also experiment on your own. The sound you produce by your interpretation of the instructions can be different from what the manufacturer intends.

To emit a sound from your own lips that will attract love-sick bulls generally requires wetting your mouth, dipping down low in pitch, then hitting the highest octave possible. Return to low with all the volume you can muster. I'm not a loud whistler by any means, and rarely attempt whistling at ball games the way many sports fans do. Yet a mouth whistle is often more effective at bringing in elk than any of the store-bought whistles. Some of them are like too many fishing lures—they're aimed more at fishermen than at fish.

Like an old bull elk, Gap also breathes in deeply, lowers his head for the beginning or lower notes, then reaches deep inside his chest cavity for all the volume he can muster. Don't be embarassed or feel self-conscious if a frightful noise pours forth. Keep working on it until the pitch is thick and unrestrained from *"EEE"* to *"OONNNKKKK."* Actually imagine yourself to be a frustrated bull elk. To reach the climactic high note, move the sound from the lungs into the throat. Start from the top down with a shrill blast which decreases to a lower, basal grunting. Repeat, if you still have wind, at least twice.

Compare this sound to the "rusty-gate"

squeal of the cow, and remember that cow squeal. You won't have much reason to repeat it, but it is a sound you'll want to recognize. When you hear it, there could be a herd bull nearby.

Another way to simulate bull-elk music is with a commercial turkey call. Place it on the tongue inside your mouth and blow. You can emit a plausible bugle with a metal or wooden pipe or even a piece of garden hose. Some of the expensive and complicated calling contraptions on the market are considered by many experts as a total waste of money. How can you tell which will work? The best way is to listen to a real or recorded elk bellow, then decide for yourself. Old-timers such as Gap like to joke that with the first false note from one of these worthless callers, the bull can detect brand, type, and serial number, if not the manufacturer's mailing address.

At first mention of bugling, many newcomers feel anguish or frustration. "You have to be born with the ability," one hunter lamented. However, the facts prove otherwise. Master bugler Gap Puche did not grow up in a lair of elk, but emigrated west in his teens from Pennsylvania. At that time the only elk he had seen were in zoos. But his days of whitetail hunting made him intrigued by the prospects of hunting elk. He acquired the art of seeking and calling elk from hours of practice, much of it done in the off-season so he wouldn't spook away game. It is something others can learn as well.

When Not To Bugle

When should you forget calling efforts altogether? If a guide has been out the week before without hearing any bugling, he may have his finger on the game's pulse

well enough to suggest putting your Acme Guaranteed Elk Call away. Day after day of wet or windy weather can dampen a bull's sense of sexual adventure. It can even delay the rut for weeks. I remember one particularly wet autumn when monsoons struck the mountains for three weeks and scarcely any bugling could be heard at all. There is no good reason for bugling at such times, and in fact doing so could stamp you for what you are, an imposter. Obviously, you'll have a better chance if you stay silent in such circumstances. There is also the slim chance you may sound like an honest threat to a herd bull, which will then quickly and silently herd his cows away. Such a sultan may issue a warning challenge; yet it is also true that the larger herd bulls are seldom lured away to look for a fight. The bull you call in may carry a massive rack, but he is probably "unattached." Harem-guarders don't usually run to every challenger. Those you call in are more likely to be sexually mature bulls looking for a harem and thus eager to fight any bull with any female following whatsoever. These bellicose bulls may be willing to travel fearlessly to your gun muzzle.

This doesn't mean bugling never brings a response from massive-racked herd bulls. It well might. But if he doesn't come to you in time, it could be because he has what he wants where he is. You'll have to go to him.

It is also possible that bulls within sound of your call may be convinced you are one of them and yet, not wanting to fight, shy away. Where I live, elk season opens October 15, well after the rut is usually finished. To blow a bugle then could cause a bull with no further amorous interest, perhaps even bedraggled and weak from the rut, to actually avoid what seems to be a challenger. Once, I observed a young bull in that situation actually run from an artificial bugle.

Certainly, if you have found no elk and all seems futile, you can try bugling even if the timing does not seem propitious. Assuming you have learned how to do a reasonable imitation, try to do the following: select a background just as you would in predator calling — so that a bush, boulder, or cliff prevents an animal's approach from a "blind" side. (You want to see him before he sees you.) Settle comfortably in a place of concealment or camouflage. If there is a wind, it should be in your face, not at your back. Be mentally ready for anything. A bull may rush in, head tossing, looking for battle, or he may steal in serenely to a brushy edge, where he peers about first. Such a bull may be urinating profusely, apparently a factor in scent-signalling to cows a masculine readiness and whereabouts. You have to be prepared for such things.

Some experienced guides say they can call in bulls anywhere, sophisticated animals or not. But the preponderance of guides I've interviewed say it is definitely much easier if the bull hasn't been fooled too many times previously. I concur. I prefer to work my calling charms on bulls which haven't been recently duped. I think any animal can lose its "callability" if spooked often enough. Thus, if bulls won't answer during the rut, perhaps you'll have to move deeper into the wilderness.

After all this, will you be ready to shoot when His Magnificence appears? The more regal bulls have a way of taking your breath away when they suddenly and entirely fill your scope at 15 yards. Guides like Puche and Duane Wiltse have watched a sizable percentage of clients,

often on their first wapiti shoot, "freeze" at the sight of a much-sought rack. I've seen this sight intimidate a hunter long enough that he either fails to get the safety off in time to shoot or forgets to move a cartridge into the firing chamber. There is also something disarming, if not frightening, about a beast charging into your lap looking for a sparring partner. You can, to a certain extent, control this situation by taking a position a dozen or so yards from elk cover so that you have a modicum of approach warning.

Don't be too surprised if you receive an answer to your bugling from deep in valley timber. Almost any call or whistle, even a beginner's lip attempt, can be heard a surprising distance away. Mountain walls can echo noises much farther than you might realize. Sound carries vibrant and clear through high, thin-aired, narrow valley openings. After listening to some bugling, you can better judge how far away the bellowing actually is.

Tonal Qualities

Always pay rapt attention to the tonal quality of a call. Is it the shrill, high voice of an eager young bull or the resonant bugle of an older bull? One day I heard two bugling bulls, one a commanding declaration to be left alone. The other was less defined, a little wishy-washy, less confident. In short time, a 3-point bull loped slowly and forlornly out of the spruces, running with head down in an attitude of inferiority, much as a whipped dog moves with tail between legs. After the young bull had moved off by itself, I saw a giant of a bull, rack held high and proud, then swept low to prod cows ahead. This bull had a harem to push along the rim of a deep chasm, and he did it with an "I'm-in-charge-here" mastery which couldn't be mistaken. I didn't see the two bulls ever match antlers, but it would appear the herd boss had effectively driven the other out. It was elk season. I could have shot either one, but I'd just filled my tag on a nice rack. I was now hunting deer. If I had shot at the smaller bull, quite likely I wouldn't have seen the larger. For the time being I was happy just to sit still and observe the world of elkdom. Selective siring was at work to produce the best bloodlines and genes for a future generation of wapiti. The giant herd bull would see to it.

If I had been interested in taking that herd bull, my best bet would have been to sit down and train my scope on the cows. It is one of the consistent vulnerabilities of a monarch bull that he will usually appear last in line, making certain the cows march directly ahead. This is of particular advantage to a shooter waiting for the last (and antlered) head to show. It is an advantage seldom enjoyed in deer hunting, since does are almost never a buck's possessions to be moved about at will as in the world of elk.

One reason a bull keeps his harem close is that various cows may come into heat at differing times. A cow may be receptive to breeding for only a half day or so, requiring the beleaguered old bull not only to keep his cows close at hand but also to concentrate more on mating than on hunters or danger.

Research shows that in the western United States cow elk are most likely to become pregnant from September 26 through early October. In Alberta and British Columbia, where it's colder, mating instincts may be triggered earlier than September 26. Apparently cooling temperatures affect the glandular structure.

Elk are not technically territorial. True, they may return to one favored slope for the rut each autumn, and possibly remain within one square mile of the area the entire time. But the bulls are more likely to move with the cows if they decide the grass is greener or the water cooler elsewhere. Little attempt is made to keep the harem in one place. The main factors seem to be that the bull stays with the harem, and that all the cows he can possibly look after remain together.

Much has been said about wallows—so much, in fact, that they seem mystical and ritualistic. I believe the wallow is simply a place which allows a bull reaching feverish emotional pitch during the rut to cool off and wash away dried, irritating urine. Some wallows are favored over others due to availability and/or depth of soothing ooze.

The Battle

At its height, the rut may lead a bull to do battle with even mock enemies—a convenient sapling or even a pile of brush, leaves, or dirt—which can be tossed about to show who's boss around here. This arduous activity, like the battle of the bulls itself, may last for a short time only. Indeed, even prodigious elk-watching by biologists reveals but a few all-out, head-locking sessions. After a few brief encounters, possibly no more than bluffing in a semicircle, most bulls seem capable of deciding who has the tenacity, experience, or brute strength to prevail. Occasionally, bulls inflict serious injury or lock horns, but it is rare. Bulls may also size each other up all year long for body strength, as head-to-head shoving matches are witnessed in the winter on any elk refuge. Nature has instilled the bull elk with a pecking order to determine who is fittest to mate. At such times a bull has such a desire to prove himself worthy that he might indeed be oblivious to a hunter creeping within rifle range. You want to be vigilant during the rut, for elk are often least wary then.

Many smaller bulls might be satisfied with keeping track of five to eight cows, but a prime bull six to nine years old could convince 15 to 30 cows that he's the leader. The most cows I've ever seen clearly in the command of one bull was 31. Remaining around, just in case a few cows slipped out of his sight, were several 3 and 4-pointers. Statistics indicate that a 2½-year-old bull is apt to be a cow-stealer. Youngest mating for a bull in the wild is recorded at 14 months, a rather rare occurrence. Biologists say most spikes and young forkhorns don't even know what is going on during the rut. Yet there are always exceptions. A yearling bull in a Colorado study was known to have 17 cows in his harem. Chances are that the larger the harem you chance upon, however, the larger the owner will be.

One of the greatest advantages of hearing elk bugle is that it acts as a hunter stimulus. I've seen groggy men mutter undecipherable complaints about getting out of bed two hours before sunup, but let a bull bugle sometime in the middle of the process and they suddenly come to life, pull on their hunting boots, and grab the rifle in a hurry. After hunters ride around sleepily on some mountain trail, a sudden burst of energy always follows what naturalist Ernest Thompson Seton labeled the "most sonorous sound in the wild." Jim Bond, who used to play recordings of bull elk on his lecture circuit, didn't have to tell the thousands of would-be hunters and nature-lovers in his audiences much about the hunt. He let them listen until they were on the hunt with him. He said that when a bull elk lays his antlers back across his shoulders to express his inner feelings,

"there is nothing to compare with it. You may not be able to make a man like getting up at four in the morning to go to work, but he will do it to go elk hunting. He will also put in the gosh-darnedest, ruggedest day you ever thought of and love every minute of it." He concludes: "When elk hunting gets into your blood, look out. You'll carry the torch the rest of your life."

Bond describes a day (September 25) in Alberta when bulls were so busy with their rutting interests that the forests rang with the sound of bugling music. The large bull he downed that day was almost anticlimactic to the enjoyment of sitting down and listening to the melodies floating on the breezes.

When you hear those eerie notes and the maker refuses to budge in your direction, how do you entice him to move closer? Some hunters beat one branch against another to simulate the eagerness of an angry bull, hoping to bring in a would-be challenger. I recommend it only if you are convinced the bugler is seeking a fight. If it's a herd bull, you could frighten him away. As Puche did, try to match the mood of the bull you are calling. If he answers belligerently and quickly, do the same.

Watch for Cows

Remember, too, that when dealing with a harem, any cow in it may signal your presence to the others. The cows are not as caught up with the whole rutting business as is a bull (some men would say there are human parallels here) and could easily precipitate a mass migration. With them you need to exercise large doses of concealment and silence.

Then, too, call into the wind, not with it at your back. Human scent can and does sober even an overly romantic bull very quickly. As for stalking a bugling bull, it makes no difference whether you try to do so uphill, downhill, or sidehill; but don't attempt it downwind. Obviously, this means you'll have to locate a bull that can be approached by walking into wind, if there be any.

Surprisingly, many western guides have never called in a bull elk, seen it done, or even place much stock in the tactic. In most cases there is a logical reason: their seasons traditionally open after the rut, in middle autumn. Therefore, they may pay little attention to your questions about hunting during the rut. If you are after lovesick or fighting bulls, you usually need to contact guides whose seasons occur somewhere from mid-September to early October.

I know of several late-October quests on which bulls were supposedly beyond the rutting period, had no cows with them, and didn't seem to be actively seeking any. Yet they were heard bugling. One guide told me how he hunted in vain for a week, heard no elk during that entire time, and was about to leave. But since he had nothing to lose, he sat down and let out a plaintive wail from his lips. Before long he heard crashing in the distance. Then branches rattled within rifle range. Upon a second bugle, a bull materialized out of dark timber 150 yards away. It never responded in voice, perhaps attracted simply by curiosity. In any event, the hunter scored. The elk's royal tines were enough to top local contests, and convinced a guide and his hunter never to give up if you have sufficient breath for one more bugle.

Bowhunters and muzzleloaders, usually blessed with seasons during the rut, have special reasons to learn the lure of elk call-ing. Primitive-style nimrods can often learn more about the process by joining an archery or mountain-man club.

Some strange things can happen when a hunter is straining his ears to catch faint wapiti rhapsodies. Was it a bull or a far-off goshawk? Of course, the more you've heard an elk bugle, the more likely you are to recognize it. I've even seen elk tilt their heads as if to discern what they think they heard. One day a car stopped on the highway near my house and men emerged to "call" two young bulls feeding with the beef cattle in the off-season. The elk strained cupped ears for several seconds, then resumed feeding in the hay windrows. Even the real thing had to take some time to check out a fake bugle.

Anytime I've ever heard bugling, I've been extra glad I was alive. It gives a feeling of elation just to be present for the concert. Carnegie Hall in the wilds. Bugling also has a ghost-like tone that's often difficult to pinpoint. One day, after eight hunters and three guides had combed a ridge, we sat beside a fire in a canyon bottom to discuss how a bull had somehow slipped through our net. Several minutes later the bull sounded again in the rain and mist, seemingly where we had just walked.

To sum it up, bugling can bring phenomenal results, done in the right place at the right time with the right skill. If you don't know how to bugle realistically, I advise hunting with a guide or companion who does. It can pay big dividends as you seek this elusive animal which might roam anywhere in the vast expanse of trees before you. When you can bugle them in, you don't have to find them. They find you. Try it with the cautions given. It works. You might decide there is no other way to hunt elk.

13

Horses and Elk

If you hunt elk for long, you will likely have something to do with horses. They're helpful in transporting you deep into elk country with enough saved-up energy left to hunt. (Getting your game out via horse will be covered in Chapter 20.)

If you have a guided hunt, of course, your contact with a mount will be less than it would be on a do-it-yourself quest. Either way, however, you'll need enough guidelines to get along with this unpredictable creature for a week or more. And how well you get along with your new hunting companion could have much to do with the success or failure of your hunt.

First of all, if you are inexperienced in hunting with a horse, admit it to a guide or someone who knows more. No need for apology. After all, you are a hunter, not a jockey. By thus going on record, others can be ready to help you. At times, though, you will be alone. When no wrangler is at your side, there are certain mistakes you want to avoid.

For example: you don't have to be a reincarnated Pony Express rider to realize there is something potentially dangerous about negotiating a steep, snowy sidehill. If it is particularly slippery, you are better off to dismount and walk. Even in routine circumstances, there are certain things to watch out for: give two or three yards of space, if possible, between you and the next horse fore and aft. If you don't, your horse may be constantly nipping or kicking to protect his "space rights." No two cayuses are precisely alike, and the steed that does tolerate crowding may not be the one you ride tomorrow.

But let's start with the No. 1 abuse of most horse hunters: overusing your beast

Hunter should always hang onto horse, as Wixom does here. Otherwise, he might have long walk to camp.

of burden to reach hot elk habitat. Be mentally and physically prepared to do plenty of walking on any elk expedition. Utilize your horse to gain desired distance and altitude. But when you want to peer over a rim or into a potential elk bedding or feeding area, get off well in advance, and tie up. How far away? That depends on what type of horse you have. Stompers, stampers, and head-shakers can spook a wary bull elk several hundred yards away, even when well out of sight. Whinniers can spook an elk a quarter mile off. So can head-tossers with bristling metal bridle. Get to know your horse. True, I have ridden a mount in soft, deep snow within 50 yards of elk without alerting them. But obviously the sound of horseshoes clinking over a rockslide can carry way out there.

The main thing is never to expect your horse to do too much for you. Yet let it do everything for you it can do. When headed out for the hunting, maintain a reasonable buffer zone between your mount and a potential quarry. Some hunters claim their steed can see, scent, or hear game before a human can—"Watch close when your horse cups his ears forward," they say. But the problem is that by the time your horse senses elk, the elk have spotted you.

One of the top guides I ever met, Roy Sanders, ties all horses near the foot of a target mountain before he ventures up. Sanders's hunters don't always like such steep climbing, but they enjoy a high rate of success, thanks partly to this guide's horse sense.

How you tie your horse is highly important. Novices have an inclination to tie loosely so the cayuse "can get at grass" underfoot. That also allows the critter to get a rope underfoot. Recently I witnessed a horse which had been tied that way. It had tripped downhill and couldn't get up. By the time guides arrived, the animal had suffocated. (With a horse it doesn't take much for that to happen.) The mare hadn't even tangled in her rope at all. She was merely unable to get all her weight off one side.

More typically, a poor tie merely allows the mount to escape, leaving you with a long walk back to camp. A few trained mounts might stand around waiting for you to get through with your business, but the only safe practice is to tie any horse properly.

Once I was assured by a steed's owner that it "wouldn't go anywhere. Just drop the reins." But while I was glassing, the critter, spooked by a gust of wind, began running toward camp. My camera was in the saddlebag. The walk wasn't so bad, just a little under two miles. But consequences could have been worse had the frightened animal smashed my camera against a tree. While we're on the subject, never leave your rifle in a scabbard after dismounting. Even after tying up at camp, any horse might decide to scratch its back by rolling over, with dire consequences for your rifle.

Use Two Knots

As for the tie itself, there are two types that veteran wranglers use. One is for use around camp where horses might panic, maybe due to confusion and close proximity to other horses or hunters. (If they get loose, they won't likely stray away from camp.) Tie a "loop slip knot," which unravels with a sharp pull from either you or the horse. Away from camp—say, on some lonely mountain—make a more solid tie such as a square knot or bowline. Here you want the horse to remain put for sev-

eral hours. He isn't as likely to spook. The last thing you want is for him to break away, because he will hightail it elsewhere. If he does, you will almost certainly have a lengthy challenge in recapturing him.

In both types of knots, always make sure you tie "short." In camp, just enough rope for the horse to move its head down to hay or oats is fine. Elsewhere, tie so the horse can move his head comfortably with, say, less than two feet of slack. Never allow enough slack for the critter to get a hoof tangled in it.

In addition, never tie a horse to anything near the ground, such as a log or low tree. On the mountain, make the tie about as high as the horse's neck. In camp, a little lower is tolerable if necessary to let the animal reach feed.

Daily horse rations include about a third of a regular 80 to 100-pound bale of hay each morning and evening. Reward the mount with a gallon of grain each time as well, if a tough day's work is ahead of or behind him. Don't be overly concerned if your horse attempts to nip at everything he can reach throughout the day. If you have time, let him have at it. And if he works hard on steep hills on a warm day, let him quaff at water as desired. Using a horse only every other or every third day is a good idea if enough mounts are available. Yet you risk losing a mount by letting him browse unattended. Even a hobbled horse can move a mile or so in a day or night. Some veteran horsemen bell their mounts at night, but this can be irritating to those attempting to sleep nearby. Whatever you do, make certain your steed receives the needed feed and water every morning and night during the time he is in your custody.

If you are on your own, it isn't necessarily wrong to leave a horse tied overnight.

They can handle it, even on a mountain-top. But if you want the best out of your mount the next day, provide freedom of movement by putting him in a small corral at night. Two ropes tied around several trees can do the trick, as will end gates from a couple of horse trailers.

Halter Ropes and Reins

Most outfitters provide a halter rope for dudes to do their tying. Use reins only in the absence of a rope. Reins break much easier and are more expensive and inconvenient to replace (especially with a tack shop 50 miles distant), and they don't hold nearly as well as a rope. Tying with reins when rope is available can only be construed as poor horsemanship, as well as lack of sensitivity to the outfitter's narrow profit margin.

A few years ago I watched a disaster occur because of tying with reins. It was precipitated by a can of soda pop falling on the ground near one nervous nag. The can broke open, soda fizzed out, and the horse jerked up sharply. The reins snapped, and the beast then stepped onto a wire fence. The wire caught between hoof and shoe, and no amount of human struggling could calm that critter down long enough to remove the wire. Half an hour later the problem was resolved with continued reassurance, plus wire cutters. At other times I've seen panicked horses rush onto cattle guards, where they caught a hoof in the metal grooves and went completely berserk. In one case, a horse had to be killed. This is an extreme case, but it is one example of what can happen.

Saddle Horse Checklist

Here are some simple things most hunters overlook, and far too often, so do the rancher-wrangler types who forget how little the average city dweller or flatlander knows about such things:

Always place a blanket (at least one for riding, two for pack animals) beneath a saddle.

When you cinch your saddle, always make certain you loop the strap at least twice through the ring. One is not enough—the saddle may slip. I've seen more than one sportsman tossed from a loose saddle. With a saddle under its flanks, the horse can kick whatever happened to be on the back of the saddle (maybe a coat or binoculars) to pieces. Again, be sure to loop twice before wrapping the saddle cinch. And when you do wrap the saddle cinch, keep it loose at first. Gather all the slack strap up before tightening the cinch—it is much easier that way.

Dismount after the first half mile or so (earlier if heading up a steep slope) to re-tighten the saddle cinch. Most horses "steel up" or "bloat" against the saddle cinch, preventing a tight wrap on the first attempt. Later they tend to let down and forget the strap, allowing a tighter saddle.

When reining, you normally need only to place leather against the horse's neck and pull gently to the side you intend to go. However, try to be consistent in your commands, to help old Bessie know if you want a gentle turn or a sharp one left or right. How hard you need to rein often depends on the horse's past experience, plus your bridle bit. (Some horses have tender mouths and need very little urging.)

If you do your own bridling, keep the chin strip underneath, and hold the bit in one hand, the ear loop in the other. When you have the bit in place, do not allow slack or the bridle will drop. Most horses will "fight" the bit somewhat, but will settle down once you have it in place.

Most rule books say always mount and dismount from the left side, but frankly, if the right side is distinctly uphill, test your mount to see if it allows you to take advantage of a right-side mount. Most will.

I'm convinced horses have a more vivid memory than elephants. Each horse is different because their experiences have been different. Few mounts are "just plain ornery"—usually they are simply concerned with their own security. Things which threaten that security might include a burned-out stump near the trail which resembles a predatory animal, a shiny motorbike reflecting sunbeams that represent demons, or just the unknown. Most horses seem to have a deathly fear of sinking beyond the fetters in mud, but this seems more a survival instinct than a phobia.

If your horse suddenly faces some fearsome bugaboo, no amount of whipping or yelling will calm him down. The opposite result is more likely. On the other hand, if your steed is plain stubborn—a bit tired perhaps and doesn't want to climb another hill—you may have to give him a stern jab. How do you tell the difference? It's a major part of the entire thing called horsemanship.

A horse that attempts to kick you while you walk around his backside can be labeled as ornery. I've seen many a cayuse disabused of some foul mood by a whap on the bottom, sometimes with a stiff pine branch. But if you fall, let's say, and try to catch yourself by grabbing a hind leg, the ensuing kick is probably done out of fear. So is a bite if you rubbed a sore spot on the horse's jaw. Now, if the nag tries to bite you when you put the saddle on, well, you are duty-bound to thump him a good one on the mouth. Punishment you mete out, however, must be like that to a pet dog. Make certain it is directed where and when it will be understood. Punishment that is not understood will do more harm than good, and can make your horse confused and difficult to manage.

I once took a nag away from his hay to go trail riding, and found myself in a profound rebellion. However, after a few minutes of bucking and cartwheeling, the horse decided the rider's spirit was stronger than his. I had no more trouble with him. But when another animal, a packhorse unaccustomed to being ridden, acted the same way, I gave ground. This mount would need some training, possibly even breaking, to accommodate a rider. There wasn't time for that. Later the outfitter decided to make it easy on all of us by leaving that recalcitrant animal to packing, the thing he did best. We needed packhorses as much as riding horses, anyway.

Ranchers soon learn which horses will make the best mounts. A stallion or "stud" horse won't do, because of his amorous interest in every nearby mare. Gelding solves some of that problem. And most mares are fine until a rope from a pack animal you are towing drops below her tail. Some mounts are definitely better than others, but you are not always given a choice. Let's say that you are the last one to be assigned a horse. You get old "Grumpy" as a permanent assignment, and have to live with it for a week.

Some Sympathy

I can sympathize. As a guide who doesn't own a horse (at this writing), I frequently have had to take what is left. On the last hunt my horse was as suspicious and skittish as could be. The second day I had no mount at all, as the mare managed to squeeze below the lower corral pole and run off. Fortunately, she found several of our hunters two miles up the trail and followed them back to camp. The next day I was ready to turn her loose all over again. She whinnied when away from certain other "companion" horses, shook and twitched when I tried to glass from her back, and spooked at every little thing.

Yet after a week of getting acquainted, during which I gave her constant reassurance and gentle persuasion via pats of appreciation, plus grain and water for good performance, my horse changed its behavior. Anxiety was replaced with confidence and obedience. Old Sheila seemed like a new horse.

After all, we'd spend time getting to know a pet before we expected obedience, wouldn't we? With a horse, it's a matter of assuaging fears and gaining its confidence. It can be done via gentle tone of voice, as well as feeding and other actions. Once I witnessed a guide abandon a horse which had slipped twice on wet shale, refusing to get up the second time. The animal had an ugly bruise on his left front shoulder. I couldn't change that for the present, but I did talk to that horse until he decided to give it another try. The rider climbed back on that horse and with a new, patient approach had no more difficulty.

Later, I was leading Sheila when I spotted a nice bull headed my way two canyons over. I pushed Sheila to one side, not tying her at all because there was nothing to tie to. Then I sat down in the snow to shoot. The elk was mine. But one of the most satisfying things about the episode is that my mount made no noise during the entire time, nor did she shy away at the crack of my rifle. She would have done both, most assuredly, at the beginning of the week.

Since then, I request to ride this now-trusted steed. But I'm sure some other mount would also work out as well, given similar time and/or effort. That horse wasn't an easily trained pony of four or five years. When I made her acquaintance, Sheila was going on 15, late middle age for any horse.

By the way, if you have to catch an errant horse and nothing else works, try rustling a bucket of grain while holding a rope in the opposite hand. As the horse digs his nose into the bucket, latch the rope's metal snap around the halter's metal ring, or drop the rope around the horse's neck to lead it to halter or bridle. If you have no grain, rustle sand or anything until you get close enough to grab the halter rope.

If there's nothing nearby to tie the horse to, try this tactic used by some forest rangers: tie a halter rope to the horse's front fetter so that it acts as a hobble on one leg. The tie must be done with the right length of rope. There should be enough slack so the head can move about, yet not so much slack that the other leg can foul in it. I wouldn't leave a horse "tied" like this for long, but it does work for brief periods, allowing you to glass or attend to a pack-horse problem.

Pack Animals

You may someday be in a position to lead a pack animal, when hauling supplies in or game out. Horses in a string can be tied several ways. It is possible to tie to the doubled-over tail of the horse in front. However, it is better to make the connection with a piece of equipment, such as the horn on a riding saddle or the sturdy bottom of a pack-saddle frame. The latter usually has a loop of rope extending from it, which places less stress on the frame itself. In any event, to avoid tying a knot that straining pack animals pull so tight you can't unloosen it at trail's end, do this: tie with a loop on the end. It is easier to unloosen a doubled-over rope than a single end.

For tying the loose end of halter rope around the saddle horn while on the trail, use a clove hitch (two half hitches with the longer part always underneath). Some experienced wranglers like to tie the loose rope around the neck and through the halter, but keep it out of the way. If you don't, it will almost certainly catch on something.

You will also want to make sure trailing animals remain behind one another. If they don't, one cayuse could walk to the north side of a tree near the trail while the one behind it trots around to the south. Keep watching closely. In addition, some horses panic or are temporarily blinded if a flashlight is used around them. In most cases you won't need a light, because horses see much better to follow a trail at night (especially one familiar to them in daytime) than we humans do. If you do use a flashlight, keep it shining on the ground, not toward the beasts' eyes.

When packing, take special pains to make sure the load is evenly distributed side to side, within a few pounds, or you'll have trouble down the trail. Veteran packers even use scales to mete out some 75 to 100 pounds per side. If one side does slip down, you can often apply a temporary remedy by placing a few rocks in the too-high side.

Slope Caution

Be especially cautious when traveling a snowy or rain-wet sidehill, especially if paralleling the top. Straight up or down doesn't seem as dangerous to a horse as sidehilling it. A horse has a tendency to slip in toward the hill. I keep my leg on that side out of the stirrup. In fact, in particularly precarious situations, I may keep both feet out of the stirrups for short periods. I can count several times when that move prevented what could have been a broken leg. I know an old sheepherder

One reason guides earn their money—packing a sportsman's gear is not always easy, especially deciding what goes where.

Horsemanship is something that comes with years, but a hunter must learn enough to get by for a week. Do you know what to do with your mount?

who broke a shoulder when his mount fell on him. He had to be helicoptered out. On dry ground horses have amazing balance, and little concern over sliding or falling. They can also handle extremely steep slopes if you "wander" to the top.

I remember one occasion when a mount's breast strap broke on steep terrain. The saddle slipped back about the same time the horse encountered slippery going. The animal began sliding backward, and the saddle inched toward his flanks. I got off. The horse soon felt the saddle too far back for his liking, and kicked. Then he began bucking, slipped, and rolled. My rifle flew out of the scabbard, landing on a rock. Several hundred yards away, the critter quivered in a fearful heap. In time, the animal stood up. Repairs were made on the breast strap from parachute cord I kept in the saddle bag. (Hay-baling twine is also strong enough.)

I loosened and recinched the saddle. We avoided that steep, wet slope, although it required a circuitous route, and had no further problems.

Another place to avoid is wet blowdown timber. Most experienced horsemen get off their mounts in such places. Even then, I've seen a hunter slip on a hidden log and plummet downhill, the horse breaking away and running off. Play it safe by tying up if you have to negotiate such places.

Another dilemma occurs when you decide to shoot near a horse. With some animals, it works out. But if you don't know your horse, you may find the animal skittering quickly off. Once a horse owner told me we could practice shooting while untied packhorses grazed a few dozen yards away. Several minutes later, the critters were nowhere to be found. My friend located them a mile away. We were lucky.

It could have been the end of the hunt. Another time, I sighted in my rifle with range horses 100 yards away across a fence. They were soon 300 yards away. One reason could have been that this was early summer and no shooting had been done nearby since the preceding autumn. The horses weren't accustomed to hearing gunfire. When I did some more shooting several days later, they paid less attention to me.

If you do have the chance of a lifetime at a big bull, with no time or place to tie your mount, try to get the horse's head away from your muzzle. Once, while leading my horse on a foggy morning, I found myself looking at a shootable buck. I dropped the reins to the ground, stepped inside them, braced my right leg to handle the expected jerk from my horse, aimed, and fired. The "jerk" was more like an explosion. My aim was true, but the horse's was not so bad either. I all but fell in a loose pile. Luckily, the reins held, the horse didn't go totally berserk, and I lived to tell about it. However, I certainly wouldn't recommend it, unless you have one of those trained "Western-movie" steeds that allow shooting from or near the saddle.

One alternative is to tell yourself that this particular bull is well worth a long walk back to camp. On the optimistic side, you might have to walk only a short distance to catch your mount—so long as you obey that one cardinal rule of getting your muzzle as far away from the horse's head as possible.

If you are on a guided hunt, just hand the reins (or halter rope) to your guide. If he is alert, he will remind you to do so.

After all this, a neophyte at horse hunting for elk might decide the four-footed help isn't worth the trouble. But you want

to know a horse's limitations as well as his advantages. I've known even ranching veterans who, temporarily careless, came to grief. One was bucked off when a loose saddle slipped forward toward his mount's head. I've had a fingertip nearly ripped off by a horse which refused to be tied; but it was my fault. If I had asked the wrangler why this horse was walking around untied, he could have told me why—the animal was incorrigible. It's a matter of horse sense. Put yourself in the place of the animal.

Saddle Comforts

When it comes to horseback comfort, I like to wear soft clothing, especially when embarking on a long ride. This means avoiding jeans or other pants with rivets on the seat. Likewise, I keep my wallet in my front pocket (you can lose a wallet that rubs a hole in your pants pocket against a saddle), or I put it in the saddle bag. I wouldn't take it at all, except that I keep my hunting licenses there. Also, make sure your stirrups fit. Any cramps you have early will turn into full-scale pain 10 miles later. A common mistake is for stirrups to be too high. If you don't know how to adjust your stirrups, let your guide do it for you. If on your own, take time to get as good a fit as you can. You'll be happy later you did.

Rifle Scabbards

There are several ways to handle a rifle scabbard. Many hunters like to dismount before extracting the rifle from the left side. Others like the scabbard on the right side with the stock near the saddle horn where they can keep a constant eye on it. Rifles have been known to be plucked right out of the scabbard when riding through dense cover, especially if the sling is allowed to droop outside the scabbard. Keep it tucked inside. Whichever position you prefer, keep the open end tilted up slightly so that the rifle can't bounce its way out and fall free.

You will also want to practice dismounting quickly enough to shoot at an elk on the move. If you don't, you might find yourself on the ground, looking up at your mount's belly. Also practice removing rifle from scabbard. Your scabbard should have a special notch for any bolt-action rifles. Freeing the bolt from the notch rapidly may require some concentration. If it seems laborious, imagine a giant bull staring back at you from 200 yards. You have perhaps three or four seconds to get an accurate shot off. Can you do it?

One more thing. Drill with your rifle on safety. That's the way you always want to do it. With gloved hands, a hunter's fingers can inadvertently press the trigger when grabbing at a rifle. On one occasion, it was nearly fatal when a hunter in front of me accidentally fired his weapon just after clearing the scabbard with it. We had spotted a bull with "aspen limbs growing from its head," and several orange-vesters went for their rifles. The rifle not on safety fired, nearly hitting a hunter and guide in front of it. Needless to say, we never saw the elk again. Much worse could have happened.

Saddle Bags

When tying something on your saddle bag, make certain ends don't hang loose. Tie your saddle bag on tightly before attaching coat or other clothing. More than one bag has been lost by someone quickly untying a raincoat and then forgetting to retie the saddle bag. If you carry anything fragile in the bag, like a camera, pad it well against the bouncing it will take. On a guided hunt, you can identify your saddle, bridle, halter rope, saddle bags, and other tack by placing a piece of adhesive tape on the saddle. Write your name on it, and hang the other paraphernalia on the saddle horn each night. Wranglers like the idea of keeping your gear with you and your horse rather than adjusting bridle, stirrups, etc., daily.

Horse Care

When feeding a horse grain (oats is a favorite), place it in a feed bag or other container (rubber dishes can be purchased for this purpose), to keep your mount from taking in excessive dirt. Otherwise, "wheezes" could possibly follow.

If without benefit of a corral, some old salts tether their horses by running a rope through a garden hose to stiffen it and make it less likely a horse could tangle in it.

It is a good idea to have someone around who knows horses and knows the particular string you're to hunt with. For one thing, he can select sure-footed, mountain-bred horses fully confident in elk country. For another, he may know of a certain mount with a sensitive scar near the left ear which should be handled gently. Such animals can bite the hand which touches any such tender spot. Before putting your gear on a horse, do your own checking for strap sores, bruises, etc. A curry comb's purpose is more than making a horse parade-pretty, or even getting burrs out. Hand and comb working together can ferret out sores or other areas of horse flesh where knots and straps should be avoided. If medical attention is required, you don't always need a veterinarian. He can often supply you ahead of the hunt with medicants in spray form to treat a horse's cuts, sores, and other minor irritations.

Watch for Signals

Watch for trouble signals from your horse. If your mount shies abruptly from a hand lifted alongside his line of vision, he will likely do the same when you attempt to extract a rifle from a scabbard near his head. Some mounts panic when you move anything rapidly near their eyes or flanks. One game biologist I know leaned over to latch a gate hurriedly, and his horse bit him severely on the buttocks. He was able to joke about the cayuse "wanting to be traded to a fisheries biologist," but he couldn't sit down for weeks. But there may be some ignored signals prior to such seemingly unwarranted attacks. As has been mentioned, much of a horse's behavior results from previous experience. It is that factor which causes some steeds to take off like a Derby winner when you drop the reins, while another must be slapped before he gets your message. I've seen an otherwise savvy game warden get knocked down when he walked behind a pack animal without letting him know he was there. Just a few words before walking around to tighten the rear harness would have saved those two hooves to his chest. Fortunately, they did not strike him in the jaw.

Sometimes horses strange to one another must be separated. When a certain

Getting your steed to hold still while glassing is not easy, but it will help if you gain his confidence, calm his fears, but also let him know he can't get away with anything out of line.

Wyoming wrangler I know bought several Utah horses, he couldn't keep the newcomers from being kicked and bitten. They had to be separated from his resident animals at night, and on the trail. Obviously, you wouldn't want such animals together while making a drive on elk. They might whinny or began bickering noisily as game approached.

Hunters can also make such mistakes. Bob Burch, outfitter-guide in Colorado's San Juan Wilderness Area out of Vallecito, told me he has placed hunters in high, timberless passes only to have their horses spook elk. One hunter let the stirrups thump his horse as he dismounted. One horse whinnied when separated from a second horse he had spent most of the hunt with. The important thing is to be observant. When you get a quiet group of horses, try to maintain your good luck in prime elk habitat by keeping them together. A veteran wrangler knows which cayuses get along. But if you are on your own, check early in the hunt to see which combinations of animals work out. Certainly there will be some packhorses which won't get along with riding horses, and this could cause trouble if you take them along while actually hunting.

Coaxing a horse into a trailer can be a challenge indeed. Most wranglers I know give the cayuse some time and room on this one, especially if the step up is a big one. If pushing and cajoling don't work, you might try placing hay or oats inside, up front. (Rustling the oats in a bucket, the same ploy used in catching a mount, can't hurt.) In most cases, you will have to use patience. Leading an experienced horse in first can help. If your truck or trailer lacks partitions to equalize weight, you will have to be careful not to tilt both horses onto one side. It could tip your vehicle. In such matters it usually is best to have a veteran horse handler around. That's a good reason in itself to hire a guide who has moxy with horses.

If you ever find yourself bucked off a horse, or beneath flailing legs, the best recourse is take up a tight fetal position. Cover your head and neck. Keep your hands in. Most horses will instinctively try to avoid contact with you as much as you do them. It is simply less likely to cause them pain. Remain still if possible, unless it is a wild stallion or other animal deliberately attempting to maim. I've looked up at horse bellies a number of times, but only once was I accidentally struck. In that one, I was simply surrounded by too many excited animals to avoid them all.

Preventive "medicine" is the best approach. Much can be avoided by repairing equipment before it breaks. A pocket knife can be used to cut new bridle-strap holes when leather wears through. Never let a saddle slip very far forward or rearward. Keep your cool. You don't have to go to pieces just because your tack does.

14

The Elk Camp

Since elk hunting usually requires a generous amount of time and preparation, the traditional wapiti camp is frequently more than a mere parking of cars at road's end. The latter situation may suffice for hunting deer or antelope, but a successful elk hunter can often be told by the camp he keeps.

I prefer the kind where you can not only take care of physical needs such as sleeping quarters and food, but also have a planned social atmosphere—a place you look forward to reaching each evening following the hunt. A place where after a rugged day you can sit back and reflect on elk and elk hunting. Some of the banter might even bear a resemblance to the facts.

Such was the camp a group of guides put together in Wyoming's Bridger National Forest during the 1984 and 1985 seasons. The region was so wild it was an adventure just reaching the end of the four-wheel-drive track that was loosely labeled a road. Then came an eight-mile horseback ride. The first ride in each year was difficult. At the campsite we faced rocks and bare ground. After the camp was up, the trail in to it, even in a bitter blizzard, wasn't nearly as formidable . . . now the path led to light and cheer and human warmth.

We set that camp up so the kitchen tent was large enough to get everyone inside by the stove, yet the cook still had room to fix supper and clean up afterward. The kitchen was at a right angle to the other tents, so there was ready access to the "mess hall." It became obvious to me then, if it hadn't been previously, that the cook tent always emerges as the camp's social center. Therefore you might as well plan it that way to begin with. As we set things up, the guide's tent was on the right side of the kitchen and the hunters' on the left, keeping the two groups apart with their separate responsibilities. Guides must usually get up well before hunters, to get fires started and horses saddled, but there is no reason to wake the hunters before their time. If the hunters preferred to get up first, they could get our attention by tossing a snowball at our tent wall. In the darkness it sounded like a sledge-hammer.

A well-organized kitchen "headquarters" provides daily necessities you'll want handy. Fruits and vegetables, for example, need to be accessible to the kitchen, but well away from heat. Our kitchen tent had a blanket partition that kept the section opposite the stove much cooler than the rest of the tent. Things like juices which had to be kept cool were placed at the far end of that partition, near the tent wall. Temperatures there day and night were about the same as in a household refrigerator. Bread and other items mice could spoil were placed beneath upside-down wooden panniers that were not needed until pack-out time. There were also hooks . . . and a place to put everything.

A stream 30 feet outside the kitchen door was our water supply. Equidistant in the other direction was a small mountain of wood. During the summer months trees, mostly pine, had been chainsawed into three-foot lengths. Later we split the logs into quarters just right for the stoves.

These stoves were 10-gallon barrels cut in half lengthwise. A metal cover was soldered onto the flat side, and a hinged door was added to seal off what was now the front of the stove. Air holes were punched in the door to provide oxygen to the fire. Metal braces were soldered to the belly of the barrel for legs. With the door closed, the fire perked. Open, it raged.

We placed a paper cup filled with a mixture of sawdust and kerosene in a far corner of the tent to soak overnight. To start a morning fire, you just tossed the contents into the fireplace atop a single paper napkin, lit a match to the napkin, and stood back. A little kindling was added, and soon split logs were blazing. Of course, we generally kept sleeping-quarter fires alive only long enough to take the chill off the tent for dressing. The kitchen stove sometimes burned all day.

We placed our tack tent for saddles and bridles about 60 feet from the kitchen. The hay-grain feed tent went nearby. To the side of our hitching post, we built a square corral enclosure by placing logs between live trees, positioning them horizontally about two and four feet high. An uphill spring fed water through a garden hose into a tub at the corner of the corral. The tub spilled and then flowed on below camp. Far enough from this area we placed our latrine, a wooden-roofed structure made of plywood and log support beams. We were overjoyed when the U.S. Forest Service approved our one-holer design on the first try, although the next year the agency did require us to move it farther away from the corral and hitching post. I never did find out why it had to be moved, nor did I ask. We also had to move the corral fencing. It was apparently in the path of wandering moose.

The Right Arrangement

Arrangement of our horse facilities made it possible to come in late from hunting, light one lamp, tie the mount, remove saddle and bridle and put them in the tack tent, and then, after supplying feed to the horse, head for the kitchen to chow down ourselves. By the time we'd had our fill, the cayuse had also. We could then lead the critter into the corral for the night. It was all relatively simple, allowing us to return kitchenward to listen to a few tall tales before bedtime.

The first year we put our camp in, it seemed enough just to hew it out of the wilderness. We had no electricity. Light came via gas lantern, flashlight, or not at all. That year our tent floors were dirt — often frozen. The next year, plywood pieces placed together for floors were an improvement much applauded.

At first, we kept the horses in a fenced three-acre meadow. It was perfect for the animals — but not for people trying to catch them. Just when you thought you had one bridled, he stepped into the icy creek with you. In addition, horses could hide in high brush even from a flashlight, slowing down the entire process of preparing to hunt.

The second year, with additional improvements, we enjoyed the hunt infinitely more. Some hardy (and in my opinion misguided) souls might prefer a primitive camp, feeling it more compatible with their Kit Carson or Jim Bridger self-image. However, our goal was to make the place a home away from home, a haven comfortable enough to relax in at night. You don't appreciate electric lights until you've gone without them. We especially used them while working with the horses and cutting wood. True, the generator did reduce wilderness silence, although ours was fairly quiet. Chores could be done much more quickly. It meant more time for evening talk — until someone looked at the kitchen clock and saw there were only a few hours remaining until predawn wakeup.

This isn't to say an elk hunter shouldn't go all "natural," including cooking done by a campfire. To each his own. But our permanent camp, with many souls bustling about each morning and evening, was my idea of an ideal home in some of America's wildest mountain terrain.

Some hunters may prefer dirt floors to keep it "frontier" style. I've had it that way. Trouble is, a little precipitation can change your outlook hurriedly. Once, when it began to rain, a guide and several hunters spent nearly an hour matching their pads and sleeping bags to the only dry spot in the tent. And then a creek washed them out during the night. No, I'll take a cot, or even pack in a sun-deck chair, provided there is space on a horse. If not, I would go with a covering of some type over the earthen floor. I've been kidded at times about using a deck lounge — "Hey, have you got that thing broke to ride?" — but I also believe in the importance of getting some sleep before going elk hunting. Of course, if you don't have packhorses, you rough it. But some ways of roughing it are easier than others.

However, an elk camp is much more than its physical components. An elk camp for the beginner or the super-hardy may be little more than a campfire with a sleeping bag and a few pots or pans and a can opener lying nearby. The main ingredient is people . . . hunters with the indomitable will to outwit an elk by day, and the same will to relax from the joust by night. Elk camp is a place to unwind and enjoy the lull between the challenge of man and beast. One of the most intense hunters I've ever known was also among the most relaxed after sundown. He didn't talk much when there was daylight to hunt. But after returning to camp, he would usually have a story to tell. Often he insisted that his every word was true. It might go something like this:

Hunter: "I looked out across the basin, saw something dark moving, stopped for a closer look, then realized the bull had seen me."

Another hunter: "Took off then, I guess?"

Paul: "Nope, ran straight toward me."

Guide: "A bull elk?"

Paul: "Bull moose."

Another guide: "Then what?"

Paul: "He got close enough to see what I was, and veered off."

Me: "See any bull elk all day?"

Paul: "Looked at what must have been a world record."

All guides together: "Well?"

Paul: "Felt sorry for you. It was down in a deep canyon. I didn't want to make you haul it out. I kept looking for a little 6-pointer you could handle . . ."

And so it went. Since you didn't always know what "enlightenment" you could believe, you picked out what you wanted. The after-dinner companionship was spiced somewhat by the fact guides were not always with every hunter at all times (we were not hunting in a declared wilderness area). Nonresident licensees often preferred to hunt down a mountain, with the guides trailing horses to the bottom. If it had been a designated wilderness area, nonresidents would have had to remain with guides. Enjoyment in many camps is heightened when different pairs of guides and hunters can exchange notes with each other. This may help a neophyte nimrod, who will be satisfied with a spike as end of the hunt nears. A veteran hunter seeking only a trophy could be happy to share locations of lesser bulls. That's serious stuff. The "environment" in any camp either encourages or discourages such valuable day's-end conversation. Maybe it would happen anyway. But the right camp makes it more fun.

Special Mission

One day, when several guides and I had to head for town to bring in more supplies, several of the hunters entreated us to bring them in some distilled spirits. The outfitter had nothing specific against whisky on the premises, but on the other hand, we didn't have much room on the horses for carrying the stuff, or the means to pad it. All the sleeping bags, blankets, and such were already in camp. But we went to town, bought the liquor, and headed back. It was well after dark when we left the road's end, and a packer who happened to be there helped out. After a mile or so in the dark, one of the loads slipped, the horses panicked, and after repacking . . . well, it was late indeed as we headed down the home stretch along a wilderness lake into camp. One slip along the lake's ledges, and we would be in deep, frigid water. Yet one thing cheered me up. Those hunters would be looking for their booze. I knew we would not be left forever at the bottom of the lake. Through the fog and the cold and the wee hours' fatigue, I envisioned the camp with its inhabitants cheering our arrival. It kept me going. And I was not disappointed. The rejoicing at our homecoming well after midnight resembled a miniature Olympics opening ceremony.

That's the spirit of elk camp as I know it. After experiencing a few like that, you can even feel it coming as you notch the lodgepoles together for the wall tent's frame. Fitting a triangle of poles together, digging holes to anchor the vertical slabs, and all the rest could be just drudgery if you forgot about the camaraderie to fill the camp later. If you really got into the mood, you willingly added doorway metal snaps to retain every ounce of precious warm air inside. You didn't just cut, hammer, and dig. You *anticipated*.

Of course, some tasks just don't have much warmth to them, such as scraping snow off the several tents each night. One day the tack-tent ceiling very nearly collapsed under melting snow pooled beside the pine supports. With the cook and sleeping tents, we had to make certain chimney sparks didn't touch canvas (or the nylon-reinforced plastic of the newer tents). This required metal plating, although the plates didn't fit well enough to keep cold entirely out. I think one of these summers I will take a month off to fit the metal perfectly to chimney size. But it didn't matter—if a fire was burning nearby, and it often was.

We had our own standards of perfection. Wooden floors so level you could play marbles on them. No one wanted to. But we could have.

I also enjoyed seeing a pot of hot water on the stove at all times, for hot drinks at any time of day as well as washing things. If there are no gloves placed near the stove to handle hot things, I'll place mine nearby. Lacking gloves, a pair of pliers will do almost as well. Smart camp managers also keep Dutch ovens cooking something while hunters are out. Raspberry cobbler may require only 20 minutes (depending on the heat of the fire and how well buried in coals the oven is); a venison roast needs hours. It doesn't take much, either, to improvise—a can of mushroom soup can save many a blackened or undercooked potato. It has for me.

A propane stove can make a tent a comfortable place to sit out a storm, reading or making repairs or sharpening a knife. It's not that a hunter needs to bring everything from home but the kitchen sink; it's just that it is wise to be prepared, something even an 11-year-old boy is reminded to do in his earliest scout training.

A Different Camp

True, camps can be something other than the above. I remember one year guiding a midwestern nimrod who was confined to a wheelchair during the hunt and a good bed at night. He paid for a suite of rooms at a mountain resort—our hunting camp. We watched the Green Bay Packers via excellent TV reception on a Monday night. I'm a football fan, but I felt uneasy with it. I yearned for a campfire with a hot front and a cold behind, and the distant sound of coyotes. A generous sort, the hunter paid for everything, including my restaurant steaks. But it didn't seem like elk hunting. In addition—and as might be predicted with our comforts reluctantly left behind in the morning—we did not score on elk, although we did bag a mule deer later on.

Camps may consist of pickup campers, trailers, fifth wheelers—temporary homes on the edge of elk country. You see it every fall. But I remember more warmly a tent camp with an Old West atmosphere you could taste. A sheepherder joined us one evening and told us of his constant war to keep coyotes from his sheep. Later that night, we heard prairie wolves seemingly closing in on a kill just up-canyon. He wailed back at them. They stopped howling.

"What did you say to them?" I asked.

"I told them to shut up," he said simply. No one could argue with that.

Another time I was in a camp where the cook was very nervous over a dead horse in the meadow below us. "Grizzly will be on that there horse before morning," he stated matter-of-factly. Next morning, sure enough, we found the horse partly eaten. Bear tracks circled a few dozen feet from the food tent as well.

"He'll be back tonight and maybe tomorrow night. Then he'll be finished. What will he eat then?" the cook wanted someone to answer.

We didn't know. But the cook was careful to prevent any cooking or garbage odors for the next two nights. Then we noticed the horse flesh was gone. Only the bones remained. The next night was not exactly filled with terror, but it was one with less sleep. No bears. The griz had apparently moved elsewhere. However, the next year, when a silvertip sow and her two cubs frequented the camp, several dudes stated unequivocally they couldn't abide the tension, asking to be packed out so they could spend the remainder of the elk quest elsewhere. I would not have done that, yet I can understand their feelings. Camps are not places to fear, but to enjoy.

Keeping a camp clean, hauling out refuse, and sleeping in quarters other than the cook tent are excellent practices in bear country. You can obtain a list of other bear-country camp tips by writing to the National Park Service in Washington, D.C., or directly to Grand Teton or Yellowstone National Parks in Moose or Mammoth, Wyoming.

Camp is also a good place to ask questions which could lead to paydirt. I asked a few one day:

"Been in this camp before?"

"Third year."

"Scored each time?"

"Yup."

That was enough to convince me I needed to hunt harder.

"Where did you eventually locate a bull?" I queried.

"About a mile out of camp, up on that mountain to the east." He hesitated, then added, "But I've also seen them from the lower camp to the west."

"Sounds like they're everywhere. But why are the other hunters having such a tough time locating bulls?"

"They're not looking in the right places."

"Where are the right places?"

"Well, not in thick timber. They could be there, but you wouldn't see much of them, let alone get a shot."

"Where then?"

"The little openings."

"There aren't many of them," I said, trying the role of a devil's advocate.

"The snowslides, old burns, south-facing ridgelines near timberline . . ."

I pondered what he said. And the next day I went out and shot a nice bull.

Another time a hunter returned to camp with tales of elk, but couldn't describe exactly where they were. Guides had to ask questions. The clue was that when he descended straight downhill from those wapiti, he hit a spot on the creek that was too wide to cross. He had to walk down-canyon to find a place to jump. Guides deduced where he had been.

The elk camp can be a wonderfully humorous place. Things that wouldn't be funny at all anywhere else are hilarious in elk camp. I recall a guide and hunter returning one day to a camp where I had just arrived.

"Don't go out hunting on Torrent Creek," a blue-in-the-face rifle-toter said in my direction when he spotted me sharpening my knife.

"Why is that?"

"I fell down out there trying to cross the creek. Went tumbling downstream."

"But you got out OK, apparently," I concluded.

"Yeah, but the guide, he knew what was most important. He saved my rifle."

The guide and hunter chuckled a few times, then laughed heartily, and finally held their stomachs with unbridled guffaws. The guide even rolled over onto the floor. As I said, it wasn't really all that funny. But this was elk camp. It's not hard having a good time there.

Camp Chemistry

One thing I do in camp is separate the pessimists from the optimists. Then I keep track of them later in the week. Sure enough, almost to a man, both groups are accurate in their outlook.

I prefer the optimists. I particularly remember three brothers in one camp: Paul, Mike, and Ed Palmer. All were excited about just being at a frontier camp. They hunted in wind, cold, heat, slush, and fog. They always headed out with a chin-out determination, and returned with a smile whatever the day's results. Many times they did not fire their rifles, or even glass any bulls. But they always found something to get excited about. One day it was two badgers, the next a bobcat or moose. Once they exulted in the trout they saw rising in a creek inlet at a lake. It could be nothing but a pile of snow glistening on yonder peaks. (Often it's the simple things that are most profound.)

Once the Palmer brothers got their bearings, they knew the landscape as well as the cartographers who drew up the local maps. After a time, they asked the guides to meet them at certain trail junctions with horses in case they scored. All three were searching for mature bulls, and although all saw them, only one elk was actually killed. One brother passed up a shot, and another glassed a big bull. It was an inspiration to see how they operated. Many mornings they skipped breakfast to get out early, taking food for the day in a pack. Often they went without horses. One day they did this after the guides had arrived late, bringing them in a special load of things from town.

"Sleep in," the brothers said. We did — until daylight. I always appreciated that.

If something went wrong, the Palmers never blamed anyone. They merely tried harder. Paul brought along his wife to cook one year. Ann did such a terrific job the outfitter paid her as much as any of the veteran "chefs" ever received, and invited her back. The outstanding hunt we had that year had much to do with the cheerfulness of this crew. I wouldn't have missed that hunt, particularly the camp banter when the hunters returned in the evenings, for anything.

There comes a time each autumn when the hunt, and therefore the camp, closes. The tents must be taken down, in most instances, just as meticulously as they were erected. If the snow isn't beaten out of the canvas wall tents, no one can lift them onto the horses. To prevent mildew, water has to be dried out of almost everything. One guide I know, Pete Reid of Billings, Montana, used to store his tents each year in a metal garbage can. Even in the bitter cold winter of Montana, those tents were none the worse for wear when we fished them out of the garbage cans to use again.

When it came time to put camp away, we always locked what we could in the solid-roofed outhouses. We tried to place nails and snaps where we could find them the next year, but it seemed the animals ate them. I never could find many of the smaller items. Perhaps wandering sheepherders made use of some.

Yet at the end of autumn we were doing much more than folding away tents. We were folding treasured, irreplaceable memories.

15

Resident and Nonresident Strategy

Whether or not you live in the state where you plan to hunt, one of the most important questions facing you is whether to hire a guide or go it alone.

If you have been primarily an eastern whitetail hunter or a midwest varmint shooter, you've probably dreamed of someday trying your stalking and shooting prowess Out West for elk. Then one day you see an ad in an outdoor magazine which seems to promise everything you've ever hoped for. You have never been to that region before, but it has a reputation for excellent wapiti hunting. Individual success is 75 percent in most years, according to the ad. That sounds pretty good to you, but first you obtain references and write to them. Some are outright gushy, and none are negative.

The guide helps you get in your applications before the deadline. And he seems

very helpful in answering your questions. Later you manage to draw out, count yourself fortunate, and gear up for the hunting opportunity of a lifetime.

When you first arrive in camp, everything seems about as expected. The food is fine, horses are sure-footed on the mountain trails, and the alpine scenery is beautiful. However, within several days you discover one problem. A new road was cut into this mountain a year ago, after the references you checked with had hunted here, and the public access has brought in enough competition to make hunting much more difficult than in the past. You might locate a shootable bull, yet it isn't quite what you had expected. Other rifle-toters are out there combing every ridge and canyon. You feel you should have been warned of this flaw in paradise, but you have to admit you might have asked other questions to bring things more up to date. In fact, armed with hindsight, you begin to wonder if you should have signed up here at all.

You did have several clues that hunting might not be all you were led to believe. One was the 75 percent hunter-success figure. Even in good years, topnotch elk states like Montana, Colorado, Wyoming, and Idaho rarely exceed 30-35 percent hunter success. And in those good years weather or luck would have a bearing on number and size of bulls taken. Thus, "75 percent" has suspicious overtones.

An outfitter I worked for several years ago watched his success rate spiral downward when warm weather kept elk from migrating into his territory. Later, mining and mineral booms mushroomed the human population, and the number of hunters. Ratio of license-holders to bulls increased alarmingly. However, instead of continuing to bemoan the situation or continue his previous publicity, he opened a camp in higher, wilder terrain. Then he could book hunters into either camp. If they didn't locate wapiti in the lower one, they might in the higher. The high camp cost him more to maintain, and therefore cost licensees more as well. They understood, willingly shelling out more money for a greater chance of scoring. The problem was solved pretty much to everyone's satisfaction.

"Guaranteed" Hunting

But that is not the way some outfitters overcome diminishing hunting success. Some continue with old but outdated publicity, not necessarily fabricating facts but simply failing to face them squarely. For example, my own outfitter could have truthfully publicized 70 percent success

for the previous few years, but he also realized — to his credit — that he couldn't guarantee it for the future. He sold his hunts as an opportunity to find elk and enjoy being in elk country. Because of his honesty, this outfitter enjoys something else: repeat business. Every one of his clients is a reference which now helps to sell his hunt each year.

But what of those outfitters who do offer a high, even 100 percent, shoot? Statistics can almost always be used to belie the truth. It's like the statement which says more people buy fishing licenses than marriage licenses each year. Does that mean fishing is more popular and worthwhile than getting married? Thus it would seem.

Then, too, what is being guaranteed? That the elk will simply be visible, or will show up within easy shooting range of 100 yards? Guarantees are for domestic animals, not wild ones.

Recently I sat down with one issue of a popular outdoor magazine to sort out ads for guides. I looked at 32 for one state alone, Colorado. I categorized them the way I felt a hunter would likely do it:

Good, but sound expensive: 5. Good, suitable for a guy on a budget, 20. Suspicious, 3. Cryptic or difficult to understand ad, 4.

The figures for Montana ads were 5, 13, 1, and 1, a similar breakdown. What was "suspicious" about the three ads in Colorado and one in Montana? Claims ranging from 95 percent success on bulls in general (apparently no one is perfect) to 60 percent on 6-point bulls. One claimant bragged 100 percent harvest. I wrote to him, receiving the following reply within a few days.

"I am pleased you are interested in hunting with us. We have 100 percent success on all our hunts. We go by the policy that we have to get your animal or animals before we earn our money. If we are unable to do that, then we haven't done our job, and will return your monies we have on deposit. This policy has been very hard to keep through the years, especially since I'm the only outfitter in _____ who does it.

"I hunt on private land where I have exclusive hunting rights. These lands are now some of the best hunting areas in central _____. We use 4 x 4 pickups to get into these areas, and then hunt on foot . . . Our elk are hunted in an enclosed area at _____. This is our own private elk herd; we take only the oldest bulls every year, 7 to 11-year-olds.

"A state license is not required on these hunts. We started our own elk herd when it became apparent we could no longer insure that every one of the folks who hunted with us would have the chance to get a mature bull elk . . . We average two or three stalks on trophies (not just "nice" animals) each day. For an elk . . . three days is plenty."

A list of references follows. And a price list. If you want a 6-pointer, you pay $1,000 more. The "pitch" is honest. But I'm certainly not interested in a shoot of this type. It reminds me of some whitetail farms I saw in the Midwest when I lived there. You pick your bragging rights, then shoot it. The chance to fail is what makes hunting an adventure rather than an accommodation. Self-satisfaction is difficult without a challenge.

I'm not talking here about hunting on private ranches where the game is free-roaming. Skills in locating the quarry are still required in that situation. The only guarantee is quality hunting where there are fewer competitors than on public land.

If you feel like sleeping in, you can do it with less fear that some other license-holder is shying your elk. (I should also mention that I have high admiration for the hunter who consistently beats the competition on the national forests and other public real estate; he has to be on his toes.)

I don't say that private-land hunting is necessarily easy. One of my toughest elk quests anywhere was on the Ute Indian Reservation of eastern Utah. In this hinterland of some half a million wild acres, my partner and I were the only rifle-toters for a week. We had the advantage of knowing no one else would spook the game we stalked. I liked that. But the thickly tined 5-point bull I took there could scarcely be tabbed as child's play. It was necessary to comb many square miles to locate any sign of wapiti. And when we did, there were dozens of exits for them to flee.

Sometimes you have to select your hunts carefully, even those called by the state fish and game departments. I know of one where weather was mild, the elk did not move into foothills, and hunters found no wapiti. Maybe it should have been called off. But that requires extra action on the part of the game department, something they may or may not take. Besides that, the responsibility of knowing what is happening must rest with you. Ultimately, you have to pay for the hunt, good or bad.

Choosing a Guide

Here is my advice, as both a hunter and guide, on what to ask any outfitter-guide before booking a hunt. Ask how many hunters who actually get out and hunt (many come for the scenery or to visit while recuperating from a broken ankle) have had an opportunity in recent years to shoot at game within rifle range. Here you are querying about the presence of elk, not how many hunters killed one, a factor often outside the guide's control. Are there 6-point (royal) and 7-point (imperial) bulls around? Guides expect to answer those questions. Avoid questions which are entirely subjective, like "Do you have good horses?" or "Do you serve good food?" Few would answer "no." Be leery of stock answers like "elk all over the place!" Are they really? Does the guide know where they are likely to go once the shooting begins? Does he have the means of reaching them after opening day when they are on the move? How many guides per hunter?

Also ask how long the outfitter has been familiar with his region. He may have just moved a camp in, but you want to be sure he knows — under various weather conditions, etc. — how to hunt the elk in this territory you are about to pay thousands of dollars for the privilege of entering under his tutelage. Make sure he answers your questions honestly, thoroughly, and sincerely rather than just tossing out "pat" replies.

Many outfitters recommend at least a 10-day hunt for trophy elk. You will be expected — in all instances not specifically excepted — to pay for the entire 10 days even if you should score on the first day. The outfitter's costs (often even food) are fixed, whether the hunt brings a 7-point bull the first hour or empty hands at its conclusion. The outfitter must also pay his guides for 10 days as contracted. Almost certainly, every guide is expected to work all 10 days. Incidentally, when an outfitter talks about a 10-day hunt, he usually means one day getting in and one

day out, leaving eight to hunt. That is standard. You might down a bull on the way out, but if getting the meat and horns out requires an extra day, the outfitter has a perfect right to charge you for it — unless you have an understanding beforehand to cover a different arrangement.

Here is a complete list of those things you as a hunter have a right to expect on a fully guided hunt:

• A variety of good food, including meat, desserts, drinks, etc. That would include hot food morning and evening, and a lunch packed for the day to take with you after breakfast. Incidentally, many outfitters or cooks will custom-purchase foods if contacted before they head to the local grocery store.

• Comfortable shelter, usually to include wooden flooring, heater stoves, pads, and cots — unless previously understood that it is a primitive-type first-year camp in a new area, which should be explained by the outfitter before you book.

• Horses familiar with the terrain.

• Guides familiar with the terrain — and willing to work for you daily in locating game.

• Packing of game to a processing plant, or your vehicle.

• Special care for trophies, such as getting antlers out in one piece. Fine points like caping or custom skinning should be worked out ahead of time. I know of some guides who cape out automatically for the quoted price, and some who do not even attempt it.

In most instances, you will be expected to bring your own sleeping bag, plus personal items. Check on transportation arrangements. Some super-friendly guides may take you into their homes for the first night, and most will help you make a reservation at the nearest motel, or locate a campsite. A few host incoming license-holders at a bar-restaurant in town. Some pick you up at your night's lodging, while others may expect you to drive to the road leading to the base camp, or to the camp itself. These are things you will want to talk over ahead of time. A place of difficult access may cost more, but it's usually worth it.

Another, somewhat intangible factor you have a right to expect from a guided hunt is sufficient optimism on the outfitter's part to help you to overcome the adversities of poor weather, a horse which might come up lame, etc. The guide should be ready to go out whenever the hunter is. True, I've tried to convince some novice that it would be better to wait until heavy rains desist, but if the client wants to go out now, it is the guide's job to take him, within reason. If the problem is fog, I see no reason not to get into position for the moment it clears. A visibility-hindering blizzard may force the guide into a weather-predicting situation. Ideally, with 10 days (or eight) at his disposal, the hunter has time to wait for better conditions. He may also begin to have enough confidence in his guide to allow the guide to say when conditions are right.

As an example, I will do what I can to convince a hunter that drizzling rain is no time to seek elk. They are seldom out of cover at such a time, and no hunter is going to be as effective with water hampering his visibility, streaking his scope, and maybe infiltrating his clothing. Nevertheless, most guides I've talked to agree that if the client is paying for the day, it is a guide's duty to get out when the hunter says, "Let's go," anytime during legal hunting hours.

Yet the hunter must expect some interruptions to his guided time. When game is down, one guide may be forced to take half a day or more to get it out. If it's the usual setup of one guide for every two hunters, one hunter will have to exhibit some patience when a guide is thus tied up. Nor can all the game be taken back to road's end at the conclusion of the hunt, for packhorses then will likely fill with hunter gear and, at season's end, the camp tents.

The "Spot Camp"

If you're willing to get along without horses or daily guide services, you can save some 50 percent in most cases on hunt expenses by going to the "spot" camp. Here, however, after being dropped or "spotted" in elk country, you may make it big or fail miserably. Two parties I watched one year had far different success. Both had ample wood, water, scenery. But the group which had scouted the terrain they were taken to tied tags to two whopping bulls. The other crew wasted much of its time searching in the wrong places. For one thing, they arrived in the dead of night and, not knowing precisely how they got in, spent most of one morning glassing over the canyon through which we had brought them. I've traveled that popular trail dozens of times without seeing a single game animal of any kind save a few slow-to-learn mule deer does. Certainly elk are smart enough to avoid the area. Although the hunters unfamiliar with this region didn't know it, elk were to be found two canyons eastward. But after a few days of wandering around, they became too fatigued to wander much more, especially in the uphill direction required to reach the elk. When picked up at the end of the week, they had turned to fishing.

The successful party had done more than merely point to a map and say, "Take us there." They knew the lay of the land well enough to go out in dense fog without fear of getting lost, and channeled their energy—whatever the weather—to take advantage of everything which could be turned to their benefit. They even knew from which direction other hunters might arrive, and placed themselves in strategic position to intercept any elk those others might move. Minus this information, spot campers would do well to hire a guide. Spot camping is no substitute for knowing the terrain. Yet it does save money and works out fine for hunters willing to scout ahead.

One variation of the above is to rent horses, then go on your own. But it is best if you know both the horses and the area. Again, you can reduce wasted time by hiring a guide.

I wouldn't begrudge a good guide his pay. One season I worked some 16 hours a day, averaging out to about $3.33 an hour. Every guide did far more than merely guide each day. Some of the "extras" included finding hunters who did not go where they were supposed to, thus becoming lost for a time; fetching lost items; repairing equipment in the middle of the night; and packing in added supplies.

In some states like New Mexico, landowners can automatically obtain a special authorization form from the fish-and-game department. When hunter and landowner come to terms, on either a guided hunt or a "trespass" fee, the landowner signs it and returns it to the fish-and-game department. When the hunter sends in his request for a license, the state issues it. The hunter must pay the department with something other than a personal check—money order, cashier's or traveler's check.

Success-ratio figures indicate this arrangement works out rather well for the hunter. New Mexico statistics show public hunts yielding 18.9 percent success in recent years, while a "landowner" hunt brings in 57.9 percent success. Check this out in the state you intend to hunt.

Power of Attorney

Another thing you can do in most states is grant your outfitter Power of Attorney. A legal document signed by you before a Notary Public is then returned to the outfitter, who applies for your license. He does everything necessary to buy your permit, perhaps even filling out the form concerning your physical description, to render the license nontransferable. The outfitter then sends in your application with others, or makes a trip to the fish-and-game office to stand in line on your behalf. You are then notified if you have a license to hunt with him.

Some outfitters also get a list of who was lucky in the lottery for certain game tags, then call those hunters to offer guiding services. This isn't unethical, but it can resemble "ambulance chasing" if such an outfitter tries to pressure you to contract with him. This is one way an outfitter can remain in business. But I wouldn't make any promises over the telephone. Tell him to put in writing what he says he can do for you. Check out references, including the clientele who were with him the year before. Some experienced hunters also make it a policy to ask for the name of a hunter or two who were unsuccessful. If the guide balks, ask why. With such references you can find out why the permittees failed to score. It can be most enlightening. Some nimrods have complaints which are not as valid as others, but at least this tactic gives you an opportunity to find out the pros and cons of going with a certain guide. You may also meet one at a trade or sportsman's show, but after you listen to the sales pitch, make certain your questions are being answered, not just gilded over.

I know of few dishonest guide-outfitters. But as in all human endeavors, there are some. I deem it a plus if an outfitter has been in business for a half decade or longer, but then, some young and eager types will make up in energy what they may lack in experience. There are a few places you can't let yourself be short-changed, however, and two of them are knowledge of horses and of terrain. Any quest for elk can sour hurriedly with the lack of either. I'd rather have to bear a problem or two in almost any other area, because the two mentioned deal directly with success. Most guides, of course, realize they must please in every area in order to remain in business.

Local Guide Laws

Canadian provinces like British Columbia require guides for all nonresident hunters. Several states including Wyoming require nonresidents hire a guide in officially designated wilderness regions. While such rulings may sound like the products of a strong outfitters' lobby, in most cases they are sound laws meant to protect the hunter. There are plenty of places in every state a newcomer can get lost, even in wilderness as yet undesignated. In places without roads or services, it is a wise idea to either hire a guide or hunt with someone who knows the terrain. Where legal, you can check with a sporting-goods dealer, game warden or other source to learn at least something of the domain. Arm yourself with a map and

a basketful of answers, especially if you go it alone. You might also improve your chances by 50 percent just by taking the time to ask someone who has bagged a bull in your intended hunting grounds how he or she did it. Always avoid going in cold.

But let's look at which states give you the best opportunity to obtain a license (resident or nonresident), and in which areas, if hunting is not allowed statewide. Remember that statistics have to be correctly interpreted. In Nevada and South Dakota, elk success may run from 60 to nearly 100 percent at times. But only a few permits are allotted for the little-hunted areas that are open.

Trophy Hotspots

Below are listed, state by state, your best chances for obtaining an elk permit. Contact each state to update the information since it can change every time a legislature or fish-and-game board meets. (Check the final chapter for addresses.)

Do not be discouraged by any of the draw systems listed. Rather than being an indication of decreasing elk populations, they may reflect an effort to provide quality hunting. Total estimated elk-hunting territory in square miles is listed (last survey: 1975) at the end of each state's or province's prospects. For details on specific trophy areas, also see Chapter 17.)

Since license costs vary annually, none are listed here. However, general fees for elk hunting are approximately $25–$35 for residents, $150 and up for nonresidents.

South Dakota — Resident licenses only, via a draw for Black Hills and Custer State Park. Annual success averages 30–35 percent. Hunting: 450 square miles.

Nevada — No nonresident permits available. A few lucky residents who draw out have enjoyed success ratios up to 92 percent in past few years. Hunting: 600 square miles.

Montana—Since 1975 elk hunting has been on a first-come, first-served basis. In the past few years 17,000 nonresident permits have been issued. The licenses have also included deer, black bears, birds, and fishing, but there are indications that in the future elk-only licenses will be sold. Permits are often gone within three weeks after they go on sale in the spring. If you send in your name and address to the state, it will send official application forms, which are usually on hand by April 15.

With the demand for Montana elk hunting, state officials estimate some type of draw may be necessary for residents in the future. But for now, upwards of 80,000 in-state hunters can buy an annual license.

Hunter-success figures run about 20 percent for residents, slightly higher for nonresidents, probably due to the added time and energy expended by nonresidents when they are able to obtain a license. Residents may score higher on occasional late, antlerless, depredation, and other special hunts called during the year. Montana officials told me they could not recommend any particular "underharvested" units. Check with landowners and guide-outfitters for additional nonresident license opportunities. Basically, the entire southwestern and western sectors to the Idaho border are open to all license-holders. Montana is traditionally popular with nonresidents. Hunting terrain: 36,400 square miles.

Wyoming—In 1984 the state issued 6,873 nonresident elk licenses via a drawing. In addition, if residents in any given year do not buy all available permits allocated for a certain unit, nonresidents have

a chance at them. That placed another 1,532 permits into the nonresident hopper in 1984.

Residents at least 14 years of age can obtain a license by shelling out $25 before September 30. No permits can be purchased after that date.

Nonresident applications should be sent in on special forms between January 1 and February 1. Write to the department ahead of time for the forms along with a booklet listing application guidelines. Once on the mailing list, you should receive a booklet each year well before January 1. A nonresident's chance of drawing a permit is good compared to other states.

Success figures run about 15–30 percent, but a relatively high number of the elk taken, compared to other states, are branch-antlered bulls. Most of the western and northern sectors contain elk, as do a few central and southeastern units. With permit in hand, elk can be hunted anywhere in the state. Hunting: 34,000 square miles.

Idaho—With emphasis on quality, Idaho allowed only 9,900 nonresident licenses in 1984, upping it to 10,500 in 1985, the figure likely to apply for the next few years. Hunters should check areas carefully, because much of the state's elk hunting is in the vast north-central wilderness. Those who are not well equipped, don't know the terrain, or lack a guide, could have difficulty. This is true even in the upper Clearwater River drainage, which has a reputation for the second highest elk population (behind Jackson Hole, Wyoming) in the world.

Residents must draw on many controlled hunts with high hunter-success ratios. General licenses are on a quota basis. A total of 68,000 nimrods went afield in 1983, 59,000 of them residents, for 14 percent success. The controlled hunts had 37 percent success. Future trends are toward quality hunting for more mature bulls in back areas. More permits are likely for backpackers and bowhunters. Hunting: 36,000 square miles.

Colorado — In this popular elk state, a draw is necessary. Colorado issued 33,460 nonresident permits in 1984. Game managers caution that with so much high country in the state, hunters are likely to require much more preparation and work to score on elk than on mule deer. Since there are so many remote places elk can be, a guide is a wise choice, even in the high-population White River area.

Residents can buy unlimited permits, but there may be a draw in the future. Depredation shoots can be called anytime.

Almost all of the western half of the state, to the eastern edge of the Rockies near Denver-Colorado Springs-Pueblo, holds wapiti. Success figures fluctuate widely according to the timing of the hunt, weather conditions, and other factors. Generally, late hunts bring higher success. Colorado evaluates each year's agricultural damage and elk-harvest figures carefully to determine which units might be "pumped up" with more license allocations. Hunting: 40,000 square miles, the highest of any state.

New Mexico — Residents and nonresidents participate together in a drawing for licenses. Landowners have special permit allocations for hunters on their lands, so if you intend to hunt private land, contact a landowner for details. In the past, anyone willing to pay the landowner his trespass or guide fees can obtain a permit from the state. For a fee, you can hunt much private land.

In 1984 a total 11,628 elk hunters harvested 3,370 elk for a 29 percent success.

New Mexico has an unusually high ratio of bowhunters who score — 33.8 percent in 1984. Elk country is in north, central, and western sectors. Hunting: 15,800 square miles.

Arizona — Equal opportunities exist in drawings for residents and nonresidents. Applications are accepted in May. Arizona hunter totals show only one percent nonresidents. Out-of-staters should contact the Apache and other Indian tribes for high-quality hunts for an extra fee.

Best elk hunting is in central and eastern sectors. Success is as high as 44 percent, depending on unit, but number of resident hunters is mushrooming and could affect such high kill figures in the future. At the same time, winters are milder than in many other states, with less impact on elk populations. Hunting: 8,750 square miles.

Washington — No limit on resident or nonresident elk permits. Seasons are liberal, from October to November. A total of 82,866 licenses were sold in 1984, but only slightly over 800 went to nonresidents. Roosevelt elk are difficult to find in densely timbered areas. However, success ratios are high in such units as Yakima, Aberdeen, Mossyrock, Siouxon, Tatoosh, Packwood, Marble, Abernathy. There is a trend toward quality hunting consistent with unlimited permit issue. Hunting: 17,600 square miles.

Oregon — Strong trend to quality hunting via a restricted permit system for nonresidents. Expect a "luck of the draw" program in the future. A total of 103,908 permits were issued in 1983, about the same as in '84, although only 2.7 percent went to nonresidents. Judging by past success figures, nonresidents should lean toward hunting the Rocky Mountain species away from the coast. Best counties for

Roosevelt elk: Clatsop, Tillamook, Coos. For Rocky Mountain species: Morrow, Union, Umatilla, Wallowa. Hunting: 26,000 square miles.

Utah—Once relied primarily on a restricted-entry philosophy. But the state has now moved rapidly into more of an "open bull" program. Anyone 16 years of age can buy a license. Some 28,500 were sold in 1984; success ratios of about 15–17 percent are realized in good-weather years. A total of 5,130 licensees scored in 1984, but only 128 were nonresidents. Competition is keen on "open bulls" in the central and eastern strips of mountains. Although success rates are not high, the number of elk in available habitat is on the increase. Hunting: 16,071 square miles.

California—Efforts are increasing to provide more huntable populations of Roosevelt elk in northern counties. Ten permits are allocated for 1986, nine-day hunt, Siskiyou County. Possibility of future Tule-elk hunting in several counties. Hunting: potential for 3,000 square miles.

British Columbia—Unlimited applications available in most areas with general seasons. Little competition, high-quality hunting, with only 743 nonresident licenses sold in 1984. One reason is that any nonresident must hunt with a guide in specified territory assigned to him. Expect higher costs for licenses and guides in Canada. In some regions, limited-entry regulations are based on the number of elk actually harvested. Hunter success has averaged about 35–40 percent in the last few years. Officials recommend contacting guides for additional information.

Residents have enjoyed less success than nonresidents (about 25 percent in the last few years). Some hunts are possible for residents in the extreme south on short notice, due to agricultural depredation. Hunting: 38,000 square miles.

Saskatchewan and Manitoba—Elk in some mountain areas. Check with fish-and-game officials. Hunting: 7,400 and 3,300 square miles, respectively. Nonresident permits not likely in future.

Alberta—In 1984, 31,773 general licenses were sold, with a few thousand others issued on special hunt authorization, all on a draw system. Although quality elk hunting exists in many wild, rugged units, the province has more hunting applicants than the present elk population can sustain. Efforts are being made to increase the estimated 15,000 elk to twice that number. Success is about 13 percent for the nonresident. Contact the Alberta Fish and Wildlife Division for a list of guide requirements. Hunting: 74,000 square miles.

Private Lands

Vermejo Ranch, NM—Beautiful conifer and aspen elk country at 13,000-foot level, in Sangre de Cristo Mountains west of Raton. Luxurious accommodations. Prices to match. This is a wonderful opportunity for the serious, well-heeled hunter. Several types of hunts are offered, including antlerless, but for 6 x 6 bulls the price tag is upwards of $5,000. Hunters are lined up two years in advance; no reservation is accepted beyond the two-year period. Management expects a 10 percent deposit at booking, plus an additional 10 percent by April 1 and the balance by July 15 in the year of the hunt. Reservations made after July 15 require full payment. The 392,000 acres of prime hunting land at Vermejo are large enough for 22 management units; a hunter is not likely to see any other rifle-toter outside his own party.

Another 100,000 acres of Vermejo, now known as "Valle Vidal," donated to the nation by Pennzoil, is available for public hunting in the Carson National Forest.

Indian Reservations — Many of these lands contain prime elk terrain and offer permits to the public. Check on the need for a state license. Some tribal councils have won court cases allowing them total autonomy in licensing, so check ahead with the reservation you plan to hunt. Best for oversized bulls are probably Arizona's White River Apache and New Mexico's Jicarilla. Check with the Department of Interior's Bureau of Indian Affairs.

Deseret Livestock — This undulating aspen and sage terrain in northeastern Utah was closed to public hunting for many years. Now it is open for a few dozen hunters each year seeking trophy bulls. Since herds here are free-roaming, a state license is required. No overnight accommodations, except camping. Fees are upwards of $4,000.

16

The Extra Edge

People who love the outdoors should be omnivorous readers. If so, they have the best of two worlds. They learn more — and enjoy life more. . . .
— Theodore Roosevelt

As an avid sportsman (and elk hunter), Teddy Roosevelt realized there were many ways to gain knowledge about any given subject. Even the outdoors. Certainly Teddy respected the Old Salt who plodded over the mountains seeing everything for himself firsthand. But such a person does not want to limit his skills or hunting horizons to only what he personally witnesses. There are many ways to become a better elk hunter — and enjoy the outing and the challenge even more — including vicariously living the experiences of others. After all, no one lives long enough to learn it all alone or make all the possible mistakes by himself.

So let's look at means of benefitting from several sources. Roosevelt acquired additional knowledge by reading energetically. But we certainly can't read everything ever written about hunting, even elk hunting. Better to carefully select those literary jewels which can best help us attain our hunting goals.

Let's start with the writings of Roosevelt himself. You might not pick up myriad specialized hunting tips by reading about his adventures in the Dakotas or anywhere else. What you will get is an insight into his big-hearted outdoor spirit, his hunting enthusiasm. In my opinion, no one enjoyed the big-game hunting challenge more than this frail and timid soul who became one of America's most courageous and dynamic presidents. Requiring thick bifocals for his weak eyesight, old "Four-eyes" rose to immense vision of his own potential.

Two of Teddy's personal traits stand out: enthusiasm, which has been mentioned, and perseverance. He once wrote: "I am not a very good hunter. But I am good at perseverance." No quality could better serve someone on an elk quest. Perseverance — patience with tenacity.

Roosevelt's enthusiasm and mental toughness in everything he did is contagious to those who read his writings. For one thing, he rarely sought out the easy. He seldom advocated hunting the fringes of civilization. Instead, he championed the hunting of "lonely lands." Despite his early poor physical health, he prepared for the hardest, the most robust challenge. Then he was also prepared for the easier ones as well. I've spent many hours enthralled by the man's intense determination which led him to lofty pinnacles in both big-game hunting and statesmanship. It also led him to be much more than a consumer of big-game resources. By founding the Boone and Crockett Club, Roosevelt also found a way to give something of value back to the outdoor way of life: to promote the "manly" sport of hunting. I believe he did so not for the respect or fame it brought him, but because of his love for the animals he hunted and the places where they were found. Naming his Long Island home site Sagamore Hill after legendary Indian chief Sagamore Mohannis, he made it almost a nature museum.

The anti-hunters, the Cleveland Amorys, might scoff that a person could "love" something he had killed. But Roosevelt, in his espousing of the conservation ethic understood the worth of

hunting as a necessary tool to remove surplus animals.

It was one reason he promoted hunting for trophies, believing that these generally older animals make up only one percent or less of a species' population, and that their removal in no way harms the resource. Roosevelt also championed the value of hunting for sport rather than meat only.

I have always liked Teddy's statement about being better off for having tried and failed . . . than merely having sat on the bench of life.

Success, Teddy says, "comes not from the critic who stands aloof from the contest, but by the man who enters into it and bears his part undeterred. . . ."

I can apply that to elk hunting. Anyone who is afraid to try elk hunting may understand the difficult odds. But he does not comprehend how much can be gained from not "standing aloof" or criticizing those who fail. More can be obtained by "entering into it."

I'm sure his philosophy about hunting the "lonely lands" has affected me. I remember one time when my 18-year-old son and I attended a state high-school championship football game in central Wyoming. It was a 7½-hour trip, so we departed the day before. We drove to Casper, near the next day's playing site, and began to register in a very comfortable hotel. Suddenly, it hit the two of us almost at once: why stay in a hotel? True, it was November, and a storm was threatening. But we could drive northward to a public canyon and sleep out. The vehicle was too small to sleep in, and we had no sleeping bags. We would have to lie out on the wet ground with only a few blankets. The night was cold, the storm occasionally pelting us with moisture. We didn't get the sleep we would have had at the downtown Hilton.

However, the next morning's events were well worth our night in the "lonely lands" away from city lights. The first thing I saw, in addition to a spectacular sunrise, was two mule deer bucks looking my way. Later I observed several wild turkeys. Then elk tracks. How much we would have missed by staying with the crowd! We got to the game on time, even seeing the home team win. We missed nothing. I also felt a little smug, sensing that I shared Teddy's gritty attitude. I hope I can reinforce his hardy ideals by saying they are a vital ingredient in any elk hunter's makeup.

Coveted Handicaps

Many other authors have helped shape my attitudes regarding the outdoors and hunting as I grew up. Quite often I focused on someone who had to overcome adversity in a special way to grasp success by the coattails as it tried to slip away. I recall reading for years the accomplishments of then *Outdoor Life* shooting editor Jack O'Connor. It wasn't so much how many African ibex or Alaskan Dall rams he slayed. Rather, it was his attitude toward overcoming a handicap. He had a problem which could have been disastrous to someone of his calling: a defect in eyesight requiring thick glasses. I didn't delve into the medical details, but O'Connor never considered his need to wear glasses as a handicap at all. He simply championed the value of a wide-brimmed hat to keep the rain and sun glare off those glasses.

I wear glasses, but only for reading. I've never had to carry them along for long-distance viewing. I'd feel handicapped if I had to worry about them falling off in brush, or, for that matter, had to don a wide-brimmed hat. O'Connor made it sound as if everyone should wear a combination of bifocals and 10-gallon fedora. It wasn't for me, yet I admired his positive outlook. Seemingly impossible hunting situations were turned around so adroitly that any O'Connor reader almost felt a loss if he did not "enjoy" a particular challenge in a given article.

My own personal headgear is a baseball cap or, in extremely cold weather, a Scandinavian no-nonsense pullover. In addition, I stayed with my 30-06 rather than going to O'Connor's beloved 270. To each his own. But I enjoyed his compelling arguments that it was trajectory and accuracy, not just 220-grain slugs and high shocking power, which downed game. In fact, the 270 usually featured a relatively light 130-grain bullet. However, the important thing I gained from O'Connor (a lesson for anyone) was the need to have confidence in what works for you. If you can't seem to get it, switch to something else. And never sacrifice one other important ingredient: optimism.

I saw the value of that even as a kid plinking at ground squirrels with a 22. The concept was refined as I read other hunting authors whose fires were fueled by the intense desire to overcome.

Only by "omnivorous" reading could I have decided how to fit the elk into a mental chart of big-game challenges. How difficult is it to outwit a bull wapiti as compared to a bighorn sheep, whitetail, or grizzly? Or small game like quail or cottontail? There are seemingly as many opinions as there are hunters. However, after hearing the best of other arguments, I've come up with my own conclusion: the elk in any truly wilderness setting is the premier hunting challenge.

Many other outdoor writers have agreed or, at worst, placed the elk a close second behind some energetic expedition after a record-book ram. However, in the opinion of many writers, there is one factor which makes the wapiti as tough as any game animal: the habitat. In many ways not even a Dall or Stone sheep lives in country as formidable and rugged as that inhabited by trophy bull elk. Many veteran game wardens I know agree that among the females of the game species a cow elk is perhaps the toughest to outguess. How many veteran hunters do you know who have eagerly put in for a cow-elk permit, only to come away skunked? Occasionally you find a brutally honest soul who admits it. Both bull and cow are elusive quarries.

One thing I've seldom read in all the literature on elk hunting is an account of an easy shot on an oversized bull. An exception is a piece by *Outdoor Life* shooting editor Jim Carmichel. "Shoot it in the eye?" he asks in the story I read several years ago. "But what part of the eye?" This dilemma, born of supreme self-confidence, is a rare one. But it's one we should all be afflicted with. If the average hunter spent the time on the rifle range Carmichel undoubtedly does, there would be fewer empty-handed licensees and less game crippled or maimed to escape and later suffer a slow death.

Some hunting writers over the years have, however, suffered from another "I" problem—one of maintaining a macho image. They seemed to believe that anyone who claims to be a Daniel Boone afield must also be Superman in his off-duty hours. *Field & Stream*'s Warren Page wonders aloud (perhaps with more than a little trepidation) why so many of his col-

leagues had succumbed at an early age. Several, he pointed out, either had high blood pressure leading to an early demise or took their own lives. I'm no doctor, and I don't know the answer. But we are entitled to our own opinion after reading all the facts available. Mine is that harboring an outer man-of-steel image must be rather hard on the health. Off the job, at least, you ought to relax and forget what portrait you present to the public. Indeed, it must be a strain to live up at all times to popular expectations. If you are a hunting writer, you must profess never to have missed a shot you really wanted to make, and never to have failed to spot the game first on any outing. Nice thing to try. But I'd rather admit to having fallen short occasionally, and be around to hunt elk when I'm 90.

Grancel Fitz

I never personally knew Grancel Fitz, but have vicariously come to regard him with much respect. As a "second stage" pioneer in developing Boone and Crockett scoring methods, Fitz almost rivaled Roosevelt in contributing to the art of pursuing and measuring game trophies. Certainly he refined and clarified our present understanding of exactly what is a trophy and how it should be fairly pursued. I think I admire Fitz most when he says he felt "lucky" in locating a giant bull in Wyoming's remote Thorofare Wilderness—after having spent 19 days looking. That's dedication with a full comprehension of the price to be paid. Both the dedication and a humble attitude were there to help him succeed at anything he set out to do. And succeed Fitz did. He is credited with being the first man in history to hunt all 24 different classes of North American big-game animals that could be legally taken. In his time he had also collected more of them (13) than any other hunter.

I also have some kinship with him when he admits feeling a twinge of buck fever in lining up his sights on the front shoulder of a monster bull he downed.

Pioneer Journals

Many of us have old, dusty ancestor journals which describe "meat hunting" a century or so ago. It is clear the nation went from huge herds of elk to unlimited and unconscionable killing . . . then to a seeming point of no return. Fortunately, the elk came back; but there are old journals I know of which describe days on end without the hunter's finding game of any kind. Some of them tell how timber wolves raided camp, or grizzlies threatened, but elk were scarce. My grandfather tells of building a floorless cabin in the Bear Lake country of southern Idaho, then trying hard to locate wapiti for winter meat. It appears from these histories that game laws came just in time.

Ed Zern of *Field and Stream* convinced many that his writing cohort, Ted Trueblood, didn't exist — presenting a plausible explanation in print as to precisely how Madison Avenue had made up the phony moniker. But Trueblood was real enough to me and millions of other American sportsmen. He had grown up near my own bailiwick in southern Idaho, and he had worked at the very newspaper and job I later did. Then, as later, he always poured his best effort into anything he wrote about the natural world.

He describes in one magazine article how he and his wife Ellen both scored on Idaho bulls. He admits it almost didn't happen. For as Ted fingered the safety on his rifle, a bull heading toward him apparently detected the artificial noise and veered sharply away. Trueblood managed to make a killing shot on the running animal, but he talked more about the elk's fantastic ears than his own shooting accomplishment. Ted always had a respect for his quarry. And he usually gave the reader, in his penchant for little details, the information necessary to feel he could go out and possibly duplicate Ted's feats. And the reader always came away with the burning desire to enjoy the outdoors as richly as Trueblood always did.

From competitive sports comes something else which can help a hunter bolster a sometimes-faltering attitude. I like to read accounts of how a football quarterback or basketball guard helped his team win a big one, or a golfer or wrestler defeated a heavily favored opponent. Even the business publications such as Napoleon Hill's *Think and Grow Rich* or a sports book like *They Call Me Coach* by UCLA's brilliant John Wooden can sharpen your approach to big-game hunting. You are after an extra edge. Such positive writing can provide it, helping you upgrade your own assets and downgrade the foe's. Sure, you need a healthy understanding of the quarry's strengths, but it should not overwhelm and make you feel you have little chance. Let's face it: the world is full of stories — from David and Goliath to any modern wrestling match, to prove that the most muscular combatant doesn't always win. Rather, it is he who gets the most of his own mental and physical abilities. Often it's "all in your head."

Vicarious Hunts

I also like reading word pictures of emerald meadows, the distant frenzy of a bull elk, the wind-riding golden eagle. They can, for example, help me remember

I ought to call a certain forest ranger, sheepherder, or guide. Someone else's experiences with such seemingly insignificant things as a barking squirrel or a rasping magpie might help me better read the backwoods signals. Of course, the reading by itself won't do much good; to gain the most from what I read, I have to get outdoors enough to fully comprehend the value of what someone else is telling me.

I have also gained much, albeit sometimes laboriously, from scientific journals like the government treatises on replacing poor ranges with better vegetation preferred by elk. Rarely do the biologists expound on the romance of the hunt, but if you are willing to work, you might discover gems of wisdom about recognizing such desired elk foods as bitterbrush and crested wheat grass.

One thing I've learned from outside sources is the vital importance of hunting courtesy. It goes farther than most of us ever realize. I don't mean the surface kind that veneers any slob hunter's face until he gets what he wants. I mean real, deep-down concern for landowners, other hunters, conservation officers, etc.

Will you go out of your way to report a stray calf to a rancher who let you hunt his far ridge? Do you carry out litter someone else left? Are you considerate of your own hunting buddies?

Being a better citizen-sportsman will do as much for you as for those you help. Let's take your guide, for instance. I can guarantee you that an elk guide is sizing you up, subconsciously if not otherwise, the second he meets you. He can get by doing merely what you ask him to do. But if he finds any reason to personally like you, if he sees beyond an immediate business deal to the genuine person, he may

well go out of his way for you. He quite likely has a secret place reserved for a deserving client . . . but why should he tell you if you won't appreciate it, aren't prepared, or care only for your own aggrandizement? Is your guide going to think enough of you to walk 1,000 vertical feet downhill for game you tell him you know you missed—just to make sure? I've seen them do it, but not for just anyone. The proverbial extra mile for a guide may be much more than 5,280 level feet. And what about landowners? Most are better judges of human character than many hunters ever realize. And I hope most landowners have read *Outdoor Life*'s Richard Starnes.

Let's take another look at Wooden's *They Call Me Coach*. In it he surprises the reader who is looking only for pointers on how to play winning basketball. This coaching wizard convinced his players they were preparing not for just a 40-minute basketball game but for a game lasting throughout life. When they practiced, results were not for the day or week but forever. Think what you could accomplish in preparing for elk hunting—from physical conditioning to mental attitude—if you thought of it as discipline benefitting your total future. That's also how winning coach Vince Lombardi taught his football team. Elk hunting is as much a mental challenge as a physical one. If you can succeed at something as demanding as elk hunting, what else is there out there to stop you?

Ranchers and hunters living in the middle of elk country ask casually in general store or street, "Didja get your elk?" The local expert seeking No. 45 or so quite possibly takes things for granted. Yet one advantage he has over the neophyte is that he knows how much preparation is needed, and has long ago committed his energies to the task. The bull could come the first day in precisely the right place, or require two weeks of saddle bouncing plus some meticulous searching. His casual "Got one yesterday" can be misinterpreted by the tourist bystander as an easy matter. But the tourist may not realize the local has spent hours with horses and rifle as a matter of course, every working day of his life for years. If you live in a large city, you probably haven't had much opportunity to either keep an eye out for elk or elk sign or talk to people who have. It is a shame more of the elk wisdom of these day-by-day experts isn't published.

Franklin's Tips

We can also learn from Ben Franklin. How about taking just one of our traits or habits and trying to make daily improvement on it? What needs work this month? From my own reading, I have compiled a list to help me become better in my hunting pursuits. Can they also help you?

• Open-minded learning from every possible source; a desire to prepare for any challenge with as much knowledge on the subject as possible.

• Genuine courtesy toward landowners and others encountered in the outdoors.

• Willingness to pay the price for the prized goal by hunting "lonely" lands.

• Respect the quarry, as well as my own abilities.

• Be a trusting friend to those I hunt with, from an old friend to a new guide.

• Be mentally alert at all times to reach my fullest potential in every endeavor.

Enjoy any hunt, whatever the material yield. I remember one day a hunter and I were returning to camp with the outfitter. A guide stepped up to ask how the day went.

Other hunter: "Didn't see anything at all to shoot at."

Guide: "Oh, a poor day, huh?"

Outfitter (and his boss): "Don't say that, now. We had a wonderful day. I know where to get 'em tomorrow because of all the beautiful scenery we looked at today without any elk in it."

And the next day, the outfitter proved he was right—we notched a nice bull. But even if we hadn't, the words of Ortega y Gasset apply: "One does not hunt in order to kill; on the contrary, one kills in order to have hunted."

17

What Is a Trophy?

Originally, the definition of trophy — "emblem in honor or victory" — was linked little with the horns or antlers on an animal. But today most hunters understand the word that way. And yet "trophy" can have many slightly different meanings to hunters. To keepers of the Boone and Crockett or Pope and Young records of North American big game, the word denotes an animal that exceeds the clubs' minimum entry standards. Furthermore, it is a prize "which has usually been won by persistence, great effort, and accurate shooting."

That definition is important to B&C officials, as any of their record books attest. One year a decision had to be made whether to give the coveted Sagamore Hill medal for best trophy to a world-record polar bear or to a wapiti. The award went to the elk. The bear had been taken after being followed in a plane. The elk had been tracked on foot for days. Truly the bull had been won with the greatest persistence and effort.

To others, a spike bull found after weeks of fruitless searching might be considered a trophy. One of my first bulls was a spike, another a 3-pointer, and I was as proud of them as I was of larger racks taken later. They were a step up. And I worked harder for them all than I had for most of my high-racked deer.

However, for the purposes of this chapter, let us call a "trophy" any Rocky Mountain elk which exceeds 300 B&C points and 250 for Roosevelt. Plenty of large 6- and 7-pointers wouldn't attain that status. Such a bull would have at least six points per side plus thick, long, sym-

Do you have a trophy? This is a proud one, no doubt about it, for any campfire discussion. But it won't quite make a score of 300 by the Boone and Crockett method because sixth tine is missing.

Records of North American
Big Game

BOONE AND CROCKETT CLUB

205 South Patrick Street
Alexandria, Virginia 22314

Minimum Score:
Roosevelt 290
American 375

WAPITI

Kind of Wapiti __American__

DETAIL OF POINT MEASUREMENT

Abnormal Points	
Right	Left
Total to E	2 5/8

SEE OTHER SIDE FOR INSTRUCTIONS		Column 1	Column 2	Column 3	Column 4
A. Number of Points on Each Antler	R. 8 L. 7	Spread Credit	Right Antler	Left Antler	Difference
B. Tip to Tip Spread	39 6/8				
C. Greatest Spread	51 6/8				
D. Inside Spread 45 4/8 Credit may equal but not exceed length of longer antler of Main Beams		45 4/8			
IF Spread exceeds longer antler, enter difference.					
E. Total of Lengths of all Abnormal Points					2 5/8
F. Length of Main Beam			55 5/8	59 5/8	4
G-1. Length of First Point			20 5/8	20 5/8	
G-2. Length of Second Point			27 3/8	25 5/8	1 6/8
G-3. Length of Third Point			20	18 5/8	1 3/8
G-4. Length of Fourth (Royal) Point			22 4/8	21 5/8	7/8
G-5. Length of Fifth Point			15 7/8	15 4/8	3/8
G-6. Length of Sixth Point, if present			11 7/8	7 3/8	4 4/8
G-7. Length of Seventh Point, if present					
H-1. Circumference at Smallest Place Between First and Second Points			12 1/8	11 2/8	7/8
H-2. Circumference at Smallest Place Between Second and Third Points			7 5/8	7 5/8	
H-3. Circumference at Smallest Place Between Third and Fourth Points			7 7/8	8	1/8
H-4. Circumference at Smallest Place Between Fourth and Fifth Points			8	9	1
TOTALS		45 4/8	209 4/8	204 7/8	17 4/8

ADD	Column 1	45 4/8	Exact locality where killed Dark Canyon, Colorado
	Column 2	209 4/8	Date killed 1899 By whom killed John Plute
	Column 3	204 7/8	Present owner Ed Rozman
	Total	459 7/8	Address
SUBTRACT Column 4		17 4/8	Guide's Name and Address
FINAL SCORE		442 3/8	Remarks: (Mention any abnormalities or unique qualities)

Scoring summary on world-record elk. (front of official form)

I certify that I have measured the above trophy on ___*8 February*___ 19 _*1962*_
at (address) _*Am. Museum of Nat. History*_ City _*New York*_ State _*New York*_
and that these measurements and data are, to the best of my knowledge and belief, made in accordance
with the instructions given.

Witness: _____ Signature: _*Elmer M. Rusten*_
                                                         OFFICIAL MEASURER

INSTRUCTIONS FOR MEASURING WAPITI

All measurements must be made with a ¼-inch flexible steel tape to the nearest one-eighth of an inch.
Wherever it is necessary to change direction of measurement, mark a control point and swing tape at
this point. Enter fractional figures in eighths, without reduction. Official measurements cannot
be taken for at least sixty days after the animal was killed.

A. Number of Points on Each Antler. To be counted a point, a projection must be at least one inch
long and its length must exceed the width of its base. All points are measured from tip of point to
nearest edge of beam as illustrated. Beam tip is counted as a point but not measured as a point.

B. Tip to Tip Spread is measured between tips of main beams.

C. Greatest Spread is measured between perpendiculars at a right angle to the center line of the
skull at widest part whether across main beams or points.

D. Inside Spread of Main Beams is measured at a right angle to the center line of the skull at widest point between main beams. Enter this measurement again in Spread Credit column if it is less
than or equal to the length of longer antler; if longer, enter longer antler length for Spread Credit.

E. Total of Lengths of all Abnormal Points. Abnormal points are those nontypical in location (such
as points originating from a point or from bottom or sides of main beam) or pattern (extra points,
not generally paired). Measure in usual manner and enter in appropriate blanks.

F. Length of Main Beam is measured from lowest outside edge of burr over outer curve to the most distant point of what is, or appears to be, the main beam. The point of beginning is that point on the
burr where the center line along the outer curve of the beam intersects the burr, then following generally the line of the illustration.

G-1-2-3-4-5-6-7. Length of Normal Points. Normal points project from the top or front of the main
beam in the general pattern illustrated. They are measured from nearest edge of main beam over outer
curve to tip. Lay the tape along the outer curve of the beam so that the top edge of the tape coin-
cides with the top edge of the beam on both sides of the point to determine the baseline for point
measurement. Record point length in appropriate blanks.

H-1-2-3-4. Circumferences are taken as detailed for each measurement.
* * * * * * * * * * * *

FAIR CHASE STATEMENT FOR ALL HUNTER-TAKEN TROPHIES

To make use of the following methods shall be deemed as UNFAIR CHASE and unsportsmanlike, and any
trophy obtained by use of such means is disqualified from entry for Awards.

 I.   Spotting or herding game from the air, followed by landing in its vicinity
      for pursuit;
 II. Herding or pursuing game with motor-powered vehicles;
 III. Use of electronic communications for attracting, locating or observing
      game, or guiding the hunter to such game;
 IV. Hunting game confined by artificial barriers, including escape-proof fencing;
      or hunting game transplanted solely for the purpose of commercial shooting.
****

I certify that the trophy scored on this chart was not taken in UNFAIR CHASE as defined above by the
Boone and Crockett Club. I further certify that it was taken in full compliance with local game laws
of the state, province, or territory.

Date_____Signature of Hunter_____
(Have signature notarized by a Notary Public)

Rules for measuring and scoring by Boone and Crockett system. (back of form)

metrical tines. For Rocky Mountain species, the main beams would need to be at least 45 inches long, with a circumference at the bases of some 10 inches minimum. Inside spread should be around 45 inches, but should not exceed that figure, for excess width means penalties.

A bull of these dimensions would quite likely approach the minimum record-book score for Roosevelt elk (wisely differentiated by Boone and Crockett and Pope and Young Club measurers, since the Roosevelt less frequently attains monumental antler length than does the Rocky Mountain species), and also be fairly close to the requirements for Rocky Mountain variety. But to make the 375 minimum B&C points, a rifleman would have to glass carefully for long tines of nearly equal symmetry.

To understand trophy quality as evaluated by B&C, let's take a closer look at the No. 1 world-record bull taken by John Plute in Dark Canyon, Colorado, in 1915. Its total 442³/₈ score (all scores are given to the nearest eighth of a point) came via the following: a right main beam of 55⁵/₈ inches; the left, 59⁵/₈. Inside spread credit of 45⁴/₈ did not exceed the length of the longest antler, so all 45⁴/₈ inches were allowed. Circumference at the smallest place between the first and second antler projections was 12¹/₈ right, 11²/₈ left. The difference cost a few penalty points for the four circumference measurements (made between antler projections on the main beam), but the girth of each was great enough to gather considerable points in the overall score.

Although the Dark Canyon bull possessed seven points on one side and eight on the right, the seventh point was not counted under column two as credit (G-7). Rather it was listed at "E" with "total of

lengths of all Abnormal Points." Rudy Drobnick of the Utah Division of Wildlife Resources, an official scorer for the B&C, explains that this is due to the location of the seventh point in an abnormal position on the rack, arising from the sixth point rather than from the main beam. Thus, the No. 1 record carries 2⁵/₈ penalty points on these three tines (2⁵/₈ inches in all). The rack also picks up penalties in comparisons of right and left antler measurements, including a whopping 4⁴/₈ difference between the unbalanced lengths of the sixth tines, the right being 11⁷/₈, the left 7³/₈. Nevertheless, so long are the tines, so thick and symmetrical the antlers, and with the spread credit of 100 percent, that it stands out above all other rivals.

The No. 2 bull wapiti, killed in Wyoming's Bighorn Mountains in 1890, is fairly close at 441⁶/₈. My own personal scrutiny at the Jackson Hole Museum indicated striking symmetry, with noticeably delicate long upper tines. The third slot is held by an Alberta bull at "only" 419⁶/₈. The fourth best in the world, from Madison County, Montana, is just ²/₈ points behind. In comparing these impressive racks, it becomes obvious just how gargantuan the Dark Canyon trophy really is.

You may have noticed that one measurement given considerable credibility by many hunters, the outside spread, was 51⁶/₈ on John Plute's bull; however, it is not counted in any B&C totals. That is an important point to remember when looking over a bull in the field. Only the inside width of 45⁴/₈ (D on chart) is allowed. Likewise, tip-to-tip spread, 39⁶/₈, is not a factor (see B on chart). Elk scoring well in those physical dimensions would certainly be the object of envy around a campfire, but if you are shooting for B&C or P&Y records, you will need to spend some time studying the aforementioned measuring system in considerable detail.

Other Records

It should be pointed out that some trophy-conscious organizations like the Safari Club International do not place as much emphasis on symmetry as B&C or P&Y. Credit is given for total size of antlers, with mass more important than a "balanced" rack. However, for simplicity here, we will scrutinize the older and more historically revered measuring system. If a bull is listed with B&C or P&Y, it almost certainly will be with all other trophy-measuring groups.

Now let's take a look at a bull down the B&C list a bit, some 50 slots away from the world record, one scoring 388 points. Right main beam is $53^2/_8$, left is $53^6/_8$. Inside spread is a whopping $48^2/_8$, and since it is less than the longest antler ($53^6/_8$), all of it counts. However, the circumference at the smallest place between first and second antler projections is a disappointing 9 and $9^3/_8$, respectively, and some point value is lost in that the bull is "only" a 6-pointer. Additional B&C points are lost due to lack of antler tine symmetry.

It all adds up to this: the difference between a world record and a very good listing is a few inches here and there in length and circumference of main beam, plus length of at least six or more tines. How do you tell from 300 yards? Look for six or more points which sweep upward some three times the length of the head from nose to ears; you want something 55 inches or more in dimension. Check for thick beams, particularly from near the base to the fourth or primary sur-royal

points. Width? It usually takes care of itself with wapiti if the other qualities are present. Also glass carefully for long tines projecting from the main beam. In my opinion, judging an elk trophy is much easier than with deer; deer fall into typical and nontypical categories, while the wapiti has only typical antlers. Also, the size horizontally is likely to be more uniform with elk, so width is not as critical a factor. Sizing up a bull on the move is not an easy task. Try to visit elk country in winter when bulls are less spooky so you can compare racks and make mental measurements. Also visit museums and other places where known trophies are on display.

If you'll be doing any unofficial measuring, be sure to note the B&C instructional chart. You will have to wait 60 days for the antlers to dry and shrink before an official measurement can be made. A steel tape is then required to determine in inches (a tine is not allowed if it's less than one inch long) all required measurements. When the rack is no longer "green," you can take it to an official measurer, usually an official with the state fish-and-game department. If you appear to be within the top 10 entries, you will then be expected to crate up the rack and ship it to measurement headquarters for a fine-tooth inspection—at your own expense. Naturally, care must be taken to protect the trophy from damage, for a chipped tine could cost critical points. A few such points can mean a dozen or more slots in the record book.

Any trophy-seeker also will want to use utmost caution in preparing antlers for future measurement. An animal known as the Black Hills "Super Bull" reportedly cannot be considered for the books due to a mistake in cutting off the skull plate.

Like splitting a fine diamond, you can ruin a lifetime's hunting accomplishment in a second's careless move. Watch out, for example, for insecure lashings when packing a trophy head on a horse. The trophy labeled as "probably the greatest bull elk ever killed anywhere or at any time" (see Chapter 16) emerged with a loose antler which forever killed its Boone and Crockett chances.

In addition, you don't want to do anything to artificialize a head. Emblazoned in memory are antelope horns "embellished" with steel rod, and a big-game head soaked in something like vinegar to widen the rack. Such things have caused the officials who measure trophies to limit spread credit.

While it is true that many of the top bulls in both the Rocky Mountain and Roosevelt categories were taken many decades ago, it is interesting that every new edition of the record books includes relatively recent entries. The top bull in Alberta—surpassing even those giants taken in the 1930s and 1940s, when far fewer hunters were afield—was bagged in 1977 by Clarence Brown on the Panther River drainage. Through aggressive transplanting efforts, Alberta (like Utah and some other states) has far more elk today than it did 100 years ago. Some herds are just getting established. If hunting pressure does not cull out the young bulls before they have an opportunity to reach full maturity, the province could offer even more oversized elk in the future. Too, a P&Y Roosevelt bull taken in Oregon (more about that one later) was field-judged No. 1 in the fall of 1985. Records are apparently still out there!

Boone and Crockett Origins

There is no doubt that when Teddy Roosevelt held that dinner party in New York City in December of 1887, leading to the formation of the "American hunting riflemen" to be an "elite guard in the conservation field" (later to be known as the Boone and Crockett Club), trophy hunting was placed on the pedestal it deserved. The philosophy was to leave the younger males of the species to grow and provide breeding stock, and to consider most shootable older animals on the downhill side as far as their ability to perpetuate the herd goes. Instead of meat hunting, and often wanton waste of game just to test rifle accuracy, there was peer pressure to seek out the stag of the herd. The B&C ideals also promoted "fair chase," in which as much attention is given to how the trophy is obtained as to the trophy's size. So popular has the pursuit of trophy animals become among big-game hunters that outdoor writers have begun to stress the ethical code championed by Roosevelt and his conservation cohorts.

Says one account: "Big-game hunting is suffering from an overburden of rewards for success." The story goes on to say that while trackmen or football players perform before large audiences, the accomplishments of a hunter are often seen only by him, or by him and a guide, whose sole job is to assist the hunter. An official measurer may get into the act later, but only one or two others know the true details of a hunter's achievement. At times I have also lamented that while the sense of accomplishment in knocking down a fleeing bull in timber is deeply satisfying, the applause of an adoring audience must in most cases be forgotten. The point is, trophy hunting can be a difficult and lonely challenge, particularly when it ties in with your profession. There is little glamor at the time in pressing on through rain and fog, walking until nearly exhausted, then luckily having a nice bull elk saunter into rifle range — only to pass it up because the left antler is not symmetrical with the right.

But such is true trophy hunting. Many times as a guide I have heard a client say he is "after nothing less than a 6-point. . . ." Time will tell. I certainly lose no respect for the hunter who decides at end of his week — perhaps after suffering through abominable weather and a little high-altitude sickness — that a spike will do. I've passed up 4-point bulls in the Washakie Wilderness of Wyoming on two consecutive sightings, but I still felt happy at end of the hunt to go home empty-handed. Yet I didn't start out that way. When I confront an inexperienced client, I may try to talk him or her into taking a lesser bull for starters. At least I want the hunter to fully understand what it means to set mental sights on a lordly stag. Not only will it almost certainly be much more difficult to locate such an animal (few bulls attain the age necessary), but also just seeing it might wilt the novice's knees. Is he truly ready for the grueling quest which may, if he's lucky, mean one shot in seven to ten days of intensive searching? Even back in 1970, a study in Colorado's White River herd indicated trophy-seeking hunters more often than not took the first bull they saw. A small bull does much to prepare a license-holder for the discipline required to score on a larger specimen. One motto might be, after taking a few bulls: "Why kill anything from here on out that's smaller than my best?" If you can truly say, "I will be satisfied only with a 6-point or better," one of life's most memorable quests is about to begin.

Part of the satisfaction of hunting alone or with one other person in a remote canyon comes in knowing you are matching wits with one of nature's craftiest crea-

tions. I believe that to be the major motivating factor, although there are many other awards which might come later as byproducts of your singular accomplishment. One of them is an honor like the Roy Weatherby recognition, conceived in 1956 to "reward the sportsman who has made the greatest lifetime achievement in hunting . . . by passing up average heads to look for record trophies." The award further spotlights "the taking of animals which are most difficult to hunt and hardest to find." This seems a worthy goal for any energetic hunter because it places the emphasis where it belongs: on those same B&C values of persistence and great effort to win an above-average head. In addition, it is not a monetary reward, but rather a symbol of a hard-won accomplishment.

Self-Inflicted Pressure

Some hunters unduly place pressure on themselves by promising someone "a winter's supply of meat," or shooting for bragging rights in some sort of peer contest. I can testify from personal experience, as can many other hunters I know, that you will put forth more determination in bagging a trophy when you do it mostly for self-satisfaction. Any medal hung around the neck or pinned on your chest will be meaningless if the sporting element is removed. Any extrinsic rewards should be merely symbolic of the enjoyment and challenge you experienced in pursuit of your quarry, not ends in themselves. Otherwise, the hunt dwindles to the level of a fisherman I know who hurriedly caught some fish for guests to dine on, then went out again on the stream "to have some fun."

So, what is a "trophy"? That can depend on the time frame involved. Back in

1951 the minimum wapiti score for the B&C book was 330. It had been 340 the year before. In 1963 it toughened to 360. Then, with more and more trophies crowding the books, the minimum was raised to 375. That in itself seems to be a tribute to the number of trophy heads being encountered nowadays.

Some old ones, too, are just now being recognized. For example, a bull elk which hung in an Afton, Wyoming, sporting-goods store for years was recently submitted for official measurement. With a 56-inch right main beam, 46-inch inside spread, and 8-plus-inch circumference, it scored well enough to place an amazing 17th. It is strange the rack wasn't measured earlier. However, many big-game trophies are similarly overlooked for long periods. At the same time the oversized elk was taken in for measurement, a bull moose which had long hung on the same store wall was adjudged third best in the world.

Do you have a book-qualifying set of elk antlers in your attic? One with a lower beam so thick you can't wrap your fingers around it? Bank presidents, service-station owners, even museum curators often hang a rack on a back wall somewhere without fully realizing its importance and value to the world of trophy treasures. Even the great Chadwick Stone ram, considered by many outdoorsmen as the top big-game trophy of all time, was found a few years ago in a Smithsonian Institution storage room. Perhaps as you become more proficient in ferreting out trophy bulls, you can contribute to wapiti mega-lore. From talking with B&C measurers, it is also clear you would be much appreciated for "rescuing" such elk, for emphasis on trophy size is a goal long sought by conservation-oriented organizations, including the Boone and Crockett Club. More hunters seeking trophy heads mean more total elk on hand.

In addition, many remarkable heads which didn't make the books have an interesting story behind them. Recently, while waiting out automobile repairs, I skipped the magazine rack to examine a head on the wall. It turned out the parts manager's grandfather outwitted the giant bull up on Idaho's Preuss Creek, named after a member of explorer John C. Fremont's party. During that hour I determined to visit Preuss Creek country, especially after hearing local elk hunters talk about the region as still producing over-sized elk.

Locating Big Bulls

Where are the top trophies to be found these days? First, let's look at some of the requirements an elk needs in order to live six to ten years and attain necessary antler growth. The gene pool is important, along with sufficient food and water, to transform calories into antler growth. If a given region has poor winter range, much of an elk's energy in late spring or early summer will go into sheer survival rather than growth of rack. Another factor is the limestone content in the soil—such mineral value goes into bones and antlers. Let's look at each of the trophy factors in detail.

1. Time needed to attain mature rack. Elk living in the farthest wilderness corners with little hunting pressure will likely live longest. Sometimes, however, a crafty old bull near metropolitan centers or popular hunting units will manage to elude hunters. Still, your chances will be best if you get well back away from the competition, a full day or even a two-day pack

into remote hinterlands. Restricted-entry hunting can help.

2. Gene pool. This factor is high in almost any written account of trophy elk hunting. However, it is often less important with elk than other big-game animals — not only because elk move around so much but also because they have been so widely transplanted. Many elk, even in Canada, originated from the top gene pool in Yellowstone. However, it must be said that the fittest progeny is most likely to be perpetuated by the healthiest and largest bulls. Fortunately, thanks to the combative and competitive nature of male wapiti during mating season, the offspring produced are generally most fit for survival, long life, and large antler growth.

3. Since most elk have little difficulty finding sufficient summer-range feed, the habitat factor narrows down to availability of caloric intake in winter. It is not likely that oversized bulls will be found with any consistency in areas of poor or nonexistent winter range. The artificial feedlots, such as in state or federal refuges, seem to help, attracting many high-tined bulls every year. Some of them are harvested during the ensuing fall hunts. But the point is, the heavy winter food requirements of a giant bull must be met. A particularly critical time is right after the rut, when a male wapiti must have ample food, so areas of early and bitter winters combined with poor range are not conducive to old age.

4. Mineral content in the soil as a factor in antler development is controversial in some circles, but it is a fact that both elk and deer seem to grow larger antlers where limestone is found in the soil. Of course, elk move around enough to take advantage of that mineral if it is available somewhere on summer-to-winter range. Inter-

estingly, salt is known to be sought out by elk — indeed, they often compete with range cattle for it — yet there is no present proof that bulls grow bigger because of its use. There is also no proof that elk deliberately seek out limestone. But in the absence of research to the contrary, limestone must be considered an important factor in antler development.

It is wise to seek out a trophy where someone took a big head sometime before. But usually the "hotspot" factor is the result of one or more of the elements named above. It is also true that in some places where *Cervus* is found, bull-to-cow ratios are greater than in others. The most vital criterion there seems to be type of terrain. In the easy, roaded areas, medium-aged or younger bulls are likely to be cropped before they can attain mature size. Even in a rough and remote hinterland, it stands to reason that the valley trails and horse-inviting ridgelines will have fewer outsized bulls. Concentrate on the regions of highest bull-to-cow ratios.

From the time of emperors and ancient civilizations, man has been enthralled by oversized horns and antlers. Cave-wall drawings show elk antlers of impossible dimensions. Such proportions indicate the trophy mentality of those long-ago hunters. Oversized antlers indicate health, energy, and virility — all the more incentive to meet the trophy challenge. After all, you can't rise to that lofty sphere without special discipline and vision. Perhaps that is a reason men seek large antlers.

With that in mind, let's take a close look around the top elk states and Canadian provinces for regions which have produced the greatest bulls. Interestingly, many are on public land. Some of those bulls have emerged relatively recently from places which yielded few monster racks before. So we should not rule any region out, especially if it is remote and roadless. Nor should we ignore private properties such as Vermejo Ranch and the Indian reservations which are managed almost exclusively for oversized animals.

Here, then, are the major public and private lands that produce trophy elk — state by state, province by province:

South Dakota and Nevada — Opportunities are there for a few residents who can get permits. Best big-bull areas aren't difficult to decipher, since very few areas have elk at all. However, neither state has any B&C listings.

Montana — The B&C book shows more entries from this state than any other — 61 in the 1981 edition, compared to next highest, Wyoming, at 42. The entire mountainous region of the southwestern sector is excellent. Best of all are Madison, Beaverhead, Gallatin, Jefferson, and Park counties. However, nearly every county in western Montana is represented in the book, including many well away from Yellowstone such as Lewis and Clark, Missoula, Granite, Sanders, and Powell. Since listings are not always by county, other identifying geography, such as the Ruby Mountains (Madison County), must be sought out.

It is clear that Montana and trophy wapiti get along very nicely together. Strangely, one county not listed in the records is Ravalli along the Idaho border, but don't let that fool you. This, too, is oversized bull country. The entire Bitterroot Mountain chain running along most of the border with Idaho is topnotch big-bull country. So is the Bob Marshall Wilderness and on northward, although it does not show up as dominant in a state with so much other blue-ribbon opportunities. With Yellowstone and Glacier National

Parks as elk sanctuaries, special "spillover" hunts for large bulls could be called in the future, along with depredation ("reduction") shoots. Montana game managers, not wanting to funnel too much pressure into any one region, don't attempt to pinpoint big-bull bailiwicks. But generally, they are anyplace access is difficult. And in Montana there is still much of that kind of country.

Check with landowners, guides, and sporting-goods dealers for other quality bull hunting areas.

Wyoming — According to the record books, the Bighorn Mountains in the north-central sector have had the most big heads. There are, in fact, more B&C entries from here than from any other mountain range anywhere. However, this is a large hunk of real estate, encompassing Bighorn, Sheridan, and northern Washakie counties. Other likely places are ranges adjacent to Jackson Hole such as Gros Ventre and Thorofare, and from the northern Wyoming Range eastward to the Wind River Mountains. (Taxidermist Rocky Vandersteen likes the Wyoming Range, where several of his recent bulls have scored 360 or better, just short of the minimum for B&C entry.) The Snowy Range and Medicine Bow National Forest near Laramie once produced many oversized racks, but today an increasing human population is taking a toll. An Outdoor Life magazine story of a few years ago, titled "Wow, What a Wapiti!" had its setting in the Medicine Bow, but trophy chances today are better in less-trammeled sectors of the state. Much elk habitat in central and eastern Wyoming, too, is being invaded by more roads for timber harvest and outdoor recreation. A less-publicized big-bull region, if seismographic exploration and oil development do not crowd out elk, is Lincoln County's Bridger-Teton National Forest. In northwestern Wyoming generally, excellent winter feed grounds at state and federal refuges should keep all of that region excellent for trophy bulls. Ditto for the Beartooth Mountains just east of Yellowstone, often overlooked for giant bulls but offering trophies from the North Fork of the Shoshone through Sunlight Basin to the Montana border. Areas southward through the Washakie Wilderness to several other wilderness and primitive areas provide big-bull security all the way to the Wind River Indian Reservation. At present it is mostly roadless, and holds some wonderful wapiti for those willing to pay the price of difficult access.

Idaho — The Salmon River drainage northward to Lochsa-Selway country and all along the Bitterroot Mountains is the best big-bull region, but naming it isn't as difficult as getting in to such places. Difficulty of access, however, is one reason Idaho will always likely be tops for B&C prospects. Even Owyhee County, more famous for chukar partridge and coyotes, has produced a B&C bull. Other good areas include Caribou, Nez Perce, Fremont, Valley, Bonneville, Kootenai, Shoshone, and Teton counties, and all of the upper Clearwater River country. Future chances for mammoth bulls are very good because Idaho is managing more and more for mature racks, and launching an educational program to combat problems associated with road building and too-easy access. But to get into the best area — the Salmon River country or Clearwater drainage — requires a long horse pack, a float down the river system, a backpack, or other strenuous effort that many hunters won't expend.

Big bulls are also taken along the Wyoming border (Caribou, Bonneville, Teton, and Fremont counties), indicating some of the possibilities outside designated wilderness or primitive areas. Much of this terrain is undulating forestland between patches of farmland. In Idaho, don't count out any reasonable elk habitat. Check with sporting-goods dealers in such communities as Montpelier, Soda Springs, Ashton, Challis, Salmon, Idaho Falls, McCall, and anywhere in Clearwater, Shoshone, or Kootenai counties.

Colorado — Any real estate tilted above the valley floor from the Utah border to the east slope of the Rocky Mountains could hold a respectable bull in the state of Colorado. Behind only Montana, Wyoming, and Alberta in numbers of B&C bulls in the 1981 listings, this state has 40 mountains over 14,000 feet in elevation — a treasure house of "hidden" bulls. The vast White River herd in the northwestern sector, the state's largest, has immense potential, as do the San Juan Mountains and Grand Mesa to the southwest.

Some other "magic" names which show in the B&C annals are Routt and Jackson counties (near Rocky Mountain National Park); the Uncompahgre Plateau in Mesa, Montrose, and Ouray counties; and the northern Sangre de Cristo Range. An elk hunter might also find a huge head in the Front Range, despite heavy human populations from Ft. Collins to Pueblo, but chances are probably better from the west slope of the range toward interior hinterlands.

Sporting-goods dealers and taxidermists seem particularly trophy-conscious in Colorado, and keep tabs on where the best racks come from. But with so much high terrain, the energetic hunters are best rewarded.

New Mexico — The Vermejo country is

widely known for its giant bulls; yet New Mexico's public land for some reason hasn't produced the quality elk hunting of, say, Montana or Colorado. The reason quite possibly lies in number of hunters afield. The regions around mushrooming cities like Albuquerque, despite their scenic mountains don't seem to have yet reached their big-bull potential. Perhaps competition is too heavy.

Nevertheless, New Mexico must be considered a prime B&C prospect if you include Vermejo, with its 5-point-bull minimum regulations, and the Jicarilla and other Indian reservations. Most of the hottest terrain is in the north and along the higher western border mountains. Top counties are Colfax, Taos, and Rio Arriba; parts of San Juan, McKinley, Valencia, Catron, and Grant; plus the center strip of mountains south of Albuquerque.

Contact the Vermejo Ranch and Jicarilla Indian Reservations (see addresses in last chapter) for additional information on quality hunting there. Both offer rich trophy opportunities.

Arizona—This state has yielded some fine, long-tined B&C bulls in the past, especially the San Francisco Mountains near Flagstaff, and the Williams, Mormon Lake, Payson, Tonto Lake, Show Low, and Sierra Blanca areas. But the best spot nowadays is easily the Apache Indian Reservation, where you'll pay an extra fee. This wild terrain (one hunter I know called it the "wildest" in the Southwest) offers excellent elk hunting mostly because man does not easily penetrate it. Some top bulls have been taken in the upper Blue and White River drainages, particularly the latter. Best counties are along Mogollon Rim, the north center, and the eastern border. Competition is keen on all public properties.

Washington—The Northwest, with its Roosevelt elk, has not shown up well in old B&C books because of a "fluke": the coastal species is slightly smaller in most antler dimensions than the Rocky Mountain species. However, with a new B&C listing for the Roosevelt, chances are much higher for a trophy worthy of the record book. In the combined 1981 listings, Washington had 2 entries while Oregon had 6, yet the future could bring more respect to the Evergreen State with its many miles of coastal and inland forests. The entire gauntlet of coastal counties could yield a record Roosevelt bull at any time, as could the Cascade Mountains. As mentioned earlier, Rocky Mountain elk are taking hold in eastern, flatland sectors.

With so much contiguous forestland and little in the way of "island" mountains (like Colorado's, for example), elk can be about anywhere. In this state elk are much like black bears—they're abundant, but you don't often see them until they decide to show for food, water, or to do battle. Highest population figures for elk, and probably the best chances for a better-than-average bull, are listed by game managers for the Yakima, Vancouver, and Aberdeen Regions. More specifically, in the Yakima try Maneum, Cape Horn, Taneum, Manastash, Wenas, Nile, and Rimrock-Cowiche units. In the Vancouver region top hunter success is in Tatoosh, Margaret, and Skamowaka. For Aberdeen, try Soleduck, Mathena, and Palix.

Oregon—In the past, Clatsop, Grant, Harney, Washington, and Umatilla counties have held the greatest potential for elk trophies. Clatsop has the No. 1 and 2 listings for the Roosevelt elk in the 1982 B&C update records. Ken Adamson's mammoth Roosevelt bull arrowed in Washington County (field-measured at a Pope and Young score of 348⅜, topping all records) gives the Clatsop-Washington Counties region just west of Portland additional respectability. If giant bulls like these can survive near the metropolitan suburbs, what else is out there among the coastal rain forest?

Highest bull-to-cow ratios for Oregon Roosevelt elk (and hence the top trophy prospects) are Saddle Mountain in Clatsop County, Siuslaw, Tioga, and Rogue. For Rocky Mountain elk, the best past bull ratios have been in the Minam, Catherine Creek, Pine Creek, Snake River, Grizzly, and White River units, the entire Ochoco Zone, and the Umatilla-Whiteman Zone, save its Northside Unit (only four percent bull ratio). The other areas listed have at least a 10 percent bull ratio, with a history of yielding oversized racks.

Taxidermist Rocky Vandersteen shows head mount of his bull, which scored 360 by the Boone and Crockett method, almost making the record book. *Photo courtesy of Rocky Vandersteen.*

Utah—No B&C or P&Y bulls on record. Most of state is under the open-bull concept, so the best chances in the future will be in the restricted-entry units. Largest heads are taken in Uinta Mountains, Book Cliffs, Fishlake National Forest, Boulder Mountains, Ogden River, Nebo, and southeastern Manti Mountain. Some units, like Ogden River, require landowner permission. Try the Wasatch Mountains on the least-accessible east side. Uintas are an excellent choice if permits can be obtained on the eastern end. Ditto the roadless Book Cliffs. Cache-Rich units have potential, but like Nebo and Manti they have more than average hunter competition. Cache has a refuge for wintering elk.

Utah, with its ambitious transplanting of elk into new habitat, is a state to watch. Excellent hunting was once enjoyed on Ute tribal lands in the eastern sector, but it is now off-limits to non-Indians. Also check with Deseret Livestock for quality hunting opportunities in northeastern Morgan and Rich counties.

California—No hunts likely for trophy bulls.

Texas—Comprised mostly of private land, this state offers hunts for transplanted elk on a fee basis. One Lone Star State entry is listed in B&C books, but nothing of recent vintage.

British Columbia—Chances exist for big bulls, yet few have made the record books. Best chance is on Vancouver Island (Roosevelt species), or the mountains bordering Alberta. Check with the province for more information and a list of guides.

Saskatchewan—Four listings in B&C books. However, fewer trophy opportunities exist here than in past. Scattered populations.

Manitoba—Three bulls have been listed in the records. Like Saskatchewan, trophy elk are scattered, with hunting competition high. There are enough wildlands, however, to provide surprises.

Alberta—Record books show clearly this is the top Canadian province—a whopping 29 entries, behind only Montana and Wyoming, with 10 bulls ranking from 3rd to 44th. Top spots are Panther River, Muddywater, Red Deer River, Rock Lake, Ram River, Elkwater, and Waterton. Many other known hotspots such as the Brazeau River drainage could yield entries in the future. With so much roadless back country plus an ambitious transplanting program, this province has high potential for trophy bulls. However, a good guide and sufficient time are necessary prerequisites.

18

Hunting and Game Management

Management of elk is much more difficult than with deer or other big game, for a major reason: the animal's mobility. Elk range widely. They do so for two primary reasons: 1) physical needs of food and water for a mammal weighing up to half a ton; 2) an almost insatiable need for emotional security.

Both needs are most difficult to satisfy in winter months when scarcity of food forces elk into more vulnerable circumstances. Thus a game manager faces his greatest challenge then as well.

Just a minute ago I looked out my front-room window, after a 24-hour snow, to observe 23 elk, including one very respectable bull, walking down from the mountain foothills. They filed across open sagebrush into a little grove of aspens. Springs there form the water supply for the ranch where I live.

With two feet of snow on the ground, these wapiti have trekked into the edge of trouble. They are within five minutes' striking distance from several haystacks, and close enough to a field where hundreds of domestic cattle are fed by tractor daily to compete with them for that food. Fortunately for these elk, they will likely be tolerated for a time. Owners of the ranch are fairly sensitive to the elk's plight. After all, residents here make part of their living by guiding big-game hunters. However, most area ranchers won't put up with elk depredations for long. In a critical winter, too much of their survival depends on those haystacks. The ranchers will likely call the nearest fish-and-game officer to come and take care of the problem. In some states, if the officer does not arrive within 24 to 48 hours, laws allow the landowner to begin

A big bull heading for a farmer's hay corral can lead to demands for damage payments or for future elk reductions.

shooting those thieving wapiti. One state words its law to read that the property owner can stop the four-footed raiders on his own if the state does not solve the problem "forthwith"—whatever "forthwith" means. Most angry landowners give it a liberal definition, oft-times meaning "now."

To their credit, most farmer-ranchers realize the esthetic value of the elk to hunters and the monetary value to state coffers. I've known ranchers who shoot deer on sight the first night they get into stacks, fields, or orchards. Yet attempts are made to scare elk away with lanterns, flashing lights, coyote-type noisemakers, cherry bombs, firecrackers, or by shooting over the animals' heads. In one state where ranchers were about to declare war on troublesome elk via calling for late-season "slaughter hunts," the sportsmen got together and insisted on some better

settlement. Commendably, these sportsmen would never even get to hunt those animals, including more than 20 lordly bulls, because the elk spent the autumn months across the state border. Yet the sportsmen helped drive the wapiti back uphill where they belonged.

In many states the main factor which prevents buildup of elk populations—by transplanting or otherwise—is a farm federation that asks: "But what will you do with the elk in a tough winter?" Most states do not have funding for massive feeding programs, or to compensate ranchers for depredation damages. Management also becomes difficult when far-ranging elk mushrooming on (or transplanted to) public national forest summer range migrate in winter smack onto the fringes of civilization. The problem can be particularly severe if the elk move onto suburban streets, front-yard fitzers, and back-yard lawns. There is then a demand for their removal. When that happens, game biologists must either "manage people" or, failing that, manage the elk by 1) immediate removal, or 2) more hunting permits issued upslope next fall. With the latter, good hunting might be enjoyed for one season, but under concentrated hunting pressure the herd dwindles.

One of the most energetic solutions attempted was at Stump Creek on the Wyoming-Idaho border. Elk which raided Wyoming ranches on winter nights retreated by day just across the border into Idaho. Obviously, the problem required the two states to cooperate, and they met the dilemma in the most desirable way possible: trapping and moving the animals to several sites in southern Idaho where there is potential habitat but as yet no elk.

Elk in Trouble

When landowners grow impatient with bureaucratic red tape, they may begin removing (shooting) elk without benefit of accurate marksmanship. Some animals may crawl away to die slowly elsewhere. Indeed a few landowners have been said to deliberately aim for the paunch so elk will die where someone else will have to dispose of the carcass. At least, when the state wardens do it, the elk can be donated to charity, with hides and meat utilized. But that is a poor second choice — hunting elk today ought to mean more than plunking meat into a stew.

At the other end of the spectrum is the activity of looking at, photographing, and just enjoying elk year-round in parks, sanctuaries, and refuges. How much attention should managers pay to this recreational activity — as opposed to hunting?

These are questions which will likely be asked by state legislators (and biologists) more and more in the future.

Another vital question is how much feeding can be done each winter in view of available funds. Purse strings are generally kept tight until deep snow forces feeding, but by then, elk may be in such poor condition that feeding does not do as much good as it would if done earlier. The feeding of wapiti each December to April-May becomes a monumental task in northwestern Wyoming — it is done on 23 state refuges, and that doesn't even count the expansive National Elk Refuge just east of the town limits of Jackson. The strategy, of course, is to let the elk first deplete natural grasses, and be ready with artificial feed when grass grows scarce or snow covers it too deeply for elk to readily paw through.

Tagging studies have indicated most elk move into the National Elk Refuge in late autumn from as far away as southern Yellowstone, up to 90 miles distant. Several thousand move in from nearby Grand Teton National Park, and the remainder from public hunting grounds. These grounds include the Bridger-Teton National Forest along such river drainages as the Gros Ventre, Buffalo, Pacific, and Pilgrim creeks, and the entire upper Snake River. Elk from several wilderness hunting units such as Thorofare and Teton winter on the refuge, complicating things for game managers, who are "politely requested" to reduce herds with "shooting gallery" hunts on the north end of the federal refuge. Irate outfitter-guides in the impacted hunting units lament such "slaughter" of game, stating that elk could be taken by "more sporting methods" off the refuge. However, a few guides have quit fighting the "system" and are accepting fees to "guide" hunters on the refuge fringes. Some large bulls are taken.

While refuge managers are the most visible people to "blame" for the reductions, they are simply abiding by an agreement between state and federal agencies to keep refuge elk down to a compromise level—a level depending heavily on how well the wintering elk remain out of haystacks and other "people conflicts."

In the past, National Refuge elk have been maintained at more than 10,000 animals, but in 1985 managers were shooting for 7,500 elk. How many are to be refuge-fed can change at any given time. Some hunters and guides have stated that lack of money should never be the main factor in the decision, because the elk are too valuable to withhold funding. However, it seems that the agricultural community is the strongest voice in wildlife management, in Jackson Hole or anywhere else.

It is so strong, in fact, that many state wildlife biologists say the No. 1 reason elk numbers cannot be allowed to grow, or new regions receive infusions of transplanted elk, is that U.S. Forest Service and Bureau of Land Management managers fear grazing conflicts with domestic livestock. One state game manager told a sportsmen's group that quality elk hunting would have to take a back seat to sheep and cattle grazing allotments. "Right now the forest can't handle more elk, because we have already given out so many AUM (animal unit month) permits," the official was quoted as saying. (An AUM is the unit of measurement used in determining grazing rights for both game and livestock on public lands.)

This is not to berate stock permittees for looking after their own interests, or the public land managers who assist them. It is meant merely to properly assess why

sportsmen often find fewer elk. Too often the complaint is laid at the feet of the state game managers. But licensees cannot overlook a problem of serious dimensions: most states have boards or commissions which set a limit on herd populations. It does seem appropriate, however, in the matter of making payments to farmers for damage done by wild game (Utah, for example, pays out hundreds of thousands of dollars a year) that such payments be withheld if the landowner does not allow a reduction of that game by some sort of hunting. One method utilized by game departments is to add a $2–$5 fee to license costs, the money going for damage payments or winter refuge feed.

State Vs. Federal

Theoretically, states—not the federal government—manage game. However, there are many ways the U.S. Forest Service in particular takes over the management role. "After all," one USFS district ranger told me, "the elk are on National Forests almost the entire year, then often spend much of the winter on BLM foothill terrain. Why shouldn't the federal agencies be in the game-management business?" Indeed they are—whether or not they set seasons, regulations, or license sales.

Some of the best outdoorsmen-wildlife biologists I've ever met are with the USFS. Or were. Phil Mooney lived with the elk herds of southwestern Wyoming. He loved his work. Yet he got out of the public agency after more than a decade at his profession. The reason he gave was politely discreet, but it boiled down to a game-management conflict with a white-collar superior. That superior later told me the Forest Service was "doing more for elk than anyone else, because we supply most of the rangeland habitat for the animals." However, his policies brought much disagreement from the state game-fish department (see the next chapter for the solutions offered), local sportsmen's clubs, and others concerned about elk management. Those conflicts involved building new roads into hot elk domain to reach timber sales, and allowing oil and gas exploration in the heart of forests which harbored thousands of elk. Since the exploration included seismographing helicopters and dynamite explosions, the animals were definitely affected.

The usual answer by public land-agency officials to wildlife interests is that they are doing what is best under the "multiple-use concept." Yet in many regions, like the northern Rockies' Medicine Bow National Forest, state game managers say timber interests are the "single-use" benefactors, even when recreation is listed as a major use.

But let's look at another challenge elk managers face due to the animal's skittish nature: maintaining a buffer zone between them and man. One of the game manager's perennial problems is that this need for a buffer is disputed by industry, often by sportsmen, and even by would-be managers in state and federal government. Yet, studies in Idaho and Oregon have proven conclusively that if you want elk to remain around, you need to provide space where overt danger (including man's presence) does not present a security threat.

Roads in themselves do not constitute so great a threat to elk as does the traffic on them. In fact, in coastal Oregon and Washington, hunters would have a difficult time locating any bulls were it not for logging roads providing the only openings

in the thick rainforest—openings that let in sunlight for maximum food growth as well as shooting opportunities. In 1985 a new potential record P&Y Roosevelt elk was taken by an archer who lured his quarry out of the timber via antler rattling and scraping along a back road. Infuriated, the giant bull stepped from cover long enough for an arrow to pierce his heart. The hunter made wise use of a road.

Likewise, controlled burns and clearcutting can provide desirable open space in a timber jungle. Such space may yield the only grass and browse around. That is often a primary objective of the U.S. Forest Service in behalf of elk and elk hunting. Controlled burning has now become so valuable a wildlife-management tool that fires are being deliberately set in more and more forests, with no apology to Smokey the Bear.

However, the problem we are talking about here is roads where public traffic is allowed. One forest supervisor I know attempted to close existing roads to all but industrial traffic, and found himself locking horns with the president of a local sportsmen's club. Yet the forest manager had a point: "The roads are already here. If vehicles on them skitter elk away, we will cut down the traffic by completely closing them during the hunting seasons, and for the remainder of the year to all but loggers or commercial users for whom the road was constructed in the first place."

Effects of Roads

Some game managers—aware of how road traffic, snowmobiles, etc., can ruin winter range elk—forbid vehicles in certain areas, especially before 8 a.m. and after 5 p.m., to avoid stressing the crowded winter wildlife. Usually a sign is placed at the mouth of a canyon forbidding use of the road at such critical times.

Studies in Idaho indicate elk are frightened away from active roads. The tagged-elk research concluded that the animals will not live on the edge of man's activities. It posed a simple question: "What do you prefer, more roads or quality elk hunting?"

In several conversations, biologists at Gulf Oil Company told me elk can live compatibly with man without a buffer zone. "They do so at Gulf and other mining interests in Colorado. One area has 600 to 1,000 elk that are not driven off by man's activities. The area is also a sanctuary, off-limits to hunters."

There's the difference—those elk are protected. It is clear that unhunted elk will abide man's proximity, as demonstrated in several national parks. But if an elk is huntable sometime during the year, he will not tolerate man's immediate presence, save when he's desperately in need of food on the winter refuge. Even then, the animal must become convinced over a period of time that man is there only to feed, not to harm him.

But let's look at an example in Idaho where the aforementioned studies were made. A forest manager sells several hundred acres of timber to a lumber company, which cannot begin cutting until it builds a road to the site. Idaho game biologists say elk might return temporarily following construction, but heavy traffic on the road shies the elk away. As long as there is any appreciable use on the roadway, elk remain from a half to three-quarters of a mile away. In other words, the elk themselves established a buffer zone and will not approach any closer to man or his threat of danger.

Not only is that region lost to hunters, but also remaining elk are crowded into smaller terrain. That, in turn, means less available feed. To provide more needed food, a game manager somewhere is faced with either regaining the lost range or vastly reducing herd size. The latter is not a pleasant option, since the reduction is likely to be permanent. But it is better than letting Mother Nature do the trimming next winter via starvation—a slow, cruel death, with no chance of meat salvage.

Closely allied to wholesale herd reductions to prevent winter die-off are the Yellowstone Park "slaughters" of a few years ago. Park rangers killed thousands of elk because they had over the years eaten themselves out of house and home. Sportsmen stood by willing to pay out handsome sums for the opportunity to hunt those elk. But the Park Service, adhering to past tradition, would have nothing to do with allowing hunters inside the boundaries of Yellowstone. The reason given sounded plausible enough: i.e., a purpose of the National Parks is to prevent artificial impacts on nature. However, total protectionism is in itself an artificialization—a fact that too many overlook. With all enemies eliminated, wapiti increased over several decades to the point that clearly something drastic had to be done. Suddenly, park rangers began shooting once-trusting elk in droves. The problem should have been solved many years before, via hunting seasons on those elk in nearby winter range outside the park, within the states of Montana, Wyoming, and, to a lesser extent, Idaho.

Trapping and Transplanting

When elk numbers anywhere exceed food supply, a cry frequently goes up for trapping and transplanting. Some of that has been done; in fact, many sectors of the North and East owe their small elk herds to a transfusion via Yellowstone. But elk are too volatile for easy trapping, holding, or moving. From helicopter herding to corral fencing, I've observed cow elk beat themselves at post, pole, or wire until exhausted. Some break a leg and are disposed of. Fewer areas these days will accept elk transplants due to the animals' damage to agricultural crops.

But even though it is not easy to trap and transplant elk anywhere, park-ranger slaughters are not the answer. Herd reduction by sportsmen can provide both recreation and more money in state coffers.

Before meaningful elk hunting can be conducted to trim herds down to carrying capacity of available range, research must first determine where to hold the hunts — that is, where the elk go in autumn and winter. To accomplish this, some tagging must be done. It is hoped that trapping and confining some of these restless animals can be accomplished without endangering their health, possibly already fragile due to oncoming winter.

Tagging operations are often bemoaned by the hunter who sights a wild animal adorned with easy-to-see-and-report bright ribbons. That astute sage of natural-resource management, Aldo Leopold, said it for sportsmen decades ago: "The recreational value of the trophy is in inverse degree to its artificiality. . . ." Again: "Proper game management seeks a happy medium between the intensity of management necessary to maintain a game supply, and that which would deteriorate its quality or recreational value." However, most game managers maintain that ribbons in ears or collars around the neck are vital to determining where these highly migratory creatures go. Indeed, the

man who has to make decisions in some capitol building must have field data with which to work. Tagging studies have told biologists, for instance, that elk on a certain winter haystack in Colorado or Montana must be harvested in the fall on a mountain 10 or possibly 30 miles away. Biologists must know whether any Yellowstone bulls are being harvested on public hunting grounds. They must know what is happening to transplanted elk. Are they flourishing where put, migrating away permanently, being killed by hunters, or dying on the site where stocked?

Such information must be readily available when elk or elk habitat is threatened. The game manager who comes to a hearing table with emotional concern, but no hard data to back him up is doomed to lose his case and cause. Can the state prove beyond reasonable doubt that the censused elk use this range? Data-less hunters are "buzzard bait" for an industrial lawyer who spends his full time paving the way for a well-heeled client. The professional politician, who scarcely ever has had any biological training or background, is easily overwhelmed with such propaganda.

The most effective state natural-resource manager I ever saw utilized a computer to combat anti-wildlife arguments. When a water conservancy district wanted to divert water from a 100-mile-long mountain slope, the governor and engineers at the bargaining table listened intently. What would be the effect upon the trout fisheries of those streams? The question had to come up sooner or later.

Instead of merely lamenting that the resource would be harmed for fishermen who flocked to those streams each season, the manager pulled out computer readouts specifying the number of trout electroshocked in the streams per mile, plus other research indicating how many fish had died in streams elsewhere with similar flow reductions. The biologist did not need to cry, wheedle or cajole to get minimum stream-flow guarantees. The computer spat out how many thousands of pounds of trout would be lost if streams were dewatered as engineers planned it.

The biologist dramatically proved his point. Minimum flow guarantees were plugged into the project. It might be mentioned that this enterprising biologist is now the head of a state wildlife resources department. And it should be added that such applied homework is the only way to combat sophisticated anti-wildlife interests these days. The competition is using detailed research. If game biologists don't do the same, the wildlife resource will suffer.

Actually, most game departments went to computers long ago for compiling harvest data, as well as issuing licenses. But the point is, research on elk herds must be an ongoing process. We need to know where the animals are going, what problems they are facing, how many should be harvested at any given time in each hunting unit, and how to reach that ideal of game management: determining the surplus each year, the elk that would die of natural means anyway—and adjusting the hunter harvest accordingly, without cutting into the seed crop.

Cropping Surplus

Most game departments have a formula of harvesting about one-third of the annual increase each year. But in the past few years much pressure has been placed on state game departments to manage their elk herds for better quality. Hunters want a chance at a branch-antlered bull.

This can seldom happen when intense hunting pressure quickly culls out spikes. It may require a bull seven to ten years to attain 6 x 6 status, and few states make any attempt to follow the practice of many private ranches or the Indian reservations, for example, prohibiting the taking of spikes.

It is also interesting to note that at Vermejo Ranch in New Mexico, quality hunting clearly began to suffer by 1980. The number of 6 x 6 bulls had decreased from 52.3 percent in 1976 to 37.3 percent in 1979. Game managers deduced it was due to removal of bulls in the six to nine-year category. As the number of mature bulls decreased, according to ranch managers, "more hunting mortality was also inflicted on the younger bulls." This caused additional problems in the quality hunting concept as number of bulls dropped as low as 17 per 100 elk.

Game managers took steps to solving the problem by banning the taking of bulls having fewer than five points per side. They also imposed a 12 percent reduction in the total number of hunter permits. In order to gain a higher calf-to-cow ratio than an approximately 35 calves per 100 cows, the ranch also concentrated more on harvesting older, "dry" females. The program worked. By 1984, the number of 6 x 6 bulls harvested rose dramatically to 92 percent. During that same period, the number of bulls improved from 17 per 100 elk to a high of 26 per 100. Calf-to-cow ratio also increased from 34 per 100 to 44 per 100. Game managers reported they would continue to decrease number of hunters, or do whatever was necessary to continue the trend.

Vermejo can get away with asking hunters not to take anything less than 5 x 5s so that there will be more trophy bulls on hand. But when a state becomes too restrictive, it can take its lumps. I saw, as an outdoor writer for a western newspaper, what can happen. Someone complains to the governor that game management is "going downhill" because he (the hunter) went out last week and saw only spike elk, "and the state won't even let me fill my license with the only bulls I saw." But it doesn't always require the governor's intervention. A letter to the editor, phone call to state tourist director, or other complaints from the average hunter who didn't locate an oversized bull during the past hunting season can bring about a liberalization of seasons.

I have witnessed the opposite happen occasionally, more so now than a decade ago. Sportsmen's groups like the Utah Hunter Federation (greatly spurred on by the leadership of a savvy hunter, Rich LaRocco, recently a field editor for *Outdoor Life*) massed their membership and then requested more emphasis on quality hunting.

The usual definition of "quality" hunting prevails: more opportunity for "mature" bulls. How large is "mature"? That depends on who you are talking to, but generally it ranges from something more than a spike up to a 4 x 4 or better.

One way game managers can achieve higher quality is via manipulation of seasons. For example, Colorado has a split shoot, with a hunter having to choose which he wants. Thus some 50 percent of the competition at any given time can be eliminated. In the past, more licensees have chosen the earlier, warmer season. Thus the way is paved for a serious elker to take the later quest, to enjoy less hunter rivalry and more large bulls pushed into lower terrain by highland snow.

New Mexico has several seasons, the later ones for mature bulls only. Of course, if a hunter is allowed to take in all the opening days, quality (fewer rifles afield) won't be attained. It would just mean more opening-day pressure in more units.

Combination hunts are popular with both guides and hunters, since the old bugaboo of sighting elk during deer season and vice versa is eliminated. In addition, when both animals are legal, some hunters will turn their attention to the easier quarry, deer. Tough, rugged terrain, most often the home of oversized bulls, will have far fewer human intruders.

Early hunts offer an opportunity to go after rutting bulls. However, most states allow only archers the opportunity. Wyoming does have a September 10 opening in and around Jackson Hole, but strangely, few other very good elk regions do. One answer may be in the strong lobby efforts by Jackson Hole-area outfitters. In any event, hunting elk at a time when you can have a reasonable opportunity to bugle them in has to be labeled "quality" hunting. And opening a hunt in September or early October is such an easy thing to do that it is peculiar more sportsmen's organizations don't petition the same from their state game managers.

At this time Montana hunters enjoy some of the longest of all U.S. elk seasons, but managers say that to retain quality, some of these seasons may have to be shortened.

Opening-Day Dilemma

According to the Utah Hunters Federation, too many bulls are killed in that state on opening day: 37 percent of the harvest occurs on the first day, 67 percent in the first four days. Members would like to see several openings to disperse the number of shooters roaming the hills, and leave some bulls for later opportunity in the fall. The Federation advocates additional seasons in areas of crop depredations, and issuance of cow permits. (Most sportsmen realize a cow elk is a fairly formidable opponent, and usually makes for good eating, perhaps better than an old bull.) Game departments might offer enticements for license-holders to take cows, by issuing more cow permits, or by reducing their cost. This is the practice at Vermejo, where a trophy bull hunt might cost $6,000, a cow $400.

But let's take a closer look at the open-bull concept. In many states the masses applaud such a liberal approach because anyone can buy a license in any year desired. Yet, many sportsmen's organizations have begun to oppose the idea, favoring a draw which reduces hunting competition. In 1985 one hunters' association was dismayed when three units where entry had been restricted were changed to open-bull—a step backward, these hunters claim. The UHF cites statistics it says prove more Utah hunters want quality hunting: "Last year there were 13,163 persons who applied for the 1,135 restricted-entry bull or hunter's choice elk permits offered. A person would have to apply an average of 11.6 years before drawing one of those permits. When demand for quality elk hunting is that great, we do not believe there is a good balance between quantity and quality elk hunting." The sportsmen also lamented transferring of draw units to open-bull status. Adds the UHF: "One of our priorities is to . . . make some current open-bull units into limited-quota areas. So we're not about to stand by and let them take away our quality units."

To their credit, Utah game managers and the top brass have promised to look closely into more quality elk hunting. Likewise, the state has prime mule deer habitat which could accept more wapiti transplants, according to wildlife officials. However, each state must decide what "quality" means. In Montana it depends on the area. In the Gravelly Range a shortage of cover and easy access can result in a high elk harvest. Too many mature bulls harvested mean fewer pregnant cows, fewer calves. Allowing the taking of spikes might be better, resulting in more mature breeding bulls, Montana game biologists suggest.

The draw system frustrates many sportsmen who have difficulty with the annual lottery, so some states have gone to a point preference system. If you fail to draw this year, you receive "points" toward the next time. Other states limit applications to every second, third, or even fifth year.

Some states with open-bull programs, like Washington and Utah, are accused of not going to a draw "because it would mean less money." State game managers reply that their elk are on the increase, and the number of permits allocated is not harming the resource. But one hunter complained that elk are so scarce he's never seen a bull in all his outings. "I might as well buy a license to hunt Bigfoot," he said.

But the states with little or no restriction on their elk-permit program usually counter with the philosophy that it is a "recreation hunt" and that "high success figures or not, everyone gets a chance."

A problem game managers must contend with, though, is that when everyone has a chance anytime they want it, quality hunting doesn't exist.

Utah big-game biologist Homer Stapley checks condition of winter range browse, one way to determine whether elk are headed for trouble.

Another difficulty faced by game managers and sportsmen is the idea, often advanced by farmers' associations, that "herd numbers should be cut down to the number which can survive the worst possible winters." Most sportsmen's organizations oppose the idea, saying, "A terrible winter may come along only once in five years; why go without any reasonable hunting opportunity for five years to satisfy one?" Usually, some type of compromise must be worked out, with the game manager functioning almost as a weather forecaster.

Pursuit of Quality

Let's take a look now at another aspect of quality hunting, one more in the hands of sportsmen than game managers. Years ago I was an officer for the American Sportsmen's Club. Although some outdoorsmen decried the manner in which the ASC sought improvement in quality hunting, I think then and now that the group had a point. Members would contact ranchers who had previously closed their lands to hunting due to litter, cut-down fences, loss of livestock, etc. Owners were promised a reduction of hunters on their lands, plus patrolmen to make certain those allowed on the land did not abuse the privilege of hunting private property. The ASC bought an insurance policy covering damage to the owner's land, and if he lost (even accidentally) one cow or sheep, he could collect on it. On top of that, the sportsmen's group paid a respectable fee for the numbers of acres patrolled and hunted.

No wonder ranchers accepted the offer! The concept even solves another problem—removing enough game animals to prevent excessive foraging in the rancher's haystacks. This is a plus if the property had previously been closed to all hunting.

For many licensees, membership in such a group is a problem. If you can't afford it, you are likely to feel critical. For those who can, it provides better-quality hunting. Among such private hunting lands, Indian reservations are often the least expensive. Check with the various tribal agencies.

Elk Decisions

The fate of hunting often rests with people who have personal biases or are not educated in elk matters. After attending hundreds of fish-and-game board meetings, I recall some where even the designated commissioners failed to follow the recommendations of the grass-roots field men who all but lived with the elk on a daily basis. Some officials literally had no interest in maintaining a maximum herd for license-buyers. At a wildlife com-

mission meeting in Oregon—according to the *Portland Oregonian* for March 25, 1985—a commissioner-rancher hearing a request to purchase winter elk range was quoted as saying: "The elk herd has to be eliminated, or reduced, or whatever you do with it."

He opposed the decision of the game department and county officials who had approved acquisition of 2,762 acres for wintering elk. The idea was also opposed by timber and livestock interests, who claimed the decision to buy the land "was an emotional one, not one based on biological reasons."

A local past president of the Izaak Walton League said the precise opposite: "Purchase of the feeding sites is a matter of survival when elk are forced to lower elevations by winter snow."

The local county officials said the purchase "would not be in conflict with county zoning" or other public interests. The commissioner who asked that the herd "be eliminated" then asked if the lands to be purchased would be lost to state taxation. He was reminded that the fish-and-game department is the one state agency which pays an in-lieu tax on all lands it holds. "Forever and forever?" the commissioner asked.

"Yes," was the reply.

In addition, biologists and sportsmen explained that if this land was not made available to wintering elk, they would cause more winter depredations on ranch land downslope. On a split vote, it was decided to spend $100,465, appraised value of the property in question. Not all voting turns out as beneficial for public and sportsmen, however.

Retaining and/or acquiring adequate habitat for elk is a vital challenge for any game manager. Dr. D. I. Rasmussen, concerned biologist who did more than sit in a swivel chair, has stated that if elk are to exist without conflict, "They require extensive wilderness area for their year-long range." This does not necessarily mean designated or even "classical" wilderness, but rather terrain without the permanent presence of man where elk can find food. Places like Wyoming's Red Desert grasslands, Utah's Book Cliffs, and Colorado's river breaks might have elk if industry or agriculture didn't crowd them out. For instance, one enemy of elk habitat is reservoir construction. The impounded waters might inundate much valuable winter range at middle and low elevations, or even summer range at higher altitudes. Airports, urban sprawl, snowmobiling paths, and many other factors can decrease usable elk habitat. Worldwide research indicates the elk's counterpart on other continents, the red deer, gets along fine in treeless Tunisia, Algeria, and elsewhere if food is present and man doesn't stay for long. So can the elk in western North America. But any land-use change can adversely affect elk and elk hunting. Game managers are sometimes hard put to convince state agencies that large roadless tracts which don't return large monetary sums may harbor valuable herds of elk.

It is in such places that quality elk hunting, seemingly a philosophy whose time has come, can flourish. Large numbers of wapiti are not always the goal, but rather places where bulls can grow to trophy size because fewer hunters seek them there.

Manager's Challenge

Wyoming's Lee Wollrab, game-and-fish department control specialist, explains a few of the things a modern elk manager must be concerned with. "As always," he says, "the main concern is loss of habitat. Try and put yourself in my shoes for a moment. Imagine, for example, that the timber industry wants to harvest timber in your favorite elk hunting spot, and you realize that they are going to clearcut 50 or 60 percent of the timber that elk use for escape cover, and that they are going to double road densities to increase access by logging trucks. Next fall, hunting may be great — lots of roads to go anywhere an elk may be, and since most of the timber is cut, killing an elk may be 'easy.'

"But what happens in two or three years? The public at large finds out that it is an easy place to kill an elk, and all of a sudden you can't draw the license anymore; and those years when you do, the elk are no longer where they used to be. To top it off, you find out that some of the taxes you paid to the IRS may have been used to subsidize the timber industry, because most, if not all, Wyoming timber is managed by the U.S. Forest Service at a deficit.

"Habitat is definitely a major concern, because game-and-fish agencies don't always have the means to protect the habitat required to support the wildlife, as in the previous example."

Wollrab says a game manager's choices often boil down to "being damned if you do and damned if you don't." Worst of all, he says, is attempting to make such vital decisions without data to back them up.

Other factors affecting game managers are anti-hunting factions, predation on elk, and poaching, to name a few. The anti-hunting groups are yet not as disruptive to sound game management in the West as elsewhere. But they do hamper managers at times. For example, when elk are starving to death in a severe winter and more licenses are allocated for the hardest-hit areas, to prevent a repeat the following year, the "save our wildlife" fanatics sometimes do all in their power to halt hunting. Obviously, selective hunting is the best management tool available to prevent an entire herd from destroying itself. No more need be said on the subject. Nonetheless, such groups (like the one which almost banned moose hunting in Maine) continue to worry, harass, and even prevent game managers from getting their jobs done. The anti-hunting factions are not as strong in rural areas where guns are used in legitimate year-round activities, it would seem, as in metropolitan regions.

Elk loss because of predators is probably not so much a problem with elk as with deer, yet some game managers still list it as a challenge. Wolves in British Columbia and Alberta cause unwanted elk reductions. Mountain lions take a few elk in many of the western states. The biggest loss is probably the number of elk calves killed by coyotes. I have witnessed a healthy adult cow elk pay no attention at all to a single coyote, but several of the prairie wolves might well gang up and kill a calf up to several months old.

Curbing Poaching

Most law-enforcement sections, though they never eliminate poaching, curtail it. I've been with conservation officers and game wardens on a number of occasions when they happened upon an illegal kill. Drag marks in the snow led to an elk's remains, and only the hindquarters had been taken. Most important is how well the state officers enlist the help of community citizens, for no warden can patrol all alone the thousands of square miles under

his care. Smart wardens talk to butchers, acquaintances of suspected poachers, and landowners, and get their statements on tape or in writing. Building a solid case against a cheater is vital as a deterrent to future violators. So is a judge or justice of the peace who tosses the book at the offender.

Too often a judge is sympathetic when he hears how the culprit was "down and out," "just a poor student," and so on. I've seen cases where a nonresident hunter who illegally bought a resident elk license was fined less than the nonresident license would have cost. A judge who confiscates firearms, vehicles, and all other accoutrements used in illegal acts soon influences potential outlaws. Many newspapers publish a weekly list of game-law violators, their crime, and the punishment. Fish-and-game departments are now doing a better job of exposing the offense for what it is, cheating on the honest sportsmen. Hunters can help by obtaining a "hotline" number to report suspected game thieves.

Game management becomes very difficult when poaching—say, the wanton killing of hundreds of elk during deer or moose seasons—leaves a biologist thinking there is more game out there than really exists. So important is the matter that some game departments just figure in about a 50 percent or higher illegal kill and reduce the number of permits allocated by a like amount.

Check-station data, hunter survey cards, and personal telephone calls give game officials much information on game killed. Idaho statisticians call thousands of hunters every year in order to gain a handle on how many elk have been harvested—and thus how many are still out there.

Another aspect of management deals

with hunting preserves and winter feed refuges. Sure, they help elk subsist in tough winters. But how early should a refuge manager allow elk on those premises? Since many bulls will head for the safety of a refuge with the first shooting, should the wapiti be allowed to remain there when feed is not yet critical—needlessly costing taxpayers and license-buyers a heap of money and probably inviting more "welfare" elk in future years?

I got a dramatic look at this situation once when I helped three out-of-state friends with their elk hunt. After we'd spent several days finding nothing but deer and moose, I kiddingly asked a road crew where the elk were. "Down at the refuge," one answered. I didn't think that was likely, given the bluebird weather we'd been having, so I paid little attention to it. But a few hours later I glassed from a high vantage point down onto the refuge and saw hundreds of elk there!

"Fellows," I said, "I just looked at a large meadow full of elk, and I'll now take you there." We drove to the edge of an elk wintering refuge. Huge bulls gaped back at the hunters through a barbed-wire fence. "Can we hunt them at all this season?" a perplexed orange-vester asked the refuge manager.

"Just around the fringes, as they come in . . . or possibly if they should venture out," he said. "But you'll have to join the crowd. Most of the elk come in over there on the timbered side, and there's a long line of hunters each morning next to the fence."

The next day my hunting friends took a look. "That's not hunting," one of them said.

"Stick around," a watching nimrod told my companions. "You never know when a straggler might wander in here during daylight."

To their credit, the hunters from Wisconsin said they had seen enough. We searched elsewhere.

I later asked a game manager if the state's best interests were being served by selling permits to hunt that region, then letting all the elk move directly into the refuge. In my opinion, the managers should have spooked the game out of there by walking among them or shooting a rifle over a few elk heads. Then hunting could have been made legal in that vicinity. From the number of cows on that refuge, it was also questionable whether enough antlerless permits were being issued. Protecting the resource was one thing; but I got the distinct impression the refuge situation was a political thing: some state legislator who had introduced a law to construct a visitors' center on the refuge may well have figured it was best to keep the elk around just for visitors to look at. Maybe. In any event, elk were seemingly not being harvested as they might have been. Feeding costs were mounting. And elk-hunting success on that general unit that year was later announced at eight percent. Protection is not always the best way of managing elk for the best interests of hunters or the animals. Protection is the philosophy of the National Elk Refuge in Jackson Hole. Since it holds the world's largest elk herd, it might be well to summarize management practices there, including efforts to hold elk numbers at a 7,500 "compromise" level.

Refuge Management

Concerted efforts are made by officials to avoid drawing elk year-round into the refuge's 23,972 acres. If that were allowed, many elk would remain on refuge grass even during the summer. During heart of

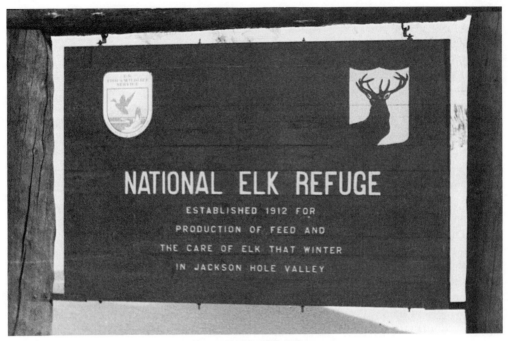

Sign at National Elk Refuge.

The National Elk Refuge is one place to winter elk and attempt to keep them out of private lands.

the winter, when too many wapiti gather for that grass, elk are fed 10 pounds of hay pellets a day per animal. Before pellets, some 12–13 pounds of hay apiece was doled out daily. Refuge managers complained much of it blew away, portions were bypassed, and some was rendered unpalatable by elk bedding and/or defecating on it. Large volumes of hay, usually in heavy bales, required much more time to move than do the high-density pellets. Refuge managers say one man in five hours can feed the pellets, whereas it once required six men all week to distribute as much food.

Ranchers frequently questioned whether the pellets contained the necessary protein and nutrients required by the elk. Refuge managers monitored the elk for several years before determining that health, pregnancy rates, ratio of healthy calves born, etc., were "normal enough." The pellets are now here to stay. Costs are also considerably less, primarily because fewer employees are needed.

But why are hunts necessary on the refuge? Managers say the herds are increasing at an annual rate of 20 percent. Some elk still spill over into Cache Creek and other residential and agricultural areas. To prevent more of it, herd size is reduced, primarily by hunting. Hunters with state licenses are allowed to put in for free refuge hunting permits to shoot elk entering the north side of the wintering grounds. Applicants must be present at a public drawing in the Jackson Rodeo Grounds. As of 1986, 120 permits are drawn each week for three hunt periods in late October and early November. For more information on the hunt, contact the Department of the Interior at P.O. Box C, Jackson, WY 83001.

Many Jackson Hole-area elk guides frankly don't like the shoot. We will examine their reasons in the following chapter.

Several other ramifications of managing elk come from managing some other animal. For example, in their zeal to protect the grizzly bear from extinction, state and federal managers have placed stringent limits on elk hunting. Elk outfitters complain that they must do many things to avoid the possibility of conflict with bears, including going to the extra expense of bringing in an extra tent so the cook can sleep away from food odors, putting up with foraging bears that may damage camps, keeping an extra hand around on guard to discourage bears from getting too close, hanging meat a long distance from camp, etc. It may seem to be only an outfitter's problem at this time, but it could be a game manager's problem in the future, especially in the hottest grizzly country in Montana, Wyoming, and eastern Idaho. If too many elk hunters are discouraged from going there, elk harvest may be inadequate. It's a thing game managers will have to keep their eyes on in the years ahead. It is hoped that both grizzly and elk can share the same habitat without either species suffering.

What else can the hunter do to help the game manager in his challenge to provide better hunting? The first thing is to join a worthy organization—to lend your ideas, absorb those of others, and present your knowledge and causes to game managers. Those managers must serve the will of the most people. However, as one game manager said, if five percent of the population wants quality hunting, the game department will try to provide five percent of the state with quality hunting.

If your organization sends a resolution of your proposals to game managers and they ignore you, go to a superior, the state

A particular threat to elk habitat in these modern times is oil exploration and development, usurping winter range.

fish and game director. If that fails, go to a natural resources director, or the governor. The main thing is to get your ideas out to those who make the decisions. But don't just rail at them. That kind of complaint is too often ignored as radical and unproductive. Be constructive enough to suggest a plan or proposal which the game manager can look good in adopting. If you feel too many elk licenses are issued in a certain region, suggest the state adopt a draw that limits licenses. If you can't get such a change made in a whole region, concentrate on one unit. Or ask for a shoot in which spikes are not legal game. Naturally, you will get farther if you have some concept of and sympathy for the game manager and the job he is expected to do. For one thing, he cannot always manage on a purely biological basis. He may have pressure from elected officials to do something other than what the data can support. This problem of "bio-politics" can't be ignored. Do you short the elk, the elk hunters, or the people who hired you?

Dedicated game managers can keep busy all year keeping tabs on fluctuating elk populations. To do so they must constantly measure and interpret range conditions, control diseases such as brucellosis, make sex ratio counts, keep elk from crop depredations (or pay for damage), set up efficient hunting regulations, take data afterward to determine success, publicize and sell the program to the public so license sales will be up, and convince the nonresident he is wanted and needed — even when residents ask him to go home. And that is only a capsule summary.

Some fish-and-game department personnel, including elk managers, must pay close attention to funding, including state and federal money needed to provide

Sheep operations share elk habitat on some public land in national forests.

sound game management. One of the top funding sources is the Pittman-Robertson Act of 1937. More information at the end of this chapter.

In order to best serve hunters, game managers must also take into consideration a gauntlet of interests. According to a survey of 5,500 elk hunters in Washington, they hunt for the following reasons, in order of importance: communion with nature, escape from the city, companionship in the outdoors, shooting, hunting skills, variety of opportunities, trophy display, harvest or bragging rights, utilization of equipment, verbal contact with other hunters, visual contact with other hunters.

Game managers cannot provide all these attractions at the same time. Priorities must be established. For example, wilderness "restricted-entry" permits allocated to only a few might minimize verbal and visual contact with others, yet would fill the needs emphasizing shooting and hunting skills.

Reasons for Hunting

Interestingly, a study in Colorado listed these reasons for elk hunting: love of the outdoors, companionship in the outdoors, challenge, recreational activity, escape.

Other studies indicate that elk hunters — many of them blue-collar workers from a city setting — feel they gain the following from big-game hunting: self reliance, initiative, instinct enhancement, ecological awareness, appreciation of cultural values, ethical training (especially of father teaching son or daughter), release of antisocial impulses, thrill of the chase, a release of tensions, bodily health, awareness of esthetic values, personal development in meeting challenges, awakening of religious beliefs.

Obvious by their absence are the factors of providing meat for the larder, and desire to kill an animal. However, many of the above hunters admitted they would hunt less or not at all if their chances for success were less than 5 to 10 percent.

Good game management is supposed to address all of the above factors.

Sometimes game managers and sportsmen's organizations face a special challenge, as indicated in this story in an Evanston, Wyoming, newspaper in 1985:

"Uinta County Evolves from Poor to Rich"

"CHEYENNE, Wyo. (UPI) — Uinta County, center of the Overthrust Belt energy boom, will evolve from one of Wyoming's poorest counties to one of the richest within five years, the head of an industry group said.

"The newfound wealth will probably make it unnecessary for the Overthrust Industrial Association, an organization of energy companies, to continue providing aid to the county by the end of the year, OIA president Owen Murphy told UPI.

"'We won't have any reason to exist in the Evanston area by the end of next year if our projections are correct,' Murphy said. 'The tax base will be tremendous.'

"'Chevron and Amoco will have two large natural-gas processing plants in operation by next year, permitting the companies to begin producing from other wells,' Murphy said. 'More severance-tax revenues will begin to pour in,' he said.

"'Within the next five years, Uinta County will go from one of the poorest counties in Wyoming to one of the wealthiest,' Murphy said. 'That may occur a good deal sooner than five years.'

"He said earlier Wyoming will make more than $2 billion from just severance taxes in the next 10–15 years from the Overthrust oil and gas. Uinta County's property taxes doubled this year and will double again next year, he said.

"The OIA has made 'considerable pro-

gress' since it was formed in June 1980, Murphy said. Membership has increased from three to 35 companies. The organization has provided $3 million in grants and other financial assistance to the area, and local and state governments have added another $20 million, Murphy said.

"'We're not through yet by a jugful,' he said. Several million dollars more in cash grants and alternative financing are possible, depending on need, and if developers can be persuaded to provide moderately priced homes, 'the total benefit could be as much as $100 million,' he said. 'That could include our cash grants, money from the state Farm Loan Board, and federal impact money if we could get it.'

"New schools are being built, highways are being improved, two extra police officers have been added in Kemmerer, funds have been provided to social-service agencies, and some housing, 'not enough but quite a bit,' has been built, he said. Housing remains a serious problem.

"Evanston had to dump raw sewage into the Bear River on some occasions, so the PIA provided $30,000 for a new pump that solved the problem, he said.

"Reaction from residents has been 'mixed,' Murphy said. A good cross-section of people have joined advisory groups, and there is 'a good feeling of cooperation,' he said. 'There will always be, though, that group of people whose families have been there for generations and are still ranching who just don't want to change. For them there is no solution. But they seem to be more in the minority than we originally supposed.'

"Uinta County has 'very self-reliant people,' Murphy said. 'Perhaps the most important service that we're rendering up there is supplying a technical assistance team. They are experts in community finance and human services, recreation, education, and health care.

"'What we do in effect is loan them to various communities to assist in providing the expertise to be able to manage a rapid-growth situation. Typically the administration in small communities just doesn't have that kind of expertise on its staff.'

"The OIA is not out to tell communities how to handle boom problems, Murphy said."

But game-management officials in Uinta County have a slightly different point of view, particularly concerning industrial development and its impacts, the money expended notwithstanding. Consider this newspaper story in the same Evanston, Wyoming, newspaper concerning a major industrial "benefit" and problem in local big-game management:

"According to Game Wardens, Wildlife Study Is 'Too Little, Too Late'"

"EVANSTON (AP) — Two Wyoming game wardens say a $1 million wildlife study of the southwestern Wyoming Overthrust Belt is 'too little, too late.'

"Uinta County Wardens Craig Sax and Jeff Smith say they believe the study is too late because impact from oil and natural gas drilling in the area is already occurring and will intensify before the study is completed.

"The two wardens, emphasizing they were speaking for themselves and not the Wyoming Game and Fish Department, said some value will come out of the study, because it will measure what already occurred. But, they said this week, it may be too little, too late to protect much of the wildlife in the hills and mountains surrounding Evanston.

"'We'll never be able to sustain the populations of animal species we once had there' in the Bear River Divide, Sax said.

"The $1 million study is being underwritten by the Overthrust Industrial Association, a group of energy companies operating in the Overthrust Belt. OIA officials were in a meeting in Denver and could not be reached for comment Wednesday evening.

"Sax was warden in the Evanston area and now covers the Bridger Valley in eastern Uinta County. Smith came to the Evanston area from Glenrock and, before that, worked on grizzly bear studies in Idaho.

"Uinta County now has two wardens, because of an $80,000 OIA grant. The association also granted $40,000 each to Utah and Idaho to upgrade game enforcement.

"The two wardens said OIA should be praised for that activity, and they also said some benefits will result from the wildlife study.

"'We're talking about a field that hasn't been explored. There is a need for research,' Sax said. 'There will be some information to be used, some good information. We'll be learning from the study what impacts have already occurred.'

"But, he said, the industrial association is 'riding both sides of the fence' by first saying wildlife would not be affected by drilling and then turning around and sponsoring a study.

"He criticized the lack of a control area or study and said there is need for an environmental impact statement for the entire Overthrust area.

"'The Game and Fish Department has said an environmental impact statement should have been prepared for the entire

Overthrust Belt, and we still contend that it's a significant impact,' he told the Herald.

"The study should have been started years ago, before drilling started, he said. 'Now it's too late to get the best use of this,' he said."

Then later came this frequently typical aftermath to the industrial dollars so welcomed at the sacrifice of big-game habitat (from the Casper, Wyoming, *Star-Tribune*, January 27, 1986):

"Evanston Begins Tightening Its Belt. Businesses, Government Try to Adjust to Oil-Price Plunge, Gas Glut By Paul Krza, Star-Tribune staff writer"

"EVANSTON — Belt-tightening has replaced black-gold rush euphoria here, where business and government are adjusting to new economic realities.

"Falling world oil prices, a natural-gas glut, and a better understanding of the limits of the Overthrust Belt are casting a new light on community operations, business, and government, officials say.

"Economic conditions still are far better than before the late 1970s and early 1980s boom, residents are quick to point out. But even with the newly found wealth, the reduced expectations and skidding energy prices are requiring readjustment.

"City-government officials, caught in a cash-flow squeeze, are trimming budgets to avoid what could be a deficit of more than $700,000 at the end of the fiscal year if nothing is done. A public hearing is scheduled January 30 to discuss proposed budget cuts.

"Housing vacancies are up, in part due to overbuilding during the boom, and the overall business climate is discouraging, some merchants say.

"Production levels are at less than capacity in the area's new economic linchpin, the oil and gas industry, which now provides more than 90 percent of the tax base, one industry official says.

"Ten years ago, the first significant discovery was logged in the Overthrust Belt in what was to become a string of oil and gas company success stories. The activity touched off a rash of exploration activity and sparked construction of two large gas-processing plants that triggered the boom in Evanston.

"But there are indications that expectations exceeded reality.

"'Anytime you have a boom like that, you always have people who come in trying to make the bucks while it's hot, and a lot of 'em end up folding because they have greater expectations than they should,' Chevron area Manager Tom Perryman said.

"A member of the City Council and longtime Evanston resident, Julie Lehman, agreed. The euphoria was fueled by people from economically depressed areas who 'came thinking they were into the gold rush,' she said.

"For Chevron, the current oversupply of natural gas means that contracting companies are taking no more than 'minimal' amounts of the fuel, Perryman said. Chevron's Carter Creek processing plant, which is capable of processing 150 million cubic feet of gas per day, operated at only half-capacity in 1983 and is still not up to its full output, he said.

"The original plan of tripling the plant's capacity also 'probably won't happen,' Perryman said.

"The Overthrust is 'still a very prolific

area with a lot of reserves and still some potential,' he said. 'But it's not like the activity back in 1981–82' when there was 'one heck of a lot of money' flowing through the Evanston area, he added.

"The net result has been a slowdown in Evanston's once-overheated economy, prompting a shutdown of some businesses and cutbacks at others."

The Pittman-Robertson Act
(Reprinted with permission from the Browning Co. catalog, October 1985)

What is Pittman-Robertson? In 1937, legislation was sponsored by Sen. Key Pittman of Nevada and Rep. A. Willis Robertson of Virginia, to direct funds of an 11 percent excise tax on the manufacturing costs of guns and ammunition specifically to programs involving wildlife management. The fundamental concept was that sportsmen would directly help pay for the needs of wildlife through mon-

ies collected by the tax. The excise tax was heartily supported by sportsmen and the wildlife management community. Recent amendments have placed the tax on archery equipment and pistols as well.

Taxes for wildlife. Each year more than $100 million is collected. Over the past 50 years of Pittman-Robertson more than $1.5 billion has been collected for wildlife.

How the fund is allocated. State wildlife agencies receive portions of the fund according to a formula involving hunting licenses sold, a state's population, and general need. States propose conservation or research programs and, if approved, Pittman-Robertson funds will cover up to 75 percent of the cost — $3 for every $1 put up by the states.

How the money is spent. More than 62 percent of the money collected goes directly into land accquisition. Since the program began, over 3,700,000 acres have been purchased to develop and operate wildlife management areas. Purchasing land and improving habitat have always

Another game-management opportunity is to let public enjoy viewing and photographing elk on the winter refuges like this one at Utah's Hardware Ranch.

been of the utmost importance. Habitat loss is the most significant cause of reduced wildlife populations. Twenty-six percent goes directly into research or surveys. A recent amendment allows about seven percent of the tax to be spent on hunter education programs. The remaining five percent goes to the states for planning and supervising the program, and for providing and distributing technical information to government agencies. Funds are used where they are needed most — for nongame, endangered, and threatened wildlife as well as for game animals.

About the wildlife case histories in this catalog. Many of the wildlife management case stories contained in this year's Browning catalog were provided by the "Un-endangered Species" program of the National Shooting Sports Foundation.

Professionally produced filmstrips, booklets, and other literature are available to teachers and individuals promoting the successes of sportsman-sponsored wildlife management and conservation in America. For further information, write Un-endangered Species, P.O. Box 59, Riverside, CT 06878.

If you'd like to know more about Pittman-Robertson. The Department of the Interior is planning an extended commemoration of the Pittman-Robertson Act beginning in 1986, and continuing throughout the anniversary year, 1987. The Fish & Wildlife Service is publishing a detailed book on Pittman-Robertson success stories. Films, posters, and exhibits are also planned. For more information contact the Fish & Wildlife Service, Washington, D.C. 20204.

19

What of the Future?

Given the management challenges outlined in the previous chapter, what can be done to protect elk habitat and ensure the future of quality elk hunting? Let's look at the following problems and decide what can be done about them.

1. Energy fuel exploration and development.

2. Construction of logging and other roads into prime elk domain.

3. Agricultural depredation and all the winter conflicts facing elk.

4. Conversion of grasslands and feed to other uses detrimental to wapiti.

5. Unchecked natural predation.

6. Mushrooming number of hunters.

7. Role of parks and winter refuges.

8. Apathy to elk, their habitat and value.

9. Antihunting influence.

10. Poaching and other law-enforcement problems.

Oil exploration-development is listed first because many game managers and sportsmen's-club officials now feel it is the major threat to the future of quality elk hunting. As energy fuel spokesmen claim, there are few proven instances of either exploration or development causing the death of a wapiti. However, the negative impacts on elk habitat (and the esthetics of elk hunting) are far-reaching. Perhaps the situation is best explained by an in-depth look at the process of seismographic exploration (with helicopters and dynamite charges) and subsequent development. I believe it is best explained in this article, "Oil vs. Wildlife, Controversy Grows," which I wrote for the March 1985 issue of *Western Outdoors* after considerable research. Permission to reprint portions of it was kindly granted by *Western Outdoors* editors:

"As a hunter you have just spent nearly four hours in the saddle. Emotionally and monetarily, you have put much into this western Wyoming elk opener. Preparations began nearly a year ago. Now, finally, you are on a mountain trail leading away from all roads, high into emerald meadows where oversized bulls graze by dawn's early light. Your muscles ache, and only the icy October wind in your eyes keeps you awake. But it will be worth it when you sight bands of undisturbed wapiti peacefully residing in backcountry as they have done for decades.

"But don't count on it. Not since a phenomenon known as seismographing is being increasingly allowed on our western public lands. This method of searching for energy fuel, usually with aid of a helicopter, lays out 'lines' of wire-connected dynamite charges on or near the ground. After detonation, resultant vibrations beneath the earth's surface are measured. If favorable 'readings' are found, development can quickly follow: Roads, rigs, processing plants, pipelines, year-round maintenance crews, 24-hour-a-day pumping, and, in some cases, signs warning of dangerous gases closing even public roads for a time.

"How widespread is seismographing? And exactly how much negative impact does it have, directly or indirectly, on wildlife? While the above example is cited from Wyoming's portion of the Overthrust Belt (energy engineers say the Belt could run down the entire western U.S. from Montana to New Mexico), the practice of seismographing has, and is, spreading far beyond the Rocky Mountains.

"Don Schultz, minerals specialist for the U.S. Forest Service's intermountain office at Ogden, Utah, says the chopper-explosion technique of seeking out oil and gas is now being used in dozens of national forests from the Dakotas to California. This type of exploration has long been used in the Canadian provinces. It could occur anywhere in the U.S. at any time. Schultz explains, 'It is within USFS policy to allow seismographing on any national forests in the entire United States.'

"But to realize fully what is happening—or could—throughout the West, let's focus on one national forest particularly abounding in big-game wildlife, western Wyoming's Bridger.

"Elk have long thrived here in remote, steep canyons and ridges rising up to well above 11,000 feet elevation. This region is not official wilderness, but wild enough to be managed by the Forest Service as 'primitive,' and roadless. What is happening to our wildlife here could be multiplied a hundredfold considering the many square miles of public land involved across the western states.

"Take the Bridger's southwestern Kemmerer District. How much of it is leased for oil exploration via seismographing? All of it. Every arroyo and rim. 'It is 100 percent leased out to the energy fuel industry,' says district supervisor Robert Riddle. 'And if favorable readings are discovered, we cannot within our guidelines from Washington deny the right to access and develop any of these leases on the national forest.'

"Such roads and permanent developments can mean major impacts on naturally suspicious wapiti. But let's look at these post-exploration factors later. Recently the writer examined the 'seismic exploration grid' on the Kemmerer District.

Multiple lines paralleled, criss-crossed, and even overlapped one another in what could pass for the sewerage blueprint of a major metropolis.

"Photographs were prohibited. Competing oil companies do not want each other to know where they have been. Thus, 'dry' holes are repetitively worked.

"Not only does this drive up the price of gasoline at the pump, but it repeatedly drives elk from favorite bedding, grazing, and watering grounds. Given the noise of choppers, explosions, and crews laying out and regathering miles of wires, it is not surprising that an animal which flees at even a hunter-snapped twig will move elsewhere."

I talked with a Forest Service supervisor about this, and he told me that elk in seismographed areas do not bed or feed much in the open anymore, "But then hunters can learn to hunt the animal like they do the whitetail deer—back in the heavy brush."

However, beyond a certain loss of hunting esthetics, most USFS managers I've talked to deny any loss of habitat via exploration and no decrease in total elk numbers. (Development, of course, is another story—it means permanent intrusion on wapiti range.)

The Forest Service also says the following steps have been taken to avoid spooking off elk under the most critical circumstances: no seismographing is allowed on elk-calving areas in May and June, during winter months when animals are yarded up, or during the hunting seasons themselves. In most instances, forest supervisors also require helicopter and dynamite activities on elk habitats to cease at least five days prior to the rifle hunting seasons. Archers do not enjoy such a

stipulation. Naturally, the bowmen and many riflemen who find no elk where they had scouted them earlier don't think the USFS is stringent enough.

One oil-industry spokesman told me that the energy fuel people "would have to kill a lot of elk to equal what the hunters do every autumn." But let's ignore that swipe at hunting to look at what effects oil exploration does have on elk and elk habitat. Not enough research has been done to combat industrial skepticism on every front, but the following was compiled by the University of Wyoming in a study titled: "Response of Elk to Seismic Exploration, Bridger-Teton National Forest, Progress Report." Begun in 1983, it immediately reports a calving impact as recorded in the aforementioned *Western Outdoors* article:

"'It has been observed that elk no longer have their calves in Snider Basin . . . apparently due to a variety of disturbance-related causes.' The report says, in part, 'Following such range and abandonment, it may take years for elk to regain old patterns of range use.' The above represents 'a reduction in recreational activities, interpreted as a loss by game managers,' the report adds.

"The study also cites previous data from Michigan across the West to Alberta indicating that the following could well occur with seismographing-oil development: (1) greater vulnerability of game to predation as crowding occurs; (2) stress at any time of year, i.e., 'If a bull, already shedding heat maximally under a hot sun, was disturbed by a helicopter, it could collapse from heat stroke after running away;' (3) displaced game has been observed not to feed as well as before, with likelihood of later and lighter calves and potentially twice the death rate of healthier ones on favored ranges; (4) death could be caused by frightening game over ledges and cliffs, as has been observed with bighorn sheep fleeing helicopters; (5) stress which might affect an adult, making it more susceptible under crowded conditions on poorer range to disease, and likewise calves born later to that adult.

"An aspect of the research is that elk were observed to flee 1,000 meters (about three-quarters of a mile) from seismic activity, and then move up to two miles away, 'usually keeping at least two ridge-lines between them and the disturbance.' Some elk returned within a few days to the general area seismographed, and some did not return at all during the testing period of one year. The study did conclude that breeding activities were adversely affected: 'Bulls were forced to spend much time regrouping scattered harems.'

"The study did not directly address impact of roads on elk. But the Wyoming Game and Fish Department says it has research linking exodus of elk when new or substantially improved old roads allowing general traffic invade buffer zones between wapiti and human activity. Elaine Raper, southwestern district WGFD supervisor, says, 'Another half-mile of new road here, upgrading of another there, and the vital buffer zone between elk and human activity is lost. Elk may then be crowded on poorer, less desirable range. This also creates problems for big-game hunters, with less habitat where the animals can be found.'

"In addition, WGFD studies show a decrease in elk harvest, particularly bulls, since 1981 on the southwestern Bridger with intensification of oil-related activity. In 1981, 19.8 hunter-days were required to bag a bull. In 1983 (latest year for which

figures are available), 28.8 days were required per hunter. Quality of the hunt, measured in number of branch-antlered bulls taken, dropped 44.8 percent. This downward trend occurred with no significant decline in numbers of hunters afield, according to WGFD statistics."

Officials of the Overthrust Industrial Association told me they see little or, in most cases, no connection between the foregoing and oil impacts. Aaron Clark, program manager for the OIA, a consortium of 26 oil companies along the Overthrust Belt, says much of the $15 million spent since 1981 on socio-economic-biological studies has directly assisted elk management.

Maybe so. But not nearly as much as if the seismographing and later oil-field development had not been thrust on Rocky Mountain elk habitat. According to a former WGFD game biologist, Don Roy, the oil industry has too often done what it wanted first, then funded a study later, with results being largely academic. "The damage is done," he emphasized. "Why don't they wait for the information to be obtained from the study before proceeding with business as usual?"

The question was put to Clark. He replied, "It is not prudent to stop first. We may find no significant impacts. And if we did, we may find no better way to mitigate or reclaim. Certainly we do find some unavoidable impacts, but oft times the value of the wildlife does not exceed the value of the mineral or goal we're after."

But back to the *Western Outdoors* report:

"Some oil representatives have also hit back at sportsmen's complaints by pointing out that elk are 'crowded on elk refuges each winter.' No one argues that this is good for the animals. But sportsmen add more may be needed 'if elk continue to be pushed off favored feeding grounds and enter winter in poorer shape.'

"Rocky Vandersteen, veteran hunter and taxidermist who talks to many other license-holders, holds to that view. He also cites elk departing open sage areas of the Overthrust Belt where wapiti had become established, 'but left coincidentally when oil activity increased in that region.'

"Vandersteen says he also feels part of the problem is philosophical. 'Many of the oil-industry people are not westerners,' he comments. 'They don't always fully appreciate the value of a big-game animal or its habitat requirements. The aesthetics of the hunt are being destroyed. We hunt on public lands to challenge a wild elk in natural surroundings, not between oil rigs and a lacework of roads leading to them. Or for a big bull with its tongue hanging out from dodging helicopters. You have to wonder if it's even worth buying a license anymore.'

"The USFS's Riddle says: 'To prevent wholesale movements of elk, we try to organize seismic activities to every other or every third canyon or ridge. That way the animals have a place of refuge during the entire disturbance.'

"One Jackson Hole guide says the Forest Service is trying to maintain an impossible juggling act in its multiple-use mandate. Guy Azevedo, who outfits south of Jackson Hole, says he finds plenty of elk in his bailiwick, except after it has been seismographed."

Jack Ourado, president of the Kemmerer, Wyoming-based Overthrust Wildlife Association, says the oil companies are pushing elk off the areas they explore and/or develop. At present there are many developments near Kemmerer on the Bridger Forest which elk will no longer use, and it represents more lost elk hunting. He noted that seismographing is no longer allowed during the actual hunting seasons, but told me: "They better not. They might find a 30-06 hole in their helicopter." He adds that he would not condone it, but that threat is a major reason exploration was halted during the hunting seasons. "Hunters were beginning to shoot at choppers that were spooking away elk they were stalking," irate sportsman's representatives explained.

To be fair, seismographing has come a long way from the early days when the nation seemed to hear no other voice but the cry for oil. But it would seem the federal land agencies need to say a polite "no" to some oil companies who want to explore and develop the heart of America's wapiti habitat. So far, according to USFS and BLM managers, no oil firm has been denied access to any potential oil field. I hope no more oil-related helicopter flights will duplicate one I know of wherein two employees bragged about swooping down at wintering wapiti for a closer look. "You should have seen them scatter," the employee said. On the Shoshone National Forest in northwestern Wyoming, a forest supervisor who says he runs a "tight ship" hauled an oil-firm chopper pilot into court for harassing winter-range wildlife, causing them stress by severely depleting a low fat reserve, which could lead to starvation later. The judge assessed an appropriate fine.

At this time, no seismographing is allowed in designated wilderness areas. However, oil exploration is knocking at the door of several—one of them in New Mexico, some in Wyoming, and even

Grand Teton National Park. In 1985 the Teton Park supervisor complained that several explorations occurred on the park's eastern boundary. In Utah, oil companies attempted to hurry exploration into the southern boundary of the newly legislated High Uinta Wilderness Area. At a 1984 hearing in Washington, D.C. I joined the Utah Wilderness Association in testifying to personally observed high-density elk populations on the East Fork of Bear River and adjoining drainages. Wildlife and conservation interests won part of that battle by gaining wilderness protection for some of that area. But much of it was lost, including East Fork calving areas, because oil had already been discovered there.

This isn't to say elk should always win out over conflicting interests. But in a democracy it is important for the public to know the issues, and too often the value of one commodity—wildlife—is downplayed or ignored outright. And unfortunately, big-game habitat is rarely reclaimed once lost.

The solution to the oil-industry threat to the future of elk and elk habitat is summed up by officers of the Wyoming Wildlife Federation, which has been following the oil vs. wildlife quandary from the beginning. Brent Bergen, WWF president, said:

"'Let us approach this threat, present and potential, to our hunting future with intelligence. The oil industry is already quite clearly impacting big game. And where facts are needed, let the burden of proof that oil *is not* harming wildlife be upon the energy fuel industry before more floodgates are opened to possible resource damages.'

"Emphasizing that many of those dam-

ages are 'irreparable,' Bergen calls for sportsmen everywhere to write state and federal decision and policy-makers. 'Tell them you are not against oil, just against it unfairly taking precedent over wildlife in the multiple-use process. These are our public lands. They belong to you and me. We ought to have a voice, a powerful one, in how those lands are managed,' Bergen advises.

"Bergen says sportsmen should 'demand now, if they haven't already,' that the public agencies be required to show all negative effects in an environmental impact statement specifically addressing detailed energy fuel impacts on wildlife in each oil-related action, rather than an assessment only on an entire forest or district, as is often now the practice. He says in summary: 'If we as western sportsmen do not stand up for wildlife interests at this very moment, we have no right to lament later when they are lost.'"

In addition, the actual process of drilling for oil can have its effects on elk hunting. One Wyoming outfitter was even moved off his traditional campsite at the head of the Greys River because "an oil company decided it wanted to drill there" on the national forest. Also consider the accompanying letter regarding the esthetics of oil drilling.

Azevedo was not compensated as requested. But Arco officials decided not to drill although denying it was due to negative publicity.

In addition, WWF President Bergen's call for a full environmental impact statement, rather than just a general forest-wide assessment, seems to have gained desired results in the courtroom. In Montana, U.S. District Judge Paul Hatfield ruled the USFS and BLM violated the Na-

To Bridger-Teton National Forest
Kemmerer Ranger District

Dear Sir:

In regards to the Arco Oil Well Coantag Creek Unit No. 1: We feel that this well will greatly reduce the number of hunters we can book because:

1. The noise from the well will easily be heard from our campsite (approx. 1 mile).

2. Most of our hunters will feel that an oil rig in the area will greatly reduce the number of game animals available, and book elsewhere.

3. We feel that the access road should be limited to oil-well employees only. If the general public is allowed to use this road, it would mean increased hunting pressure in the heart of our area, and this would also affect our ability to book hunters.

We feel this road should be permanently closed at the conclusion of the drilling process.

We also feel we should be compensated for the number of hunters we lose because of this project.

Sincerely

(signed)
Guy and Debbie Azevedo
Wolf Mountain Outfitters
Afton, Wyo.

tional Environmental Policy Act and the Endangered Species Act. Hatfield said the federal agencies had failed to prepare an EIS needed to explain the effects of oil and gas activity on the Flathead and Gallatin National Forests. As might be expected, it didn't happen in a vacuum. The suit was brought via intense efforts by the Montana Wildlife Federation. The victory was more than locally important for it meant a precedent for the EIS process on other national forests where elk habitat could be impacted.

Roads and Elk

Threat No. 2: new or substantially improved roads bringing more vehicular traffic into prime elk terrain. This concern is a relatively new one, but it is nonetheless real. Nearly every state lists roads, particularly logging roads, as a top problem for the future. Typical of concerns everywhere is this news story from the Wyoming Wildlife Federation's "Pronghorn" publication: "The Medicine Bow National Forest is currently bulldozing a major road through the heart of essential elk habitat

. . . Elk calving grounds, summer forage, and fall hiding cover will be destroyed. The Forest Service claims the roading and clearcutting will benefit wildlife."

The Federation claims the road building on this forest is part of a 50-year timbering program which may be illegal under the Forest Service's own guidelines.

But let's take a look at the timbering-roading philosophy within another forest, Wyoming's Bridger. The USFS scoping statement on the Scotty Creek area says:

1. The recently enacted Wyoming Wilderness Bill released the area in which the proposed sale is located to uses other than wilderness.

2. Management direction in this zone is to obtain *optimum* sustained production of quality timber, forage, and *wildlife habitat* . . ."

Roads are being equated with optimum wildlife habitat. How is not explained. The USFS adds that "the timbering roads will also improve hunting access."

The Boone and Crockett Club has often said: "We must think twice before encouraging local land managers to build roads into prime big-game hunting areas to facilitate access. There seems a direct correlation between mechanical access and the decline of big-game populations."

The State of Washington's "Green Dot" program seeks to close existing roads to vehicular traffic in elk habitat. If the road is not marked with a green dot, it is closed "to benefit both elk habitat and elk hunting." Washington's big-game proclamation invites hunters "to get out and walk the roads, but not drive them." A number of studies in Idaho and Oregon reinforce this concern about roads in elk country and also indicate that the Forest Service is at odds with other game managers in its "build roads to help big-game hunting" philosophy.

Of course, the USFS must operate under the multiple-use concept. But any attempt to equate better hunting with roads has to be a trifle strained at best.

"Consider that roads can bring motorcyclists, snowmobilers, Sunday drivers, picnickers . . . As road densities increase, elk retreat from this disturbance until eventually there is no escape left. . . ." So says a Wyoming Forest Study Team, quoted by USFS wildlife research biologists in the book *Elk of North America*, by Thomas and Toweill. Not all forest managers agree.

Also consider this statement in the aforementioned USFS scoping statement for the southwestern Bridger forest: "Improvement could be made in existing wildlife habitat through money derived from timber sales."

Why not just "improve" the big-game habitat by skipping the roads? If the roads are constructed, the Forest Service may take aggressive steps to do as Washington has done and manage the roads for benefit of wildlife and hunting. That would mean closing them to vehicles most of the year.

In addition, the USFS leaves the impression that an honest profit is made from the timber sales and attendant road construction. But this is not the case at all thus far. Considerable taxpayer money would be saved if the Forest Service scrapped the timber sales. (Since they do not pay their own way, the USFS turns to "wildlife benefits" as a justification for the costly roads to timber operations.) A number of news stories in 1985 said that every thousand board-feet of timber the USFS has sold since 1981 cost the U.S. taxpayer (us) from $33 to $114. "Cash losses from one forest totaled a minimum of $1.36 million," said the Casper, Wyoming, *Star-Tribune*. The administrator of this forest admits the program is a money-loser, but claims "the losses must be viewed in the context of other benefits, and as an investment in the forest's future." Cash income was listed at about $1.54 million from the timber sales, yet administrative costs were listed at $2.6 million, including $485,000 paid to timber companies for road construction. Interpreted, it means sportsmen are paying for deterioration of elk habitat.

The Forest Service has its side to the controversy. One supervisor commented, "Why do we have to justify everything we do with a profit?" Unfortunately, the outdoor recreationist talking esthetics and hunting seldom gets far unless he can cite some economic benefits. The Wyoming game-and-fish department proved the major use on the Medicine Bow National Forest was outdoor recreation, yet the USFS said the forest was to be logged anyway. The local wildlife federation sums it up this way: "We can kiss the area's elk goodbye . . ."

Recently I stood on the crest of a ridge looking down into Scotty Creek. Bedded down there in the snowy timber were several bull elk of respectable size. The nearest road was several miles away, and the wapiti seemed secure in their backcountry bailiwick. A cow moose trudged down past one 5-point bull, which merely turned to look at the black animal, then squirmed tighter into his bed. How is a road and cutting of the timber on that slope going to provide an "improvement"?

Granted, the multiple-use management idea does have some benefits to elk. Clear-cutting has often helped wildlife by con-

verting foodless jungle to grass and browse by letting sunlight in. Controlled burns by the USFS have transformed conifer and deciduous forests into new browse and grass species palatable to both livestock and big game. Roads in the Northwest's coastal rainforests have benefitted the hunting of Roosevelt elk—provided the roads are managed for some restrictions in vehicular use.

In the West and elsewhere, driving back roads is a popular American pastime. In one study, "Sunday driving" came in second only to camping among major uses of forests (with hunting third). Yet it would seem that under the Forest Service's own announced camping and hunting uses studies that new-road construction would be weighed most carefully before the bulldozers are turned loose. And I think Teddy Roosevelt and Gifford Pinchot, stalwart pioneers in the National Forest concept, would agree that reducing usable habitat for elk violates a primary forest use. Hunters in Oregon at first used access roads into elk-hunting terrain, then later voted for a ban on vehicles when they discovered that elk don't mix well with cars and trucks.

The value of the roadless philosophy was dramatically pointed out to me several years ago on a hunt I took near the Colorado-Utah border. Our party, new to the region, chose to camp near a good gravel road. We didn't have horses, so we attempted to hike in to the elk. We did not find any. At first we assumed we were in a poor unit, and decided never to return. However, in talking later to a conservation officer who had been in this terrain, I learned that our hunters had actually been relatively near known elk-bedding grounds. If we had camped farther down that road, where it was a mite rougher and more challenging (with less traffic), we'd have been within three-quarters of a mile of the elk. I located dozens of them later on, including several nice bulls. They were one buffer zone away all the time.

In many instances the greatest problem with federal-agency road construction is that it can slip by as a wildlife benefit when it is precisely the opposite. At least with oil development, the industrial assessment says it plainly (Exxon LaBarge Project, page 27): "The major impact will be the disturbance of elk critical winter range and elk calving grounds . . ." That is one reason sportsmen must be skeptical about wildlife "improvements" or so-called enhancements. As one sportsmen's leader put it, "We could be improved right out of the elk business."

Actually, the USFS and other federal agencies must, under the National Environmental Policy Act, comply with a number of safeguards before making land-management decisions. One of these is a public hearing. However, hunting interests must alertly watch newspapers for notices of hearings and, when attending, be able to pick out the chaff from the wheat. A disadvantage of such hearings is that the citizen must appear on his own time and money, while a commercial interest is usually paid well to be there. But in the end, federal agencies are duty-bound to do that which will be in the best public interest. Too often, public input is not received on things like wildlife values, sometimes because sportsmen think the importance of big game is obvious. But it's not unless you say so!

There are some indications the USFS has recently become more sensitive to public outdoor recreation interests. In the beginning of 1986 several forest man-

agers, following continued research, announced cutbacks in timber felling and road construction. Officials of the Bridger-Teton forest stated that "recreational and wildlife uses are growing in importance" to such an extent that traditional timber cutting could no longer be justified. Reductions were so extensive that a lumber mill in the region faced shutdown. However, even though jobs will be lost, several local newspaper columnists blamed the community leaders for not diversifying economically. "To keep that mill running," said one newsman, "this entire sector of the state would suffer more loss of income from outdoor recreation and tourism, including hunting and fishing. Why should any one group have carte blanche to destroy that?"

Sometimes the road proponents are hunters. One forest supervisor told me that local sportsmen objected when he attempted to close a forest road frequently used to reach prime elk terrain. The group's leader later voiced the concern that the closure might not be fairly administered, giving some interests access but keeping others out. Such reactions require fortitude on the part of public agency leaders. But they are a part of an administrator's job.

Nuisance Wapiti

Threat No. 3: agricultural depredation. Colorado's Public Services Officer Peggy Cabiness puts it this way: "What do we see as the main problem facing elk? Loss of habitat caused by an unwillingness of landowners to tolerate increasing elk populations." That sums up the problem for most game managers.

Game managers understandably hesitate to allow herd increase, or transplant elk into any area already suffering from agricultural damage by game animals. The public and political pressure is exerted to reduce populations, not increase them. Sometimes these reductions, like the "thinning out" process on the National Elk Refuge, also precipitate a problem. Many veteran nimrods complain vociferously that elk should be "earned" with greater effort than parking a vehicle near a refuge entrance and then waiting. One guide told me he would like to have some of those elk up in the wilds "where they have some value. Down there, they're just a cheap shot and a pile of meat." However, federal refuge managers defend the hunt, saying most of the elk on public hunting grounds move to state refuges and don't even winter at the National Elk Refuge. In addition, National Refuge officials say some guides are getting fancy fees for guiding nonresidents to large bulls in the "refuge reduction" hunts—this despite the fact that finding a refuge firing line isn't very hard.

I don't agree with the nationally televised "Sixty Minutes" that this shoot is an unnecessary slaughter. The decision to reduce elk is a valid one. However, I would prefer to see the elk removed via trapping, which in that situation shouldn't be as difficult as usual. If a hunt is deemed the only way, I would like to see it done in some more sporting way. Maybe it should be reserved for hunters over age 65, disabled veterans, or something of that nature.

The value of an elk, monetarily and esthetically, should always be kept in mind. By paying out $500 for information leading to the arrest of anyone poaching an elk, many states have placed that value on a single wapiti. Nothing should be done to cheapen the value by making what

could be a sport hunt into an annihilation. To make this work, game managers must decide when a herd could potentially face starvation. A hunt not held early enough translates later to the "cheap slaughter." However, to hold a November hunt on a herd likely to ravish a given haystack or two in January, a game manager must have ample data on elk movements.

Some have advanced the idea that the refuge and other hunts are held simply for economic reasons, to cut down on the number of animals which must be fed. But I hope the value of an elk is sufficiently understood these days that a bull wapiti is not destroyed for the cost of a little hay. If elk can be kept away from landowner haystacks by a feeding process, we ought to find the governmental wherewithal to feed them. If the herd size is such that the elk cannot be kept out of private property, more hunting season permits should be allocated before animals are winter-weakened.

Because of these possible conflicts with man, game managers are often reluctant to transplant elk into any but the wildest backcountry. Several Yellowstone transplants into eastern states—including Michigan, Pennsylvania, North Dakota, and Minnesota—might grow to huntable size if landowner complaints are few. In Utah, several transplants have made game managers look good, particularly in the Boulder Mountains. Old-time stockman J. J. Casey Bown (later a legislative specialist with the Utah Division of Wildlife Resources) watched this remote range deteriorate from a place abounding with elk hunted only by local Indian tribes to one where white men overkilled the animals in the absence of game laws. Where Casey had looked at many elk, he later witnessed few. He and others with the state recommended elk be restored to the Boulders, and the area has since flourished with wapiti to the point where Utah has changed it from "limited entry" to open-bull hunting. With ample highland grass and conifer cover, this rugged plateau has "held" the elk well, with few local rancher complaints, save in a severe winter. Every state needs to determine whether it has any "Boulder Mountains."

Much of what any state management program can do depends heavily on such federal funding as Pittman-Robertson, through which sportsmen help defray costs of big game and its enhancement. It is usually only with such funding that a state can afford to do the "extra" things like conduct in-depth tagging research, pay for elk transplants, and acquire winter rangelands.

However, not all elk herds get along as well as the one above. Consider the following excerpts from the November 24, 1985, "Utah County Journal," titled "The Killing Fields":

"Beginning Saturday, 90 hunters will begin killing cow elk forced by snow out of their rugged Nebo Mountain habitat . . . There are residents, however, who don't like the idea when some of the cows are three months pregnant and are handicapped by deep snow when fleeing hunters' bullets . . . but wildlife officials say, 'You should hear the calls we get from farmers and fruit growers when the elk come out of the mountains this time of year.'"

When asked why the state doesn't just issue more cow permits during the regular autumn hunts, the answer is: "The late hunt is targeted to the specific animals causing the damage, and when we know they are causing it." Utah started a herd on Mt. Timpanogos, but had to terminate the elk for similar reasons: local land-

owners complained they couldn't sustain the damages, and the state decided it couldn't pay them.

When asked why Utah did not initiate an extensive feeding program like those in Wyoming, an official is quoted as saying: "Hunters line up around that preserve . . . shooting the elk like cattle whenever they step over the line." However, conclusion of the article is that if Utah wants to provide elk hunting in that area, it had better begin a feeding program. It would appear the Journal has a point. (However, one study in Idaho found each elk cost $222 per winter to feed, with costs rising.)

In addition, the newspaper suggests contacting legislators and other high government officials, plus television media, to look at the problem and see if there is any better way than feeding. If so, the solution would likely be to buy up winter rangelands (if available) and then plant them in vegetation that is more attractive to elk than the adjacent farms and orchards. The agricultural lands, however, with tender shoots in the early spring, are magnetic to both elk and deer. Another possibility is an eight-foot fence surrounding the private land. Where this has been done, flooding and erosion have sometimes washed out land beneath the fence, allowing animals in. One game biologist told me it is uncanny how an elk can find a small opening in a fence to get through if he wants in badly enough. In addition, "sportsmen" sometimes want in and will cut holes, along with other vandalism. Even if it works, a fence is expensive. Game departments rarely have enough funding for such things.

A problem with feeding elk on winter refuges in areas of high human population is conflict with traffic and dogs, accessibility for poaching, and other activity that stresses the wapiti. And once elk are dependent on the feeding, stopping is almost impossible.

During one elk controversy it was discovered that 22 elk were apparently killed by landowners and left to rot. Perhaps a hunt called earlier would have been better for everyone concerned; some elk would have been harvested and used and others spooked away.

I have a neighbor who hosts 200 elk in his yards and haystacks each winter night. They compete directly with the cattle for every bale of hay. The rancher is given funding to construct a high board fence around the stacks, but he must remove them every time he wishes to feed the stock. "Yesterday," he told me, "a 7-point bull got an antler tine caught in a fence crack and nearly tore the place apart getting untangled. I love the wildlife, but I can't stand by to see my cattle lose out. I figure hay at $80 a ton—if I could even buy it in the winter. One elk eating an average of 13 pounds a day would consume a ton during the five months of a severe winter's duration. With some 200 elk, it would cost me $16,000 from mid-November to the middle of April."

The game manager must have an idea of how many acres per elk will be needed to sustain the animals without artificial feeding. Wapiti will often head for an easy handout before buckling down to available natural feed that requires added effort, so the manager must also know when to "force" elk from the man-supplied calories without causing bodily stress or harm. Feeding too early is wasting dollars; feeding too late is wasting elk.

Some states compensate landowners for game damage by allowing them extra elk hunting permits. These are usually for nonresidents, who must pay trespass or guide fees to hunt on the landowner's property. Some states provide coupons on

hunting licenses; the landowner hands in the coupons later for cash redemption. The sportsman has nothing to lose in helping the landowner in such ways.

Elk, owned by the public, have as much right on public property as do private livestock. Yet landowners also hold many of the private land acres. The hunting fraternity might as well recognize it, and sit down to work with them. No legislature in this land is likely to vote for more elk benefits when even a single major landowner steps to the podium to complain that the wild animals are forcing him out of business.

However, hunters should swallow no shenanigans when it comes to posting or shutting off access to public lands or roads. In a court case pitting the Wyoming Wildlife Federation vs. Red Rim private landowners, a final decision required a rancher to remove fences that were preventing game animals from migrating to public winter range. Fortunately, the WWF wouldn't give up, even after several years of being told to forget it by courts handing out rulings sought by landowners. One thing which helped was that the BLM stepped in to hear the Federation's argument, then sided with it. Yet the main credit for championing the victory goes to a group of tenacious sportsmen who believed in their cause.

Another key to landowner toleration of hunters is horse-sense courtesy: closing gates, picking up your own litter, avoiding contact with livestock. It can go a long way to allowing big game on private land. Another element here is to have the right maps showing pertinent private-public boundary lines. Know where you are at all times. In most states it is your responsibility, even in the absence of signs, to avoid trespass.

State game departments should be allowed to make recommendations concerning placement of haystacks; landowners who don't comply could be denied damage payments. Some stacks are magnets that lure elk across busy roads or into known conflicts. I know of one eight-mile-long canyon which is a winter graveyard now for deer, with up to a thousand killed each winter. It is the same, potentially, for elk, depending on stack placement. One farmer I know offered to let game officials move his stack to the mountain side of a busy highway, in an effort to save animal and, potentially, human lives. The offer was declined. If the state must pay depredation claims anyway, it might as well be realistic and help the elk (or deer) get the hay without their being threatened in the process. In addition, plants *not* desired by game should be planted along roadways.

The entire problem of wintering elk must be met with boldness. Action must frequently be taken before problems heighten. Legislators need to be appraised of elk vs. agriculture problems when it comes time to appropriate funds for winter range acquisition. Sportsmen should meet with game managers, landowners, and legislators to expedite such explanations. For some reason lawmakers often give more credibility to sportsmen's leaders than they do to state game biologists. If there is any ax to grind, however, it should be shared by both hunters and game managers. With biologists providing technical data and sportsmen getting it to the right people, both sides can benefit.

Habitat Losses

Threat No. 4: increased loss of grassland habitat via land developers, ski resorts, city sprawl, etc. This problem is separate from wintering elk depredations because it can occur on summer or winter range, and it directly robs elk habitat. And it is complicated, because some seeming intrusions into elkdom also bring benefits—as when a pipe or power line cut through heavy forest opens the terrain up to sun and water, producing needed grass and browse. Freeways often do the opposite, however, even usurping prime winter habitat. In addition, freeways may prevent game from reaching lower winter range. Funnels and expensive bypass tunnels indicate a helpful spirit on man's part, but their design is not always understood by elk. Poor land-use practices can transform public land into juniper "junklands" which offer little feed for elk. To its credit, the BLM has "chained out" (pulled a chain between two tractors to root up undesired vegetation) junipers or scrub sage, replanting with desirable species such as bitterbrush and crested wheat grass.

Whenever a change is proposed in the status quo, government officials must often make a rapid evaluation of elk habitat in comparison with what would replace it. In Montana a few years ago a huge recreational complex was allowed apparently because government decision-makers felt it would serve the state better than would the existing elk habitat. At least in that case the full value of the wildlife was taken into consideration. Too often it is not. Ski resorts frequently replace elk habitat (usually summer range), and again it is a decision based on which interests are most important. In some areas, managers need more research to determine the elk's fate if the range is lost. Only then can they convince zoners and planners what is in the best public interest.

Predation Problems

While Threat No. 5, natural predators, is often listed by hunters as a reason elk numbers are down, game managers less often agree. Studies seem to indicate one of the worst predators on elk is pet dogs unchained and running loose on winter range. There is some predation on elk, particularly calves, by coyotes, bobcats, and on occasion, bears and lions. When an elk is road-killed, both bald and golden eagles, plus other creatures of prey, may feed on the carrion. Eagles have been known at times to attack live fawns. Coyotes on the National Elk Refuge appear to bother only the weak and aging, but many stockmen say the critters take anything they can get, and actually seem to prefer the healthiest. There seems little question that a pack could distract parent elk long enough to kill calves. The federal edict against the broadcasting of the coyote poison 1080 has undoubtedly allowed greater numbers of coyotes, yet most people interested in elk would also laud the restriction because it prevents loss of other wildlife often found dead near 1080 stations. At present, predators are listed as a serious problem only in British Columbia, where timber wolf cause problems on Vancouver Island. It also likely occurs in Alberta. Yellowstone managers have actually considered reintroducing wolves to help curtail elk populations. At present, black and grizzly bears are observed gorging on dead elk, but in almost every case the carcass was already known to be dead by park personnel.

Too Much Pressure

Threat No. 6, increasing numbers of hunters, isn't one likely to go away. It is best offset by shifting away from quantitative hunting to more emphasis on quality. If the range won't support 50 bulls, maybe it can harbor half that many twice as mature. A 4-pointer doesn't eat that much

more than a spike. Consider the state of Oregon and its obvious trend. In 1940 there were 6,152 elk hunters afield, and they had a 41 percent success ratio; in 1970 it was 73,568 for 17 percent; in 1983, 128,905 for 14 percent. These figures are for both Rocky Mountain and Roosevelt elk, but the former dropped much more dramatically, from 48 to 16 percent in hunter success over the 43-year period. The coastal species dropped from 17 to 8 percent. Granted, some "hotspots" in certain states retain a high hunter-kill ratio, and those states with limited permits like Nevada and South Dakota still look good on paper. The private ranches, tribal lands, etc., don't have so much of a challenge, because they can manage for quality—and charge for it. States attempting to provide general bull hunting for the masses face the major obstacle in elk management, particularly where quality is concerned.

Quality control can be achieved in one of two ways—limit either the number of licenses sold or the harvest. Thus, the ratio of rifles to elk must somehow be reduced. States with open elk hunting usually enjoy less than 20 percent success, and in some years below 15 or even 10. But sportsmen claim they would be satisfied with less hunting opportunity, even fewer elk, if the animals were mature bulls pursued by reduced competition.

"The truth is," game managers sometimes counter, "that those who push for quality don't always represent the majority." A beginner or inexperienced hunter (and they might represent over 50 percent of the elk license-buyers at any given time) may want whatever gives him the best chance of scoring. A spike could be a trophy to many such licensees. How do game managers provide for them? First of all, only in rare instances is an elk hunt the most economical way to obtain a winter supply of meat. Beef would almost certainly cost less. The hunter should realize this from the beginning. Rural hunters often talk about filling the freezer, but most are veterans, and understand their chances. Elk are not like gamefish, which can be caught and released. And an elk is too valuable to be slain only for its meat. The sport aspects should be elevated to a pedestal by state game departments.

While limited quotas are seldom popular with elk hunters, they are almost certainly a management tool of the future. In Utah, where hunters have their choice of limited entry or open bull, the former can be downright discouraging. For example, the chances of drawing out in the Oquirrh Mountains near metropolitan Salt Lake City are about 80 to one. In one prime roadless unit far from civilization, only 30 permits are allocated, though many hunters apply. However, if everyone who wanted to hunt here was allowed a license, a relatively fragile elk resource could quickly diminish. Few bulls would likely make it to trophy size. At the least, hunter success would falter.

Serious nimrods can increase their chances of success by taking advantage of late hunts wherever offered. Colorado has split seasons with the following hunter-success figures for early and late hunts: Snake River unit, 38 percent and 64 percent; Williams Fork, 26 and 91; Miller Creek, 31 and 88; Grand Mesa, 23 and 82. All are figures from 1984 hunts, but are typical of any given year in the past few seasons.

Some states are also moving to primitive-weapons quests (archery or muzzle-loader) in order to place more emphasis on quality. It is one way to provide more opportunity with less harvest. Almost all such license-holders fully realize their lower success odds. Win or lose, these customers tend to be more satisfied. "Primitive" hunters generally represent a small minority, but ought to be encouraged by game managers. Primitive hunting isn't as tough on the resource, provides recreational opportunity, and usually adds to license-sale revenue since it doesn't diminish the number of rifle hunters.

Some nonresidents have long sought license prices equal to resident fees for hunting on federal lands belonging as much to any one American as another. However, the well-known Sagebrush Rebellion notwithstanding, residents still enjoy much lower prices than out-of-staters—generally around $25–$35 as compared with $150 up. In addition, if states seek to reduce hunting numbers in a search for quality, the cuts likely will occur in nonresident licenses.

Quality-conscious Idaho game managers are doing the following to ensure good elk hunting in future years: (1) aiming for harvest of more mature bulls; (2) reducing numbers of hunters; (3) providing a variety of hunts—early, late, split, primitive weapon, etc.; (4) utilizing funds more carefully for quality hunts; (5) applying modern data-gathering techniques to keep a "pulse" on elk herds. The public is allowed to value its opinion on all points via public meetings. One idea meeting with increased favor is early backpack quests for mature bulls only. Idaho also refers to elk as a "prized big-game animal," which promotes the sport attributes over meat hunting.

Game managers of the future must also address the variety of reasons sportsmen hunt elk (cited in Chapter 18). Ranging all the way from observing nature and social interrelationships to religious awakening, they seem to suggest that not all hunting seasons should be held in primitive backcountry. One study indicated most young elk hunters are introduced to the sport by their fathers. For situations like the teenager and his Dad or uncle or grandfather, some hunts offered should be simple and relatively inexpensive. This is especially challenging when you consider the wilderness nature of the wapiti.

Many states rely heavily on federal Pittman-Robertson funding (federal tax money paid by sportsmen) to match state money. Some sort of financial assistance will probably always be needed by states, since expenses usually exceed license revenues. If funding cutbacks become necessary, alert sportsmen should keep vigil on the budget to see whether vital elk interests are being slighted. Income can drop anytime elk sales dwindle.

In Oregon, some 5,000 citizens attending hunting workshops — plus 16,000 more answering survey questions — came up with several methods of providing restricted elk hunts: vary the number of licenses by (1) issuing permits this year to applicants born in certain months, while the others get their turn another year — or people of even age can apply this year, the balance getting an opportunity next season; (2) using last name in an alphabetical lottery, A-I this year, J-R next year, S-Z the year after that; (3) allowing hunters to go after deer in one year, elk the next; (4) reduce the number of rifle permits, issuing more to low-harvest licensees like archers and muzzle loaders.

Quite clearly, the public realizes that permits need to be trimmed to achieve quality hunting. Limiting permits or harvest seem to be acceptable means to the man in the street.

Parks and Refuges

Threat No. 7 is the role of parks and winter refuges in hunting. Professional outfitters say that protecting elk until they reach huntable numbers is good management. But they also feel that elk are too valuable to be "stockpiled" until they reach such numbers that they are eradicated in "cheap hunts." Park or refuge managers should consider themselves as more than caretakers, those outfitters say. The elk are esthetically important to view and sleigh-ride among, but harvesting surplus animals should be part of the management plan. To be sure, some elk may not be "surplus" until a severe winter comes along. But managers must always anticipate when that weak link in the chain might occur: too many months for too little feed. Rarely does it happen overnight.

In some cases, parks or other sanctuaries are not as vitally needed as winter range in the right place. That may require federal intervention, since state land planning seems almost always to equate the best use with the highest monetary gain. In other words, the land used in winter for big game survival, if nothing else, may have no higher use, or value.

In any event, states with hopes for future elk hunting had better get into the real-estate business; if they lack a budget for feeding, they should at least acquire a place for the animals off private lands. In many ways, that situation is better than a costly park or refuge because the wapiti move off the winter range to cheaper summer and autumn feed, where they can also be managed by hunting.

Apathy and Elk

No. 8: apathy. It's a tragic word and an enemy — past, present, and future — to elk and elk hunting. Grass-roots apathy filters up into high places. High-ranking political leaders seldom have much background in the natural sciences, and they may be rather easily swayed by seemingly intelligent arguments from one side or the other in matters concerning elk.

Let me give a perfect example. I have no interest in singling out any one person or group, but let's look at an application from an industrial firm to construct a huge processing plant in elk winter range. The firm, Exxon Oil, has spent millions to mitigate impacts of their work on adjacent communities. But when it comes to wildlife, consider these statements extracted from the Wyoming Industrial Siting Administration (WISA) staff review of the Exxon application:

"In the permit application, Exxon acknowledges that impacts to hunting and fishing will be extensive, and yet no mitigation measures are proposed. Rather the company suggests the Wyoming Game-and-Fish Department could . . . simply allow wildlife-fisheries populations to decline. . . . There is little doubt that wildlife/fisheries populations *will* [author's italics] decline due to direct and indirect disturbances of habitat due to the project."

Fortunately, WISA did not buy Exxon's suggestion to just let things deteriorate. WISA goes on to say: "These suggestions are not consistent with WGFD planning objectives or with concepts of multiple-use management. Further, wildlife and fisheries are resources of the people of Wyoming, and Exxon is asking the state's wildlife-fisheries users to accept severe negative impacts without compensation." State officials didn't accept the "everything-get-out-of-the-way-of-progress" concept—fortunately so for hundreds of thousands of license buyers and other members of the general public who enjoy wildlife but may not hunt.

WISA stipulated that Exxon reach agreement with the WGFD, and that the agreement be incorporated into any industrial siting permit for the Exxon project.

Conditions were also outlined for curtailing poaching. Many of the oil-firm workers moving in were unfamiliar with the game and its value. Developers were asked to pay for the hiring of an extra game warden. Many oil firms voluntarily agreed to hold rigidly to a policy of firing employees found guilty of poaching.

However, it is not likely that any of the above safeguards would have happened without the intervention of state agency people who cared about wildlife resources—and said so on behalf of their constituency. Lethargy and apathy would have been easy, and in fact was almost invited. Edmund Burke said it well: "All that is necessary for the triumph of evil is for good men to do nothing."

Perhaps "evil" is too harsh a term here. The question is whether developers are looking out for the general public as well as their own private profit. Often they are not, and only a caring love for wildlife values, esthetics, and economics will save the day.

One philosophy sportsmen must constantly watch out for is the idea that "money replaces elk habitat." An infusion of dollars may be better than nothing, a mitigation of sorts. But about the only thing which can replace an acre of elk habitat is another acre of it. I've seen fish-and-game departments accept money or another study or extra employees or vehicles in lieu of vigorous game management. But the true measure of such a decision must always be: how will this help sportsmen who buy the licenses?

In addition, decisions about habitat protection may have to be made repeatedly. In the Exxon vs. Wyoming case, permission was granted for a Phase Two development, to begin in July 1985. However, after getting the green light from the Industrial Siting Administration, based on promises to the state game-and-fish department, Exxon was charged with trying to get around the commitments by simply claiming never to have entered Phase Two! The WGFD statement says: "It was clearly understood that Phase Two would commence in July 1985 . . . Game and Fish negotiated in good faith with Exxon to mitigate wildlife problems . . . said contract was adopted. Mitigation measures agreed to include an elk habitat enhancement program, and installation of stack yards to offset elk damage to private land caused by wellfield construction on public land which will displace elk and hunting-fishing recreation tied to the increased population associated with Exxon expansion. In fact, the population expansion has occurred, and the wellfield activity continues apace, but Exxon now asserts that Phase Two has not begun and may not begin in the foreseeable future. Accordingly, Exxon refuses to supply funding for the mitigation measures agreed to with the Game and Fish . . ."

Exxon continued to maintain it had not entered Phase Two. This report is not meant to supply a judgment or guess who was correct. It is only meant to point out that the state game managers were not guilty of apathy in looking out for sportsmen.

In summary, since elk herds range over a wide mosaic of boundaries and jurisdictions, wildlife interests simply cannot adopt a "let George do it" mentality.

Antihunting Groups

No. 9: antihunting groups usually have three arguments: (1) it is immoral to kill things; (2) hunting is cruel; and (3) hunting does not serve any useful purpose anyway.

Let's examine them without wasting words. (1) If hunting or killing animals/birds is immoral, why is it mentioned so frequently and with such acceptance in the Bible? (2) It is obvious, given the documented proof of almost every state game manager, that hunting is worlds less cruel than slow starvation on poor or nonexistent winter range; (3) Answered in No. 2, since hunting is the ideal alternative to natural demise and its attendant waste of meat, revenue from license sales, plus recreation.

It rarely does any good to talk with antihunting groups; too often their minds are closed. Hunters should expend their energies with those who make hunting decisions. Generally, the greatest threats to hunting come from heavily populated areas such as metropolitan California, the East Coast, and large Midwest cities. Educational efforts should be concentrated there.

At the same time, "slob" hunters must be forced to clean up their act before landowners close even more private property. Then, too, hunters should realize that more practice on the rifle range can help make the harvest more humane.

If you discover any activities which could tarnish the hunter's image or endanger elk or its habitat, contact an organized sportsmen's group in your area or an official of the fish-and-game department. But before you begin a campaign to protect elk and/or elk hunting, become armed first with all the facts. Chances are the competition has some—and hunting's future could depend on how well we gather the vital facts and how energetically we disseminate them.

Illegal Kills

No. 10, poaching and other illegal kills, requires organized sportsmen's groups to assist state law-enforcement officers. There should be a well-publicized telephone number to call to report suspicious vehicles on back roads, game meat being transported, spotlighting, and the like. Game laws need to be tightened. If necessary, a "special witness" program used to report and/or apprehend criminals while retaining the witness's anonymity should be utilized. In event of conviction of such a poacher, rewards are paid through an arranged code. Sportsmen can become more involved by pointing out to the public that the elk stolen out of season could be the very bull they might have put in their sights.

Game managers can also subtract the number of known or estimated illegal or accidental kills from the total number of permits to be allocated for the coming sea-son. That usually drives the point home—these are *our* elk the thieves are poaching.

Efforts should also be put forth to recover wounded game. The end effect of unrecovered (and wasted) game may be worse than that of poached game. Many states provide low-cost rifle ranges and marksmanship training that can lessen crippling and excessive loss of game animals.

Other problems can arise, particularly actions that endanger valuable elk habitat. Whenever that happens, sportsmen and game managers alike must be willing to take their own action.

Our elk are at a critical crossroads in many states. Hunters must be mature enough to see them as a reflection of our value system, our ecological quality of life. Will our management of them now be a tribute to our wisdom and foresight? Time will tell.

20

Care of Meat and Mount

"Good shot!" a companion says, and you bend over your bull three miles from the nearest road. Now what?

First of all, is it dead? Place the rifle muzzle near the eyes and wave it to see if they blink. If you detect any movement there, wait a minute or two. You don't want the touch of the knife to "wake" the animal up.

Now, should you cut the bull's throat? Most taxidermists say "No!" If it was a beef in the slaughterhouse, the reply would be "yes." But experts say that by the time you walk a few hundred yards to a game animal, turn its head downhill, and get the cutting done, the heart has probably ceased pumping. The only blood that might drain is in the immediate throat area—if you managed to knife the jugular directly on target. Of course, it is easier to hit the jugular if you cut deeply across the throat. But if you may want to have the bull mounted or save any part of the cape, don't make a throat cut. If you have perfect conditions, as in the slaughterhouse, for a quick draining of blood after the kill, make any cut parallel with the throat hair, not against the grain.

What about the musk gland? Some hunters have been told by older companions, who should have learned better, to cut off the gland on the inside of the rear legs so that the musk smell does not get into the meat. Master big-game taxidermist Merlin Anderson of Sandy, Utah, says this: "The only way the musk gland can affect meat is if you touch it with hand or knife prior to cleaning the animal. So don't touch it. Just leave it alone."

Cleaning should be accomplished immediately after the animal is down. If you must leave the carcass in the field

265

overnight, fine; but first get it properly dressed. The sooner you get the hot entrails out and cool air in, the better.

Cleaning Your Elk

Some neophytes consider cleaning an elk a formidable task, and it is admittedly more difficult than a deer, simply because of the elk's size. However, if you have ever dressed a beef cow, an elk is much easier. For one thing, you can reach in hand-to-backbone to get the job done. Place your coat or other bulky outer clothing out of the way, and then, says meat processor Wayne Anderson of Georgetown, Idaho: "Get the elk on its back, and if at all possible tilt the carcass so the head is slightly downhill. Remove the bottom half of the leg, using a 'break joint' about one inch below the knee on each leg. Then start at the anus and cut along the belly from the rectum to the lower throat (if the trophy will be mounted, don't cut beyond the front shoulder area), being careful not to puncture through the paunch and spill the entrails.

"Take a hand saw or hatchet and split through the large 'aitch bone' between the hind legs. Then cut the brisket bone between the front legs until you can reach the lungs and windpipe. Grab hold of the windpipe and pull, using your knife to help free it. You will have to cut through muscle around the diaphragm so you can begin the pull from the forward area to remove the entrail mass. Now you are at the heart and liver. If you wish to save these items for a gourmet meal, cut them out and place in a plastic bag.

"Continue cutting away tissue along the ribs and backbone so that the entire entrail mass can be pulled out of the stomach area. You will need to cut carefully around the genitals to prevent any spillage of urine or excrement. Cut out the entire genital area without cutting into it, and move it well away from the meat."

Unless you'll be caping out the animal later, you will likely want to cut off the head to facilitate loading on a horse. Many outfitters would prefer to pack quarters out without the head. The neck's "break joint," says Anderson, "is just below the jaw. Cut all the way around the neck, then spin the head until you can finish with your knife. Don't give up. The head will come off quickly if you learn to do it right."

If there will be a delay in packing out, try to tie the hind legs to a pole, and get the animal off the ground. If you don't have someone to help you with this task, first quarter the animal to make the job lighter. The main thing is to get the meat where it can cool. Avoid letting meat touch other meat. Usually the first place to spoil is the upper chest, lower neck region. Use several game bags if you have them to keep flies away.

Should you remove the hide? Anderson says no, unless the weather is exceptionally warm and you can't get to a locker within a reasonable time. The hide helps keep dust and grime out. Washing with water from a creek or hose will help cool meat down, and does the meat no harm. Unless you are an expert at aging meat, get it as soon as possible to the processor. Let him age it, if he has room.

Skinning should not be attempted unless you have help from a processor or someone like a veteran rancher who has skinned an elk before.

In the field, especially with an animal which must be left overnight, try to get the meat into the shade. Cover it with branches or boughs to keep crows, magpies, and other predators away. Pinpoint the spot well. Many outfitters mark trees with one color of ribbon from trail or road to the general site of the kill, another color of ribbon near the carcass to let them know they're close. Aspens, pines, and sage can all look the same when you attempt to return to your downed elk.

Outfitter's Approach

Big-game outfitter Sharon Dayton has horse-packed hundreds of elk out of western Wyoming mountains. He adds these important details:

"Bringing home the game is the highlight of the trip. I know of no more colorful and warming sight than to see a string of hunters and horses loaded with elk antlers and meat. Good news! But let's go to the beginning.

"You've examined the downed bull with awe and respect for its size. With pictures to prove how big it was before you cut it down to packing size, you gather equipment from a saddle bag. I like to have on hand a sharp knife, brisket saw, two axes, small rope, paper towels, and a pair of plastic gloves. After cleaning and skinning many game and domestic animals, I have learned the value of protecting skin against blood and sharp bones. The small rope is especially useful if I'm alone. Balancing an elk where you want it is much easier if I can tie a leg to a tree or bush to keep it where I want it. As for the head, I like it slightly downhill to start with. This allows the entrails to slip forward toward the chest cavity.

"As you begin the cut between the hind legs on a bull, you want to cut around the scrotum (most states say you must leave the scrotum, or other visible evidence of sex, attached to the carcass), leaving it with the belly skin. The hide is then split from the scrotum to the center of the belly so the penis and entire sheath can be re-

moved and discarded. This is a good time to trim any urine-contaminated skin from the animal.

"When you cut to the aitch bone between the hind legs, continue right on through to the anus. Make short saw strokes when cutting this bone to avoid puncturing the nearby bladder. If necessary, hold the bladder away with one hand. During this time, of course, your plastic gloves will help keep blood and body wastes from getting beneath fingernails or in cuts. If you lack such gloves, you will want to wash hands when possible.

"When the legs can be spread easily, cut through the hide in a circle around the anus to remove it. When finished aft, go forward and finish cutting up the belly to the neck region. As mentioned previously, stop behind the front legs if you envision a shoulder mount. Cut to the jaws if you're not heading to a taxidermist.

"As you use your knife to cut away the stomach muscles, do so carefully. I like to use the two fingers nearest the thumb, along with the thumb, to spread and lift the muscles as they are cut. This will expose the innards from the ribs on back. At this point, I like to turn the animal around so the hind legs are downhill. This allows everything I've trimmed to slide away between the back legs. Keep trimming right to the rear, being sure-fingered all the way to avoid perforating any of the gut material which might spill out onto the meat. Make certain that you remove all windpipe material in the throat to prevent it from spoiling forward-area meat. If you have anyone around to help, have him hold the carcass open for you while doing the above knife work.

"After pulling the entrails downhill, you may find that one organ, the large intestine, 'catches' in the pelvic cavity. To remove, just slice the tissue holding it to the backbone area.

"In the process of cleaning, some blood is likely to remain. In heart, lung, or back shots, the blood drains into the body cavity. While the blood begins congealing quickly after the kill, it usually remains fluid enough to be swept by hand (and paper towels) out the rear of the pelvis. You can also pump the limbs to force more blood into the body cavity for removal. This is especially recommended when your shot-slug did not cause internal bleeding to any degree. If there is snow present, you can use it with the towels to complete a thorough cleaning, which prevents blood from contributing to spoilage."

If caping, be sure to prevent blood from drying on the cape. Salt the flesh side of the hide generously. More on that later as taxidermists tell us precisely how they like to see it done to protect a cape.

As for loading elk onto horses, Dayton recommends the following: "If you must pack out meat on a day other than the kill, be sure to split the carcass with sticks so it can cool, particularly the upper chest area. Use stout sticks to prop it open. If possible, also get a log or something under the carcass to prevent it from 'lumping' on the ground. The idea is to let air circulate all around it until you can return."

Horse Packing

"Horse packing," Dayton says, "is a science which can be simplified to a relatively easy challenge if you know how. I am aware of one day when 23 elk were transported 10 miles by horseback, with few hitches. A calf elk can be carried to camp on a riding saddle. A big horse can carry a spike or younger bull a considerable dis-tance that way, but mature cows or bulls are usually halved or quartered, with each horse packing two quarters. (Incidentally, mules or South American llamas are often used for packing, but the llama is often limited to smaller game due to its size.) In any event, for packing heavy game like elk, avoid animals that are only partly broken, or easily spooked. Use the best-dispositioned members of your string for packing any game.

"Tie your pack animals securely before turning your attention to the game on the ground. Remove the panniers (large canvas bags with loops) from the pack saddles, and unload your axes, lash ropes, and other items. If you have not done so previously, you will want to make certain all four elk legs are removed at the knee joints. To make the front quarters fit into most panniers, you will also have to make sure the neck is trimmed off. If the neck is to be transported for any reason, do so with the head, not the front quarters. Next, the animal is halved by cutting between the second and third ribs, counting from the rear. (Note: some outfitters cut between the first and second ribs, but the idea is to obtain a balanced load.) Use your knife to cut through the skin, then two axes (one for cutting, one for hammering with the blunt side) to sever the backbone itself.

"Now, to split the backbone lengthwise on each section before you, hold the axes firmly in hand. Elk bone is tough, but will sever with a sharp blow directly down the middle. On the backbone in particular, you do not want the cutting ax to slip away from its duty. A saw will help get through stringy gristle. Use your knife to cut through the skin on the back. Have a whetstone handy. If you don't plan to load quarters in panniers, but instead intend to

Outfitter Sharon Dayton shows how to begin the quartering process for loading meat onto horse.

Most outfitters make the quartering cut between either first and second or second and third ribs.

drape an elk half over the saddle, do not slice through this backside skin. Leave it intact to hold the sides of meat together. If desired to hold the load in place, you can slit a hole in the center to fit over the saddle horn or extension. (This is sometimes done in extremely cold weather after the carcass has frozen, rendering it difficult to cut for loading into panniers.) Keep hide toward horse. With the front half, keep the elk shoulders forward toward the horse's head; with the rear half, point the legs to the rear.

"Load quarters in panniers this way: hide side toward the horse, preventing meat bones from gouging the pack animal. Load front quarters with the leg up and toward the front of the horse; load hind quarters with the leg up, angling toward the rear. Before loading, make sure all straps and cinches are tight to prevent panniers from slipping, which can spook a horse. Talk to the cayuse in reassuring tones as you load. Outfitters are accustomed to loading alone, but because of the weight of the meat, hunters may need help.

"Some outfitters tie with antlers down, but I like to keep the tines up, well away from the horse. Tie them tightly so there will be no rattling, slipping, or gouging. One thing which helps is to tie a branch tightly between the antlers so they can be lashed down by the branch itself. Keep checking the load along the trail."

There are other ways to tie on meat, one of them without panniers, as Jim Bridger did it 150 years ago. The master of this tie is Gap Puche, who balances an elk quarter on the side of a horse, then loops beneath the ribs and cinches it all tight. I've seen both this method and Dayton's used to pack elk dozens of miles without any problems, so long as care is taken not to allow the load to catch on tree trunks or other obstacles. Maintain a vigil along narrow trail corridors; skirt them whenever possible. Never tie anything onto another rope, for then both may loosen. Always make ties onto something solid, like the saddle or rings. Avoid tying to straps because they loosen with the horse's gait.

Load all equipment such as axes and extra ropes into the panniers before the meat takes up all the room. Also be careful about laying knives down in loose snow. They can be difficult to locate later on.

Here are some taxidermist don'ts regarding the care of meat and antlers:

1. Don't cut or split the throat.

2. Don't make any cuts on the front of the throat or neck.

3. Don't drag unskinned animals, since the hair will rub off quickly.

4. Don't leave the care of your trophy until tomorrow.

5. Don't cut the cape too short — leave all of the front legs.

6. Don't cut through the lip line.

7. Don't leave fat or meat on the skin.

8. Don't try to skin in the sun, or near fire.

9. Don't wait too long to get the head to the taxidermist.

10. Don't leave the skin unsalted.

11. Don't brush the hair in the wrong direction.

12. Don't be discouraged.

(Note: from "Hints for Hunters and Fishermen," courtesy Merlin Anderson.)

If a hide or scalp is spoiled, throw it away. But save the antlers. The taxidermist can make an attractive panel mount to display the antlers, or, if you can afford it, he can buy up another cape to provide a front shoulder mount for your trophy rack.

Gap Puche and helper show how to tie meat on as Jim Bridger did it, without panniers.

Neither a trophy rack nor the meat of an elk should be wasted. I consider elk meat as good as meat can get. One winter, when I had my two freezers filled with both beef and venison from a spike bull, I asked my family which of several steaks, roasts, and hamburger they preferred. I did this several times. More often than not, they chose the elk.

There is simply no reason it shouldn't be as good as beef or better, particularly if you killed it cleanly and took good care of the carcass from the kill site to the butcher. That includes cutting out wound

If head and antlers remain together, most outfitters prefer to keep the tines riding high to avoid gouging horse. Sharon Dayton shows how.

"splotches" where the bullet has bloodied the meat. Most care of meat is just common sense.

Caping Techniques

Caping should be done by skilled hands. If yours are not, you can get the job done by meticulously following this procedure:

Begin to cut on the back well behind the front shoulders. You want to retain all of the front shoulders for a head mount. Make no cuts at all on the throat. Using a sharp knife, make an incision on the back from just aft of shoulders to the base of the ears. Make a "Y" cut from there to the base of each antler. Trim the hide around the pedicle of each antler; some experts use a screwdriver to work the skin loose at those two points at top of skull. When you skin down the skull, be certain to include the entire tear-duct cavities below the eyes. Skin the ears to the tips. Allow plenty of room around the lips, particu-

larly on top. Remember that any cuts you make on the lower half of the animal will be seen from below as the mount hangs on the wall. Pull the hide gently but firmly to avoid tears or cuts anywhere in cape skin. Remove all flesh from the hide.

A taxidermist needs measurements from the head before you throw it away. He can give you a much more lifelike mount resembling the original if you use a flexible tape to measure from tip of nose to eyes, distance between eyes, ear to ear, etc. Remember that your cape only provides an approximation of those valuable measurements, especially since it has probably lain in storage for several months. I have never heard a taxidermist complain about having too many head measurements, or about having too much cape to work with. You can always throw unneeded parts away; it is much more difficult to "resurrect" something that just isn't there.

When you have finished caping, salt the skin until it is slightly white; then roll it

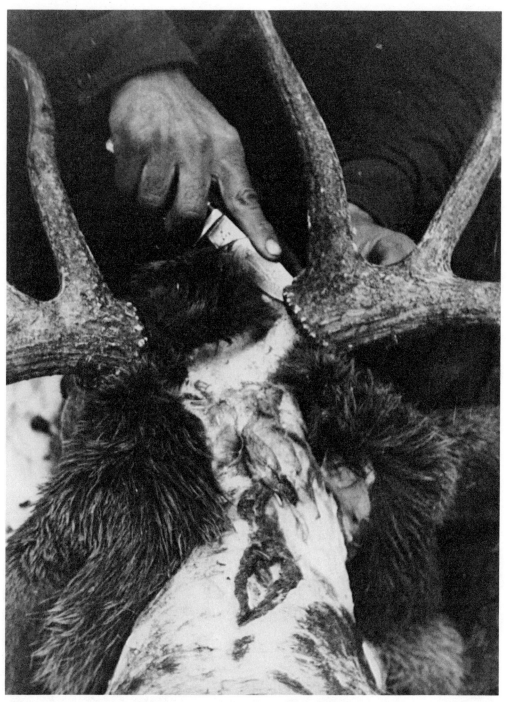
Cutting around the antler base while caping mount.

hair side out for delivery to the taxidermist. Keep it away from sunlight and
moisture in the interim. If you cannot get
to a taxidermist for several days, scrape
off the loose salt, which will draw up excess blood, grease, and moisture in the
hide, discard all excess, then re-salt. If
possible, place the skin where air can circulate to it.

Incidentally, if you are not certain
about the caping process, experiment first
on an elk you do *not* want to have

mounted. The experience can be invalu-
able later when you have a nice bull you
do want to hang over the fireplace. Another thing you can do is "short cape."
After making all cuts to the lower neck
region of the animal, do not continue
toward the head at all. Cut off the neck so
that you have the shoulder hide removed
as before; but leave it attached to the entire neck, head, and antlers for delivery to
a taxidermist, who will finish the caping.
This makes an awkward load for horse

Branch tied across antlers often helps in tying package down to horse.

Before heading home with 6-point bull, Wyoming hunter Steward Petersen shows how the entire load looks. *Edward Ellsworth Photo.*

transporting, but it will work if you fold the hide under the head and tie the load with head and antlers up, as you would normally. You can tie it extra tight by using the "D" rings, those metal devices near the top of the stirrups on most saddles. If the antlers project high from horse, especially with some elk hide showing, be sure to attach a red ribbon somewhere on the rack!

If you do not want a shoulder and head mount, instead planning to display only the rack on a plaque, saw through the skull plate just below the bottom of the eye sockets. When you cut through the bone to less solid matter, pull up gently to separate. Continue until the skull plate is free, but be careful not to angle the saw too high toward the antler bases. If you do, the antlers may be loosened, making it impossible to measure for record scoring and also causing a wobbly mount. The taxidermist will later fit the antlers to a wooden or other plaque. You need not save any hide at all for this mount, but do remove any blood or foreign matter which might have touched the antlers.

Horseless Packing

Outfitter Sharon Dayton tells of the time he watched a lonesome horseless hunter attempt to haul out elk quarters, plus head with antlers, nearly a mile uphill to camp. He had made no attempt to debone the animal or remove the antler plate from the head. He had no backpack either. He would first struggle uphill a bit, then take a long rest. Many hours later, he had made little progress. An elk quarter can weigh well over 100 pounds, and is awkward to find a handle on. The hunter would have been far better off to hike out to get help or rent a horse; perhaps he could have dragged the load *downhill,* then driven a vehicle to it.

Use your head when challenged with getting an elk out! It isn't the same as hauling any deer. To load an elk whole into a vehicle, you'll need at least three strong people. Four is even better.

Here are some additional tips from meat processors:

If you don't want to pay the going rate per pound for nonedible items like head and lower legs, don't bring them in. Be cautious about floating the carcass down a stream, not because of the water but because sand and grit can attach to the meat. If you encounter any "boils" or strange growths in the meat when cleaning, cut them out, then wash your knife before proceeding. Be sure to wash manure off meat and blood off cape; especially do not allow blood and salt to stain the cape.

When it comes to salting, taxidermists recommend rubbing salt over the entire skin, using the flat of the hand to push it in. There is no danger in using too much salt, says Utah taxidermist Merlin Anderson. Be generous around nose, lips, eyes, base of tail, and the folding or wrinkled parts. Some 15 pounds of common table salt should be used over the skin of an entire elk, a little more than half that amount for a shoulder mount.

In a pamphlet entitled "Hints for Hunters and Fishermen," Anderson and other taxidermists suggest selecting a skilled craftsman to preserve the memory of your trophy hunt. I agree. You don't want to just choose one from the phone book. Be certain to examine a sample of the work. Are the details realistically done? Check the little things such as tear ducts below eyes, texture of throat hair, and alert posture of eyes.

Sporting-goods stores, museums, banks, and other public establishments often have mounts on display for you to scrutinize. Many hunters or outfitters can recommend a good taxidermist, but even then, make certain it is not just a business arrangement. By the time you have concluded your hunt, you have likely learned whether you can trust your outfitter. Be sure you can trust a taxidermist before you turn over your trophy to him. Most people don't want to trust an amateur because the mount may wind up in the garbage. The motto of many good taxidermists bears serious thought: "The bitterness of poor quality remains long after the sweetness of low price is forgotten."

Consider, too, this statement from expert J. Strebel: "A professional taxidermist's greatest problem is his constant battle against time. Most customers cannot understand why it takes so long to complete work. The work often comes in a seasonal rush just after the hunting period. After skinning and preparation, the hide may remain at the tannery for six months before the taxidermist sees it again."

Strebel goes on to say that tanning is a full-time profession, and most taxidermists leave it up to a pro. He says that many amateur taxidermists try to do it themselves, but it rarely works out. A taxidermist worth his salt, so to speak, places the emphasis on quality rather than speed. Expect to give up your trophy for a year or so to get the job done right.

Cleaning a Mount

Anderson suggests you pay close attention to the mount after receiving it. If it is subject to dirt or smoke (as when it is positioned near a fireplace), you may want to clean it periodically. He suggests the following: "Remove it from the wall without touching the pelt. Handle it around the horns, base of neck, or nose, not by the ears or neck. If the head is a large one, get help to remove it.

"If you're inexperienced, don't apply water or water solutions to heads or skins. Dampness can do a great deal of harm. Dust should be removed by blowing with a vacuum cleaner with the airflow reversed, while beating the hair lightly with a limber switch. Use a hair brush to work the hide in the direction of the hair. After the dust has been removed, moisten a rag or sponge well with white gas or carbon tetrachloride, and wipe the hair to remove the last film of dirt. A comb suitable to the texture of the hair, along with the flat of the hand, may then be used to rearrange the hair. After cleaning, polish the glass eyes with a soft cloth. Keeping the mount clean will do much to protect it against insects."

For further reading on the subject, I suggest the latest Boone and Crockett record book, since this organization probably has more to do with preservation of trophy heads than any other.

What about cooking the elk venison you have so conscientiously packed to processor and storage locker? Most gourmet cooks say elk is especially easy to prepare. You don't have to resort to tricks or "disguises" in order to render it deliciously palatable. Those who love elk venison have many favorite recipes. Some of my favorites follow.

Favorite Recipes

Venison Swiss Steak with Variations
(3 to 4 servings per pound)

Round steak 1 in. thick
Basic flour mixture:
  ½ cup flour
  2 tsp. salt
  ½ tsp. pepper

2 tbsp. fat
1 cup water

Pound flour into round steak, using the edge of a plate or mallet. Brown steak in hot fat in a heavy skillet. Turn and brown other side. Add water, cover with tight lid. Cook in moderate oven at 350° for 1½ hours, or simmer on top of stove for same length of time.

Variations:
Spanish Steak
1 cup canned tomatoes, 1 onion chopped, 1 green pepper chopped, ¼ cup chopped celery. Use this mixture in place of the water.

Smothered Steak-with-Onions
Proceed as for Swiss Steak. Add 3 onions thinly sliced when steak is about half cooked.

Swiss Steak with Mushroom Sauce
Add cream of mushroom soup and ½ cup water in place of cup of water above.

Stroganoff Steak
Proceed as for Swiss Steak. Add ½ cup cultured sour cream just prior to serving.

Teriyaki Venison

2 lb. sirloin or round steak, 1½ to 2 in. thick
1 can beef consommé (condensed)
1 clove garlic
½ cup soy sauce
¼ cup chopped onion
2 tbsp. lemon juice
1 tsp. seasoned salt
2 tbsp. brown sugar

Slice meat diagonally across grain, about ¼ in. thick. Prepare marinade by combining remaining ingredients. Pour marinade over the meat, and refrigerate overnight. Drain meat and broil 3-4 in. from heat for about 5 minutes. Baste with marinade, and broil other side. Simmer remaining marinade to serve hot with meat.

Pot Roast Mexicano

4 lb. pot roast
2 onions sliced thin
8 oz. tomato sauce
¼ cup corn oil
½ tsp. ginger
¼ tsp. pepper (plus pinch of cayenne)
1 cup water
⅛ tsp. allspice
⅛ tsp. garlic powder
2 tsp. salt
⅛ tsp. cloves
¼ tsp. powdered thyme

Brown meat in fat. Combine other ingredients, and cook in a lightly covered pan for about 3 hours or until the elk venison is completely cooked and tender. Use the sauce for the gravy.

Elk Venison Parmesan

*1½ lb. venison round steak, pounded
    thin*
3 eggs, well beaten
2 cups dry bread crumbs
½ tsp. dried oregano
½ tsp. salt
½ tsp. freshly ground black pepper
½ tsp. garlic salt (or minced garlic)
½ tsp. dried basil
½ tsp. dried parsley
1 lb. shredded mozzarella cheese
½ cup parmesan cheese
tomato sauce
oil for cooking

Preheat oven to 350°. Pat steaks dry on absorbent paper. Mix together bread crumbs, basil, parsley, oregano, salt, and pepper. Roll meat slices in bread crumbs, then in beaten eggs, then again in bread crumbs.

Heat the oil in a large skillet. Fry the seasoned slices, a few at a time, for about 3 minutes, or until golden.

Arrange meat, without overlapping, in a shallow baking dish. Cover with tomato sauce, and top with a layer of mozzarella cheese. Pour on remaining tomato sauce, and sprinkle evenly with grated parmesan. Cover and bake for 15 minutes. Good served with rice.

Wigwam Stew

2 lb. stew meat
1 cup water
2 spoon drippings
4 chopped green peppers
*6 carrots, thickly sliced
    dash of thyme, rosemary, and basil*
*1 head cauliflower (broken into
    flowerlets)*
2 onions, chopped
¼ tsp. garlic powder
2 large potatoes, cubed
2 bay leaves
1 can tomato sauce

Sauté onions in drippings until transparent. Add meat and garlic, and brown. Cover with tomato sauce and cup of water, and simmer for 1 hour. Add vegetables except for cauliflower, which should be put in about 15 minutes before serving. Add additional water as necessary.

Tastes even better if cooked one day, refrigerated overnight, and then heated for the next day's meal.

Meatballs in Sauce (Serves 6)

1½ lb. ground venison
¼ cup chopped onion
2 cups grated raw potatoes
1½ tsp. salt
⅛ tsp. pepper
1 cup evaporated milk
1 egg
⅓ cup butter
3 cups water
2 tbsp. flour
2 cups dairy sour cream
½ tsp. dill seed
1 pkg. frozen peas (10 oz.)

Combine meat, onion, potatoes, salt, pepper, milk, and egg, and shape lightly into 1½-in. balls. Brown slowly in butter in large skillet. Add ½ cup water and cover; simmer until meat is done—about 30 minutes. Remove meatballs. Stir in flour, then remaining water, and simmer to thicken. Reduce heat, stir in cream and dill, add meatballs and peas. Heat, but do not boil. Delicious served over rice or biscuits.

NOTE: Many of the above recipes can be adapted to dutch-oven cooking.

21

Resources and Contacts

Listed are the names and addresses of organizations or persons, which can be of further help to elk hunters. Many are mentioned in this book.

Fish and Game Departments

ARIZONA Game and Fish Dept.
2222 W. Greenway Rd.
Phoenix, AZ 85023

CALIFORNIA Fish and Game Dept.
State Capitol Bldg.
Sacramento, CA 95814

COLORADO Dept. of Natural Resources
6060 Broadway
Denver, CO 80216

IDAHO Dept. of Fish and Game
600 So. Walnut
P.O. Box 25
Boise, ID 83707

MONTANA Dept. of Fish, Wildlife &
  Parks
1420 E. 6th Ave.
Helena, MT 59620

NEVADA Fish and Game Dept.
State Capitol Bldg.
Carson City, NV 89701

NEW MEXICO Fish and Game Dept.
State Capitol Bldg.
Sante Fe, NM 87501

OREGON Fish and Game Dept.
State Capitol Bldg.
Salem, OR 97308

SOUTH DAKOTA Fish and Game Dept.
State Capitol Bldg.
Pierre, SD 57501

TEXAS Dept. of Fish and Wildlife
State Capitol Bldg.
Austin, TX 78710

UTAH Div. of Wildlife Resources
1596 W. North Temple
Salt Lake City, UT 84116

WASHINGTON Dept. of Game
600 North Capitol Way
GJ-11
Olympia, WA 98504

WYOMING Game and Fish Dept.
2424 Pioneer Avenue
Cheyenne, WY 82002

Canada

ALBERTA Energy & Natural Resources
Fish-Wildlife Div.
P.O. Box 2223
Edmonton, Alberta, Canada TSJ-2P4

BRITISH COLUMBIA Wildlife Branch
Ministry of Environment
Parliament Building
Victoria, BC, Canada V8V-1x5

MANITOBA Dept. of Natural Resources
1495 St. James Street
Winnipeg, Manitoba, Canada R3H-0W9

SASKATCHEWAN Dept. of Tourism
   and Renewable Resources
3211 Alberta St.
Regina, Saskatchewan, Canada S4S-5W6

Private Ranches

Deseret Land and Livestock
Woodruff, UT 84086

Vermejo Park
Raton, NM 87740

Federal Government Offices

Agriculture, Dept. of
14th St. & Jefferson Dr. SW
Washington, DC 20250

Fish & Wildlife Service
C & 19th Sts. NW
Washington, DC 20240

Forest Service
P.O. Box 2417
Washington, DC 20013

Indian Affairs, Bureau of
C & 19th Sts. NW
Washington, DC 20240

Interior, Dept. of
C & 19th Sts. NW
Washington, DC 20240

Land Management, Bureau of
C & 19th Sts. NW
Washington, DC 20240

National Park Service
C & 19th Sts. NW
Washington, DC 20240

Representatives, House of
Capitol Bldg.
Washington, DC 20001

Senate
Capitol Bldg.
Washington, DC 20001

Outdoor Magazines

Field & Stream
1515 Broadway
New York, NY 10036

Outdoor Life
380 Madison Ave.
New York, NY 10017

Sports Afield
250 W. 55th St.
New York, NY 10019

Western Outdoors
3197 E. Airport Loop Dr.
Costa Mesa, CA 92626

Outdoor Services

Browning Co.
Route One
Morgan, UT 84050-9749

Dwight Schuh School of Bowhunting
175 No. Center
Wellsville, UT 84339
(also check for northern Utah guide
    services.)

Matsons
Box 308
Milltown, MT 59851
(Elk aging by tooth sample)

Elk Refuges

National Elk Refuge
Box C
Jackson Hole, WY 83001

State of Utah
Hardware Ranch
Hyrum, UT 84319

Sportsmen's Organizations

Utah Hunter Federation
175 No. Center
Wellsville, UT 84339

Wyoming Wildlife Federation
P.O. Box 106
Cheyenne, WY 82002

Record Keepers

Boone and Crockett Club
205 So. Patrick St.
Alexandria, VA 22314

Safari International
515 E. Broadway
Tucson, AZ 85711

Guides and Outfitters

Burch, Bob
Vallecito, CO 81122

Dayton, Sharon
Box 244
Cokeville, WY 83114

Puche, Gaspar "Gap"
Crystal Creek Outfitters
Star Rt., Box 44A
Jackson Hole, WY 83001

Robb, Val
Paragonah, UT 84760

Wiltse, Duane
Cabin Creek Outfitters
1313 Lane 10, Rt. 1
Powell, WY 82435

Taxidermists

Anderson, Merlin
9119 So. 150 West
Sandy, UT 84070

Vandersteen, Rocky
1650 Dewar Dr., Lot 28
Rock Springs, WY 82901

National Parks

Grand Teton Nat'l. Park
Moose, WY 83012

Yellowstone Nat'l. Park
Mammoth, WY 83020

Bibliography

America's No. 1 Trophy, Jim Bond, Portland, OR, 1964

Complete Book of Shooting, Jack O'Connor, Stackpole Books, Harrisburg, Pa., 1965

Elk of North America, Olaus Murie, Stackpole Books and Wildlife Management Institute, Harrisburg, Pa., 1979

Elk of North America, Ecology and Management, compiled and edited by J.W. Thomas and D.E. Toweill, Stackpole Books with WMI, 1982

Field Guide to American Wildlife, Henry Hill Collins Jr., Harper and Row, New York, NY 1959

North American Head Hunting, Grancel Fitz, Oxford University Press, NY 1957

North American Big Game, Boone and Crockett Club, 1981 edition, edited by Wm. Nesbitt, Alexandria, VA, 1985

Outdoor Guide to the Pacific Northwest, John Gartner and Mel White, Van Nostrand Co., NJ, 1968

Ted Trueblood Hunting Treasury, Ted Trueblood, David McKay Co., NY, 1978

Theodore Roosevelt Autobiography, Scribners, New York, NY, 1913

Theodore Roosevelt, Sayings and Quotations, Donahue Press, Chicago, IL, 1903

Index

Some other fine hunting books
from America's Great Outdoor Publisher

Badge in the Wilderness
My 30 dangerous years combating wildlife violators.
by David H. Swendsen

Grouse Hunter's Guide
Solid facts, insights, and observations on how to hunt the ruffed grouse.
by Dennis Walrod

Art and Science of Whitetail Hunting
How to interpret the facts and find the deer.
by Kent Horner

Hunting Rabbits and Hares
The complete guide to North America's favorite small game.
by Richard P. Smith

White-tailed Deer: Ecology & Management
Developed by the Wildlife Management Institute. Over 2,400 references on every aspect of deer behavior.
edited by Lowell K. Halls

Bowhunting for Whitetails
Your best methods for taking North America's favorite deer.
by Dave Bowring

Deer & Deer Hunting
The serious hunter's guide.
by Dr. Rob Wegner

Elk of North America
The definitive, exhaustive, classic work on the North American elk.
ed. by Jack Ward Thomas and Dale E. Toweill

Pronghorn, North America's Unique Antelope
The practical guide for hunters.
by Charles L. Cadieux

Spring Turkey Hunting
The serious hunter's guide.
by John M. McDaniel

How to Plan Your Western Big Game Hunt
All you need to know to plan a do-it-yourself or guided hunt in the 11 Western states.
by Jim Zumbo

Available at your local bookstore, or for complete ordering information, write:

Stackpole Books
Dept. EEH
Cameron and Kelker Streets
Harrisburg, PA 17105

For fast service credit card users may call 1-800-READ-NOW
In Pennsylvania, call 717-234-5041